Humanitarian intervention
in the long nineteenth century

Manchester University Press

HUMANITARIANISM
Key debates and new approaches

This series offers a new interdisciplinary reflection on one of the most important and yet understudied areas in history, politics and cultural practices: humanitarian aid and its responses to crises and conflicts. The series seeks to define afresh the boundaries and methodologies applied to the study of humanitarian relief and so-called 'humanitarian events'. The series includes monographs and carefully selected thematic edited collections which will cross disciplinary boundaries and bring fresh perspectives to the historical, political and cultural understanding of the rationale and impact of humanitarian relief work.

Calculating compassion: Humanity and relief in war, Britain 1870–1914
    Rebecca Gill

Humanitarian intervention in the long nineteenth century

Setting the precedent

Alexis Heraclides and Ada Dialla

Manchester University Press

Copyright © Alexis Heraclides and Ada Dialla 2015

The rights of Alexis Heraclides and Ada Dialla to be identified as the authors of this work have been asserted by them in accordance with the Copyright, Designs and Patents Act 1988.

Published by Manchester University Press
Oxford Road, Manchester M13 9PL
www.manchesteruniversitypress.co.uk

British Library Cataloguing-in-Publication Data
A catalogue record for this book is available from the British Library

Library of Congress Cataloging-in-Publication Data applied for

ISBN 978 0 7190 8990 9 hardback

First published 2015

The publisher has no responsibility for the persistence or accuracy of URLs for any external or third-party internet websites referred to in this book, and does not guarantee that any content on such websites is, or will remain, accurate or appropriate.

Typeset in Arno and Univers by R. J. Footring Ltd, Derby
Printed in Great Britain

For Argyris

Contents

	Preface and acknowledgements	ix
1	Humanitarian intervention today	1

Part I: Theory

	Introduction	11
2	The origins of the idea of humanitarian intervention: just war and against tyranny	14
3	Eurocentrism, 'civilization' and the 'barbarians'	31
4	International law and humanitarian intervention	57
5	Intervention and non-intervention in international political theory	81

Part II: Practice

	Introduction	101
6	Intervention in the Greek War of Independence, 1821–32	105
7	Intervention in Lebanon and Syria, 1860–61	134
8	The Bulgarian atrocities: a bird's eye view of intervention with emphasis on Britain, 1875–78	148
9	The Balkan crisis of 1875–78 and Russia: between humanitarianism and pragmatism	169
10	The US and Cuba, 1895–98	197

Part III: Conclusion

11	Assessment	225
	Select bibliography on international law until 1945	231
	Select bibliography	234
	Index	241

A table summarizing the stance of publicists regarding humanitarian intervention, 1830–1939, appears on pages 60–2

Preface and acknowledgements

The nineteenth-century precedent of humanitarian intervention was little known until recently. Most international relations and international law scholars as well as diplomats are unaware that humanitarian intervention has a longer history and is not simply a post-Cold War phenomenon. In the nineteenth century it was invoked and recognized by European states, public opinion and international jurists, from the three-power intervention in the Greek War of Independence (1821–32) until the more controversial US intervention in Cuba in 1898, but also with regard to other instances short of the use of armed force in cases of humanitarian plight from Peru to the Congo and from Naples to Russia.

But even among the few who are aware of the nineteenth-century experience there has been a reluctance to include it as a precedent, in view of the different circumstances and standards reigning prior to 1918, not least the embarrassing 'civilized–barbarians' dichotomy. Only a handful of international lawyers have used the nineteenth-century 'doctrine' of humanitarian intervention to butttress contemporary thinking on the idea.[1]

In recent years the claim that the nineteenth century was a heyday of humanitarian intervention has been made more convincing with Gary Bass's *Freedom's Battle: The Origins of Humanitarian Intervention* (2009). Lesser known is a lengthy paper by Tonny Brems Knudsen given at a conference in 2009.[2] These two works, as well as a lecture by André Mandelstam[3] in the inter-war period and a chapter by Martha Finnemore[4] in the mid-1990s, convinced us that a book on our part was in order.

The idea for this book matured following a workshop on humanitarian intervention at the University of Malmö in March 2010, where a paper on humanitarian intervention in the nineteenth century by one of the authors of this volume was well received.[5] By the time we had secured a contract with Manchester University Press, a second book appeared, edited by Brendan Simms and D. J. B. Trim, *Humanitarian Intervention: A History* (2011) and when writing our book, a third book was published, Davide Rodogno's *Against Massacre: Humanitarian Intervention in the Ottoman Empire, 1815–1914. The Emergence of a European Concept and International Practice* (2012). Ours is the fourth book in English. Why yet another volume on the history of humanitarian intervention?

The book by Bass, well researched and written in an engaging manner to reach a wide audience, brings to life three cases of intervention in the nineteenth century, but does not deal with international law and the views of international jurists in those days (which is basic, for humanitarian intervention evolved as a concept or doctrine of international law), or with political theory and philosophy (for instance making only passing mention of J. S. Mill).

The Simms and Trim edited volume is an important scholarly book but is not focused on the nineteenth century: it begins with the sixteenth century and ends with interventions in the 1990s. 'Humanitarian intervention' is understood very broadly to include humanitarianism, and not as understood in the study of international law and international relations, namely as armed intervention to end suffering in humanitarian plight or protracted internal wars. Moreover, that book is not concerned with international law and the views of international lawyers in the nineteenth century. Having said this, we have benefited from several excellent chapters in the book, notably those by Trim on the Renaissance roots of humanitarian intervention, Rodogno on the Lebanon/Syria case, Schulz on the 1875–78 Balkan crisis and Sewell on the 1898 US intervention in Cuba.

Rodogno's book is crisp and persuasive as regards its subject matter, humanitarian intervention in the Ottoman Empire and the Orientalist gaze of the Europeans, and its overall thrust is closer to what we had in mind when we started writing our book, though ours is broader; we cover not only the Ottoman Empire but also include specific chapters on political theory and the thinking behind international law.

This book is an attempt at a comprehensive presentation of humanitarian intervention in theory and practice. It starts with a brief presentation of the present situation and debate and then moves centuries back in time, with the genesis of the idea in the Renaissance followed by the nineteenth-century civilization–barbarity dichotomy, with its concomitant Eurocentric/Orientalist gaze towards the Ottomans. We continue with the pivotal international law dimension, examining the arguments of advocates and opponents of humanitarian intervention from the 1830s until the 1930s, concluding the first part of the book with international political theory and intervention. In the second part, four case studies are examined in detail in five chapters: the Greek case (1821–32), the Lebanon/Syria case (1860–61), the Balkan crisis and Bulgarian case (1875–78) in two chapters and the US intervention in Cuba (1895–98).

This volume is of course a joint venture. This is the case with five chapters, namely chapters 3, 6, 7, 8 and 11. The other six chapters have been written by one author, namely chapter 9 by Ada Dialla and chapters 1, 2, 4, 5 and 10 by Alexis

Preface and acknowledgements

Heraclides. Note that all the translations from the original languages are by the two authors unless otherwise stated.

We would like to thank a number of individuals for their advice and support. Special thanks are due to the Mill scholar Professor Georgios Varouxakis for his help and advice and to Professor Bertrand Taithe for his valuable comments and suggestions. We would also want to thank international law Professor Antonis Bredimas, Hegel scholar Professor Georges Faraklas and, at the LSE, Professor Kevin Featherstone and Dr Spyros Economides. Alexis Heraclides would also like to thank his Panteion colleague Dr Chrisafis Iordanoglou and his schoolmate and oldest friend John N. Faraclas for their generous hospitality in London when the research for the study began in the first part of 2011, and Ismini Demades, Ioanna Antonopoulou and Tena Prelec for technical assistance during two fruitful sojourns at the LSE in 2011 and 2013. Ada Dialla would like to thank the personnel of the Russian State Library and the State Archive of the Russian Federation for their assistance during her research trips in Moscow.

Notes

1 See e.g. J.-P. L. Fonteyne, 'The Customary International Law Doctrine of Humanitarian Intervention: Its Current Validity Under the U.N. Charter', *California Western International Law Journal*, 4 (1973–74), 203–36; R. B. Lillich, 'Humanitarian Intervention: A Reply to Ian Brownlie and a Plea for Constructive Alternatives', in J. N. Moore (ed.), *Law and Civil War in the Modern World* (Baltimore: Johns Hopkins University Press, 1974), 229–51.
2 T. B. Knudsen, 'The History of Humanitarian Intervention: The Rule or the Exception?', 50th ISA Annual Convention, New York, 15–18 February 2009.
3 A. Mandelstam, 'La protection des minorités', *Recueil des cours de l'Académie de droit international*, 1 (1923), 369–82, 388–91.
4 M. Finnemore, 'Constructing Norms of Humanitarian Intervention', in P. J. Katzenstein (ed.), *The Culture of National Security* (New York: Columbia University Press, 1996), 153–85.
5 See A. Heraclides, 'Humanitarian Intervention in the 19th Century: The Heyday of a Controversial Concept', *Global Society: Journal of Interdisciplinary International Relations*, 26:2 (2012), 215–40.

1

Humanitarian intervention today

Humanitarian intervention – that is, military intervention aimed at saving innocent people in other countries from massive violations of human rights (primarily the right to life) – entered public consciousness around 1990 as never before in the course of the twentieth century. It has earned a central place in scholarly research and in the preoccupations of decision-makers and international organizations and has captured the imagination of the wider public in a fashion few other political subjects have achieved in the post-Cold War world.[1] Ironically, it is in the limelight not due to its general acceptance but because of its controversial character, which has led to acrimonious debates. At the two ends of the scale there is, on the one hand, rejection, with the notion seen as nonsensical, an 'oxymoron',[2] the hallmark of deceit and, on the other, its acceptance as one of the clearest manifestations of altruism, the epitome of human solidarity and compassion (the 'good Samaritan'), the willingness to face great risk and considerable loss to save the lives of 'strangers', with no gains.

Interestingly, rejection of, and sheer incredulity with, 'humanitarian intervention' is shared across the ideological spectrum, from realist scholarship in international relations to Marxism and other forms of leftist critique, as well as pacifism. From the realist line of reasoning, which has its origins in Thucydides, Machiavelli, Hobbes and Spinoza, so-called 'humanitarian' or other ethical concerns have no place in international politics and are damaging to rational foreign policy. More scathing is a critique from Carl Schmitt, who argued that 'war in the name of humanity, is not war for the sake of humanity, but a war wherein a particular state seeks to usurp a universal concept against its military opponent', identifying itself with humanity and denying it to the enemy.[3] He adds (as if he were a Marxist) that it has been used as 'an ideological instrument of imperialist expansion, and in its ethical-humanitarian form it is a specific vehicle of economic imperialism ... whoever invokes humanity wants to cheat'.[4]

The question of intervention for humanitarian reasons poses agonizing dilemmas. There is the tension between the sanctity of life (saving human beings) and the veneration of sovereignty and independence; and there is the tension between doing something salutary in a humanitarian crisis if the United Nations Security Council is paralysed and abuse in the name of humanitarianism by intervening states. Most liberals opt for saving lives[5] and for intervening, exceptionally, even without the authorization of the United Nations, provided the intervention has gained wide international legitimacy and the plight is so appalling that the interest in global humanity overrides narrowly defined national interest.[6] Realists of course discard ethics in foreign affairs (with exceptions, such as those realists who take seriously the 'morality of states'[7]) and regard only threats to vital interests worthy of intervention, and intervention for humanitarian reasons a delusion, or as bogus. Most leftist thinkers, such as Noam Chomsky,[8] Edward Said, Tariq Ali,[9] Jacques Derrida or Jean Baudrillard denounced the 1999 intervention in Kosovo and the whole idea of 'humanitarian intervention', as have other critical thinkers in more scholarly manner, such as Anne Orford,[10] Antony Anghie[11] and Costas Douzinas.[12] For them, intervention is by definition abusive, the *diktat* of the powerful, a form of blatant neo-imperialism and neo-colonialism. But a minority of leftist thinkers, who put a premium on self-determination and saving the weak from the strong, are favourable to such interventions, albeit in very exceptional cases, such as Jürgen Habermas,[13] Michael Walzer[14] and the more controversial Bernard Kouchner, with his *droit d'ingérence*.[15]

Most international lawyers are opposed to such interventions, emphasizing state sovereignty and independence. There has, though, been a shift, which is far from insignificant, in that during the Cold War, among those opposed, the majority were against the whole notion, while in the post-Cold War era most are opposed to intervention only if it does not obtain UN authorization. Students of international relations are more nuanced, especially non-realists,[16] with those in the field of international ethics, cosmopolitans in particular, who tend to be less burdened by sovereignty, supporting unilateral humanitarian intervention, followed more guardedly by communitarians, from Michael Walzer in the late 1970s onwards.[17] They, together with international lawyers supportive of humanitarian intervention even without a UN mandate, disagree mainly as to the level of onslaught that warrants intervention, which ranges from systematic violations of fundamental human rights to a situation akin to genocide,[18] and the point at which to intervene: early on or late in a conflict, when all attempts to stop the humanitarian plight peacefully have failed.

During the Cold War, humanitarian intervention was generally considered beyond the pale, although even then a minority of international lawyers supported armed intervention on humanitarian grounds.[19] Some states, notably the US in the cases of the Dominican Republic (1965) and Grenada (1983), Belgium in Congo (1960–61), Belgium and the US in Congo (1964) or France in the Central African Republic (1979), had justified their actions on humanitarian grounds. But the near consensus is that only three military interventions qualify as humanitarian given that they put an end to widespread loss of life: India's intervention in East Pakistan (1971) (hundreds of thousands of civilians dead and almost nine million refugees fleeing to India), which led to the creation of Bangladesh; Vietnam's overthrow of the heinous Khmer Rouge regime under Pol Pot in Cambodia (1979) (with up to two million civilian deaths mainly from disease and malnutrition in forced labour camps); and the overthrow of Amin's odious regime in Uganda (with 300,000 citizens murdered by Amin's thugs) by Tanzania (1979). Interestingly, all three intervening states did not justify their action on humanitarian grounds (with the partial exception of India[20]) but on grounds of self-defence, and all three intervened mainly for instrumental reasons, especially Vietnam. The first two interventions faced heavy wind internationally, notably in the UN (especially the Vietnamese invasion), even though they both saved many lives.[21]

Following the end of the Cold War, the first post-bipolar decade witnessed unprecedented interventionism on humanitarian grounds: safe haven for the Kurds of northern Iraq (1991), Somalia (1992), Bosnia (1992–95), the intervention of the Economic Community Of West African States (ECOWAS) in Liberia (1990–96), the US-led intervention in Haiti (1994), French-led forces in Rwanda (1994), NATO's intervention in Serbia and Kosovo (1999) and the Australian-led intervention in East Timor (1999).

In Rwanda effective French intervention came very late, following three months of genocidal massacre by the Hutus of more than 800,000 Tutsis and many moderate Hutus.[22] The peacemaking intervention of ECOWAS in Liberia headed by Nigeria[23] and NATO's Kosovo/Serbia operation took place without authorization by the UN Security Council. NATO's Kosovo/Serbia operation gave rise to a heated discussion not only because of its lack of UN endorsement but also due to the choice of means (high-altitude aerial bombardment), which led to hundreds of civilian deaths, more intense ethnic cleansing by the repugnant Milosevic regime, thousands of refugees, considerable destruction of infrastructure and environmental pollution.[24] Many had feared that this Kosovo precedent would open a Pandora's box but this did not come about, partly due to these unintended consequences. In the second part of 1999, the Australian-led peacekeeping operation in East Timor took place with UN sanction, with no mismatch between the military means and humanitarian ends, and it turned out to be peaceful.[25] With the onset of the new millennium – and with '9/11' and its repercussions as far as US priorities were concerned (the 'war on terror') – the idea of humanitarian intervention seemed to have 'evaporated',[26] although there were at least two candidates, Sierra Leone and Sudan's Darfur. The next humanitarian interventions took place more than a decade later: the NATO-led operation in Libya (February–October 2011) and the French peacekeeping operation in the Central African Republic (December 2013), both authorized by the UN Security Council.[27]

In the wake of the Kosovo experience, UN Secretary-General Kofi Annan pondered: 'On the one hand is it legitimate for a regional organisation to use force without a UN mandate? On the other is it permissible to let gross and systematic violations of human rights, with grave humanitarian consequences, continue unchecked?'[28] Addressing the UN General Assembly in September 1999, he expressed his strong reservations about NATO's unauthorized intervention in Kosovo and Serbia but added: 'If in those dark days and hours leading to the genocide [in Rwanda] a coalition of States had been prepared to act in the defence of the Tutsi population, but did not receive prompt Council authorization, should such a coalition have stood aside and allowed the horror to unfold?'[29] And he challenged the member-states to come up with a new vision of sovereignty.[30]

The Annan challenge was taken up by the Canadian-sponsored twelve-person International Commission on Intervention and State Sovereignty (ICISS), which responded by subsuming humanitarian intervention under the novel concept of 'responsibility to protect' (R2P or RtoP).[31] The aim of the R2P approach was to 'shift the terms of the debate';[32] it amounts to a 'rhetorical trick' of flipping the coin and shifting the emphasis from the controversial right to intervene for humanitarian reasons to the 'less confrontational idea of a responsibility to protect',[33] but the substance remains the same.

In 2005 at intergovernmental level, the *Outcome Document* of the UN World Summit (15 September) made it a primary responsibility of states to protect their population against 'genocide, war crimes, crimes against humanity and ethnic cleansing'; if they fail to do so, a 'timely and decisive response' becomes the responsibility of the international community. The ICISS had suggested that the permanent members of the Security Council refrain from using the veto in such cases as long as their vital interests are not at stake but this was unacceptable to the US, Russia and China.[34] The first test case of R2P was the intervention in Libya.[35]

Given the situation during the Cold War and the interventionism of the 1990s and the ongoing debate, the general impression is that humanitarian intervention is basically a recent phenomenon, but in fact the concept of humanitarian intervention had been established in the nineteenth century.

Before moving back in time (in chapter 2), let us identify the main issues at stake in the present-day debate on the question of intervening or not intervening militarily for humanitarian reasons. Putting aside the proverbial question of whether 'violent means can ever serve humanitarian ends',[36] today's debate includes six main questions and at least three secondary ones.

The first question concerns the legality–legitimacy spectrum. Is legality through UN authorization indispensable? Is non-authorized intervention by definition illegal or is it perhaps legal given an alternative reading of the UN Charter?[37] Can intervention be condoned if it appears legitimate even though it is technically illegal, as the Independent International Commission on Kosovo concluded in its detailed report?[38] Another tack is the contention that one is faced with a complex legal problem[39] which may or may not be resolved on an ad hoc basis.

A second question is where to place the threshold for intervening with or without UN authorization: on systematic human rights violations (such as systematic discrimination akin to apartheid or 'internal colonialism'), on something more grave, such as so-called egregious crimes (i.e. ethnic cleansing, war crimes, crimes against humanity), or only at the level of mass extermination and genocide?[40]

A third issue is in which cases to intervene (with or without UN authorization): in a protracted internal war (Liberia, Syria), in a Hobbesian 'war of all against all' (Somalia), a separatist war (Kosovo) or only to put an end to one-sided onslaught (Rwanda), or in all four cases?

A fourth problem is abuse (wrong intentions and ulterior motives) and how it can be checked, if at all. UN authorization, collective intervention and intergovernmental supervision may do the trick but what if they are not forthcoming? And even if they are, they may still be seen as suspect, for the permanent members of the Security Council (as in the case of the Concert of Europe in the nineteenth century) can hardly be counted upon – or live up – to being the moral consciousness of the world. A related factor is the presence of tangible interests as motives and how they can be reconciled with humanitarian motives and intentions, especially since 'saving strangers' on its own is unlikely to provoke intervention.[41]

Another question is timing. Should intervention take place only after the exhaustion of all peaceful means (i.e. as a last resort) or should there be early, anticipatory intervention and preventive deployment once egregious crimes have been spotted, such as ethnic cleansing, so as to forestall a humanitarian disaster (the Kosovo model) and to avoid greater use of military force later, even though early intervention would be more difficult to justify internationally?[42]

There is also the need for a reasonable estimate of a successful outcome, that is, of attaining the humanitarian goals, avoiding 'noble intentions and bloody results',[43] with few deaths of civilians and little destruction of infrastructure (sparse 'collateral damage').[44] There is also the related issue of ensuring that less damage is done by intervening than by not intervening.[45]

The three secondary questions concern: a quick exit strategy or a longer stay for fear that the bloodbath and anarchy will resume;[46] how many casualties of 'our soldiers' are acceptable;[47] and the fact that the intervening states are by definition more powerful, which smacks of the powerful bullying the weak under a smokescreen of righteousness.[48]

The recent tendency of advocates of humanitarian intervention is to borrow from the well developed 'just war' doctrine of the Middle Ages and Renaissance (see chapter 2), with the criteria for a just war remodelled to fit modern conditions. The following 'just war' criteria are all regarded as essential for a humanitarian intervention to be contemplated: right authority, in the sense of 'legitimate authority' and not simply legal (factual) authority, which also alludes to 'failed states' as illegitimate and not worthy of sovereignty;[49] just cause (massive suffering); right intention (humanitarian motives genuine and not a ruse); last resort; proportional means (good over harm); and a reasonable prospect of success, leading to a 'just peace'.[50]

Notes

1. B. Jahn, 'Humanitarian Intervention – What's in a Name?', *International Politics*, 49:1 (2012), 36.
2. A. Roberts, 'Humanitarian War: Military Intervention and Human Rights', *International Affairs*, 69:3 (1993), 429.
3. C. Schmitt, *The Concept of the Political* (New Brunswick: Rutgers University Press, 1976, translated from the German, with Introduction and notes by G. Schwab) [1932], 54.
4. Ibid., 54.
5. M. J. Smith, 'Humanitarian Intervention: An Overview of the Ethical Issues', *Ethics and International Affairs*, 12:1 (1998), 73.
6. M. Walzer, 'The Politics of Rescue', *Social Research*, 62:1 (1995), 59.
7. D. C. Hendrickson, 'In Defense of Realism: A Commentary on *Just and Unjust War*', *Ethics and International Relations*, 11 (1997), 19–53; M. Wesley, 'Toward a Realist Ethics of Intervention', *Ethics and International Affairs*, 22:1 (2008), 55–72.
8. N. Chomsky, *A New Generation Draws the Line: Kosovo, East Timor and the Standards of the West* (New York: Verso, 2001).
9. T. Ali (ed.), *Masters of the Universe? NATO's Balkan Crusade* (New York: Verso, 2000).
10. A. Orford, *Reading Humanitarian Intervention: Human Rights and the Use of Force in International Law* (Cambridge: Cambridge University Press, 2003).
11. A. Anghie, *Imperialism, Sovereignty and the Making of International Law* (Cambridge: Cambridge University Press, 2004), 274–308.
12. C. Douzinas, *Human Rights and Empire: The Political Philosophy of Cosmopolitanism* (Abingdon: Routledge-Cavendish, 2007).
13. J. Habermas, 'Bestiality and Humanity: A War on the Border Between Legality and Morality', *Constellations*, 6:3 (1999), 263–72.
14. Walzer, 'The Politics of Rescue', 53–66; M. Walzer, 'The Argument About Humanitarian Intervention', *Dissent*, 49:1 (2002), 29–37.
15. See S. Hoffmann, 'The Politics and Ethics of Military Intervention', *Survival*, 37:4 (1995–96), 34–6; Smith, 'Humanitarian Intervention', 70–5; T. Allen and S. Syan, 'A Right to Interfere? Bernard Kouchner and the New Humanitarianism', *Journal of Development*, 12 (2000), 825, 828–36, 840; G. J. Bass, *Freedom's Battle: The Origins of Humanitarian Intervention* (New York: Vintage Books, 2009), 11–24.
16. See e.g. Hoffmann, 'The Politics and Ethics of Military Intervention', 29, 37–41; Smith, 'Humanitarian Intervention', 63–79; N. J. Wheeler, 'Legitimating Humanitarian Intervention: Principles and Procedures', *Melbourne Journal of International Law*, 2:2 (2001), 550–67.
17. M. Walzer, *Just and Unjust Wars* (New York: Basic Books, 1977), 101–8.
18. For a low threshold see W. M. Reisman, 'Sovereignty and Human Rights in Contemporary International Law', *American Journal of International Law*, 84:4 (1990), 866–76; A. D'Amato, 'The Invasion of Panama Was a Lawful Response to Tyranny', *American*

Journal of International Law, 84:2 (1990), 516–24; F. R. Tesón, 'Eight Principles for Humanitarian Intervention', *Journal of Military Ethics*, 5:2 (2006), 95–100, 105–6. For a high threshold, a 'spike test', see T. Farer, 'Cosmopolitan Humanitarian Intervention: A Five-Part Test', *International Affairs*, 19:2 (2005), 215–19.

19 They included some major figures from an older generation, such as Lauterpacht, Guggenheim, de Visscher, Reisman, McDougal and Jessup, as well as Lillich, D'Amato, Moore, Chilstrom, Levitin, Umozurike, Sornarajah and Tesón.

20 N. J. Wheeler, *Saving Strangers: Humanitarian Intervention in International Society* (Oxford: Oxford University Press, 2000), 64 n.43.

21 M. Leifer, 'Vietnam's Intervention in Kampuchea: The Rights of States Versus the Rights of People', in I. Forbes and M. Hoffman (eds), *Political Theory, International Relations, and the Ethics of Intervention* (Basingstoke: Macmillan, 1993), 145–56; F. Hassan, '*Realpolitik* in International Law: After Tanzanian–Ugandan Conflict, "Humanitarian Intervention" Reexamined', *Willamette Law Review*, 17 (1981), 897; Wheeler, *Saving Strangers*, 65–71, 80–106; M. Akehurst, 'Humanitarian Intervention', in H. Bull (ed.), *Intervention in World Politics* (Oxford: Clarendon Press, 1984), 95–9; S. Chesterman, *Just War or Just Peace? Humanitarian Intervention and International Law* (Oxford: Oxford University Press, 2001), 71–4, 77–80.

22 B. D. Jones, '"Intervention without Borders": Humanitarian Intervention in Rwanda, 1990–94', *Millennium: Journal of International Studies*, 24:2 (1995), 225, 230–1.

23 See H. Howe, 'Lessons of Liberia: ECOMOG and Regional Peacekeeping', *International Security*, 21:3 (1997), 145–76.

24 For the international law debate see: R. A. Falk, 'Kosovo, World Order, and the Future of International Law', *American Journal of International Law*, 93:4 (1999), 847–57; B. Simma, 'NATO, the UN and the Use of Force: Legal Aspects', *European Journal of International Law*, 10 (1999), 1–22; A. Cassese, '*Ex injuria jus oritur*: Are We Moving Towards International Legitimation of Forcible Humanitarian Countermeasures in the World Community?', *European Journal of International Law*, 10, (1999), 23–30; L. Henkin, 'Kosovo and the Law of "Humanitarian Intervention"', *American Journal of International Law*, 93:4 (1999), 824–8; R. Wedgewood, 'NATO's Campaign in Yugoslavia', *American Journal of International Law*, 93:4 (1999), 828–34. More generally see Independent International Commission on Kosovo, *Kosovo Report: Conflict, International Response, Lessons Learned* (Oxford: Oxford University Press, 2000); A. Schnabel and R. Thakur (eds), *Kosovo and the Challenge of Humanitarian Intervention* (Tokyo: United Nations University Press, 2000).

25 N. J. Wheeler and T. Dunne, 'East Timor and the New Humanitarian Interventionism', *International Affairs*, 77:4 (2001), 805–37.

26 T. G. Weiss, 'The Sunset of Humanitarian Intervention? The Responsibility to Protect in a Unipolar Era', *Security Dialogue*, 25:2 (2004), 135.

27 J. Pattison, 'The Ethics of Humanitarian Intervention in Libya', *Ethics and International Affairs*, 25:3 (2011), 271–7.

28 K. Annan, 'Two Concepts of Sovereignty', *The Economist*, 18 September 1999, 49.

29 Press release SG/SM/7136, GA/9596 (20 September 1999), 2.

30 R. Thakur, 'Outlook: Intervention, Sovereignty and the Responsibility to Protect: Experiences from ICISS', *Security Dialogue*, 33:3 (2002), 325.

31 G. Evans and M. Sahnoun, 'The Responsibility to Protect', *Foreign Affairs*, 1:6 (2002), 99–100; T. G. Weiss, 'R2P after 9/11 and the World Summit', *Wisconsin International Law Journal*, 24:3 (2006), 741–60.

32 International Commission on Intervention and State Sovereignty (ICISS), *Responsibility to Protect* (Ottawa: International Development Research Centre, 2001), 16–18; Thakur, 'Outlook', 327–8.
33 C. Stahn, 'Responsibility to Protect: Political Rhetoric or Emerging Legal Norm?', *American Journal of International Law*, 101:1 (2007), 102.
34 A. J. Bellamy, 'Whither the Responsibility to Protect? Humanitarian Intervention and the 2005 World Summit', *Ethics and International Affairs*, 20:2 (2006), 146–7, 151–2, 167.
35 J. Welsh, 'Civilian Protection in Libya: Putting Coercion and Controversy Back into RtoP', *Ethics and International Affairs*, 25:3 (2011), 255–62.
36 Wheeler, 'Legitimating Humanitarian Intervention', 556.
37 For the alternative reading see e.g. W. D. Verwey, 'Humanitarian Intervention Under International Law', *Netherlands International Law Review*, 32 (1985), 357–418, especially 406–18; C. F. Amerasinghe, 'The Conundrum of Recourse to Force – To Protect Persons', *International Organizations Law Review*, 3 (2006), 7–53, especially 37–9, 47–53.
38 Independent International Commission on Kosovo, *Kosovo Report*, 2.
39 I. Hurd, 'Is Humanitarian Intervention Legal? The Rule of Law in an Incoherent World', *Ethics and International Affairs*, 25:3 (2011), 293–313.
40 M. J. Bazyler, 'Reexamining the Doctrine of Humanitarian Intervention in Light of the Atrocities in Kampuchea and Ethiopia', *Stanford Journal of International Law*, 23 (1987), 598–601; Hoffmann, 'The Politics and Ethics of Military Intervention', 37–8; D. Fisher, 'The Ethics of Intervention', *Survival*, 36 (1994), 51–9; Farer, 'Cosmopolitan Humanitarian Intervention', 215–17; M. Fixdal and D. Smith, 'Humanitarian Intervention and Just War', *Mershon International Studies Review*, 42:2 (1998), 296–9.
41 R. B. Lillich, 'Forcible Self-Help by States to Protect Human Rights', *Iowa Law Review*, 53 (1967–68), 53; Walzer, *Just and Unjust Wars*, 101–4; Wheeler, 'Legitimating Humanitarian Intervention', 238–9.
42 Hoffmann, 'The Politics and Ethics of Military Intervention', 44; Fixdal and Smith, 'Humanitarian Intervention and Just War', 301–2.
43 M. Ignatieff, 'The Seductiveness of Moral Disgust', *Social Research*, 62:1 (1995), 78.
44 G. Levy, 'The Case for Humanitarian Intervention', *Orbis*, 37:4 (1993), 624; A. Roberts, 'The Crisis in U.S. Peacekeeping', *Survival*, 36 (1994), 109.
45 Fixdal and Smith, 'Humanitarian Intervention and Just War', 305; Farer, 'Cosmopolitan Humanitarian Intervention', 219; B. Parekh, 'Rethinking Humanitarian Intervention', *International Political Science Review*, 18:1 (1997), 67.
46 Walzer, 'The Politics of Rescue', 56–7, 61; Hoffmann, 'The Politics and Ethics of Military Intervention', 41, 43.
47 Walzer, 'The Politics of Rescue', 58–9; Hendrickson, 'In Defense of Realism', 46.
48 Hassan, '*Realpolitik* in International Law', 910.
49 Fixdal and Smith, 'Humanitarian Intervention and Just War', 291–2; A. Coates, 'Humanitarian Intervention: A Conflict of Traditions', in T. Nardin and M. S. Williams (eds), *Humanitarian Intervention* (New York: New York University Press, 2006), 62–3.
50 J. B. Hehir, 'Expanding Military Intervention: Promise or Peril?', *Social Research*, 62:1 (1995), 46–8; Fixdal and Smith, 'Humanitarian Intervention and Just War', 283–312; Wheeler, 'Legitimating Humanitarian Intervention', 550–67; Thakur, 'Outlook', 332–3; G. Reichberg and H. Syse, 'Humanitarian Intervention: A Case of Offensive Force?', *Security Dialogue*, 33:3 (2002), 309–22; J. Boyle, 'Traditional Just War Theory and Humanitarian Intervention', in Nardin and Williams (eds), *Humanitarian Intervention*, 31–57.

Part I
Theory

Introduction

Throughout the long nineteenth century and until 1939, 'intervention' (originally a French term) or 'interference' (the original British term) was 'Protean', covering an array of manifestations 'from a speech in Parliament by Palmerston to the partition of Poland'.[1] Not only was the scope of intervention wide, but its meaning and consequences remained contentious.

The Argentinean diplomat and jurist Carlos Calvo points out, in his acclaimed 1870 treatise, that on intervention 'there are almost as many different opinions as there are authors. Some admit it, approving intervention; others condemn it, repudiating it; for some it has become a right, others add the idea of duty; others see nothing else but a simple fact, a brutal fact, which has its place in history'.[2] The situation remained the same well into the twentieth century. As Percy Winfield put it in the early 1920s, '[t]he subject of intervention is one of the vaguest branches of international law. We are told that intervention is a right; that it is a crime; that it is the rule; that it is the exception; that it is never permissible at all'.[3]

Following the Second World War the problem with intervention continued to be discussed in the international law and international relations literature.[4] In the post-Cold War era, with increasing interventionism, interest hardly diminished, the main focus now being on humanitarian intervention, which is even more contentious.[5]

But two things are clear. Intervention meant then – and today[6] – 'coercive', 'dictatorial interference by a State in the [internal or external] affairs of another State for the purpose of maintaining or altering the actual conditions of things'.[7] Moreover, non-intervention was – and is – the rule, intervention the exception.[8]

It is often assumed that the non-intervention norm was established in the Treaty of Westphalia (1648). In fact non-intervention was established as a principle of international law in the first half of the eighteenth century by jurists Christian Wolff and Emer de Vattel.[9] Thereafter non-intervention became a fully fledged legal principle associated with the principles of sovereignty and independence. Half a century later, Kant lent considerable weight to this new norm in his quest for principles assuring peace, with his Preliminary Article 5 on non-intervention in his *Toward Perpetual Peace* (see chapter 5).

In the course of the long nineteenth century, five positions on the matter can be discerned in international law and international political theory: (1) strict adherence to non-intervention; (2) exceptions limited to instances of threats to national interests; (3) exceptions to include protracted civil wars when a state has collapsed into anarchy; (4) exceptions to include national struggles against alien rule, especially in order to offset a previous intervention in support of the incumbent government; and (5) exceptions to include intervening in order to stop massacres and other atrocities.

The English term 'humanitarian intervention' was coined by the British jurist and aesthete William Edward Hall in 1880 in his acclaimed *International Law* (renamed the very same year *A Treatise on International Law*).[10] It appears in a footnote and not in the main text,[11] which might imply that the author was unaware of having launched a new term or was reluctant to do so. In fact he had not conceived a new concept but the English term that was to stick, for other terms had previously been used, such as 'intervention in the general interests of humanity'[12] and 'intervention for humanity', which correspond to the French term in use, *intervention d'humanité*,[13] or 'intervention on the ground of humanity', intervention 'on behalf of the interests of humanity',[14] all with the same meaning.[15]

From the 1830s until the 1930s humanitarian intervention was understood as interfering 'for the purpose of vindicating the law of nations against outrage',[16] 'in the interests of humanity for the purpose of stopping religious persecution and endless cruelties in times of peace and war'.[17] According to Antoine Rougier (in a seminal 1910 survey of the literature), 'intervention on the grounds of humanity is properly that which recognizes the right of one state to exercise an international control over the acts of another in regard to its internal sovereignty when contrary to the laws of humanity'.[18] Ellery Stowell (in 1921) defined humanitarian intervention, with the nineteenth-century experience in mind, 'as the reliance upon force for the justifiable purpose of protecting the inhabitants of another state from treatment which is so arbitrary and persistently abusive as to exceed the limits of that authority within which the sovereign is presumed to act with reason and justice'.[19]

Unquestionably, humanitarian intervention as such is a nineteenth-century concept and doctrine. But the wider idea of rescuing those tyrannized and maltreated has older roots. It was arguably a Renaissance idea, though admittedly within a different normative context, when theology intermingled with the 'law of nations' (international law), then just taking its very first steps.

Introduction

Notes

1. P. H. Winfield, 'The History of Intervention in International Law', *British Year Book of International Law*, 3 (1922–23), 130, 135–6, 141.
2. C. Calvo, *Le droit internationale: théorie et pratique* (Paris: Guillaumin et Cie, G. Pedone-Lauriel, 1880, 3rd edition) [1870], 237, para. 134.
3. Winfield, 'The History of Intervention in International Law', 130.
4. See C. G. Fenwick, 'Intervention: Individual and Collective', *American Journal of International Law*, 39:4 (1945), 645–51; R. J. Vincent, *Nonintervention and International Order* (Princeton: Princeton University Press, 1974); R. Little, *Intervention: External Involvement in Civil Wars* (London: Robert Robertson, 1975); H. Bull (ed.), *Intervention in World Politics* (Oxford: Clarendon Press, 1984).
5. See e.g. J. Macmillan, 'Intervention and the Ordering of the Modern World', *Review of International Studies*, 39 (2013), 1039–56; C. Reus-Smit, 'The Concept of Intervention', *Review of International Studies*, 39 (2013), 1057–76.
6. See H. Bull, 'Introduction', in Bull (ed.), *Intervention in World Politics*, 1; S. Hoffmann, 'The Problem of Intervention', in *ibid.*, 7–28; R. Higgins, 'Intervention and International Law', in *ibid.*, 30–2.
7. L. Oppenheim, *International Law: A Treatise* (London: Longmans, Green and Co., 1937, 5th edition, edited by H. Lauterpacht) [1905], vol. I, 249.
8. Winfield, 'The History of Intervention in International Law', 139.
9. *Ibid.*, 132, 135.
10. See E. C. Stowell, *Intervention in International Law* (Washington, DC: John Byrne, 1921), 51 n.7; S. Chesterman, *Just War or Just Peace? Humanitarian Intervention and International Law* (Oxford: Oxford University Press, 2001), 24.
11. W. E. Hall, *International Law* (Oxford: Clarendon Press, 1880), 247 n.1; and W. E. Hall, *A Treatise on International Law* (Oxford: Clarendon Press, 1884, 2nd edition) [1880], 266 n.1.
12. H. Wheaton, *Elements of International Law: With a Sketch of the History of the Science* (Philadelphia: Carey, Lea and Blanchard, 1836), 91.
13. Stowell, *Intervention in International Law*, 51.
14. R. Phillimore, *Commentaries upon International Law* (London: Butterworth, 1879, 3rd edition) [1854], vol. I, 568; E. S. Creasy, *First Platform of International Law* (London: John van Voorst, 1876), 300.
15. Chesterman, *Just War or Just Peace?*, 24.
16. Stowell, *Intervention in International Law*, 51.
17. Oppenheim, *International Law*, vol. I, 255.
18. A. Rougier, 'La théorie de l'intervention d'humanité', *Revue générale de droit international public*, 17 (1910), 472 (quote translated by Stowell, *Intervention in International Law*, 53 n.9).
19. Stowell, *Intervention in International Law*, 53.

2

The origins of the idea of humanitarian intervention: just war and against tyranny

The just war doctrine

The original just war doctrine was not concerned with intervening in other states for humanitarian reasons, but with providing just reasons for resorting to an inter-state war. It was only by the sixteenth century, coinciding with the birth of international law, then known as *jus gentium* or law of nations, under the sway of natural law, that support for those suffering from tyranny and maltreatment was seen as one of the reasons for a just war.

The just war (*bellum justum*) doctrine has its origins in ancient Greek and Roman thought, and was developed in early Christian and more specifically medieval Catholic thinking. This first normative phase regarding war was followed by the period between the Peace of Westphalia (1648) until 1918 in which waging war, even without a pretext, was deemed an attribute of state sovereignty.[1] It consisted mainly of *jus ad bellum* (when resorting to war is justified and just) but later included *jus in bello* (appropriate conduct in the use of force). The idea of a just war can be seen as a middle road between the tradition of *Realpolitik*, which regards moral dilemmas and the ethics of war as irrelevant in international politics, and the alternative world view of pacifism. According to this middle road, war is deplorable but under certain circumstances justified and necessary as a last resort.[2]

Aristotle is credited with having first used the term 'just war' (*dikaios polemos*) in his *Nicomachean Ethics*.[3] For 'the Philosopher', as he was known in the Middle Ages and the Renaissance, war is just if we are victims of aggression, if we have been wronged and if the purpose of the war is to end up with peace. He also regarded a war as just if it was waged against those destined by nature to be governed by others, 'slaves by nature'.[4]

The Romans rendered the just war idea a clear legal theory, most of all Cicero, who maintained that there are two just causes for resorting to war: redressing an injury and repelling an invader, with peace the ultimate aim of war.[5]

The early Christians condemned war as evil and opposed to the will of God. But when Christianity became the official religion of the Roman Empire with the Edict of Milan (313), a more positive stance regarding war was called for.[6]

In this context Augustine maintained that war may be evil but nevertheless some wars are ordained by Providence because they are just. The essence is a just cause: to defend a state from invasion, to safeguard its safety and honour, to avenge injuries or to punish another state for its wrongdoing, provided the war is not aimed at territorial aggrandizement or revenge and not motivated by a delight in violence. The arbiter of whether a war is just is God, which amounted to human conscience.[7] The aim of all wars should be the restoration of peace, order and tranquillity.[8]

Thomas Aquinas in the thirteenth century presented the just war tradition as a coherent set of rules. For Augustine, the injury provided the just cause for war, while for Aquinas it was the culpability of the wrongdoer.[9] The great scholastic, in his *Summa Theologica*, presented three conditions as necessary for just war: (1) declaration of war by the proper authority; (2) just cause, avenging wrongs committed by another state and punishing the guilty state (which is unwilling to make amends); and (3) right intention, the motive of resort to armed force being 'to do the good and avoid the evil', to secure peace, rather than lust for power, thirst for revenge or a readiness to injure.[10]

Aquinas distinguished between the 'guilty' and those who were 'innocent', though he acknowledged that in a war situation the innocent could unintentionally be killed. He is also known for the famous 'double effect': if an action results in both good and bad effects it is permitted, if the latter are not disproportionate to the good and insofar as the good effects are intended, while the bad effects are unintended and if there is no other way to achieve the good results.[11]

The next major contribution to just war came from the four founders of international law as they tend to be regarded today: the Spaniards Francisco de Vitoria and Francisco Suarez of the University of Salamanca, the Italian Alberico Gentili of Oxford University, and Hugo Grotius.

Vitoria, prompted by the Spanish conquest and cruel treatment of the 'Indians' in the New World, tried to follow a middle path between the justification for conquest, as put forward by Spain and by the Aristotelian philosopher Juan Ginés de Sepúlveda, and the doubts about the conquest on ethical grounds raised by jurists of the University of Salamanca, such as Domingo de Soto and Diego de Covarruvias, and more scathingly by Bartolomé de Las Casas,[12] who did his utmost to abolish Indian slavery and stop the barbarities committed by his Spanish compatriots.[13]

According to Vitoria, Spain's justifications for the conquest were inadequate, but the conquest was ultimately beneficial to the 'American aborigines' (whom he did not regard as slaves by nature) for it brought to the New World a higher culture.[14] Resort to war should be reluctant, not aimed at the destruction of the other country, with moderation in victory. Both sides may believe in the justice of their cause, but it is impossible objectively for both to have a just cause: one side was objectively righteous while the other was under 'invisible ignorance'. Vitoria is also known for the principle of distinction (non-combatant immunity): that the innocent should not be the object of deliberate killing in a war.[15]

Suarez stressed that the method used must be 'proper', with 'due proportion' at the start, during its prosecution and after victory is attained. The innocent should be spared and he did not condone waging war against backward non-Christian peoples.[16]

For Gentili, a war could be just if based on honour, necessity or expediency and if it is a last resort. In essence, war 'cannot be just, unless it is necessary'.[17] He stressed the sparing of the innocent and prisoners of war, and conducting war justly with no excesses and cruelty. He also argued that it is possible for both belligerents to have a just cause, especially in instances of a 'disputed right'.[18]

For Grotius, just causes are (1) defence of persons and territory, (2) recovery of what is due to the aggrieved state, (3) inflicting punishment on the wrongdoer, (4) sufficient justification, (5) costs and evil from the war not greater than the good that would come about from the war, and (6) war as a last resort. Grotius, like his predecessors, was also concerned with the *jus in bello* aspect. Unjust causes were the desire to acquire rich lands and conquer others on the pretext that it is for their own good.[19]

Against tyranny: the monarchomachs, Bodin, Vitoria, Gentili, Grotius

Humanitarian intervention's possible Renaissance roots

On the Renaissance roots of humanitarian intervention there is disagreement as to the progenitors and as to whether such roots exist in the first place.

From 1945 until recently, the conventional view was that Grotius was the precursor. This tendency is largely due to Hersch Lauterpacht, who had stated (in 1946) that in Grotius one finds 'the first authoritative statement of the principle of humanitarian intervention – the principle that exclusiveness of domestic jurisdiction stops when outrage upon humanity begins'.[20] When humanitarian intervention was hatched in the nineteenth century, jurists referred to their contemporaries as the fathers of the concept (see chapter 4) but some also mentioned Grotius,[21] others Emer de Vattel[22] and some mentioned both.[23]

Peter Haggenmacher and Theodor Meron regard the concept as pre-Grotian and see Gentili as the progenitor,[24] from whom Grotius had picked up the idea without mentioning Gentili, despite his obvious debt to him.[25] The first to point to Gentili's contribution on this question is probably Gezina van der Molen, in the inter-war years, who referred to his idea of 'the right of intervention on behalf of subjects, who are treated cruelly and unjustly by their prince'.[26] Meron also refers to Suarez as being almost on a par with Gentili. More recently Vitoria has been mentioned as the progenitor by an increasing number of scholars. However, the view that Grotius is the progenitor lingers on.[27]

There are also two other proposed progenitors, whose contribution has not gained wide acceptance: the 'monarchomachs', mainly with the work *Vindicae contra tyrannos* (*Defence Against Tyrants*), and Jean Bodin.

But other commentators regard the presumed Renaissance roots of the idea as far-fetched, given (1) the different contingent and ethical-religious rather than juridical basis of action; (2) the absence of the vital non-intervention principle; (3) that its advocates had an axe to grind (to save Protestants from religious persecution); and (4) that it amounted to 'cloaked imperialism', in that humanitarian reasons functioned as a justification for the conquest of those labelled 'infidels', 'barbarians' or 'aborigines'.

According to Antoine Rougier, prior to the nineteenth century the idea 'to combat tyranny in a neighbouring State' as propounded by Grotius and others was 'a vague theory based on examples from Greek antiquity, with a moral rather than a juridical character', within a school of thought (natural law) 'which did not separate law from its ethical foundation'.[28]

John Vincent points out that taking up arms 'on behalf of oppressed subjects is plainly to make war on another sovereign', while the development of the idea of humanitarian intervention is closely linked to the modern concept of 'intervention', a term not used or known to Grotius.[29]

In the same vein, Luke Glanville has argued that 'this right of war to punish tyranny and rescue the oppressed was not articulated in terms of an exception to a sovereign right of non-intervention in any clear and recognizable sense';[30] it was rather a manifestation 'of the right of the sovereign prince to wage war' and punishment for 'grievous violations of the law of nature'.[31]

According to Wilhelm Grewe's reading of Grotius, his approach is 'nothing other than the doctrine of religious intervention expressed in the language of natural law'.[32]

The argument that saving people from maltreatment was a justification for colonialism and imperialism is levelled mainly at Vitoria and Grotius (see below).

Antiquity and the Middle Ages

Interestingly, Renaissance writers, notably Gentili and Grotius, believed that their views on assisting the oppressed had roots in Greek and Roman antiquity. In particular they harked back to Cicero and especially to Seneca, whom they used to buttress their stance. Grotius also mentions another precursor, Pope Innocent IV, and he names Vitoria and three of his Spanish contemporaries as being opposed to this view.[33]

For Cicero there were two kinds of injustice, one resulting from injury and the other from not averting injury to others, if one has the power to do so.[34] He asserted that 'those who say that we should think about the interests of our fellow citizens, but not those of foreigners, destroy the common society of the human race'.[35]

Gentili and Grotius quote the following dictum by Seneca: that if another sovereign 'remote from my nation harasses his own ... the duty which I owe to the human race is prior and superior to that which I owe [that sovereign]'.[36] Grotius also refers to two other Seneca maxims: 'Men have been born to aid one another',[37] and 'I shall come to the aid of the perishing'.[38]

In the early thirteenth century, Pope Innocent IV, an eminent canon lawyer, justified the Crusades on the grounds that the use of armed force was permissible in order to prevent or punish the persecution of Christians in 'infidel' kingdoms and enforce natural law if it was violated (the Saracens were also bound by natural law according to Innocent) but this should not lead to wars of conversion to Christianity or annexation. Aware that this was open to abuse, he added the need for papal authorization.[39]

The views of Innocent were obviously self-serving at a time when the papacy's power was at its zenith. Innocent referred to Christians vis-à-vis 'infidels' – contrary to Gentili, Suarez and Grotius, who referred to humankind – thus it is difficult to treat his view through the logic of humanitarian intervention.

Lesser-known origins: the monarchomachs and Bodin

To begin with, there is an earlier possible progenitor, Thomas More, in his *Utopia* (1516).[40] The Utopians loathe fighting and fail to see anything glorious in war but 'go to war only for good reasons: to protect their own land, to drive invading armies from the territories of their friends, or to liberate an oppressed people, in the name of humanity, from tyranny and servitude'.[41] However, More's tentativeness as to whether *Utopia* is in all respects 'the best state of a commonwealth'[42] (note that the Utopians had abolished property and were heathens, contrary to More, who was a devout Catholic), not to mention his at times playful approach to the Utopians, and the fact that he does not elaborate on this particular point, make him a very elusive precursor, if one at all.

The first to draw attention to the contributions of the monarchomachs (those who fight monarchs, as coined by the contemporary Scottish jurist William Barclay) as well as of Bodin to the theory of intervention is probably the French legal historian Adhémar Esmein, in 1900.[43] The contribution of the author of *Vindicae* was also alluded to by William Archibald Dunning in his *History of Political Thought from Luther to Montesquieu* (1905),[44] and in the 1920s by Ellery Stowell,[45] by the Calvinist theologian Marc Boegner[46] and by Harold Laski.[47]

Vindicae was published in 1579 in Basle, at the height of the religious wars in France and as a reaction to the St Bartholomew's Day massacre (24 August 1572). The author wrote under the pseudonym Stephanus Junius Brutus Celta (the Celt). The writer was undoubtedly a Huguenot (French Calvinist) but the authorship of the book still remains a mystery. The most likely authors are two distinguished personalities of the time, Hubert Languet, a French lawyer and diplomat, and

Philippe de Mornay (known as Duplessis-Mornay), a French theologian and activist (the two were close friends).[48] The work was mainly known in Europe for its 'resistance theory', and the doctrine of tyrannicide[49] and republicanism as popular sovereignty.[50]

Other notable works in this tradition were the anonymous pamphlet *De jure magistratuum* (*The Right of Magistrates*) by theologian Theodore Beza (Calvin's successor in Geneva) and *Franco-Gallia*, by François Hotman, Professor of Law at the University of Geneva, which called for representative government and elective monarchy.[51] Note that Beza and Hotman were both initially regarded as the author of *Vindicae*.[52]

Vindiciae and *De jure magistratuum* advocated outside intervention if a prince persisted in his violent course and if other remedies had been tried but had failed.[53] According to both texts intervention was both a right and a duty of all princes, if another prince was a tyrant and 'persisted in his violent courses'.[54] A prince who stood idly by 'and beholdeth the wickedness of a tyrant, and the slaughter of the innocent ... is worse than the tyrant him selfe'.[55]

Are we then to surmise that Languet or Mornay and Beza are the progenitors or among the progenitors of the concept? We need to bear in mind that we are dealing with polemical tracts, whose agenda was to save Protestants being persecuted for religious reasons.[56] As Trim points out, 'the monarchomach authors conceived of "tyranny" in narrow confessional terms. Roman Catholic regimes were *assumed* to be tyrannical, because of the way they "oppressed" Protestants'.[57] This included the Pope. Hotman, for instance, characterized Rome as 'innately, permanently tyrannical'.[58] True, the monarchomachs were primarily concerned with the plight of their fellow Protestants. However, in their works they also referred to people in general and especially to suffering women and children. According to Garnett, *Vindicae* is not 'straightforwardly partisan', at least 'not overtly so', but addressed to all those who profess the Christian religion, 'whether papal or reformed', pointing to the 'evil arts' and 'pestiferous doctrines' of Machiavelli.[59] And Trim acknowledges that 'whatever the propagandists and apologists intended, what many readers would surely have taken away from their reading was that extreme violence was intrinsically wrong because of the human suffering involved, and this was true for all (or at any rate most) human beings'.[60]

Now let us examine Bodin, who has been bypassed on this question even more than the monarchomachs.[61] The fact that he was (together with Hobbes) the father of the concept of sovereignty makes his contribution even more intriguing. Bodin was a moderate Catholic vexed by the French onslaught against the Huguenots.[62] In his *Six livres de la République* (1576) he took a middle road between absolute sovereignty without moral considerations and resistance theory, by equipping the state or rather a single individual, the monarch, with sovereignty that was absolute, indivisible and perpetual. The sovereign had to be just, his rule not arbitrary, and the monarch's sovereignty derived from the sovereignty of the people.[63]

On the question 'whether a sovereign prince ... can be killed if he is cruel, oppressive, or excessively wicked', Bodin asserted that '[i]t makes a great difference whether we say that a tyrant can be lawfully killed by a foreign prince or by a subject' and added that 'it is a most beautiful and magnificent thing for a prince to take up arms in order to avenge an entire people unjustly oppressed by a tyrant's cruelty, as did Hercules, who travelled all over the world exterminating tyrant-monsters and was deified for his great feat'.[64] This was probably Bodin's answer to the St Bartholomew's Day massacre. As an enlightened royalist he agreed with the Huguenots that the conflict had been provoked by the monarch, but he feared for the existence of the sovereign state and regarded sanctioning resistance as the recipe for chaos and anarchy.[65] As he had put it for good measure: 'I conclude then that it is never permissible for a subject to attempt anything against a sovereign prince, no matter how wicked and cruel a tyrant he may be'.[66]

Arguably Bodin cannot be excluded as one of the earliest progenitors, given his more detached and less *engagé* approach by comparison with the monarchomachs and the fact that he placed it within the new principle of sovereignty.

Mainstream origins: Vitoria, Gentili, Suarez and Grotius

Vitoria in recent years has been singled out (*contra* Grotius's view) by an increasing number of scholars as the earliest proponent of the idea.[67] We will contest this view.

Vitoria pondered whether the practice of 'human sacrifice', 'cannibalism' and other abominable acts by the Indians justified armed intervention and replied in the affirmative.[68] Las Casas took the opposite line, that interfering to rescue a few by killing many was disproportionate and immoral, a remedy worse than the disease.[69] Vitoria, with reference to the American Indians, asserted that any Christian ruler could justifiably intervene to halt the injury of innocent people, though that ruler could not eject the adversary from his ancestral lands and property.[70] For him it did not matter that the Indians fully accepted such religious rules and rituals as human sacrifice and did not seek Spanish help to save them.[71]

Thus what for Innocent was the rescuing of Christians from 'infidels', for Vitoria it was rescuing innocent victims from 'barbarians'. In view of Vitoria's rationale – above all his 'insidious justification' of the Spanish conquest,[72] presenting it as for the good of the 'Indians',[73] and 'intervention in the name of humanity'[74] as one of the main arguments justifying the overseas Spanish conquest[75] – it would seem far-fetched to regard him as a genuine progenitor of the idea, on any sort of par with Gentili, Grotius and a few others. Vitoria was well aware and distressed by the news of the horrible deeds of the *conquistadors*,[76] the sheer 'destruction of the Indians' (major discussions were taking place on this very subject in Spain, not least in the University of Salamanca)[77] and was deeply shocked by the 1533 'butchery' of the Incas by Pizarro that freezes the blood in one's veins (as he put it).⁷⁸ Such acts could hardly be compared, as stressed by Las Casas, to occasional ritualized human sacrifices based on the Aztec religion and accepted by the people in question.⁷⁹ In fact Vitoria acknowledged that the slaughter of innocent Indians 'undermined the claim that they were engaged in a humanitarian endeavour'⁸⁰ but did not appear to modify his views on intervention on humanitarian grounds. His prudent stance may have been due to the fact that, at the time, Charles V demanded that there should be no writing or lecturing on the Indian question.⁸¹

Gentili, based on Ambrose's postulate 'fulsome is the justice that protects the frail', regarded the subjects of other states as not 'outside of the kinship of nature and the society formed by the whole world', adding that 'if you abolish that society, you will destroy the union of the human race, by which life is supported'.⁸² According to his *De jure belli libri tres* (1589), 'if men clearly sin against the laws of nature and of mankind, I believe that anyone whatsoever may check such men by force of arms'.⁸³ He asserted that 'if subjects are treated cruelly and unjustly, this principle of defending them is approved by others as well. And they bring forward the familiar instance of Hercules, the subduer of tyrants and monsters'.⁸⁴ By 'others' Gentili almost certainly meant Bodin, whom he greatly admired⁸⁵ (for Bodin's similar phrase see above). Referring to a blood-thirsty tyrant in another country, he stated that 'If he does not assail my country, but is the bane of his own', then, on the basis of 'the duty that I owe to the whole human race ... I am free to act as I please toward him, from the moment when by violating all law he put himself beyond the pale of the law'.⁸⁶

Suarez was more circumspect and barely fits the role of precursor attributed to him by Meron. He suggested, albeit reluctantly, that a prince could resort to war when 'a state worshipping the one God inclines towards idolatry through the wickedness of its prince' to the extent that the prince in question compels his 'subjects to practice idolatry'.⁸⁷

Now we come to Grotius. The Dutch jurist and diplomat argued that war is lawful against those who offend the law of nature,⁸⁸ but made no reference in this regard to Gentili, despite his more than obvious debt to him. He is best known on this question for two passages in his celebrated *De jure belli ac pacis* (1625).⁸⁹

The first passage starts thus:⁹⁰

> Kings ... have the right of demanding punishments not only on account of injuries committed against themselves or their subjects, but also on account of injuries which do not directly affect them but excessively violate the law of nature or of nations in regard to any persons whatsoever.

He adds further down:⁹¹

> Truly it is more honourable to avenge the wrongs of others rather than one's own.... And for this cause Hercules was famed by the ancients because he freed from

> Antaeus, Busiris, Diomedes and like tyrants the lands which ... he traversed, not for the desire to acquire but to protect, becoming ... the bestower of the greatest benefits upon men through his punishment of the unjust.

But he also makes the following curious point: that 'wars are justly waged against those who act with impiety towards their parents ... against those who feed on human flesh ... and against those who practise piracy'.[92]

The second passage runs thus: 'If, however, the wrong is obvious, in case some Busiris, Phalaris, or Thracian Diomede should inflict upon his subjects such treatment as no one is warranted in inflicting, the exercise of the right vested in human society is not precluded'.[93]

Grotius was aware of the danger of abuse[94] and was against wars of liberation from tyranny, advocating instead 'a rigid doctrine of non-resistance'.[95] As Vincent has put it, he 'made a remarkable concession to the sovereign by denying his subjects the right to take up arms when wronged by him', although he did compensate by not denying other states the option 'to take up arms on their behalf'.[96] But as Lauterpacht has pointed out, Grotius mentions no less than seven exceptions, including a right of resistance if that sovereign has become the enemy of a whole people.[97]

Is Grotius, plagiarism apart (given today's scholarly standards[98]), one of the main progenitors, though not *the* progenitor, of the idea of interfering for humanitarian reasons? Grewe and others[99] dispute this and regard Grotius's stance as no more than 'a doctrine of religious intervention', especially in view of the historical examples he gives, which are cases of religious persecution.[100] This may be too harsh an assessment, but Grewe may have a point, as seen by Grotius's reference to Innocent as his precursor on this question. But Grotius also mentions examples from antiquity and the views of ancient thinkers, trying to give his approach a wider, centuries-old validity; further, religious persecution was the main form of onslaught during his lifetime. There is, however, another, harsher criticism levelled against Grotius, which has come from several authors, who accuse him of being an accomplice of European colonialism by widening the scope of punishment, and, not least, of being an ideologue of Dutch colonialism in the East Indies.[101] Richard Tuck argues that '[t]he idea that foreign rulers can punish tyrants, cannibals, pirates, those who kill settlers [which appears only in the 1625 edition] ... neatly legitimized a great deal of European action against native peoples around the world'.[102]

With reference to Grotius as well as Vitoria, one could go even further by referring to a pithy comment by Carl Schmitt: that by defining the enemy as 'an outlaw of humanity' because he presumably eats human flesh, a war against him can 'be driven to the most extreme inhumanity'; hence the extermination of the indigenous populations.[103]

From Westphalia to the French Revolution

The Peace of Westphalia is regarded a landmark, the beginning of a new age in international relations and international law.[104] This is the conventional view held from the nineteenth century onwards, mainly based on the association of Westphalia with the principle of sovereignty.[105] Upon closer scrutiny, however, one cannot discern any reference to sovereignty in its treaties of Münster and Osnabrück. Even sovereignty's implicit endorsement (via the limitation of the authority of the Pope and Holy Roman Emperor) is very doubtful.[106] Not surprisingly, given the absence of sovereignty, the non-intervention norm is simply 'not reflected at all' in Westphalia.[107]

The meaning attributed to Westphalia is a myth, a retrospective social construction due to the emphasis on sovereignty from the nineteenth century onwards.[108] In any event, from the early or mid-eighteenth century onwards, sovereignty and independence, coupled with non-intervention, become cardinal principles of international law. Thus by the time 'humanitarian intervention' per se entered the scene, in the nineteenth century, it had to cope with the principles of sovereignty, independence and non-intervention.

Now let us take the thread from the seventeenth century, where we left it off. After Grotius, the German naturalist Samuel Pufendorf opined that anyone 'may justly assist any victim of oppression who invites assistance'.[109] Coming to the assistance of the oppressed is not only a right but a duty, though an 'imperfect duty' and not an obligation, as in the case of a contract.[110]

The German philosopher and jurist Christian Wolff, exponent of *civitas maxima* (a universal system of law cum universal union of states)[111] was against any form of intervention or 'punitive war',[112] even if a ruler treated his subjects harshly. Nevertheless, he allowed for peaceful intercession when subjects were harshly treated.[113]

The main contribution after Grotius on this question came from the Swiss diplomat and jurist Emer de Vattel, in his influential *Le droit des gens où principes de la lois naturelle* (1758). For Vattel, states are free and independent and no foreign power has the right to intervene or judge their conduct.[114] But, he added, 'if a Prince, by attacking the fundamental Laws, gives his people a legitimate reason for resisting; if the Tyranny, having become insupportable, brings about an uprising of the Nation; any foreign Power has a right to succour an oppressed people who ask for its assistance'.[115] Intervention can take place if requested by the oppressed (as with Pufendorf) and provided that the oppressed have already taken up arms and have justice on their side.[116]

Worth alluding to also is intervention in the 'regicidal' French Revolution as conceived by Edmund Burke.[117] Burke, 'in defending magnificently an historically doomed position',[118] tried to make it more convincing by referring to the arguments of Vattel on intervening on the side of the just party.[119] Burke also advocated a 'law of civil vicinity' as he called it: that if a state insisted on intervening in other states, its 'civil neighbours' had the right to intervene against it militarily.[120]

Notes

1. A. C. Arend and R. J. Beck, *International Law and the Use of Force* (London: Routledge, 1993), 17; K. J. Holsti, *The State, War, and the State of War* (Cambridge: Cambridge University Press, 1996), 4.
2. J. B. Elshtain, 'Just War and Humanitarian Intervention', *American University International Law Review*, 17:1 (2001–02), 2–4; J. T. Johnson, 'The Just War Idea: The State of the Question', *Social Philosophy and Policy*, 23:1 (2006), 167–8. See more generally on the just war tradition through the ages, J. T. Johnson, *Just War Tradition and the Restraint of War: A Moral and Historical Inquiry* (Princeton: Princeton University Press, 1981).
3. See P. Christopher, *The Ethics of War and Peace* (Saddle River: Prentice Hall, 2004, 3rd edition) [1999], 10 and 15 n.11.
4. Ibid., 10; J. von Elbe, 'The Evolution of the Concept of the Just War in International Law', *American Journal of International Law*, 33:4 (1939), 666; A. Nussbaum, 'Just War – A Legal Concept?', *Michigan Law Review*, 42:3 (1943), 453; Arend and Beck, *International Law and the Use of Force*, 12–13.
5. Christopher, *The Ethics of War and Peace*, 10; Elbe, 'The Evolution of the Concept of the Just War in International Law', 666; Nussbaum, 'Just War – A Legal Concept?', 454; Arend and Beck, *International Law and the Use of Force*, 13.
6. J. Eppstein, *The Catholic Tradition of the Law of Nations* (London: Burns, Oates and Wahsbourne, 1935), 38–43, 53; F. H. Russell, *The Just War in the Middle Ages* (Cambridge: Cambridge University Press, 1975), 11–13.
7. Eppstein, *The Catholic Tradition of the Law of Nations*, 80.
8. Ibid., 69–80; G. Goyau, 'L'Église Catholique et le droit des gens', *Recueil des cours de l'Académie de droit international*, 6 (1925), 133–7; J. M. Mattox, *Saint Augustine and the Theory of Just War* (London: Continuum, 2006), 1–4, 45–85; Elbe, 'The Evolution of the Concept of the Just War in International Law', 667–9; L. H. Miller, 'The Contemporary Significance of the Doctrine of Just War', *World Politics*, 16:2 (1964), 254–5; Russell, *The Just War in the Middle Ages*, 16–39; R. B. Miller, *Interpretations of Conflict: Ethics, Pacifism, and the Just War Tradition* (Chicago: University of Chicago Press, 1991), 18–23; Christopher, *The Ethics of War and Peace*, 30, 40–2.
9. Elbe, 'The Evolution of the Concept of the Just War in International Law', 669.
10. Christopher, *The Ethics of War and Peace*, 49–51; Eppstein, *The Catholic Tradition of the Law of Nations*, 83–8; Goyau, 'L'Église Catholique et le droit des gens', 138–40; Nussbaum, 'Just War – A Legal Concept?', 456–7; Russell, *The Just War in the Middle Ages*, 259–64, 268–73; Miller, *Interpretations of Conflict*, 23–7; R. R. Gorman, 'War and the Virtues in Aquinas's Ethical Thought', *Journal of Military Ethics*, 9:3 (2010), 245–6, 251–2.
11. Christopher, *The Ethics of War and Peace*, 52; R. S. Hartigan, 'Noncombatant Immunity: Reflections on Its Origins and Present Status', *Review of Politics*, 29:2 (1967), 209–11; Russell, *The Just War in the Middle Ages*, 273–4, 278.
12. For the famous Valladolid debate (August–September 1550) summoned by Charles V, between Sepúlveda, who invoked Aristotle in claiming that the Indians were 'natural slaves', and Las Casas, who argued that the Indians were clever human beings and should

be treated on the basis of Christian ethics, see L. Hanke, *All Mankind Is One: A Study of the Disputation Between Bartolomé de Las Casas and Juan Ginés de Sepúlveda* (DeKalb: North Illinois University Press, 1974), 67–112; T. Todorov, *The Conquest of America: The Question of the Other* (New York: Harper Perennial, 1992, translated from the French by R. Howard) [1982], 151–7, 186–90.

13 C. van Vollenhoven, *The Law of Peace* (London: Macmillan, 1936), 61–3; Elbe, 'The Evolution of the Concept of the Just War in International Law', 674–5; Nussbaum, 'Just War – A Legal Concept?', 458–9; R. Tuck, *The Rights of War and Peace: Political Thought and the International Order from Grotius to Kant* (Oxford: Oxford University Press, 1999), 73–5.

14 T. Nardin, 'The Moral Basis for Humanitarian Intervention', in A. F. Lang (ed.), *Just Intervention* (Washington, DC: Georgetown University Press, 2003), 14–15; A. Anghie, *Imperialism, Sovereignty and the Making of International Law* (Cambridge: Cambridge University Press, 2004), 21–8; B. Bowden, 'The Colonial Origins of International Law. European Expansion and the Classical Standard of Civilization', *Journal of the History of International Law*, 7 (2005), 9–13; P. Keal, *European Conquest and the Rights of Indigenous Peoples: The Moral Backwardness of International Society* (Cambridge: Cambridge University Press, 2003), 70–1.

15 Elbe, 'The Evolution of the Concept of the Just War in International Law', 674–6; Christopher, *The Ethics of War and Peace*, 53–6, 58; Goyau, 'L'Église Catholique et le droit des gens', 182–9; Hartigan, 'Noncombatant Immunity', 215–16; G. M. Reichberg, 'Preventive War in Classical Just War Theory', *Journal of the History of International Law*, 9 (2007), 6–7.

16 B. Kingsbury and A. Roberts, 'Introduction', in H. Bull, B. Kingsbury and A. Roberts (eds), *Hugo Grotius and International Relations* (Oxford: Clarendon Press, 1990), 20; Goyau, 'L'Église Catholique et le droit des gens', 190–4; Arend and Beck, *International Law and the Use of Force*, 14.

17 G. H. J. van der Molen, *Alberto Gentili and the Development of International Law: His Life and Times* (Amsterdam: H. J. Paris, 1937), 116–17.

18 Ibid., 116–20, 125–6, 143–9; M. Forsyth, 'The Tradition of International Law', in T. Nardin and D. R. Mapel (eds), *Traditions of International Ethics* (Cambridge: Cambridge University Press, 1992), 31–3; W. G. Grewe, *The Epochs of International Law* (Berlin: Walter de Gruyter, 2000, translated from the German and revised by M. Byers) [1984], 211–14; Reichberg, 'Preventive War in Classical Just War Theory', 15–19; B. Kingsbury, 'Confronting Difference: The Puzzling Durability of Gentili's Combination of Pragmatic Pluralism and Normative Judgment', *American Journal of International Law*, 92:4 (1998), 713–23.

19 Elbe, 'The Evolution of the Concept of the Just War in International Law', 678–9; C. Edwards, 'The Law of War in the Thought of Hugo Grotius', *Journal of Public Law*, 19 (1970), 377–80, 390–7; Christopher, *The Ethics of War and Peace*, 82–8; G. I. A. D. Draper, 'Grotius' Place in the Development of Legal Ideas About War', in Bull et al. (eds), *Hugo Grotius and International Relations*, 194–5; A. Nussbaum, *A Concise History of the Law of Nations* (New York: Macmillan, 1947), 106–7; P. Haggenmacher, 'Sur un passage obscure de Grotius', *Revue d'histoire du droit*, 51 (1983), 164–6; Reichberg, 'Preventive War in Classical Just War Theory', 19–21; R. Jeffery, *Hugo Grotius in International Thought* (Basingstoke: Palgrave Macmillan, 2006), 13, 35, 39–40.

20 H. Lauterpacht, 'The Grotian Tradition in International Law', *British Year Book of International Law*, 23 (1946), 46.

21 See e.g. G. Carnazza Amari, 'Nouvel exposé du principe de non-intervention', *Revue de droit international et de législation comparée*, 5 (1873), 551; A. Mérignhac, *Traité de droit public international* (Paris: Librairie générale de droit et de jurisprudence, 1905), part i, 298.
22 See C. Calvo, *Le droit international: théorie et pratique* (Paris: Guillaumin et Cie, G. Pedone-Lauriel, 1880, 3rd edition) [1870], 231, para. 111; H. Bonfils, *Manuel de droit international public (droit des gens)* (Paris: Librairie nouvelle de droit et de jurisprudence, 1905, 4th edition by P. Fauchille) [1894], 156, 165.
23 See P. Fiore, *Nouveau droit internationale public suivant les besoins de la civilization moderne* (Paris: A. Durant et Pedone-Lauriel, 1885, 2nd edition, translated and annotated by C. Antoine) [1865], vol. I, 520–1; G. Rolin-Jaequemyns, 'Note sur la théorie du droit d'intervention, à propos d'une letter de M. le professeur Arntz', *Revue de droit international et de législation comparée*, 8 (1876), 677–80.
24 Haggenmacher, 'Sur un passage obscur de Grotius', 313 and 313 n.78; T. Meron, 'Common Rights of Mankind in Gentili, Grotius and Suarez', *American Journal of International Law*, 85:1 (1991), 40. See also Kingsbury and Roberts, 'Introduction', 40 n.136.
25 P. Haggenmacher, 'Grotius and Gentili: A Reassessment of Thomas E. Holland's Inaugural Lecture', in Bull et al. (eds), *Hugo Grotius and International Relations*, 137–8, 145–56.
26 Molen, *Alberto Gentili and the Development of International Law*, 131.
27 See e.g. T. B. Knudsen, 'Humanitarian Intervention Revisited: Post-Cold War Responses to Classical Problems', in M. Puch (ed.), *The UN, Peace and Force* (London: Frank Cass, 1997), 147–8; N. Wheeler, *Saving Strangers: Humanitarian Intervention in International Society* (Oxford: Oxford University Press, 2000), 45; S. Chesterman, *Just War or Just Peace? Humanitarian Intervention and International Law* (Oxford: Oxford University Press, 2001), 9.
28 A. Rougier, 'La théorie de l'intervention d'humanité', *Revue générale de droit international public*, 17 (1910), 472.
29 R. J. Vincent, 'Grotius, Human Rights, and Intervention', in Bull et al. (eds), *Hugo Grotius and International Relations*, 248.
30 L. Glanville, 'The Myth of "Traditional" Sovereignty', *International Studies Quarterly*, 57:1 (2013), 82.
31 Ibid., 81.
32 Grewe, *The Epochs of International Law*, 180.
33 H. Grotius, *De jure belli ac pacis libri tres* (Oxford: Clarendon Press, 1925, Classics of International Law, Carnegie Endowment for International Peace, translated by F. W. Kelsey), vol. II, book II, chapter XX, section XL, para. 4, 506.
34 See Eppstein, *The Catholic Tradition of the Law of Nations*, 61.
35 Quoted in Tuck, *The Rights of War and Peace*, 36.
36 Quoted in Meron, 'Common Rights of Mankind in Gentili, Grotius and Suarez', 115.
37 Grotius, *De jure belli ac pacis*, vol. II, book II, chapter XXV, section VI, 582.
38 Ibid., section VII, para. 2, 582.
39 Russell, *The Just War in the Middle Ages*, 199–200. See also Haggenmacher, 'Sur un passage obscure de Grotius', 301–2; Nardin, 'The Moral Basis for Humanitarian Intervention', 13–14; Bowden. 'The Colonial Origins of International Law', 4–5.
40 As pointed out by Tuck and Nardin. See Tuck, *The Rights of War and Peace*, 42; Nardin, 'The Moral Basis for Humanitarian Intervention', 13.
41 T. More, *Utopia* (Cambridge: Cambridge University Press, 1989, eds G. M. Logan and R. M. Adams) [1516], 87–8.

The origins of the idea of humanitarian intervention

42 See Q. Skinner, 'Sir Thomas More's *Utopia* and the Language of Renaissance Humanism', in A. Pagden (ed.), *The Language of Political Theory in Early Modern Europe* (Cambridge: Cambridge University Press, 1987), 123–6, 152.

43 A. Esmein, 'La théorie de l'intervention internationale chez quelques publicists français du XVIe siècle', *Nouvelle revue historique, de droit français et étranger*, 24 (1900), 558, 562, 564–6.

44 Referred to in E. C. Stowell, *Intervention in International Law* (Washington, DC: John Byrne, 1921), 465.

45 *Ibid.*, 55.

46 M. Boegner, 'L'influence de la Réforme sur le développement du droit international', *Recueil des cours de l'Académie de droit international*, 6 (1925), 280–1.

47 H. J. Laski, 'Historical Introduction', in *A Defence of Liberty Against Tyrants: A Translation of the Vindicae contra Tyrannos by Junius Brutus* (London: G. Bell and Sons, 1924), 38, 43–4.

48 E. Barker, 'The Authorship of the *Vindiciae contra tyrannos*', *Cambridge Historical Journal*, 3:2 (1930), 164, 167–80. Ernest Barker's conclusion is that Languet is more likely to have been the author, given his older age and greater familiarity with the issues discussed in the book. George Garnett regards three possibilities as being equally convincing: Languet was the author, Mornay was the editor, or that it was a joint book. See G. Garnett, 'Editor's Introduction', in Stephanus Junius Brutus, the Celt, *Vindicae contra tyrannos* (Cambridge: Cambridge University Press, 1994, edited by G. Garnett), lv–lxxvi. See also on this question Laski, 'Historical Introduction', 57–60.

49 The need to kill a tyrant goes back to Aristotle. See R. Boesche, 'Aristotle's "Science" of Tyranny', *History of Political Thought*, 14:1 (1993), 4.

50 Boegner, 'L'influence de la Réforme sur le développement du droit international', 278–80; Laski, 'Historical Introduction', 34, 37–56; Lauterpacht, 'The Grotian Tradition in International Law', 44.

51 Barker, 'The Authorship of the *Vindiciae contra tyrannos*', 166; A. McLaren, 'Rethinking Republicanism: *Vindiciae contra tyrannos* in Context', *Historical Journal*, 40:1 (2006), 24–7; D. J. B. Trim, '"If a Prince Use Tyrannie towards his People": Intervention on Behalf of Foreign Populations in Early Modern Europe', in B. Simms and D. J. B. Trim (eds), *Humanitarian Intervention: A History* (Cambridge: Cambridge University Press, 2011), 32–4.

52 See Barker, 'The Authorship of the *Vindiciae contra tyrannos*', 165–6, 171.

53 Trim, 'If a Prince Use Tyrannie towards his People', 34.

54 *Ibid.*, 34.

55 Quoted *ibid.*, 34 (from both texts).

56 Grewe, *The Epochs of International Law*, 180.

57 Trim, 'If a Prince Use Tyrannie towards his People', 36 (original emphasis).

58 *Ibid.*, 37.

59 Garnett, 'Editor's Introduction', xxi.

60 Trim, 'If a Prince Use Tyrannie towards his People', 38.

61 Stowell refers to Bodin in passing in his annotated 'Bibliography of Intervention'. See Stowell, *Intervention in International Law*, 465. There is also a reference by Grewe to Bodin, under 'intervention', though not 'humanitarian intervention'. See Grewe, *The Epochs of International Law*, 178. For a reference to Bodin and intervention see A. Gardot, 'Jean Bodin. Sa place parmi les fondateurs du droit international', *Recueil des cours de l'Académie de droit international*, 50 (1934), 677–9.

62 H. Legohérel, 'Jean Bodin et l'Europe de son temps', *Journal of the History of International Law*, 1 (1999), 38–9.
63 Nussbaum, *A Concise History of the Law of Nations*, 56; Legohérel, 'Jean Bodin et l'Europe de son temps', 41; F. H. Hinsley, *Sovereignty* (Cambridge: Cambridge University Press, 2nd edition, 1986) [1966], 134; J. H. Franklin, 'Introduction', in J. Bodin, *On Sovereignty: Four Chapters from The Six Books of the Commonwealth* (Cambridge: Cambridge University Press, 1992, translated from the French and edited by J. H. Franklin) [1576], xiii.
64 Bodin, *On Sovereignty*, 112–13 (book II, chapter 5).
65 Franklin, 'Introduction', xxiii.
66 Bodin, *On Sovereignty*, 120.
67 See B. Parekh, 'Rethinking Humanitarian Intervention', *International Political Science Review*, 18:1 (1997), 50–1; F. K. Abiew, *The Evolution of the Doctrine and Practice of Humanitarian Intervention* (The Hague: Kluwer Law International, 1999), 33–4; G. Reichberg, 'Just War or Perpetual Peace?', *Journal of Military Ethics*, 1:1 (2002), 21–2; Nardin, 'The Moral Basis for Humanitarian Intervention', 14–15; J. Muldoon, 'Francisco de Vitoria and Humanitarian Intervention', *Journal of Military Ethics*, 5:2 (2006), 123–43; Trim, 'If a Prince Use Tyrannie towards his People', 32; B. Jahn, 'Humanitarian Intervention – What's in a Name?', *International Politics*, 49:1 (2012), 44–5; W. Bain, 'Saving the Innocent, Then and Now: Vitoria, Dominion and World Order', *History of Political Thought*, 34:4 (2013), 590.
68 Anghie, *Imperialism, Sovereignty and the Making of International Law*, 22.
69 Hanke, *All Mankind Is One*, 92–5; Todorov, *The Conquest of America*, 186.
70 Nardin, 'The Moral Basis for Humanitarian Intervention', 14–15; Tuck, *The Rights of War and Peace*, 73–4.
71 Anghie, *Imperialism, Sovereignty and the Making of International Law*, 22; Keal, *European Conquest and the Rights of Indigenous Peoples*, 92–3.
72 Anghie, *Imperialism, Sovereignty and the Making of International Law*, 28.
73 For Vitoria and Grotius as apologists of colonization, see Todorov, *The Conquest of America*, 149–50; Anghie, *Imperialism, Sovereignty and the Making of International Law*, 13–31; A. Pagden, 'Stoicism, Cosmopolitanism, and the Legacy of European Imperialism', *Constellations*, 7:1 (2000), 7–9; Bowden, 'The Colonial Origins of International Law', 9–13, 22–3; P. Keal, '"Just Backward Children": International Law and the Conquest of Non-European Peoples', *Australian Journal of International Affairs*, 49:2 (2008), 196–7. For a more nuanced assessment see G. Cavallar, 'Vitoria, Grotius, Pufendorf, Wolff and Vattel: Accomplices of European Colonialism and Exploitation or True Cosmopolitans?', *Journal of the History of International Law*, 10 (2008), 181–209.
74 Vitoria was probably the first to have used these very words, in a lecture at the University of Salamanca. See G. Sulyok, 'Humanitarian Intervention: A Historical and Theoretical Overview', *Acta Juridica Hungarica*, 41:1–2 (2000), 83 n.12.
75 Cavallar, 'Vitoria, Grotius, Pufendorf, Wolff and Vattel', 188.
76 Muldoon, 'Francisco de Vitoria and Humanitarian Intervention', 139, 141.
77 F. Murillo Rubiera, 'The School of Salamanca and Human Rights', *International Review of the Red Cross*, 32:290 (1992), 454–64.
78 Cavallar, 'Vitoria, Grotius, Pufendorf, Wolff and Vattel', 191.
79 Todorov, *The Conquest of America*, 186–90.
80 Muldoon, 'Francisco de Vitoria and Humanitarian Intervention', 139.
81 See Cavallar, 'Vitoria, Grotius, Pufendorf, Wolff and Vattel', 191.
82 Quoted in Chesterman, *Just War or Just Peace?*, 14.

83 Quoted in Meron, 'Common Rights of Mankind in Gentili, Grotius and Suarez', 114.
84 A. Gentili, *De jure belli libri tres* (Washington, DC: Carnegie Endowment for International Peace, 1933, translated from the 1612 edition by J. C. Rolfe and Introduction by Coleman Phillipson) [1589], 75.
85 Forsyth, 'The Tradition of International Law', 27.
86 Quoted in Tuck, *The Rights of War and Peace*, 39–40. On Gentili's overall position regarding defence of the suffering, see Molen, *Alberto Gentili and the Development of International Law*, 127–31.
87 Quoted in Meron, 'Common Rights of Mankind in Gentili, Grotius and Suarez', 113.
88 Tuck, *The Rights of War and Peace*, 103.
89 Meron, 'Common Rights of Mankind in Gentili, Grotius and Suarez', 110–12; Kingsbury and Roberts, 'Introduction', 30–42.
90 Grotius, *De jure belli ac pacis*, vol. II, book II, chapter XX, section XL, para. 1, 504.
91 *Ibid.*, paras 1 and 2, 505.
92 *Ibid.*, para. 3, 505–6.
93 *Ibid.*, chapter XXV, section VIII, para. 2, 584.
94 *Ibid.*, section VII, para. 4, 584.
95 Edwards, 'The Law of War in the Thought of Hugo Grotius', 391.
96 R. J. Vincent, *Nonintervention and International Order* (Princeton: Princeton University Press, 1974), 24. See also Jeffery, *Hugo Grotius in International Thought*, 41.
97 Lauterpacht, 'The Grotian Tradition in International Law', 45; Edwards, 'The Law of War in the Thought of Hugo Grotius', 391–4.
98 Haggenmacher points out that practices which seem to us questionable 'were not then exceptional. Humanist vanity and "elegance" induced scholars to hide their real, direct sources, in order to show only the pure wisdom of antiquity'. In Haggenmacher, 'Grotius and Gentili', 148. Molen points out that 'Gentili shows as little appreciation of the work of his predecessors, as Grotius showed afterwards for his'. See Molen, *Alberto Gentili and the Development of International Law*, 113.
99 See e.g. P. Malanczuk, *Humanitarian Intervention and the Legitimacy of the Use of Force* (Amsterdam: Het Spinhuis, 1993), 8.
100 Grewe, *The Epochs of International Law*, 180–2.
101 See summary and relevant bibliography in Cavallar, 'Vitoria, Grotius, Pufendorf, Wolff and Vattel', 192, 194–7.
102 Tuck, *The Rights of War and Peace*, 103.
103 C. Schmitt, *The Concept of the Political* (New Brunswick: Rutgers University Press, 1976 translated from the German, with Introduction and notes by G. Schwab) [1932], 54 and 54 n.23.
104 L. Gross, 'The Peace of Westphalia, 1648–1948', *American Journal of International Law*, 42:1 (1948), 28; Grewe, *The Epochs of International Law*, 159; Nussbaum, *A Concise History of the Law of Nations*, 86; A. Watson, *The Evolution of International Society* (London: Routledge, 1992), 186.
105 F. H. Hinsley, *Power and the Pursuit of Peace: Theory and Practice in the History of Relations Between States* (Cambridge: Cambridge University Press, 1963), 168.
106 D. Croxton, 'The Peace of Westphalia of 1648 and the Origins of Sovereignty', *International History Review*, 21:3 (1999), 569–72, 581–2, 589.
107 S. D. Krasner, 'Sovereignty and Intervention', in G. M. Lyons and M. Mastanduno (eds), *Beyond Westphalia? State Sovereignty and International Intervention* (Baltimore: Johns Hopkins University Press, 1995), 235–6.

108 Croxton, 'The Peace of Westphalia of 1648 and the Origins of Sovereignty', 569–91; S. Beaulac, 'The Westphalian Legal Orthodoxy – Myth or Reality?', *Journal of the History of International Law*, 2 (2000), 148–77; A. Osiander, 'Sovereignty, International Relations, and the Westphalian Myth', *International Organization*, 55:2 (2001), 251–87.
109 Nardin, 'The Moral Basis for Humanitarian Intervention', 16.
110 *Ibid.*, 16–17.
111 A. Nussbaum, *A Concise History of the Law of Nations*, 150–1; H. Legohérel, *Histoire du droit international public* (Paris: Presses Universitaires de France, 1996), 69; Grewe, *The Epochs of International Law*, 358.
112 Vincent, *Nonintervention and International Order*, 27–8.
113 Tuck, *The Rights of War and Peace*, 189–90; Nardin, 'The Moral Basis for Humanitarian Intervention', 17.
114 Vincent, *Nonintervention and International Order*, 29.
115 Our translation from the French version cited in M. Wight, 'Western Values in International Relations', in H. Butterfield and M. Wight (eds), *Diplomatic Investigations: Essays in the Theory of International Politics* (London: Allen and Unwin, 1966), 119.
116 On Vattel and intervention see *ibid.*, 119; P. H. Winfield, 'The History of Intervention in International Law', *British Year Book of International Law*, 3 (1922–23), 132–3; Vincent, *Nonintervention and International Order*, 29–30.
117 I. Hampsher-Monk, 'Edmund Burke's Changing Justification for Intervention', *Historical Journal*, 48:1 (2005), 65–100; B. Simms, '"A False Principle in the Law of Nations": Burke, State Sovereignty, [German] Liberty, and Intervention in the Age of Westphalia', in Simms and Trim (eds), *Humanitarian Intervention*, 89–110.
118 R. J. Vincent, 'Edmund Burke and the Theory of International Relations', *Review of International Studies*, 10 (1984), 215.
119 *Ibid.*, 211; Hampsher-Monk, 'Edmund Burke's Changing Justification for Intervention', 66–8.
120 Parekh, 'Rethinking Humanitarian Intervention', 51.

3

Eurocentrism, 'civilization' and the 'barbarians'

In the nineteenth century, the idea of European cultural and moral superiority was at its peak, with a presumed historical mission to civilize the rest of the world by expanding European influence and by colonization.[1] At the level of the self-defined Eurocentric international society and law, countries and peoples were distinguished as either 'civilized' or 'uncivilized' ('barbarians'), with Europe the basis of comparison, in what came to be known as the 'standard of civilization'.[2]

European international society and the 'standard of civilization'

International society as it emerged from the Renaissance was the Christian society of states, despite the fact that the classic jurists from the sixteenth to the mid-eighteenth century (Vitoria, Suarez, Gentili, Grotius, Pufendorf, Wolff and Vattel)[3] had spoken in terms of universal society, though probably not in the sense that we use it today.[4] Las Casas and Montaigne and, in the eighteenth century, Montesquieu, Diderot, Rousseau, Smith, Kant and 'virtually all the thinkers of the Enlightenment'[5] referred to the existence of humanity as a whole, though they regarded European culture and civilization to be the forefront of progress.[6] It was in the nineteenth century that a (self-)conception of 'European society' replaced the one of 'Christian society' (though it still had a strong Christian component) and civilization.[7]

The novel concept of 'civilization' (as distinct from the civilized–barbarians dichotomy, which is ancient) had been coined in 1757 by Victor Mirabeau, in a treatise on population, and a decade later it was used by Ferguson in his *Essay on the History of Civil Society* (1767). 'Civilization', once unleashed, took on a life of its own, being incorporated into the self-concept of European-centred international society.[8]

Charles Alexandrowicz has argued that the shrinking of international society's scope to 'Eurocentrism' was due to the switch from natural law, which was universal, to positivism, with its emphasis on treaty law, sovereignty, international personality and recognition (as constitutive of statehood) confined to the so-called 'civilized states' as original members of the 'family of nations'.[9] This is arguable, for many nineteenth century jurists remained partly naturalists[10] and, more crucially, the previous universality of international law under naturalism is debatable, given the foundation of Christianity as a 'limiting' and 'excluding concept'.[11] There may not be a proven causal correlation between legal positivism and Eurocentrism but there is an obvious correlation and interaction between them.[12] International law for most of the nineteenth century remained mainly the law between European states and those of European extraction, and treaties with states outside Europe (and America) were unequal, with the sovereignty and independence of the Ottoman Empire, China, Siam, Persia and Japan thereby limited.[13]

Civilization linked with progress 'became a scale by which the countries of the world were categorized into "civilized", barbarous and savage spheres',[14] a distinction adhered to by Montesquieu in *The Spirit of the Laws*,[15] which was common among Enlightenment thinkers from Wolff ('civilized' and 'barbarous' nations) to Smith and Kant ('civilized' and 'savage' nations).[16] There was also a fourth category in vogue, 'wild men'.[17] For nineteenth-century publicists (lawyers and other influential commentators on international affairs with a legal dimension), only 'civilized nations' qualified as full members of the family of nations, while 'barbarous nations' had less legal capacity and even less the 'savages'. Those in the 'barbarous sphere' enjoyed only partial recognition and inferior membership in the family of nations.[18] As for 'savages', the belief prevailed that they were 'vanishing', that they 'were doomed to fall by the wayside'.[19] As the esteemed British Liberal politician Charles Dilke had put it, '[t]he gradual extinction of inferior races is not only a law of nature, but a blessing to mankind'.[20]

In general, nineteenth-century European and American views ranged from racialist (differences due to stage of development, which could be overcome) to racist (innate unbridgeable differences) intertwined with the concept of civilization. The new concept of 'race', introduced in eighteenth-century anthropology by Georges Buffon and Johann Blumenbach, came to rank peoples as 'races' hierarchically. The races of mankind were innately unequal according to Arthur de Gobineau, with the 'Aryans' as the master race. Such racist views were lent greater credibility with the advent of social Darwinism.[21] The Asians, Africans and native Americans were regarded 'inferior races', with the so-called 'white race' superior intellectually, culturally and otherwise.[22]

The idea of progress, coupled with the standard of civilization, provided the European powers with a handy justification for their global expansion.[23] From the 1830s onwards, even several liberal thinkers, such as J. S. Mill, Alexis de Tocqueville, Giuseppe Mazzini and Henry Sidgwick, supported colonization in order to bring to these backward peoples the benefits of civilization.[24] This was also the case with most liberal international lawyers (see below). In the eighteenth and early nineteenth century, the opposite had been the case: Wolff, Smith, Hume, Burke, Diderot, Voltaire, Kant, Bentham, Condorcet and Constant had been critical of the European imperialist project.[25]

Jennifer Pitts mentions only two alternative thinkers in nineteenth-century Britain critical of British imperialism: the linguist Henry Stanley and the polymath Francis Newman (brother of the famous cardinal Newman).[26] But the most widely known liberal critics of the British Empire were Richard Cobden, John Bright and Herbert Spencer.[27] In France, Gaston Jèze and Charles Solomon were critical of colonial rule but they did not suggest abandoning it, so long as it was not brutal.[28] It was at the turn of the century that critics of imperialism attained a critical mass, comprising mainly radicals, such as John A. Hobson in Britain[29] (who did not regard imperialism as necessary for capitalism), and Marxists, such as Lenin and Bukharin (who regarded imperialism necessary for capitalism in its last stage).[30]

But let us address the standard of civilization. From the 1860s until 1914 the law of 'civilized' states was the law between states that met the 'standards of civilization'[31] or 'standard of civilization'.[32] The 'standard' was not clearly defined and remained 'open-ended',[33] but there was a general understanding of its criteria. According to Gerrit Gong, they included the following: (1) safeguard of basic rights, such as life, dignity, property, religion; (2) organized bureaucracy and a capacity for military self-defence; (3) adherence to the rules of international law, including the laws of war; (4) diplomatic relations and communication; and (5) conformity with the norms and practices of 'civilized' society.[34] The minimum test according to Georg Schwarzenberger was a stable government capable of undertaking 'binding commitments under international law and whether it was able to and willing to protect adequately the life, liberty and property of foreigners'.[35] More generally, the level of civilization was judged with reference to religion, technological development, ascribed racial characteristics, economic capacity, political institutions, morality, intellectual competence, and sense of nationhood.[36]

Towards the end of the nineteenth century the religious and racial aspects lapsed and emphasis was put on the other 'minimum standards of civilization' and in this sense the standard opened the way for the inclusion of Japan and other non-Christian and non-European states to the 'family of nations' and international law.[37]

The family of 'civilized nations': the views of publicists

The dominant view

In the 1860s and 1870s international law was established as a distinct discipline, with the launching of the *Revue de droit international et de législation comparée* and the formation of the Institut de droit international, whose ultimate aim was for international law to become the 'juridical consciousness of the civilized world' (see chapter 4).[38] From then on, international lawyers became increasingly influential in international affairs, at a time when international relations as a discipline did not exist, and thinking in the foreign policy establishment had a legal bent, in a deliberate quest for legality or legal rationalization, even on matters of war, territorial expansion and imperialism, where *Realpolitik* considerations dominated the scene.[39]

International law was a matter for the 'civilized states', which set the standard of entry into the 'charmed circle',[40] as put by Thomas Erskine Holland, the second Chichele Professor of Public International Law at Oxford University. According to William Edward Hall, relations between states were akin to a Victorian social club: admission was granted to a state if it enjoyed a sufficient degree of European culture for its internal rules to be 'understood or recognized by countries differently civilised'.[41]

From the 1830s until the First World War, one can discern a spectrum among publicists, from exclusion to inclusion: (1) permanent exclusion; (2) acceptance of certain former 'barbarous' states but exclusion of Muslim countries; (3) grudging acceptance of former 'uncivilized' states once they attained the standard, but even then less than equality; (4) entry for all non-Europeans states that met the standard and full membership; and (5) questioning the distinction or the standard. We will refer to the views of key publicists, all of them also influential in the humanitarian intervention debate (see chapter 4).

Among those presuming permanent exclusion, the US diplomat Henry Wheaton (the pioneer of international law in his country together with James Kent), in his widely read treatise, with eight editions up to 1866[42] (translated into French, Italian, Spanish as well as Chinese and Japanese), asserted that there is 'no universal, immutable law of nations, binding upon the whole human race.... Hence the international law of the civilized, Christian nations of Europe and America, is one thing; and that which governs the intercourse of the Mohammedan nations of the East with each other, and with Christians, is another and very different thing'.[43] It was 'the international law of Christendom' as 'understood among civilized Christian nations'.[44]

Similar views were held by Wheaton's near contemporary, August Wilhelm Heffter, of the University of Berlin, author of the most widely read international law treatise in Europe until the mid-nineteenth century (translated into many European languages, including Greek and Serbian).[45] Like Wheaton, he stressed Christianity as a basic feature in international law and relegated the relations of European states with non-Christian ones to the level of morality and politics rather than law.[46]

This overall trend continued even in the last decades of the nineteenth century. According to Henri Bonfils, one of the earliest French international lawyers, whose international law treatise ran into several editions after his death,[47] international law was the product of European and Christian principles and it applied only to the civilized nations of European origin. He shared J. S. Mill's idea that international law cannot apply to barbarians, for they cannot reciprocate (see chapter 5). Interestingly, however, Bonfils did not subscribe to the domination of Europeans over non-Europeans and asserted that civilized states could not breach the law in relation to uncivilized nations.[48] Ernest Nys of the University of Brussels, a distinguished legal historian, divided the world into civilized, barbaric and savage peoples and argued that international law as a European creation could not be compared to the few agreements between the civilized states and barbarians or savages.[49]

The second category (exclusion of Muslim states) had several adherents. Travers Twiss of King's College London and Oxford University, a publicist active in the Institut and intimately involved in British colonial policy as a consultant of the Foreign Office,[50] toyed with the exclusion of 'barbarians' from international law, on the grounds that their 'minds' are incapable of reciprocity.[51] He concluded that reciprocity did not arise with Buddhist or Confucian nations, but only with Islamic nations, for their moral code, based on the Koran, prohibits relations of equality and reciprocity.[52]

The Scottish James Lorimer, the Edinburgh Professor of the Law of Nature and Nations, though 'eccentric'[53] and extreme even by the standards of the age, was highly regarded on the Continent and within the Institut. He was influenced by Gobineau's racist ideas[54] and widely known for his tripartite division of civilized–barbarians–savages.[55] Lorimer, like almost all of his contemporary publicists, was convinced that international law was Christian and Christianity the highest civilization. Oriental communities were akin to immature or irrational individuals deprived of legal capacity.[56] He believed that non-Christian states based on Hinduism and Buddhism could qualify as civilized states, but this was not the case with Muslim states, for they sought to become universal.[57]

From the 1860s onwards, the third category (entry into the coveted club, but with fewer rights and capabilities) wielded the widest acceptance and included many heavyweight publicists. The Swiss jurist Johann Caspar Bluntschli, professor at Heidelberg University, a revered figure in international law circles during his lifetime and one of the main driving forces of the Institut and the *Revue*[58] (he was also consulted by Bismarck), argued that international law is the creation of the Christian civilized world of Europe, mainly a product of the 'Germanic' and 'Romanic races'.[59] The superiority of the 'Aryan races', he claimed, was evident in the development of higher science, higher culture, in their respect for women and human rights and in statecraft.[60] The civilized nations of Europe and America were called upon to develop 'a common legal conscience of mankind'. Yet international law was destined to be extended to the entire globe and not limited to Christian nations, as seen with the admission of the 'Turkey'[61] to the 1856 Paris Congress.[62]

Robert Phillimore was the first major British jurist to write on international law, in the nineteenth century, a naturalist rather than a positivist, attached to Christian principles. He was a Member of Parliament, a High Court judge, held other influential posts, and was a close friend of William Gladstone, whom he influenced on matters of international politics, especially with regard to intervention on behalf of Christians in 'Mohametan' states like the Ottoman Empire.[63] Writing in 1854[64] he argued that 'International Comity, like International Law, can only exist in the lowest degree among Independent States; in its next degree among Independent Civilized States, and in its highest degree among Independent Christian States'.[65] Christianity, according to Phillimore, was the highest form of civilization and Christian nations deserved a privileged position in international law.[66] However, non-Christian nations should not be refused recognition as members of the international community.[67]

Similar views were held at the time by the Italian jurist Pasquale Fiore, of Cremona and Naples universities, whose work was highly acclaimed in Europe during his lifetime, and translated into French and English.[68] Fiore, whose work anticipated the international law of human rights,[69] was of the view that the ultimate source of international law was the juridical conscience of European peoples.[70] Human society was 'universal' but only fully civilized states could be members of what he called the *Magna civitas*, the juridical community. He had doubts whether civilization could extend uniformly to all parts of the world.[71] Beyond Europe there was a clear distinction between the somewhat civilized cultures of Asia (such as 'Turkey' and the 'great Oriental Empires') and the less civilized peoples, perhaps barbarians, of Asia and Africa, who did not possess a stable political organization.[72]

F. F. Martens, of the University of St Petersburg (an ethnic Estonian), legal adviser to the Russian Foreign Ministry and the most acclaimed Russian international lawyer of his time, held similar views. International law was based on common values and reciprocity, hence could not apply to relations with 'non-civilized peoples', as pointed out by John Stuart Mill (see chapter 5), despite commercial relations with such states or treaties. Relations with such entities were based only on natural law and morality. However, he reluctantly accepted that international law applied to non-Christian peoples if they are prepared to accept the rational aims of humanity as elaborated by the civilized European states.[73]

The eminent Swiss jurist Alphonse Rivier, of Brussels University, Secretary-General of the Institut, argued (in the 1890s) that the sphere of international law extended to the family of nations that shared the Christian faith. He claimed that the law of nations could not function properly between Europeans and 'inferior races' for the gulf between them was similar to that between ancient Greeks and barbarians. However, the family was not closed but open, consisting of European nations as well as 'Turkey' (accepted in 1856). But other Asian states and Christian

Abyssinia were excluded from the so-called 'family of nations'.[74]

A decade later, John Westlake, one of the founders of the *Revue*, President of the Institut and third Whewell Professor of International Law at Cambridge University, held similar views. He argued that the international society comprises those states equipped with 'European civilization',[75] that is, all the European and American states as well as 'Turkey' and Japan. Some backward Christian countries, such as Abyssinia or Liberia, could not contribute to the development and enforcement of international law.[76] A country 'with an old and stable order of its own' might be considered 'civilized', as in the case of China or Japan, whose 'leading minds' were 'able to appreciate the necessities of an order different from theirs'.[77] He regarded Japan an equal member of the family of nations and Morocco, 'Turkey' Muscat, Persia, Siam and China as enjoying only parts of international law.[78]

Moving onto the fourth category (eventual acceptance by all), worth mentioning is the British jurist Thomas Erskine Holland, a pure positivist,[79] who posited that international law need not be restricted to Christian nations, for this was a 'question rather of Civilisation than Creed'.[80] For him, 'civilized states' were those states that were well organized and effective,[81] even if they were non-European.[82] Participation in international conferences, such as the Hague Peace Conferences, did not automatically confer 'civilized' status but was a move forward, bringing China, Persia and Siam to the 'outer courts of the charmed circle'.[83] He accepted that Japan had become a full member of the family of nations.[84]

Lassa Oppenheim, Westlake's successor at Cambridge University, one of the most authoritative international lawyers of his time and author of the most widely read international law treatise of the twentieth century (with nine editions up to 2005), defined international law as 'the body of customary and conventional rules which are considered legally binding by civilized States in their intercourse with each other'.[85] For a new member to be admitted 'into the circle of the Family of Nations', three conditions had to be met: (1) to be civilized and 'in constant intercourse with members of the Family of Nations', (2) expressly 'or tacitly consent to be bound for its future international conduct by the rules of International Law', and (3) states of 'the Family of Nations must expressly or tacitly consent to the reception of the new member'.[86] Following 'the reception of Turkey' in 1856, international law was no longer limited to Christian states, but the position of the Ottoman Empire remained 'anomalous, because her civilization was deemed to fall short of that of the Western States'.[87]

Contemporary criticism

Very few publicists questioned the overall distinction between civilized and uncivilized countries. The earliest dissenting voices did not question the distinction but rather forceful intervention in the name of civilization. Terenzio Mamiani, the father of the Italian school of international law and actively involved in Italian unification, warned (in 1859) that 'to introduce civilization amongst barbarians, and to take them out of their savagery ... at the point of the spear, and by force of arms, as the Romans chose to do, was an uncivilized and tyrannical proceeding'.[88] His compatriot Giuseppe Carnazza Amari, of the University of Catania, pointed out that civilizing the barbarian peoples was an act of 'high philanthropy' but it should be accomplished by civilized means, as 'imposing [civilization] by force is a barbarity greater than the one that we want to destroy'.[89] Similarly, Bonfils was against intervening to educate barbarians and savages: 'For if in the name of humanity we claim to have the right to mingle in the affairs of Negro kings of Africa how could we contest such occurrences in Europe, as in the case of those who intended to invade France in 1793?'[90]

David Dudley Field, a US legal reformer and one of the founding members of the Institut, argued that a lack of neither Christianity nor 'civilization' supplied a justification for exclusion from international law. Referring to China he made the following pertinent point: 'Can it be justly claimed that a nation which has maintained a regularly administered government, over hundreds of millions of human beings, for thousands of years ... is uncivilized?'[91]

The Swiss professor Joseph Hornung referred to acts of barbarity and inhumanity by various 'civilized' states (Russia, Britain, France, Spain, Portugal, Holland) against so-called 'barbarian' and 'savage races', and concluded that 'all the Christian States have committed more or less the same crimes. In general they have proceeded towards other races by conquest, brutality and egoistical exploitation'.[92]

Another dissenting voice was that of Alexandre Mérignhac, of Toulouse University. As he put it: 'on the basis of what sign can they recognize civilized States and distinguish them from those that are not? ... seeing things from a higher level, if we do not limit civilization on the basis of this or the other criterion, which is more or less arbitrary we may arrive at the conclusion that perhaps these nations simply have a distinct civilization from our own, for in addition they, in turn, consider us barbarians'.[93]

It was only following the First World War, when the 'civilized' world clashed in the most uncivilized manner imaginable, that reference to 'civilized states' was largely abandoned. Now international lawyers and diplomats were 'wary of the language of civilization',[94] although it did continue to crop up in various texts of the inter-war period.[95] It found its echo in the trusteeship system of the League of Nations, with its notion of the 'sacred trust of civilization', and in the statute of the Permanent Court of International Justice of the inter-war period, and more embarrassingly in the statute of the International Court of Justice (1945), which still refers to 'the general principles of law recognized by civilized nations' (article 38, 1c).[96]

Eurocentrism, 'civilization' and the 'barbarians'

The reactions of the outsiders: China and Japan

But what was the reaction of those on the receiving end of the 'standard of civilization'? These states, initially not accepted into the family of nations, were not participants in international conferences, were party to unequal treaties against their interests and suffered military interventions to boot. Three cases are well documented: China, Japan and the Ottoman Empire (the last is treated under its own heading in the next section of this chapter).

China

China's reaction and adaptation to the modern world were greatly delayed. In order to understand this inertia one must bear in mind that for thousands of years and well into the nineteenth century the Chinese held a Sinocentric concept of the world. They regarded their country as the centre of the world, the 'Middle Kingdom', the Celestial Empire under the 'Son of Heaven' (the Emperor) as a universal ruler, reigning over the entire world. The Middle Kingdom was the quintessential country of virtue, the embodiment of civilization, indeed the only civilized country, hence their sense of superiority, huge pride and utter contempt for foreigners, invariably regarded as 'barbarians' (akin to 'dogs and sheep'). Barbarian entities, namely the various small states near China, were, at best, vassals in a tributary system, and then only provided they showed obedience and their representatives performed the famous *kowtow* ritual (three kneelings and nine prostrations) before the Son of Heaven. Some authors have called this a distinct 'East Asian society' or 'family of nations' with China as the centre, though it was hardly an international society in which some form of equality reigned, but was more like the Roman Empire and its relations with its neighbours. From the late eighteenth century onwards, with China's first contacts (through trade) with Britain and other Western states, the ruling Chinese regarded Westerners as 'Western barbarians' and this remained the case past the mid-nineteenth century. The Son of Heaven ruled with the mandarins, officials trained in the Confucian classical tradition (in the famous Hanlin Academy), who knew almost nothing else, for all other knowledge or practical expertise was seen as being beneath their dignity. Trade and foreign affairs (called 'barbarian affairs', which included knowledge of other countries and peoples) were regarded as a waste of time, and demeaning.[97]

This mentality and sense of superiority, together with China's size, long history and self-sufficiency (intellectually and economically) and lack of knowledge or interest for the rest of the world, made China impervious to foreign influence and even to the much more intrusive Western influence until it was too late. The 'immobile empire' moved at tortoise pace when confronted with the West, which initially was not regarded for what it was, the greatest challenge and existential threat ever faced by China, which called for quick reactions and far-reaching reforms in education, government and foreign policy.[98]

In this tragic meeting, or rather clash, of civilizations, one can discern three stages on the part of the Chinese ruling elite:

(1) *1840–60.* Following the Opium War of 1840–42, with Britain, China's defeat and the 'unequal' Treaty of Nanking, China ceded Hong Kong and opened five ports to British residence and trade; it was also made to accept a 'most favoured nation' clause for Britain. The resultant trauma and humiliation led to a 'closed-door foreign policy' in what were two 'lost decades' for the Chinese Empire. The defeat by a much smaller army was seen as resulting merely from the superior fire-power of the 'Western barbarians' instead of being seen as pointing to the urgent need for radical change in the name of survival. Thus, acquiring Western weapons and manipulating the 'Western barbarians' through trade were regarded as the ways to manage the West, along with the age-old Confucian strategy towards 'barbarians', known as the 'loose-rein policy'.[99]

(2) *1860–80.* After the 1857–60 War (with the invasion by Britain and France and huge shock of the burning of the Summer Palace in 1860), it dawned on the Chinese that the situation was unprecedented and 'unalterable'.[100] Thus the 'self-strengthening' policy was adopted, stressing knowledge of the West ('Western learning', though it made limited inroads). This new phase saw the formation of the equivalent of a foreign ministry (the *Tsungli Yamen*) under enlightened officials Prince Kung and Wen-hsiang, the formation of the Interpreters College (for learning foreign languages, again with limited inroads made), the sending of the first permanent diplomatic mission to London in 1877, under Kuo Sung-too (a Confucian scholar like the rest but forward-looking), followed by missions in Paris, Berlin, Madrid, St Petersburg, Washington and Tokyo, the translation of several international law treatises and the sending in the 1870s of the first student to study international law in Paris (Ma Chien-chung, who was to prove a valuable adviser on international affairs). China opened a new era in its relations with the West but continued to be torn between tradition and modernity.[101] Western learning, the initiatives by Prince Kung and the positive appraisal of Britain by Kuo in his reports in London faced heavy criticism from traditionalists on Confucian grounds and on the grounds of Chinese superiority.[102]

(3) *1880–1900.* According to Sinologist Immanuel C. Y. Hsü, by '1880 China had belatedly taken her place in the family of nations'[103] (this was not accepted by Western international lawyers, who placed the date later, at the turn of the century). What is more than clear is that Sinocentrism was now on the wane, the term 'barbarians' regarding the Westerners was dropped, 'Western learning' was now 'new learning', the Japanese Westernization example was

Eurocentrism, 'civilization' and the 'barbarians'

seen in a positive light and by the 1890s 'Western knowledge' had entered the school curricula (previously it had been scanty to non-existent). The defeat in the war with Japan (1894–95), a lesser power, was a great shock and, with continued foreign expansion in the region (by Britain, France, Russia, as well as Germany), China felt threatened with dismemberment, with 'being cut up like a melon'.[104] Yet despite the urgency of the situation, there was backlash on the part of conservative officials, including the reactionary mother of the Emperor (the Empress Dowager), who ran the state given the weakness of her son. This period ended dramatically with a tug of war for China's soul: on the one hand, there was the famous 'hundred days' when the Kuang-hsu Emperor asserted himself under the influence of the reformists, headed by scholar K'ang Yu-wa, who convinced him, for the good of the country and its survival, to take a series of major reforms, possibly including constitutional monarchy; and on the other, there was the Empress Dowager's coup, which deposed her son and ushered in the reactionary Boxer Rising (with its call to 'expel the barbarians').[105]

As regards international law, on the eve of the Opium War, in 1839, commissioner Lin Tse-hsu, in charge of abolishing the opium trade, had extracts from Vattel's treatise (see chapter 2), on a state's right to control foreign trade, translated into Chinese. He also sent two eloquent letters to Queen Victoria (which she never read), in which he pointed out that she would no doubt 'be bitterly aroused' if people from another country 'carried opium to England and seduced your people into buying and smoking it'.[106]

In the 1860s and 1870s, under the guidance of Kung, works of international law were translated into Chinese, starting with Wheaton's treatise and followed by those of Woolsey, Martens, Bluntschli and Hall (all of them translated by W. A. P. Martin, who initially wanted to translate Vattel's but found it too antiquated) as well as the *Manuel de lois de la guerre* of the Institut.[107] Martin, an American missionary and member of the Institut who lived in China for sixty years, taught international law and tried to present it as compatible with Confucian tradition. But his translations and teachings had limited influence prior to the 1890s. No doubt China's self-concept as the abode of civilization did not allow it to emulate Western-inspired international law, though it was obliged to do so in its relations with the Western powers. It was to incorporate international law and respect for the laws of war in its foreign behaviour mainly after the Sino-Japanese War of 1894–95.[108]

Japan

Japan was isolated and autarkic for centuries, styling itself as an empire under the 'Son of Heaven of the country where the sun rises', implying that it was the equal of China (under 'the Son of Heaven of the country where the sun sets'), much to the Chinese Emperor's anger, but, by and large, and despite Japan's sense of superiority even in comparison with China, it fell under the Chinese 'sphere of civilization', together with Korea, Vietnam and other smaller countries of the region.[109]

From the early seventeenth century until Commodore Perry's arrival in Japan in 1853, Japan, under the ruling Tokugawa warrior clan (with the Emperor powerless), had opted for a policy of complete seclusion (but for limited trade with Korea, China and the Dutch, and with no Japanese allowed to leave the country or foreigner to enter the country). When from Perry's arrival onwards the Japanese were confronted with the West and obliged to sign unequal treaties (as in the case of other 'uncivilized states') their initial reaction to humiliation was to build Japan's power and repel the 'Western barbarians'.[110] But with the advent of Emperor Meiji (and the 'restoration' of imperial power), seclusion was officially abandoned and Japan declared its willingness to become a member of international society. Indeed, it was deemed desirable to become Westernized, comply with Western rules and practices and to follow the Western 'standard of civilization'. Major intellectuals such as Fukuzawa Yukichi (the Enlightenment theorist) and Uchimura Kanzō (who introduced Christianity to Japan) were at the forefront of this process, together with the Meiji leaders. Students were sent to Europe and the US to study international law in a deliberate attempt to emulate the West. Various treatises on international law were translated into Japanese (far more than the number translated in China into Chinese), including those by Wheaton, Heffter, Bluntschli, Kent, Halleck and Hall, and were very influential (far more so than in China), making Japan better able to defend itself on the basis of Western international law.[111]

No doubt this overall pro-Western approach was stimulated by Japan's apprehension that this was a one-way street: if it did not follow this course it was bound to lose its independence to the imperialist Western powers, which were spreading their colonies and influence across the world, including East Asia. The 1857–60 defeat of China in particular was a turning point for the Japanese.[112]

For Japan, the 1894–95 Sino-Japanese War provided the opportunity to join the 'family of nations'. After an initial bad start with its onslaught on Port Arthur (with 3,000 dead civilians), the Japanese followed the laws of war, unlike the Chinese. Fukuzawa dubbed it 'a war between civilization and barbarism' and Uchimura claimed that the war was righteous, aimed at Korean independence.[113] Two international law professors, Ariga Nagao and Takashaki Sakue, were appointed to the Japanese army and navy to make sure that no transgressions occurred and they wrote two international law books on the war, Ariga in French and Takashaki in English, the latter with an introduction by Holland and a preface by Westlake. These two British authorities claimed that, apart from the Port Arthur incident, Japan had followed the laws of war and merited being regarded as 'civilized' and a member of the family of nations, a line taken by other European and US international lawyers.[114]

The acclaimed jurist and diplomat Kaneko Kentaro (a Harvard graduate), an associate of the Institut de droit international, in an article in the *Revue* argued that the Japanese laws and institutions were of as a high standard as those in Europe and America. He distinguished between the European standard of civilization as a mere European juridical device and the wider, more substantial concept of civilization as such, which had a long history in Japan,[115] concluding that the characteristic trait of the Japanese was that, when in contact with a worthy foreign civilization, they assimilated it, but this hardly amounted to simple imitation.[116]

In Japan, criticism of the standard was rare. One of the very few dissenting voices was international lawyer Tsurutaro Senga, who criticized the standard as unscientific, beyond jurisprudence and ideologically charged and untenable.[117]

The downside to Japan joining the 'family of nations' was that it started to act as an expansionist imperialist power, trying to emulate the Western imperialists, regarding itself as the only 'civilized country' in the region and its Asian neighbours fit to be under its hegemony.[118]

The Ottomans

The European 'Other': the 'Turks'

The Ottoman Empire was officially accepted as a member of the European family of nations, of international law ('the public law of Europe') as well as of the European Concert itself at the 1856 Congress of Paris, following the Crimean War, but was rarely treated as an equal.[119] This was the case above all because the Ottomans were for centuries the quintessential 'Other' in the history of the European state system.[120]

From the Renaissance onwards, the 'Turks' superseded the 'Saracens' as the European 'Other'. They were depicted initially as 'unbelievers' (infidels) and later as 'barbarians'.[121] When Constantinople fell in 1453 to the Ottomans, King Christian I of Denmark spoke of the 'grand Turk' as 'the beast rising out of the sea described in the Apocalypse'.[122] The 'Turks' were seen 'as a pernicious force sent by God to scourge Christendom from its sins'.[123] Yet in the next century an exception was made: the first alliance between a European state and the Ottoman Empire, upon French initiative, during the struggle between the Habsburg Charles V and Francis I of France, the latter concluding several treaties with Suleyman the Magnificent.[124] Moreover, in the course of the sixteenth and seventeenth century the image of the 'Turk' was more nuanced, with many European travellers praising the Ottomans for their administration, for promoting people on the basis of merit and not birth, as well as for their cleanliness and good manners.[125]

From the eighteenth century onwards, the negative image dominated the scene. For Edmund Burke, they were 'wholly Asiatic', 'worse than savages', people who 'despised' all Christians as infidels and wished to subdue and exterminate them.[126]

In the nineteenth century, Lorimer, expressing a widely held sentiment of his time, opined that 'the rights of civilization' should not have been extended to the 'Turks' in Paris in 1856, for 'bitter experience' had shown that they are incapable of performing their duties and 'possibly do not even belong to the progressive races of mankind',[127] adding that 'there is probably no other instance of a people that has been so long in contact with civilization without producing one single individual who has been distinguished in any intellectual pursuit. The art of war is the only art that they seem capable of acquiring'.[128]

Following the Congress of Vienna (1815), no less than five options were entertained by public figures regarding the fate of the Ottoman Empire and the so-called 'Eastern Question':[129] (1) upholding its territorial integrity; (2) dismemberment and division of the spoils by the great powers; (3) expulsion from Europe; (4) Russian conquest of part of the Empire, including the Straits and Constantinople; and (5) major reforms that would make the Ottoman state like the other modern 'civilized' European states.

The first option was advocated by, among others, Austrian Chancellor Clemens von Metternich and British Foreign Secretary Castlereagh in the 1820s, and in the 1870s by Prime Minister Benjamin Disraeli and his Foreign Secretary Lord Derby, though they hardly regarded the Ottoman Empire as an equal state.

The second option, dismemberment, suggested to be the ultimate aim or wish (or wishful thinking) by several personalities in Europe, and not least in Russia, was impractical, for it meant a general war, with unpredictable consequences. One of the few explicit presentations of this option by a public figure was in 1829, by the ultra-royalist Jules de Polignac, the last premier of King Charles X of France.[130]

The third possibility (expulsion from Europe) was supported across the political spectrum: in France by the writer and politician Chateaubriand, the French historian and statesman François Guizot (the dominant figure of the July Monarchy) and the writer and politician Alphonse de Lamartine, one of the founders of the French Second Republic; in Britain by Stratford Canning in the 1820s and many Liberals; in Prussia in the 1820s by the historian Friedrich Ancillon as Director of the Prussian Foreign Ministry; and in Russia in the 1820s by Ioannis Capodistrias, as co-Foreign Minister of Russia, and in the 1870s by Russian ambassador Nikolay Ignatiev, both advocates of the creation of independent Christian states in all the Balkans. This was also the approach of Giuseppe Mazzini.

The fourth option (Russian conquest) was entertained not only by Russian nationalists and pan-Slavists, such as Ivan Aksakov or Fiodor Dostoevsky in the 1870s, but also by Richard Cobden (see below). By and large, however, this option was seen as unrealistic, even by the pan-Slavists who fantasized about capturing Constantinople.

For a time from 1839 until 1875, the Tanzimat reforms made the fifth option – reforming the Ottomans, based on the conviction that the Ottoman Empire could indeed be reformed and follow the European model – a distinct possibility.[131] This minority view was held by several Orientalists, including British diplomat and politician David Urquhart in the 1840s and 1850s and two pro-Ottoman British ambassadors to the Porte in the 1870s, Henry Elliot and Austen Henry Layard. However, the 1875–78 Balkan crisis and the Bulgarian atrocities were decisive in convincing most of the elite in Europe that the Ottoman Empire was perhaps 'unreformable'.[132]

Stratford Canning, the long-serving British ambassador to the Porte, is the first to have used the expression about driving the Sultan 'bags and baggage into the heart of Asia'.[133] Guizot maintained that the 'Turks will go out of Europe' and that that day 'would be a triumph for humanity'.[134]

The French diplomat and jurist Édouard Engelhardt, a frequent contributor to the *Revue* and acclaimed Ottomanist, argued that 'the Ottoman Porte finds itself in a situation of subordination vis-à-vis the continental powers', in a state of 'tutelage' and 'surveillance'.[135] As for the Tanzimat reforms, he concluded, in his two-volume study, that they had not transformed the Empire into a secular state. It remained under Islam's doctrine, 'primitive', 'fanatic', 'Asiatic', 'corrupt', 'inferior', 'despotic' and 'virtually at war' with the Christians and Europeans, whom they hated for their 'superiority'.[136]

Such views were not limited to conservatives but resonated among liberals, socialists and other progressive thinkers and public figures of the long nineteenth century.

A striking case is Cobden, the important Radical and Liberal politician and scathing critic of British imperial rule, who, in damning the 'Turks', went as far as supporting a Russian conquest of Constantinople. According to Cobden, the 'backwardness' of the 'Turks' was due: (1) to Islam, for it teaches its followers 'to despise all other fields of learning than the Koran';[137] (2) to 'a fierce, unmitigated, military despotism' under the Sultan, which 'enables him to sway the lives and destinies of the people, with an absoluteness greater than was ever enjoyed by any tyrant of ancient times';[138] (3) to their disdain for commerce and industry, and the forbidding of communication with the 'infidels';[139] and (4) to a distinctive characteristic of the 'Turkish' and 'Mongolian races', compared with the Russian and 'Sclavonic' (*sic*), 'the former unchanging and stationary, the latter progressing and imitative'.[140]

Gladstone, in his famous pamphlet *Bulgarian Horrors and the Question of the East* (1876), written as an impassioned reaction to the 1876 Bulgarian atrocities (see chapter 8), claimed that this instance of barbarity was not a question of 'Mahometanism simply':[141]

but of Mahometanism compounded with the peculiar character of race. They [the 'Turks'] are not like the mild Mahometans of India, nor the chivalrous Saladins of Syria, nor the cultured Moors of Spain. They were, upon the whole, from the black day when they first entered Europe, the one great anti-human specimen of humanity. Wherever they went, a broad line of blood marked the track behind them, and, as far as their dominion reached, civilization disappeared from view. They represented everywhere government by force, as opposed to government by law.

This frame of mind continued until the eve of the First World War. Georges Scelle, for instance, one of the most innovative French international lawyers of the inter-war period (he discarded sovereignty and regarded individuals as the subjects of international law),[142] claimed (in 1911) that 'the Turks' were a 'living anachronism', that their 'particularly energetic methods of repression' were not used in modern times by European states, and that 'the Turk', well known for his massacres and plunders, had 'never more than camped in Europe'.[143]

David Lloyd George, the last Liberal Prime Minister of Britain, confided before the outbreak of the First World War that he was all for the expulsion of 'the Turk' from Europe, bag and baggage, adding that 'personally, I don't want him even to keep Constantinople'.[144]

The admission of the Ottoman Empire

The admission of the Ottoman Empire to the 1856 Congress of Paris had been mainly political: keeping the Ottoman Empire formally outside was seen as counterproductive. There were obvious advantages to making it a titular member of the European legal structure and thus partaking in the stability of the continent.[145]

There was also the tricky question as to whether the Ottoman Empire was now an equal member of the Concert of Europe, actually the sixth European great power (with Italy later as the seventh).[146] The wording is more than clear ('et du concert Européens') and Turkish Ottomanist scholars claim that in 1856 the Ottoman Empire had indeed become 'a member of the European concert'.[147]

Yet for the next decades there was considerable disagreement about the Ottoman Empire's legal status.[148] Lorimer regarded the admission a major mistake, 'Turkey' a 'phantom state', its recognition a 'farce', and he urged the Europeans to conquer Constantinople and civilize the country.[149] Few jurists were so extreme but even moderates such as Twiss,[150] Martens, Westlake and Rivier regarded the admission premature and incomplete, given the capitulation system.[151]

For the great majority of European and US publicists and diplomats the Ottoman admission was provisional. It was to remain inside Europe conditionally, the condition being improving the living conditions of the Christians in the Ottoman Empire.[152] The 1856 Treaty of Paris also referred to respect for the independence and territorial integrity of the Ottoman Empire by the signatory states. Yet after 1856, interventions in the Ottoman Empire increased rather than diminished, on humanitarian or other grounds. Indeed, the 'maltreatment of Christian minorities' provided 'an excuse for foreign intervention in Ottoman affairs' and such deficiencies in 'civilization' limited the Ottoman Empire's ability to participate in the European international system as a full legal personality.[153]

The Ottoman response

To begin with, the universalist Islam-centred approach during the Ottoman golden age (from 1453 until the end of the seventeenth century) left little ground for international legal relations among equals. But with the Empire's decline the Ottoman rulers had grudgingly to accept their inferior position, at least technologically and militarily, and the need for reforms, starting in the reigns of sultans Selim III (1789–1807) and Mahmud II (1808–39).

The Ottoman reaction to the nineteenth-century humanitarian interventions and other intrusions in the Empire's internal affairs warrants a separate study. One can approach this theme, which has wider ramifications, by delving into the Ottoman archives and by examining what has been written by present Turkish and other specialists on the Ottoman Empire's troubled relations with Europe. On both counts, the overall thrust is that the European powers were biased, anti-Ottoman and, according to modern scholars, Orientalist. Moreover, the massacres committed by the Ottomans were grossly exaggerated, while those committed by the Christians were downplayed or even justified, and there was no concern whatsoever for the plight of the Muslims at the hands of the Christian insurgents.[154]

Here we will limit ourselves to a few cursory remarks on the official Ottoman response and on the stance of the Ottoman opposition.

When intervention was afoot, the attitude of the Porte was, at times, one of rejection and outrage, as we will see in the Greek case of great power involvement in 1821–32 (chapter 6) and with the Balkan uprisings of 1876–78 (chapter 9), or, at other times, one of bending with the wind, as we will see in the case of the Lebanon/Syria crisis of 1860–61 (chapter 7). These two contrasting postures correspond to the reigns of Mahmud II and Abdulhamid II, with their haughty reaction, which was counterproductive for the Ottoman Empire, and Abdulmecid, who was the most reformist Sultan of the nineteenth century and who followed a careful approach vis-à-vis the European great powers.

Special reference is due to the Tanzimat reforms, which commenced in 1839, the very year that Abdulmecid succeeded his father, Mahmud II, as sultan. These reforms started with the 1839 Rose Chamber Edict and the process lasted nearly four decades; they were headed by committed reformist statesmen, in particular by Mustafa Reshid Pasha, Mehmed Emin Ali Pasha, Mehmed Fuad Pasha and

Ahmed Shefik Midhat Pasha, as Foreign Ministers and Grand Viziers, until 1877. The aim was to render the Ottoman state modern, more effective and more legitimate to its subjects, not least to its non-Muslim minorities, but above all the aimed was to save the Empire from collapse, by not permitting further external meddling in its domestic affairs.¹⁵⁵ Presumably, in an Ottoman Empire where equality and the rule of law reigned – where previously all were either *reaya* (flock) or *kul* (servants-slaves of the Sultan) – there would be fewer pretexts for foreign admixture. If European interference was threatened it could be dealt with more convincingly by the Porte as unwarranted. One of the aims of the reforms from the start was also Ottoman accession to the Concert of Europe.¹⁵⁶

Under Abdulmecid, several Ottoman officials, some of whom, like Mehmed Fuad Pasha (Foreign Minister and Grand Vizier), had studied in Europe and were proficient in international law, were aware of the humanitarian intervention discourse in Europe and tried to adjust the policy of the Empire accordingly. European diplomacy was entrusted to Ottoman diplomats, many of them Ottoman Greeks, trained as lawyers in Western Europe, such as John Aristarchis and Constantine Mousouros (who served as Ottoman ambassador in London for thirty-five years) and Alexander Karatheodori Pasha (under-secretary at the Foreign Ministry and briefly Foreign Minister in 1878).¹⁵⁷

The other side of the coin is the stance of the Ottoman opposition, namely the 'Young Turks' (as they were known in Europe), headed by the Committee of Union and Progress (CUP) in exile (mainly in Paris, Geneva, Cairo and in various British cities), whose avowed aim was the overthrow of absolutism and the formation of a democratic and modern Ottoman Empire. The CUP in exile was not limited to educated radical young men who could not stand Abdulhamid's Islamist turn and onslaught against all forms of opposition, but came to include some major high-ranking Ottoman officials, such as Murad Bey (briefly the main figure of the CUP in exile), Ismail Kemal Bey, Basil Mousouros Gkikis (the leader of the Ottoman Greek Young Turks) and none other than the Sultan's brother-in-law, Damad Mahmud Pasha, and his two sons, Princes Sabahaddin Bey and Lutfullah Bey.¹⁵⁸

With the advent of the twentieth century the liberal wing of the Young Turks was headed by Sabahaddin, who was close to Greek and Armenian Young Turks. He advocated foreign armed intervention, mainly on the part of Britain and France, the 'liberal great powers' as he called them, in order to overturn Abdulhamid's authoritarian rule. This foreign intervention would allow the liberal Ottomans to address the Armenian plight and bring about a modern, liberal, multi-ethnic, quasi-federal Ottoman state. This was known as the majority view of the Young Turks, though it was in the ascendency for only a brief period. And there was the minority view (soon to become the dominant view), headed by the conservatives and would-be nationalists under Ahmed Rıza, who opposed any notion of European armed intervention.¹⁵⁹

At the First Congress of Ottoman Opposition, held in Paris in February 1902, Sabahaddin urged the acceptance of 'the benevolent mediation of the Great Powers' in order 'to execute the terms of the treaties, and to bring force to bear against the present absolutist regime that rules against the general will in our fatherland'.[160] He called for intervention on behalf of all 'Ottoman nations' (including the Ottoman Greeks, the Ottoman Armenians and the Ottoman Jews).[161] When the question was put to him whether the intervention was to be military, Sabahaddin's response was 'How many times have [the great powers] intervened in our domestic affairs, how many times even have parts of our country been taken away? Why do we not want to transform these interventions, which most of the time took place without even a military action, into one favoring our own interests?'[162] Rıza retorted that 'every nation is free to conduct its domestic affairs in conformance to its own will'; foreign interventions in the affairs of the Ottoman Empire had always taken place in order to advance the interests of those intervening; seeking European intervention amounted to accepting 'our inability and impotence'; and if Europe intervened it would be to advance its own 'material interest' and any gains for 'us' would be far less than the losses; moreover, calls for intervention would bring about malign Russian intervention.[163]

The end result of the debate was a compromise formula calling the great powers for *concours morale*, taken from a wording used by the reformist Grand Vizier Midhat in the 1870s. At the Second Congress of Ottoman Opposition, in Paris in 1907, with the conservatives under Rıza now the majority, the use of armed force to topple the Addulhamid regime was approved but it was to be achieved without foreign assistance.[164]

Notes

1. G. Delanty, *Inventing Europe: Idea, Identity, Reality* (New York: St Martin's Press, 1995), 95–6.
2. G. W. Gong, *The Standard of 'Civilization' in International Society* (Oxford: Clarendon Press, 1984); M. B. Slater, *Barbarians and Civilization in International Relations* (London: Pluto Press, 2002), 8–63.
3. M. Wight, 'Western Values in International Relations', in H. Butterfield and M. Wight (eds), *Diplomatic Investigations: Essays in the Theory of International Politics* (London: Allen and Unwin, 1966), 94–5, 103; G. Cavallar, 'Vitoria, Grotius, Pufendorf, Wolff and Vattel: Accomplices of European Colonialism and Exploitation or True Cosmopolitans?', *Journal of the History of International Law*, 10 (2008), 186–204.
4. A. Pagden, 'Stoicism, Cosmopolitanism, and the Legacy of European Imperialism', *Constellations*, 7:1 (2000), 3–18.
5. A. Pagden, *The Enlightenment and Why It Still Matters* (New York: Random House, 2013), 294.
6. Ibid., 149–292.
7. H. Bull, *The Anarchical Society: A Study of Order in World Politics* (New York: Columbia University Press, 1977), 28–9, 33–4.

8   B. Bowden, 'The Ideal of Civilization: Its Origins and Social-Political Character', *Critical Review of International Social and Political Philosophy*, 7:1 (2004), 25–37; B. Mazlish, 'Civilization in a Historical and Global Perspective', *International Sociology*, 16:3 (2001), 293–300; J. Goudsblom, 'Civilization: The Career of a Controversial Concept', *History and Theory*, 45 (2006), 288–93.

9   C. H. Alexandrowicz, 'Doctrinal Aspects of the Universality of the Law of Nations', *British Yearbook of International Law*, 37 (1961), 506; C. H. Alexandrowicz, 'New and Original States: The Issue of Reversion to Sovereignty', *International Affairs*, 45:3 (1969), 466–9.

10 M. Koskenniemi, *From Apology to Utopia: The Structure of International Legal Argument* (Cambridge: Cambridge University Press, 2005, reissue with a new epilogue) [1989], 131–43.

11 H. Steiger, 'From the International Law of Christianity to the International Law of the World Citizen – Reflections on the Formation of the Epochs of the History of International Law', *Journal of the History of International Law*, 3 (2001), 184, 187.

12 See J. Donnelly, 'Human Rights: A New Standard of Civilization?', *International Affairs*, 74:1 (1998), 6 and 6 n.26.

13 Alexandrowicz, 'New and Original States', 466–70; Bull, *The Anarchical Society*, 34–5; A. Anghie, *Imperialism, Sovereignty and the Making of International Law* (Cambridge: Cambridge University Press, 2004), 54–6, 65–6, 100–7.

14 Gong, *The Standard of 'Civilization' in International Society*, 55.

15 Pagden, *The Enlightenment and Why It Still Matters*, 249–50.

16 On Wolff and Kant see L. Obregón Tarazova, 'The Civilized and the Uncivilized', in B. Fassbender and A. Peters (eds), *The Oxford Handbook of the History of International Law* (Oxford: Oxford University Press, 2012), 919.

17 H. White, 'The Forms of Wildness: Archeology of an Idea', in E. Dudley and M. E. Novak (eds), *The Wild Man Within: An Image in Western Thought from the Renaissance to Romanticism* (Pittsburgh: Pittsburgh University Press, 1972); P. Keal, *European Conquest and the Rights of Indigenous Peoples: The Moral Backwardness of International Society* (Cambridge: Cambridge University Press, 2003), 67.

18 Gong, *The Standard of 'Civilization' in International Society*, 55–7; A. Anghie, 'Finding the Peripheries: Sovereignty and Colonialism in Nineteenth-Century International Law', *Harvard International Law Journal*, 40:1 (1999), 7, 10.

19 P. Brantlinger, *Dark Vanishings: Discourse on the Extinction of Primitive Races, 1800–1930* (Ithaca: Cornell University Press, 2003), 3.

20 Quoted in R. J. Vincent, 'Race and International Relations', *International Affairs*, 58:4 (1982), 660.

21 On social Darwinism's hierarchy of races and the survival of the fittest race (the 'Aryans'), a view shared by Darwin, see M. Hawkins, *Social Darwinism in European and American Thought* (Cambridge: Cambridge University Press, 1997), 36, 138–45, 184–215.

22 L. L. Snyder, *The Idea of Racialism* (Princeton: D. Van Nostrand, 1962), 7–75; B. McGrane, *Beyond Anthropology: Society and the Other* (New York: Columbia University press, 1989); M. Banton, *Racial Theories* (Cambridge: Cambridge University Press, 1998, 2nd edition), 17–80; T. Todorov, *On Human Diversity: Nationalism, Racism, and Exoticism in French Thought* (Cambridge: Harvard University Press, 1993) [1989]; Vincent, 'Race and International Relations', 659–62.

23 Gong, *The Standard of 'Civilization' in International Society*, 7; Delanty, *Inventing Europe*, 95.

24 J. Pitts, *A Turn to Empire: The Rise of Imperial Liberalism in Britain and France* (Princeton: Princeton University Press, 2005); 133–61, 204–38; C. B. Welch, 'Colonial Violence and the Rhetoric of Evasion: Tocqueville and Algeria', *Political Theory*, 31:2 (2003), 235–64; D. Bell and C. Sylvest, 'International Society in Victorian Political Thought: T. H. Green, Herbert Spencer, and Henry Sidgwick', *Modern Intellectual History*, 3:2 (2006), 236–7; M. Wight, 'Mazzini', in G. Wight and B. Porter (eds), *Four Seminal Thinkers in International Theory: Machiavelli, Grotius, Kant and Mazzini* (Oxford: Oxford University Press, 2005), 109.
25 Pitts, *A Turn to Empire*, 1–100; Pagden, *The Enlightenment and Why It Still Matters*, 329–41.
26 J. Pitts, 'Boundaries of Victorian International Law', in D. Bell (ed.), *Victorian Visions of Global Order: Empire and International Relations in Nineteenth-Century Political Thought* (Cambridge: Cambridge University Press, 2007), 78–82.
27 D. S. A. Bell, 'Empire and International Relations in Victorian Political Thought', *Historical Journal*, 49:1 (2006), 286; Bell and Sylvest, 'International Society in Victorian Political Thought', 233, 236–7.
28 M. Koskenniemi, 'Nationalism, Universalism, Empire: International Law in 1871 and 1919', paper presented at the conference 'Whose International Community? Universalism and the Legacies of Empire', Columbia University, 29–30 April 2005, 20.
29 B. Porter, *Critics of Empire: British Radicals and the Imperial Challenge* (London: I. B. Tauris, 2008) [1968].
30 W. C. Olson and A. J. R. Groom, *International Relations Then and Now* (London: Routledge, 1991), 39, 47, 51–2.
31 G. Schwarzenberger, 'The Rule of Law and the Disintegration of the International Society', *American Journal of International Law*, 33:1 (1939), 64–5.
32 G. Schwarzenberger, 'The Standard of Civilization in International Law', *Current Legal Problems*, 8:1 (1955), 212–34; Gong, *The Standard of 'Civilization' in International Society*; A. Becker Lorca, 'Universal International Law: Nineteenth-Century Histories of Imposition and Appropriation', *Harvard International Law Journal*, 51:2 (2010), 495–6.
33 Koskenniemi, 'Nationalism, Universalism, Empire', 23.
34 Gong, *The Standard of 'Civilization' in International Society*, 14–15.
35 Schwarzenberger, 'The Standard of Civilization in International Law', 220.
36 Bell and Sylvest, 'International Society in Victorian Political Thought', 232–3.
37 Schwarzenberger, 'The Rule of Law and the Disintegration of the International Society', 65–6; Becker Lorca, 'Universal International Law', 495–6.
38 M. Koskenniemi, *The Gentle Civilizer of Nations: The Rise and Fall of International Law 1870–1960* (Cambridge: Cambridge University Press, 2002), 41.
39 See *ibid.*; C. Sylvest, '"Our Passion for Legality": International Law and Imperialism in Late Nineteenth-century Britain', *Review of International Studies*, 34 (2008), 403–23.
40 Gong, *The Standard of 'Civilization' and International Society*, 19.
41 Koskenniemi, *The Gentle Civilizer of Nations*, 81–2.
42 H. Wheaton, *Elements of International Law: With a Sketch of the History of the Science* (Philadelphia: Carey, Lea and Blanchard, 1836); H. Wheaton, *Elements of International Law* (Boston: Little, Brown and Co., 1866, 8th edition, edited by R. H. Dana).
43 Wheaton, *Elements of International Law: With a Sketch of the History of the Science*, 45.
44 *Ibid.*, 46.
45 A. W. Heffter, *Le droit international de l'Europe* (Berlin: H. W. Muller; Paris: A. Cotillon et Cie, 1883, 4th French edition, translated from the German by J. Bergson) [1844].
46 A. Orakhelashvili, 'The Idea of European International Law', *European Journal of International Law*, 17:2 (2006), 323.

47 H. Bonfils, *Manuel de droit international public (droit des gens)* (Paris: Librairie nouvelle de droit et de jurisprudence, 1905, 4th edition by P. Fauchille) [1894].
48 Orakhelashvili, 'The Idea of European International Law', 324, 326.
49 Ibid., 325; D. Rodogno, *Against Massacre: Humanitarian Intervention in the Ottoman Empire, 1815–1914. The Emergence of a European Concept and International Practice* (Princeton: Princeton University Press, 2012), 292 n.53.
50 Koskenniemi, *The Gentle Civilizer of Nations*, 50.
51 Pitts, 'Boundaries of Victorian International Law', 71.
52 Ibid., 72.
53 Koskenniemi, *The Gentle Civilizer of Nations*, 33.
54 I. B. Neumann, *Uses of the Other: 'The East' in European Identity Formation* (Minneapolis: University of Minnesota Press, 1999), 57.
55 Bull, *The Anarchical Society*, 38.
56 Koskenniemi, *The Gentle Civilizer of Nations*, 77–8.
57 J. E. Noyes, 'Christianity and Late Nineteenth-Century British Theories of International Law', in M. W. Janis (ed.), *The Influence of Religion in the Development of International Law* (Dordrecht: Martinus Nijhoff, 1991), 91–3.
58 For Bluntschli's contribution and views see Koskenniemi, *The Gentle Civilizer of Nations*, 40, 42–7.
59 Ibid., 74.
60 Ibid., 77, 103–4; Orakhelashvili, 'The Idea of European International Law', 322.
61 'Turkey' was chiefly a term used by Europeans and Americans to refer to the Ottoman Empire (including by many publicists in their works). The term 'Turk' was deeply resented by the Ottomans, who did not call themselves 'Turks' or their state 'Turkey' or 'Turkish Empire'. For them 'Turk' meant a vulgar individual, a peasant from Anatolia (this until the late nineteenth century and even into the twentieth). See B. Lewis, *The Emergence of Modern Turkey* (London: Oxford University Press, 1968) [1961], 1, 332–3; G. Lewis, *Modern Turkey* (London: Ernest Benn, 1974), 55; D. Kushner, *The Rise of Turkish Nationalism* (London: Frank Cass, 1977), 20–1.
62 Koskenniemi, *The Gentle Civilizer of Nations*, 77, 103–4; Orakhelashvili, 'The Idea of European International Law', 322.
63 C. Sylvest, 'International Law in Nineteenth Century Britain', *British Year Book of International Law*, 75 (2004), 27 n.87; C. Sylvest, *British Liberal Internationalism, 1830–1930: Making Progress?* (Manchester: Manchester University Press, 2009), 77.
64 R. Phillimore, *Commentaries upon International Law* (London: Butterworths, 1879, 3rd edition) [1854], vol. I.
65 Quoted in Sylvest, 'Our Passion for Legality', 407.
66 Noyes, 'Christianity and Late Nineteenth-Century British Theories of International Law', 86.
67 Ibid., 99.
68 P. Fiore, *Nouveau droit international public suivant les besoins de la civilization moderne* (Paris: A. Durant et Pedone-Lauriel, 1885, 2nd edition, translated and annotated by Charles Antoine) [1865], vol. I. For Fiore's contribution see Koskenniemi, *The Gentle Civilizer of Nations*, 54–7.
69 On human rights ('Man's rights') see P. Fiore, *International Law Codified and Its Legal Sanction or the Legal Organization of the Society of States* (New York: Baker, Voorhis, 1918, translated from the 5th Italian edition with introduction by E. M. Borchard) [1890], 40–1.
70 Fiore, *Nouveau droit international public suivant les besoins de la civilization moderne*, 54.

71 Gong, *The Standard of 'Civilization' in International Society*, 63.
72 Koskenniemi, *The Gentle Civilizer of Nations*, 56 and 56 n.210.
73 F. Martens, *Sovremennoe Mezhdunarodnoe Pravo Tsivilizovannykh Narodov* (St Petersburg: Tipografiya A. Benke, 1904, 5th revised edition) [1883], vol. I, 184–7.
74 Koskenniemi, *The Gentle Civilizer of Nations*, 53; Orakhelashvili, 'The Idea of European International Law', 324–5.
75 Koskenniemi, *The Gentle Civilizer of Nations*, 49.
76 Orakhelashvili, 'The Idea of European International Law', 320.
77 Quoted in Gong, *The Standard of 'Civilization' in International Society*, 16, 59.
78 Susumu Yamauchi, 'Civilization and International Law in Japan During the Meiji Era (1868–1912)', *Hitotsubashi Journal of Law and Politics*, 24 (1996), 21.
79 C. Sylvest, 'The Foundations of Victorian International Law', in Bell (ed.), *Victorian Visions of Global Order*, 56.
80 Gong, *The Standard of 'Civilization' in International Society*, 55.
81 Ibid., 16.
82 Ibid., 60.
83 Ibid., 19.
84 Becker Lorca, 'Universal International Law', 532.
85 L. Oppenheim, *International Law: A Treatise* (London: Longmans, Green, 1937, 5th edition, edited by H. Lauterpacht) [1905], vol. I, 4–5.
86 Ibid., 44.
87 Ibid., 44–5.
88 Count Mamiani, *Rights of Nations, or the New Law of European States Applied to the Affairs of Italy* (London: W. Jeffs, 1860, translated from the Italian by R. Acton) [1859], 195.
89 G. Carnazza Amari, 'Nouvel exposé du principe de non-intervention', *Revue de droit international et de législation comparée*, 5 (1873), 555.
90 Bonfils, *Manuel de droit international public*, 169.
91 Pitts, 'Boundaries of Victorian International Law', 74–5.
92 J. Hornung, 'Civilisés et barbares', *Revue de droit international et de législation comparée*, 17 (1885), 7.
93 A. Mérignhac, *Traité de droit public international* (Paris: Librairie générale de droit and de jurisprudence, 1905), part i, 300–1.
94 Koskenniemi, 'Nationalism, Universalism, Empire', 4–5.
95 See e.g. J. L. Brierly, *The Law of Nations: An Introduction to the International Law of Peace* (Oxford: Clarendon Press, 1936, 2nd edition) [1928], 1; Oppenheim, *International Law*.
96 Gong, *The Standard of 'Civilization' in International Society*, 69, 76.
97 J. K. Fairbank and E. O. Reischauer, *China: Tradition and Transformation* (Boston: Houghton Mifflin, 1973), 195, 258, 271; J. K. Fairbank, 'A Preliminary Framework', in J. K. Fairbank (ed.), *The Chinese World Order: Traditional China's Foreign Relations* (Cambridge: Harvard University Press, 1968), 1–19; J. K. Fairbank, 'Introduction: The Old Order', in J. K. Fairbank (ed.), *The Cambridge History of China, Volume X: Late Ch'ing 1800–1911, Part 1* (Cambridge: Cambridge University Press, 1978), 2–6, 12. See also Y. Onuma, 'When Was the Law of International Society Born? An Inquiry of the History of International Law from an Intercivilizational Perspective', *Journal of the History of International Law*, 2 (2000), 11–17, 28–30.
98 Fairbank, 'Introduction', 4–6; G. W. Gong, 'China's Entry into International Society', in H. Bull and A. Watson (eds), *The Expansion of International Society* (Oxford: Clarendon Press, 1984), 172–6.

99 Fairbank and Reischauer, *China*, 277, 282–3; S. Teng and J. K. Fairbank, *China's Response to the West: A Documentary Survey 1839–1923* (Cambridge: Harvard University Press, 1979), 23–60; Y. P. Hao and E. Wang, 'Changing Chinese Views of Western Relations, 1840–95', in J. K. Fairbank and K.-C. Liu (eds), *The Cambridge History of China, Volume XI: Late Ch'ing 1800–1911, Part 2* (Cambridge: Cambridge University Press, 1980), 142–56; J. K. Fairbank, 'The Creation of the Treaty System', in Fairbank (ed.), *The Cambridge History of China, Volume X*, 218–19, 226; Gong, 'China's Entry into International Society', 172–3, 175–6.

100 Hao and Wang, 'Changing Chinese Views of Western Relations', 156–7.

101 I. C. Y. Hsü, 'Late Ch'ing Foreign Relations, 1866–1905', in Fairbank and Liu (eds), *The Cambridge History of China, Volume XI*, 70.

102 *Ibid.*, 70–5, 84; I. C. Y. Hsü, *China's Entrance into the Family of Nations: The Diplomatic Phase, 1858–1880* (Cambridge: Harvard University Press, 1960), 108, 132–45, 163–210; T. Y. Kuo, 'Self-Strengthening: The Pursuit of Western Technology', in Fairbank (ed.), *The Cambridge History of China, Volume X*, 500–7, 517, 529–31; Hao and Wang, 'Changing Chinese Views of Western Relations', 160–5, 167–87, 196–8; H. Chang, 'Intellectual Change and the Reform Movement, 1890–8', in Fairbank and Liu (eds), *The Cambridge History of China, Volume XI*, 275–7; Teng and Fairbank, *China's Response to the West*, 61–107; Gong, 'China's Entry into International Society', 180–1; J. D. Frodsham, 'Introduction', in *The First Chinese Embassy to the West* (Oxford: Clarendon Press, 1974, translated and annotated by J. D. Frodsham), xxviii–lxv.

103 Hsü, 'Late Ch'ing Foreign Relations', 84. See for more details Hsü, *China's Entrance into the Family of Nations*, 121–210.

104 Chang, 'Intellectual Change and the Reform Movement', 274.

105 *Ibid.*, 277–338; Hao and Wang, 'Changing Chinese Views of Western Relations', 188–9, 194, 198, 200–1; Teng and Fairbank, *China's Response to the West*, 118–95; Fairbank and Reischauer, *China*, 373–8.

106 L. H. Liu, *The Clash of Empires: The Invention of China in Modern World Making* (Cambridge: Harvard University Press, 2004), 118–19. For the full text of Lin's letter to Queen Victoria, see Teng and Fairbank, *China's Response to the West*, 24–8.

107 Liu, *The Clash of Empires*, 113–24; Hao and Wang, 'Changing Chinese Views of Western Relations', 196–7; Gong, 'China's Entry into International Society', 180–1.

108 R. Svarverud, *International Law as World Order in Late Imperial China: Translation, Reception and Discourse, 1847–1911* (Leiden: Brill, 2007); Hsü, *China's Entrance into the Family of Nations*, 125–31; S. Kawashima, 'China', in Fassbender and Peters (eds), *The Oxford Handbook of the History of International Law*, 455–9; Gong, 'China's Entry into International Society', 180–1.

109 Onuma, 'When Was the Law of International Society Born?', 11, 13; M. Yanagihara, 'Japan', in Fassbender and Peters (eds), *The Oxford Handbook of the History of International Law*, 479–80.

110 H. Suganami, 'Japan's Entry into International Society', in Bull and Watson (eds), *The Expansion of International Society*, 185–91; R. P. Anand, 'Family of "Civilized" States and Japan: A Story of Humiliation, Assimilation, Defiance and Confrontation', *Journal of the History of International Law*, 5 (2003), 12–16; D. Howland, 'Japan's Civilized War: International Law as Diplomacy in the Sino-Japanese War (1894–1895)', *Journal of the History of International Law*, 9 (2007), 183.

111 Suganami, 'Japan's Entry into International Society', 191–2; Howland, 'Japan's Civilized War', 184–5, 200–1; Susumu, 'Civilization and International Law in Japan during the Meiji Era', 2–3, 6; Anand, 'Family of "Civilized" States and Japan', 16–19.

112 Susumu, 'Civilization and International Law in Japan During the Meiji Era', 7; Anand, 'Family of "Civilized" States and Japan', 22.
113 Anand, 'Family of "Civilized" States and Japan', 26–7.
114 Suganami, 'Japan's Entry into International Society', 192–3, 195; Howland, 'Japan's Civilized War', 180–2, 186–201; Anand, 'Family of "Civilized" States and Japan', 26–32; Susumu, 'Civilization and International Law in Japan During the Meiji Era', 4, 8–15. See also Holland's assessment in T. E. Holland, *Studies in International Law* (Oxford: Clarendon Press, 1898), 128–9.
115 Becker Lorca, 'Universal International Law', 497–98.
116 K. Kaneko, 'Les institutions juridiciaires du Japon', *Revue de droit international et de législation comparée*, 25 (1893), 338–9, 356.
117 Becker Lorca, 'Universal International Law', 501–2.
118 Anand, 'Family of "Civilized" States and Japan', 24–6; Howland, 'Japan's Civilized War', 181–2; Susumu, 'Civilization and International Law in Japan During the Meiji Era', 24.
119 H. McKinnon Wood, 'The Treaty of Paris and Turkey's Status in International Law', *American Journal of International Law*, 37:2 (1943).
120 Neumann, *Uses of the Other*, 39–40.
121 Ibid., 52.
122 Ibid., 45.
123 Ibid., 45.
124 H. Inalcik, *The Ottoman Empire: The Classical Age 1300–1600* (London: Phoenix, 2000) [1973], 35; S. Faroqhi, *The Ottoman Empire and the World Around It* (London: I. B. Tauris, 2007), 33.
125 D. Livanios, 'The "Sick Man" Paradox: History, Rhetoric and the "European Character" of Turkey', *Journal of Southern Europe and the Balkans*, 8:3 (2006), 305.
126 Neumann, *Uses of the Other*, 53.
127 J. Lorimer, *The Institutes of the Law of Nations: A Treatise of the Jural Relations of Separate Political Communities* (Edinburgh: William Blackwood and Sons, 1883), vol. I, 102.
128 Ibid., 102–3 n.1.
129 Rodogno refers to three of the five options. See Rodogno, *Against Massacre*, 24–7.
130 G. Bodiner, 'Le projet français d'intervention militaire en Grèce', in E. Chrysos and C. Farnaud (eds), *La France et la Grèce au XIXe siècle. Actes du colloque franco-hellénique* (Athens: Fondation du Parliament Hellénique pour le Parlementarisme et la Démocratie, 2011), 104.
131 In Russia this aspect had been discussed in the late eighteenth century but with a different twist: it was accepted that the Ottoman state could reform substantially and become European but that would not be to Europe's benefit. See V. Taki, 'Orientalism on the Margins: The Ottoman Empire under Russian Eyes', *Kritika: Explorations in Russian and Eurasian History*, 12:2 (2011), 330–6.
132 Rodogno, *Against Massacre*, 27.
133 Quoted in C. W. Crawley, *The Question of Greek Independence: A Study of British Policy in the Near East, 1821–1933* (New York: Howard Fertig, 1973) [1930], 48 n.14.
134 Quoted in Rodogno, *Against Massacre*, 24.
135 É. Engelhardt, *Le droit d'intervention et la Turquie. Étude historique* (Paris: A. Cotillon et Cie, 1880), 61.
136 É. Engelhardt, *La Turquie et le Tanzimat ou histoire des réformes dans l'Empire Ottoman depuis 1826 jusqu'à nos jours* (Paris: Librairie Cottillon, 1884), in particular vol. II, 299–328.

137 R. Cobden, 'Russia: Chapter I. Russia, Turkey, and England', in R. Cobden, *Political Writings* (London: Routledge/Thoemmes Press, 1995), vol. I, 168–9.
138 *Ibid.*, 170.
139 *Ibid.*, 171–4, 187.
140 *Ibid.*, 187.
141 Right Hon. W. E. Gladstone, M.P., *Bulgarian Horrors and the Question of the East* (London: John Murray, 1876), 12–13.
142 On Scelle's contribution see Koskenniemi, *The Gentle Civilizer of Nations*, 266, 316–17, 327–38; H. Thierry, 'The Thought of Georges Scelle', *European Journal of International Law*, 1 (1990), 193–209.
143 G. Scelle, 'Studies on the Eastern Question', *American Journal of International Law*, 5:1 (1911), 148–9.
144 Quoted in M. Llewellyn Smith, *Ionian Vision: Greece in Asia Minor 1919–1922* (London: Allen Lane, 1973), 13.
145 McKinnon Wood, 'The Treaty of Paris and Turkey's Status in International Law', 274.
146 J. C. Hurewitz, 'Ottoman Diplomacy and the European State System', *Middle East Journal*, 15:2 (1961), 152.
147 See e.g. M. Ş. Hanioğlu, *A Brief History of the Late Ottoman Empire* (Princeton: Princeton University Press, 2008), 82.
148 Pitts, 'Boundaries of Victorian International Law', 72.
149 *Ibid.*, 72–3.
150 *Ibid.*, 72.
151 Martens, *Sovremennoe Mezhdunarodnoe Pravo Tsivilizovannykh Narodov*, vol. I, 186–7; McKinnon Wood, 'The Treaty of Paris and Turkey's Status in International Law', 274; Rodogno, *Against Massacre*, 51.
152 Rodongo, *Against Massacre*, 45.
153 Gong, *The Standard of 'Civilization' in International Society*, 51, 107.
154 For a thorough study of the recent trends of Turkish scholarship regarding this question see L. Karakatsanis, 'Turkish Historiography on the Long 19th Century: The Cases of European Interventions for "Humanitarian Disasters"' (forthcoming).
155 R. Davison, *Reform in the Ottoman Empire, 1856–76* (Princeton: Princeton University Press, 1963); N. Berkes, *The Development of Secularism in Turkey* (London: Hurst, 1998) [1964], 144–200; Lewis, *The Emergence of Modern Turkey*, 105–28; Lewis, *Modern Turkey*, 44–5; E. J. Zürcher, *Turkey: A Modern History* (London: I. B. Tauris, 1993), 52–69; Hanioğlu, *A Brief History of the Late Ottoman Empire*, 72–102.
156 Hanioğlu, *A Brief History of the Late Ottoman Empire*, 73.
157 A. Alexandris, *The Greek Minority of Istanbul and Greek–Turkish Relations* (Athens: Centre for Asia Minor Studies, 1983), 28–9.
158 M. Ş. Hanioğlu, *The Young Turks in Opposition* (New York: Oxford University Press, 1995), 64–7, 76–84, 90–104, 142–50.
159 *Ibid.*, 186–92.
160 *Ibid.*, 191.
161 *Ibid.*, 191.
162 Quoted *ibid.*, 191.
163 *Ibid.*, 190.
164 *Ibid.*, 192; Zürcher, *Turkey*, 93.

4

International law and humanitarian intervention

Advocates and opponents of humanitarian intervention

From the 1860s onwards, international law became an academic discipline in its own right in Europe and the Americas, taught separately from philosophy, natural law or civil law, and came to be written by professional academics or theoretically inclined diplomats.[1] Until then what existed was the *droit public de l'Europe* or 'external public law'. Britain in particular had to face the 'spectre of Austin',[2] who dominated British jurisprudence in the first part of the nineteenth century. For John Austin, 'laws properly so called' were 'established directly by command'[3] and those lacking command were 'positive moral rules which are laws improperly so called ... *laws set* or *imposed by general opinion*'[4] and this was the case with the 'so called law of nations [which] consists of opinions or sentiments current among nations generally'.[5]

Two landmarks for international law are the founding of its first scholarly journal and of an institute/association of international lawyers (see chapter 3). The journal, the *Revue de droit international et de législation comparée*, was launched in Belgium in 1868, by the Belgian Gustave Rolin-Jaequemyns, the Dutch Tobias Asser and the British John Westlake, with the support of the Italian Professor Pasquale Mancini.[6] Rolin-Jaequemyns was also at the forefront of the creation of the Institut de droit international in 1873, with the help of Bluntschli, Holtzendorff, Calvo, Mancini and a few others.[7]

At its inception, the ultimate aim of the Institut was '[d]e favoriser le progrès du droit international, en s'efforçant de devenir l'organe de la conscience juridique du monde civilisé'.[8] The wording in question had come from Bluntschli, who had used such language before in his publications.[9] As Martti Koskenniemi points out, the reference to 'legal conscience', or 'consciousness', seems to us today 'old-fashioned and difficult to take in full seriousness'.[10] But in those days this aim was taken in all seriousness and voiced by worldly publicists, many of them with hands-on experience as politicians, diplomats, lawyers or judges.

Interestingly, humanitarian intervention entered the scene as international law was developing into a scientific discipline, as in the case of another science in its modern form, history, which matured hand in hand with the rise of nationalism (hence the emergence of national historiography in the nineteenth century).[11]

From the 1830s until the 1930s most publicists addressed the question of intervening or not for humanitarian purposes to stop 'the effusion of blood', with a clear majority favouring the use of armed force for humanitarian purposes in certain exceptional cases, thereby bypassing the cardinal norm of non-intervention (see table 4.1). According to Wilhelm Grewe's assessment, in the nineteenth century 'the principle of humanitarian intervention increasingly absorbed all other grounds of intervention (with the exception of contractual permission and self-help)'.[12] This tendency in law and practice is striking, for, prior to the UN Charter and the international law of human rights, there was no international legal ban on acts of inhumanity by states, and sovereignty and independence, including the norm of non-intervention, were the cornerstones of international law. On the other hand, aggressive war was permitted and was a manifestation of sovereignty.[13] The 'paradoxical outcome' was that 'the greater threat to the integrity of states (waging war) was widely regarded as legitimate, but the lesser (intervention) was not';[14] thus, 'in the absence of a clear distinction between intervention and war any regulation of the former could be circumvented by resort to the latter'.[15]

There was also the parallel development of the laws of war aimed at humanizing warfare initiated by Henry Dunant in the wake of the suffering in the Crimean War and the 1859 Battle of Solferino during the Second Italian War of Independence.[16] The laws of warfare were the first branch of international law to be codified[17] and these mention the concept of 'humanity'. The 1899 and 1907 Hague Conventions on land warfare adopted, in 'the interests of humanity', what came to be known as the 'Martens clause', proposed by F. F. Martens, 'that in cases not included in the Regulations adopted ... the inhabitants and the belligerents remain under the protection and the rule of the principles of international law, as they result from the usages established among civilized peoples, from the laws of humanity, and the dictates of the public conscience'. Thus, at the turn of century, the humanitarian idea had entered general international law.[18]

The advocates of humanitarian intervention, within a period of about a century, from the 1830s to the 1930s, regarded it as legitimate, but only if it fulfilled the following criteria: (1) intervention was needed to counter gross mistreatment and massacres 'shocking the moral consciousness of mankind', (2) the intervention was collective or quasi-collective, so as to acquire international legitimacy and limit the abuse factor; and (3) disinterestedness or that humanitarian concern was one of the main motives and justifications for intervening.[19]

Those opposed to such interventions based their case on the principles of sovereignty and independence, with non-intervention as their corollary, as well as on practical grounds, especially abuse by powerful states, with total disinterestedness regarded as unrealistic and by definition bogus. Some also alluded to the double standard of singling out only 'barbarous' states for intervention.

International law and humanitarian intervention

We have identified no less than 100 publicists who had addressed the question from the 1830s up to the 1930s, mainly with the historical examples of the nineteenth century in mind.[20] Sixty-two were supportive of humanitarian intervention (that is, 62 per cent of the total). Of the publicists supportive of armed humanitarian intervention, forty-eight claimed a right to intervene in exceptional circumstances only and fourteen invoked moral or political reasons. There is also a substantial minority against any such legal or moral right: thirty-eight publicists (that is, 38 per cent of the total) (see table 4.1).[21]

To make our presentation as lucid as possible, we will divide our material into five periods, from the 1830s until the 1930s, and present it, to the degree possible, in the form of a debate.

1830–50: from Wheaton to Heffter

In the 1830s and 1840s, eleven publicists addressed the question, more or less equally divided into advocates and opponents of humanitarian intervention (see table 4.1).

In the first decades of the twentieth century, Egide Arntz, of the University of Brussels, was credited as the first to formulate the theory of humanitarian intervention, this in the mid-1870s.[22] Arntz's thesis was presented in a letter he sent to Rolin-Jaequemyns, which the latter published in the *Revue*.[23] But most commentators in the second part of the nineteenth and today regard Wheaton as the initiator of the concept, on the basis of the following statement, made a few years after the end of the Greek independence struggle, in his 1836 treatise:[24]

> The interference of the Christian powers of Europe, in favor of the Greeks, who, after enduring ages of cruel oppression, had shaken off the Ottoman yoke, affords a further illustration of the principles of international law authorizing such an interference, not only where the interests and safety of other powers are immediately affected by the internal transactions of a particular state, but where the *general interests of humanity* are infringed by the excesses of a barbarous and despotic government.

Wheaton's view on intervention was put to task by the Italian–French jurist, economist and politician Pellegrino Rossi and by the British lawyer and economist Nassau William Senior. Rossi advocated neutrality in civil wars, save when a neighbouring state was menaced by the conflict.[25] Senior, a frequent writer on political affairs and governmental adviser, commented that 'interference for the mere purpose of preventing the oppression of Subjects by their Prince' was unlawful[26] and dangerous, and made the lasting point that it was 'the privilege … of the strong against the weak'.[27]

In the 1840s, three advocates of non-intervention allowed for a slight opening for exceptional intervention in instances of humanitarian plight. The Norwegian

Table 4.1 The stance of publicists regarding humanitarian intervention, 1830–1939

	Advocates on legal grounds	Advocates on moral or political grounds	Opponents
Publicists with works in 1830–50	(3) Pinheiro-Ferreira (1769–1846) Wheaton (1785–1848) Heiberg (1802–78)	(2) Heffter (1796–1880) Rotteck (1816–45)	(6) Kent (1763–1847) Reddie (1773–1852) Rossi (1787–1848) Senior (1790–1864) Taparelli (1793–1862) Wildman (1802–81)
Publicists with works in 1851–70	(5+1) Woolsey (1801–89) Bluntschli (1808–81) Phillimore (1810–85) Berner (1818–1907) Fiore (1837–1914) + Heiberg active from previous period	(3+1) Bernard (1820–82) Abdy (1822–99) Harcourt (1827–1904) + Heffter active from previous period	(3+3) Mamiani (1799–1885) Halleck (1815–72) Calvo (1824–1906) + 3 active from previous period: Senior, Taparelli, Wildman
Publicists with works in 1871–90	(11+6) Manning (1809–78) Creasy (1812–78) Arntz (1812–84) Lorimer (1818–90) Hornung (1822–?) Engelhardt (1828–1916) Amos (1835–86) Rolin-Jaequemyns (1835–1902) Martens (1845–1909) Komarovskiy (1846–1912) Kebedgy (1865–1947) + 6 active from previous period: Heiberg, Bluntschli, Woolsey, Phillimore, Berner, Fiore	(2+3) Hall (1835–94) Pomeroy (1828–85) + 3 active from previous period: Bernard, Abdy, Harcourt	(10+3) Twiss (1809–97) Pradier-Fodéré (1827–1904) Geffcken (1830–96) Funck-Brentano (1830–1906) Bonfils (1835–97) Carnazza Amari (1837–1911) Strauch (1838–1904) Sorel (1842–1906) Renault (1843–1918) Cimbali (1862–1934) + 3 active from previous period: Mamiani, Halleck, Calvo

Publicists with works in 1891–1918	(14+5)	(4+3)	(13+11)
	Westlake (1828–1913)	Oppenheim (1858–1919)	Holland (1835–1926)
	Rivier (1835–98)	Moore (1860–1947)	Pereira (1834–1917)
	Mérignhac (1843–1918)	Hershey (1867–1933)	Pierantoni (1840–1911)
	Lawrence (1849–1920)	Hodges (1888–?)	Liszt (1851–1919)
	Woolsey (1852–1929)	+ 3 active from previous period: Hall, Abdy, Harcourt	Nys (1851–1920)
	Pillet (1857–1926)		Despagnet (1857–1906)
	Le Fur (1870–1943)		Walker (1862–1935)
	Lapradelle (1871–1955)		Wilson (1863–1951)
	Lingelbach (1871–1962)		Floeckher (1867–?)
	Fedozi (1872–1936)		Maxey (1869–?)
	Rougier (1877–1927)		Smith (1872–1930)
	Basdevant (1877–1968)		Hyde (1873–1952)
	Cavaglieri (1880–1935)		Gareis (1889–1921)
	Borchard (1884–1951)		+ 11 active from previous period: Twiss, Calvo, Pradier-Fodéré, Geffcken, Funck-Brentano, Bonfils, Carnazza Amari, Cimbali, Strauch, Sorel, Renault
	+ 5 active from previous period: Engelhardt, Rolin-Jaequemyns, Martens, Komarovskiy, Kebedgy		

Table continues over

Table 4.1 Continued

Publicists with works in 1919–39	(15+12)	(3+3)	(6+8)
	Fauchille (1858–1926)	Dupuis (1863–1939)	Higgins (1865–1935)
	Snow (1859–1920)	Fenwick (1880–1973)	Winfield (1878–1953)
	Streit (1868–1948)	Potter (1892–1981)	Brierly (1881–1955)
	Taube (1869–?)	+ 3 active from previous period: Moore, Hershey and Hodges	Redslob (1882–1962)
	Mandelstam (1869–1949)		Strupp (1886–1940)
	Pinon (1870–1958)		Accioly (1888–1962)
	Politis (1872–1942)		+ 8 active from previous period: Holland, Nys, Cimbali, Walker, Wilson, Maxey, Smith, Gareis
	Séfériadès (1873–1951)		
	Hyde (1873–1952)		
	Vollenhoven (1874–1933)		
	Stowell (1875–1958)		
	Scelle (1878–1961)		
	Dickinson (1887–1961)		
	Lauterpacht (1897–1960)		
	Guggenheim (1899–1977)		
	+ 12 active from previous period: Lawrence, Woolsey, Pillet, Kebedgy, Le Fur, Lapradelle, Fedozi, Lingelbach, Rougier, Basdevant, Cavaglieri, Borchard		

The above is based on the works cited in the notes. For those publicists not cited in the notes see their works listed in the Select Bibliography on International Law until 1945 and the following works reviewing the literature: A. Rougier, 'La théorie de l'intervention d'humanité', *Revue générale de droit international public*, 17 (1910), 468–97; E. C. Stowell, *Intervention in International Law* (Washington, DC: John Byrne, 1921); J.-P. L. Fonteyne, 'The Customary International Law Doctrine of Humanitarian Intervention: Its Current Validity Under the U.N. Charter', *California Western International Law Journal* (1973–74), 203–32; S. Chesterman, *Just War or Just Peace? Humanitarian Intervention and International Law* (Oxford: Oxford University Press, 2001), 7–28, 35–42; A. Heraclides, 'Humanitarian Intervention in International Law 1830–1939: The Debate', *Journal of the History of International Law*, 16 (2014), 33–53, 59–62.

authority Johan Heiberg (in 1842) regarded intervention for humanity 'inevitable', when 'assured rights and reciprocally recognized principles' were 'endangered'.[28] His German contemporary, Heffter, opined that nations 'have incontestably the right to put an end, after common consent, to a civil war which devours one or more countries' and this could also be done by 'armed interference';[29] he added that 'foreign powers can assist the party whose position seems to them to be founded on justice, if it invokes their help'.[30] Herman Rodecker von Rotteck asserted that '[h]umanitarian intervention should be considered as a violation of law, but sometimes excused, or even applauded, as we excuse a crime'.[31]

1851–70: from Phillimore, Woolsey and Mamiani to Fiore and Bluntschli

In the 1850s and 1860s at least eleven publicists addressed the question for the first time, with the supporters more than double the opponents, eight against three, and if to them we add those from the previous period who had not passed away (and presumably had not retracted their views), the numbers are ten as opposed to six jurists (see table 4.1).

In the mid-1850s, Phillimore argued that a limitation of the principle of non-intervention 'may possibly arise from the necessity of Intervention by Foreign Powers in order *to stay the shedding of blood* caused by a protracted and desolating civil war in the bosom of another State'.[32] He regarded it as 'an accessory' to other factors and on its own not in the code of international law, 'since it is manifestly open to abuses'.[33] Despite his misgivings he concluded that intervention by a Christian state 'on behalf of the subjects of another upon the ground of Religion' is not 'a violation of International Law … as an armed Intervention to prevent the shedding of blood and protracted internal hostilities'.[34]

In the US, the Yale Professor Theodore Dwight Woolsey maintained, in his 1860 treatise, that interference can be justified if 'brought about by the crime of a government against its subjects',[35] adding that in the case 'of extraordinary crimes committed by a government against its subjects … the danger of erring is less than in the other instances, because interference here is more disinterested; and the evil results of a mistake are less, because such cases are comparatively rare'.[36] In the same year, Professor Albert Friedrich Berner of the University of Berlin asserted that there were reasonable exceptions to non-intervention, such as continued acts of inhumanity, for '[m]an is the highest right before which all other right must incline'.[37]

The end of the 1850s saw one of the most elaborate rebuttals of humanitarian intervention, by Terenzio Mamiani. After a detailed presentation of the various reasons for intervention he concluded that 'all forcible intervention in the internal affairs of a people is to be deemed unjust and oppressive'.[38] As he put it, '[t]he doings or misdoings of a people … within the bounds of its own territory, and without detriment to others' rights, never afford any ground for legitimate intervention'.[39]

However, Mamiani allowed for two exceptions to non-intervention, which he did not associate with intervention in humanitarian plights: (1) intervention when a war was waged by a subject people;[40] and (2) 'opposing the wrongful intervention of others, and undoing the certain and immediate effects which it has induced',[41] that is, counter-intervention.

Mountague Bernard, the first Professor of International Law in Britain, occupant of the newly created Chichele Chair of International Law and Diplomacy at Oxford University, is hard to pinpoint. In a lecture at All Souls College at Oxford University on the principle of non-intervention, he argued against intervention, referring extensively to Mamiani's arguments.[42] But then he made an about-face by distinguishing between 'rebellion' and 'revolt', defining the former as successful change of government or dynasty and the latter as the splitting of a state into two parts. He claimed that in the latter case 'interference ceases to be intervention when this is done', as in the case of the Battle of Navarino during the Greek War of Independence (see chapter 6), which could not be seen as 'simply an intervention in the internal affairs of the Turkish empire'.[43] Another remark by Bernard makes his overall position even more baffling: that 'for the protection of the weak ... there may be the most powerful inducements to shake off the restraints of the rule [of non-intervention]. Nay, there may even be cases in which it becomes a positive duty to transgress it'.[44]

Henry Wager Halleck, an American Civil War general better known as a jurist, maintained that interference on humanitarian grounds was lawful only if it amounted to 'pacific mediation', that is, 'one State merely proposing its good offices for the settlement of the intestine [sic] dissensions of another State'.[45]

The important Liberal politician Sir William Vernon Harcourt, repeatedly cabinet minister under Gladstone and one-time Professor of International Law at Cambridge (the first occupant of the Whewell Chair in International Law), made the following oft-quoted remark: 'Intervention is a question rather of policy than of law. It is above and beyond the domain of law, and when wisely and equitably handled by those who have the power to give effect to it, may be the highest policy of justice and humanity'.[46] But he cautioned: 'I am not insensitive to the respectable sentiments of humanity ... but I also know that, of all things, the most cruel is a mistaken and useless interference'.[47]

Pasquale Fiore, the leading Italian authority, criticized the publicists who remained indifferent spectators of the affairs of other countries if their interests were not directly threatened[48] and added graphically (in 1865):[49]

> Let us suppose ... that a prince, in order to quell a revolution, violates all the most recognized laws of war, kills the prisoners, authorizes plundering, rapine, arson, and encourages his supporters to commit those odious acts and others of the same kind.... The laissez-faire and indifference of other States constitutes an egoistic policy contrary to the rights of all; for whoever violates international law

International law and humanitarian intervention

...violates it not only to the detriment of the person directly affected, but against all civilized States.

His conclusion is that under these circumstances collective intervention is 'obligatory'.[50]

Bluntschli of Heidelberg University asserted that '[t]he civilized nations in particular are called upon to develop the sentiment of the common laws of humanity'[51] and that '[o]ne is authorized to intervene to ensure respect for the individual rights recognized as necessary ... an oppressed minority could ... provoke foreign intervention, not in the name of the state, but in the name of international law'.[52]

1871–90: from Arntz and Martens to Carnazza Amari and Renault

In the 1870s and 1880s many authorities advocated a legal right of humanitarian intervention, with a majority in favour, thirteen against ten, and if we add those from the previous period who were still active, the numbers are twenty-two to thirteen publicists (see table 4.1).

In the 1870s Arntz set the pace with the following oft-quoted passage:[53]

> When a government, although acting within the limits of its sovereign rights, violates the rights of humanity ... by an excess of injustice and cruelty, which deeply wounds our mores and civilization, the right of intervention is legitimate. For however worthy of respect may be the rights of sovereignty and the independence of States, there is something even more worthy of respect, and this is the law of humanity, or of human society, which must not be outraged.

Arntz specified that intervention in the name of humanity should be sanctioned by the greater number of civilized states, which should arrive at a collective decision, for only in this manner could intervention be reconciled with state independence.[54]

Rolin-Jaequemyns concurred with Arntz, and asked 'what would happen if in the place of a despotic monarch who is an outrage to the law of humanity, a victorious faction acts, in the name of a republic or a democracy, with analogous excess ... [embarks on] a civil war of extermination, massacring the prisoners and hostages and threatening to plunge again into barbary all the parts of the country that have not already become a desert'?[55] Elsewhere he made the following pertinent point: for 'a State to lay claim to the principle of non-intervention it should be a State worthy of its name and a viable one'.[56]

F. F. Martens, the major Russian jurist, referred in 1877, apropos of the Russian intervention in the Balkans (see chapter 9), to the 'interests of humanity' as a reason for intervention, 'in order to safeguard the interests recognized as worthy of sympathy by all the civilized nations', namely 'the life and honour of Christians'.[57] A few years later he elaborated the point thus:[58]

> In the relations of civilized peoples with the non-civilized ... the intervention by civilized states is in principle legitimate, in the case of a Christian population of those countries being exposed to barbaric persecutions or massacres. In this particular case intervention is justified by common religious interests and considerations of philanthropy.

This view regarding non-civilized states had first appeared in 1874 in a study in Russian by Leonid Komarovskiy, Martens's colleague at the University of Moscow, who was a student of Bluntschli and a frequent writer in the *Revue*.[59]

Those supportive of humanitarian intervention during this decade included Sheldon Amos,[60] Professor of Jurisprudence at University College London, and the British judge Sir Edward Shepherd Creasy.[61] Those decidedly against included the Catania professor and Italian politician Giuseppe Carnazza Amari, the French international lawyers Henri Bonfils[62] and Louis Renault and the Luxembourgian French sociologist Théophile Funck-Brentano, together with the French historian Albert Sorel,[63] Professor of Diplomatic History and co-founder of the École libre des sciences politiques.

As forcefully put by Giuseppe Carnazza Amari, Fiore's main rival in the Italian school on this question, a champion of *non-intervention absolue*:[64]

> No case exists where a foreign sovereignty has the right to substitute national sovereignty; consequently intervention is never possible, neither as a rule nor as an exception.... All coercive influence from abroad constitutes a violent intrusion of one's domain, a supreme tyranny of the powerful against the weak, the usurpation and the rapine of the sovereign powers on which we have no right, an exercise of illegitimate power, a servitude imposed by the oppressor on the oppressed.

As for civil wars, he maintained that 'whatever the good intention may be of the one who wants to intervene, he lacks the right, for he has no sovereign authority over other nations ... the man with the best of intentions in the world cannot reconcile by force another family which leads a life of hate and troubles'.[65] Yet he allowed for three exceptions, which he did not regard as interventions and contraventions of non-intervention: assistance to a people who cannot on their own get rid of foreign domination; aid to a people who want to separate from a people with whom they have been forcefully united; and aid to a people to deliver themselves from foreign intervention and its results.[66]

Louis Renault of the University of Paris, the doyen of French international lawyers in the last two decades of nineteenth century, was equally averse to the idea of humanitarian intervention. As he tersely put it (in 1879): 'Very often the nations called civilized have abused their power with regard to the so-called barbarian peoples, having declared unjustified wars and having violated the most elementary rules of international law'.[67] Referring to Bluntschli's view on

International law and humanitarian intervention

humanitarian intervention he notes that 'this may happen, but I think that it is not desirable, for the slope will be slippery'.[68]

In the period 1880–90, those supporting humanitarian intervention include the British William Edward Hall and James Lorimer,[69] the French diplomat Édouard Engelhardt,[70] the Swiss Joseph Hornung[71] and the Greek Michel Kebedgy, of the University of Berne.[72]

Hall at the start of the 1880s was circumspect in his widely read treatise of 1880 (with eight editions up to 1924),[73] putting commentators at a loss where to place him in the debate.[74] According to Hall, '[t]yrannical conduct of a government towards its subjects, massacres and brutality in a civil war, or religious persecution, are acts which have nothing to do directly or indirectly with such [inter-state] relations'.[75] But he concluded that intervention 'for the reason or upon the pretexts of cruelty, or oppression, or the horrors of civil war … could only be excused in rare and extreme cases in consideration of the unquestionably extraordinary character of the facts causing them, and of the evident purity of the motives and conduct of the intervening state'.[76]

The 1880s also saw one of the clearest presentations of the arguments against humanitarian intervention, by the French jurist Paul Louis Pradier-Fodéré, one-time Professor of International Law at the University of Lima and author of a multivolume treatise on international law, who referred to the views of Arntz, Rolin-Jaequemyns, Woolsey and Fiore in support of intervening for humanitarian reasons, but concluded that 'it is impossible to accept such a doctrine',[77] for:[78]

> A nation could still be in such a backward stage as to accommodate absolutism, to voluntarily suffer despotism; on the basis of what right can foreign Powers claim that they can impose liberty? A nation, even a backward one, is the only one competent to regulate its political, civil and religious organization; it is free to adopt its form on the basis of its customs and ideas; foreign peoples are not entitled to impose them.

For Pradier-Fodéré, humanitarian intervention 'is illegitimate for it constitutes an infringement upon the independence of States…. The acts of inhumanity, however condemnable they may be, as long as they do not affect or threaten the rights of other States, do not provide the latter with a basis for lawful intervention, as no State can stand up in judgment of the conduct of others'.[79]

1891–1918: from Lawrence and Rivier to Westlake, Oppenheim and Nys

In the 1890s and until the end of the First World War, the advocates total eighteen and the opponents thirteen, and if we add those from the previous period who were still active, the numbers are nearly equal, twenty-six advocates and twenty-four opposed (see table 4.1).

During the 1890s the jurists supportive of humanitarian intervention include the British Thomas Joseph Lawrence, the Swiss Alphonse Rivier, the French Antoine Pillet,[80] Louis Le Fur[81] and Albert de Lapradelle,[82] and the Americans Amos S. Hershey[83] and Theodore S. Woolsey.[84] Those against in the 1890s include the French Frantz Despagnet, the Germans Franz von Liszt[85] and Adolphe de Floeckher[86] and the British Thomas Alfred Walker.[87]

In 1895 Lawrence of Oxford University put it thus:[88]

> Should the cruelty be so long continued and so revolting that the best instincts of human nature are outraged by it, and should an opportunity arise for bringing it to an end and removing its cause without adding fuel to the flame of the contest, there is nothing in the law of nations which will condemn as a wrong-doer the state which steps forward and undertakes the necessary intervention. Each case must be judged on its own merits ... I have no right to enter my neighbor's garden without his consent; but if I saw a child of his robbed and ill-treated in it by a tramp, I should throw ceremony to the wind and rush to the rescue without waiting to ask for permission.

Rivier, a year later, referred approvingly to the views of Arntz and Rolin-Jaequemyns and asserted that '[t]he law of human society ... represented by the Society of nations is superior to the law of a nation on its own. When a State violates the law of humanity, it is not for one state to intervene, on its own, and without a mandate. But States as a whole, representing human society, which is injured ... have the right to intervene as in the case of one State on its own which intervenes when its proper right of preservation is injured'.[89]

Among opponents, Despagnet of the University of Bordeaux argued that intervention against a government 'which in its exercise of internal sovereignty violates the laws of humanity ... cannot be accepted, as it gives rise to abuse and, under the pretext of safeguarding the interests of populations, it completely ruins the respect of State sovereignty; a government could, for example, not permit slavery or halt the traffic of slaves in all the domains that fall under its own authority, but it cannot impose the suppression [of slavery] to other States in their territory'.[90]

In the early twentieth century and until the end of the 'Great War', supporters of humanitarian intervention include John Westlake, Lassa Oppenheim, the French Alexandre Mérignhac[91] and Antoine Rougier, the Italian Arrigo Cavaglieri,[92] and the Americans William Ezra Lingelbach,[93] Edwin Borchard[94] and Henry Green Hodges.[95] Those against include the British Thomas Erskine Holland[96] and Frederick Edwin Smith,[97] the Belgian Ernest Nys, the German Karl von Gareis,[98] and the Americans George Grafton Wilson and Charles Cheney Hyde.[99]

Westlake referred to anarchy and misrule as grounds for intervention[100] and stated '[i]t is idle to argue in such a case that the duty of neighbouring peoples is to look on quietly. Laws are made for men and not for creatures of the imagination, and they must not create or tolerate for them situations which are beyond the endurance'.[101]

Oppenheim was more circumspect in his monumental 1905 treatise, contending that '[m]any jurists maintain that intervention is ... admissible, or even has a basis of right, when exercised in the interest of humanity for the purpose of stopping religious persecution and endless cruelties in time of peace and war' and he referred to intervention in the Greek case.[102] And added '[b]ut whether there is really a rule of the Law of Nations which admits such intervention may well be doubted ... and it may perhaps be said that in time the Law of Nations will recognise the rule that interventions in the interest of humanity are admissible, provided they are exercised in the form of *collective* intervention of the Powers'.[103]

Rougier argued that collective humanitarian intervention was preferable to individual intervention for it is more able to establish 'disinterestedness and greater authority'.[104] He was the first jurist to present a list of criteria for humanitarian intervention, including 'a violation of the law of humanity and not merely a violation of positive national law'[105] and 'exceptionally grave cases, as when the life of an entire population is menaced, when the barbaric acts are often repeated, when their character is particularly horrible that it violently shocks the universal consciousness'.[106] He also refers to considerations of opportunity, appeals by the victims and favourable conditions for intervening.[107]

On the side of the opponents, worth referring to are the points raised by Nys and Wilson. Nys argued that 'independence for States is like liberty for the individual'[108] and referred approvingly to the views of Renault and Pradier-Fodéré against intervention.[109] As for the admixture of the European powers in the Eastern Question, he maintained that 'it cannot be invoked to justify the doctrine of intervention', for it was something else: 'the establishment of a protectorate regarding the Christian nations under the sultan'.[110]

Wilson, Professor of International Law at Harvard University and at the Fletcher School of Law and Diplomacy, pointed out that '[f]or a state to set itself up as a judge of the actions of another state and to assume that it has the right to extend its powers to settling and regulating affairs of morals, religion, and the relations of public authority to the subjects in another state, on the ground of maintaining the rights of mankind as a whole, is to take a ground which the conduct of any modern state, even the most civilized, would hardly warrant'.[111]

1919–39: from Stowell and Higgins to Lauterpacht and Politis

Surprisingly, during the inter-war period, at a time when no humanitarian intervention took place, the overwhelming majority of advocates who addressed the question for the first time is in support, at eighteen, as opposed to only six opponents, and if we add those from the previous period who were still active, the advocates total thirty-three as opposed to fourteen against (see table 4.1).

Supporters include the Polish-British Hersch Lauterpacht, the French Paul Fauchille[112] and Georges Scelle,[113] the Americans Ellery Stowell, Charles

Fenwick[114] and Pitman Potter,[115] the Greeks Nicolas Politis[116] and Stélio Séfériadès[117] (father of Nobel Laureate poet George Seferis), and the Russians André Mandelstam[118] and Michel Taube.[119] Those against include the British Alexander Pearce Higgins, Percy Winfield[120] and James Leslie Brierly,[121] the French Robert Redslob[122] and the German Karl Strupp.

We will start with the opponents this time round. Strupp, of Frankfurt University and later Istanbul University, discussed the views of Cavaglieri in support of collective humanitarian intervention[123] and concluded that it is unacceptable and dangerous, and given the fact that 'no one can say how many States suffice to constitute a collectivity, we are led to practically authorize the great Powers to interfere in the affairs of smaller States'.[124]

According to Higgins, Whewell Professor in Cambridge, interventions in instances of social upheavals and civil wars 'constitute a grave danger to international harmony because they offer an opportunity to an unprincipled state to take undue advantage of the internal weakness or maladministration of such a state to increase its own power'.[125] Thus it may acquire 'a *de facto* protectorate while protesting that its intervention is in the interests of humanity'.[126]

Moving on to the advocates, Stowell, of Columbia University, advocated humanitarian intervention, for no state 'may persist in conduct which is considered to violate the universally recognized principles of decency and humanity'.[127] He accepted that 'recourse to intervention on the ground of humanity may at times offer a cloak for interference and aggression',[128] but maintained that 'a deliberate violation of that minimum of security and justice to which every individual in a civilized community is entitled' made it 'the right and duty of other states to intervene'.[129]

Lauterpacht, one of the greatest international lawyers of the twentieth century, then in his thirties, who succeeded Higgins as Whewell Professor, had the following to say on the matter: [130]

> The sovereign and independent State receives from international law absolute autonomy as regards the treatment of its inhabitants.... But this exclusive right could be abused, in which case it ceases to be a right and the competence of international law to protect the individual reasserts all its force ... humanitarian intervention is both a juridical as well a political principle of international society.

Politis, one of the most innovative international jurists of the inter-war period and a key figure in the League of Nations,[131] Professor at the University of Paris and later Greek Foreign Minister, made the following important point in his book on international morality, written just before the Second World War and published posthumously:[132]

> Every people has the right to organise itself as it wants ... without other countries being in the position to oppose or to intervene in what are internal affairs.... But ... such a right will merit due respect on the principle that it makes reasonable use

of it. If, on the contrary, it gives ground to abuses of power ... and, in general, if the prescriptions of international morality and of international law are downtrodden, other countries are entitled to intervene; they could put into play the rules of international responsibility.

Overall assessment

As we have seen, most of the issues for and against humanitarian intervention raised today were developed in the period 1830–1939:[133] the moral drive to do something for the oppressed in instances where the moral consciousness of humankind is shocked, the abuse factor, a level of disinterestedness, the need to maintain the principle of sovereignty and independence, the assuredness of a successful outcome stopping the bloodshed and so on.

It has been suggested that the Anglo-Americans were more supportive than the continental schools.[134] In fact there is an even split within the British and French schools of thought. Most US jurists supported intervention on legal or moral grounds, though a substantial minority were against. Russian publicists (apparently with the Ottoman Empire in mind) as well as those from the small states of Europe, such as Switzerland, Belgium and Greece, were all, with no exception, advocates of humanitarian intervention. The Italian school tilts more towards non-intervention, though with the proviso of support for liberation movements and counter-intervention. The only group that was for the most part against is the German school, which may perhaps be attributed to the fact that Prussia, Germany and Austria–Hungary refrained from intervening militarily in humanitarian plights or in internal wars.

Until 1914 all publicists, with very few exceptions, adhered to the civilized–barbarian distinction (see chapter 3), but most advocates avoided any distinction as to its application, which implies that they considered, as a matter of principle, that intervention for reasons of humanity is applicable to all, irrespective of degree of civilization.

Some of the supporters of humanitarian intervention were explicit in this regard. Hornung posited that such intervention had to be raised 'above considerations of religion or race' and become 'truly humanitarian in character'.[135] It should apply if need be 'against the Christian, in favour of the Muslim, the Buddhist or the pagan'.[136]

According to Fauchille, humanitarian intervention is practised 'vis-à-vis civilized States as well: after all is not the violation of the right of humanity more grave when it emanates from a civilised State?'[137]

Kebedgy referred to the difficulty of distinguishing between civilized and non-civilized states, pointing out that atrocities could be committed by a state called civilized; if its actions indeed made it barbarous, it would lose 'all title to respect for its independence'.[138]

But some publicists supportive of humanitarian intervention claim, as we have seen, that it is applicable only to 'civilized states' against 'non-civilized states'. They include Martens, Komarovskiy, Lorimer, partly Bluntschli[139] and, in the early twentieth century, Edwin DeWitt Dickinson,[140] Phillimore regarding the Muslim states, and Engelhardt and Rolin-Jaequemyns regarding the Ottoman Empire per se.[141] According to Phillimore, 'the right of Christian Intervention on religious grounds in a Mohammedan State rests upon an obviously stronger foundation'.[142] But he adds, to his credit, that '[t]he converse of this, viz., Mohammedan Intervention with Christian States, has, it is believed, never yet arisen in practice, but it would be subject on principle to the same law'.[143]

Ironically, the double standards of humanitarian intervention and the singling out of non-Christian states for intervention were criticized by opponents of the concept of humanitarian intervention, who presented their supportive peers as unprincipled. They include Pradier-Fodéré,[144] Funck-Brentano and Sorel,[145] Bonfils,[146] Renault,[147] Despagnet, Floeckher[148] and Winfield.[149]

Despagnet, for instance, referred to 'an alleged *right of civilization* that permits European peoples in particular to act against barbarian governments so as to impose upon them more ethical and humane institutions',[150] adding that it was open to abuse 'under the cover, often hypocritical, of a disinterested civilizing mission'.[151]

Now we come to the fundamental question whether *armed* humanitarian intervention had become part of customary international law at the time, the majority view of legal authors from 1920 until today.[152] This overall trend is accepted even in some of today's polemics on the concept.[153] Clearly, a majority (more than three-quarters) were in favour of humanitarian intervention, be it on legal or moral grounds. However, in order to claim that a *legal* right did exist, one has to wrongly lump those advocating a legal right with those invoking moral or political grounds,[154] even though the latter explicitly deny such a legal right. It would be more accurate to say that from 1830 until 1939 the views were 'divided';[155] it was 'debatable'[156] or 'doubtful'[157] whether such a right existed in positive international law.

But when it comes to humanitarian intervention as conceived in the pre-UN Charter period, which also included peremptory demands and forms of dictatorial interference short of the actual use of armed force,[158] it appears that humanitarian intervention *lato sensu* was part of customary international law from the 1860s or 1870s onwards. In itself this is a striking finding, for the international law of human rights was yet to come, with the exception of the minority treaties regime in the peace treaties signed in Paris (1919–20) and Lausanne (1923), which hardly gave ground for intervention (their whole philosophy was minority rights in exchange for loyalty on the part of the minorities[159]).

We will conclude by reverting to the double-standard aspect. From an international law perspective, one view is that of Komarovskiy, Martens and others, that such a right exists only with regard to civilized states towards barbarous states if Christians are harshly treated. Another line is to regard it as a *lex specialis* in the relations of European states with the Ottoman Empire or China, as advocated by Bluntschli,[160] Rolin-Jaequemyns,[161] Westlake,[162] Nys[163] and Rougier.[164] A third option is to regard the possibility of humanitarian intervention as a 'special custom' applicable only in the relations of Europe with the Ottoman Empire.[165] By today's criteria this approach is problematic, for special (or regional) customs have to be applied reciprocally and not for the benefit of one party at the expense of the other. Clearly, none of these options would carry the day in current international law, but international law as conceived in the long nineteenth century was, for better or worse, the law of the European states (and those of European extraction), those with the 'standard of civilization' to boot, hence the double standards that come out naturally from this perspective, however antiquated. If we draw such a conclusion we also avoid the danger of retrospective thinking.

Notes

1. M. Koskenniemi, *From Apology to Utopia: The Structure of International Legal Argument* (Cambridge: Cambridge University Press, 2005), 122–3. For the state of play of international law in France, Germany and Britain, see M. Koskenniemi, *The Gentle Civilizer of Nations: The Rise and Fall of International Law 1870–1960* (Cambridge: Cambridge University Press, 2002), 30–3.
2. C. Sylvest, 'The Foundations of Victorian International Law', in Duncan Bell (ed.), *Victorian Visions of Global Order: Empire and International Relations in Nineteenth-Century Political Thought* (Cambridge: Cambridge University Press, 2007), 48; C. Sylvest, *British Liberal Internationalism, 1830–1930: Making Progress?* (Manchester: Manchester University Press, 2009), 63–6, 69.
3. Sylvest, *British Liberal Internationalism*, 48.
4. J. Austin, *Lectures in Jurisprudence or the Philosophy of Positive Law* (London: John Murray, 1885, 5th edition) [1861], 182 (original emphasis).
5. Ibid., 184.
6. Koskenniemi, *The Gentle Civilizer of Nations*, 12–14.
7. Ibid., 40–1; C. Sylvest, 'International Law in Nineteenth Century Britain', *British Year Book of International Law*, 75 (2004), 46.
8. 'To promote the progress of international law, striving to become the organ of the legal conscience of the civilized world'. Quoted in Koskenniemi, *The Gentle Civilizer of Nations*, 41.
9. Ibid., 42. Fiore used similar language. See chapter 3.
10. Koskenniemi, *The Gentle Civilizer of Nations*, 41.
11. See on the link between the discipline of history and nationalism, J. Hutchinson, *Modern Nationalism* (London: Harper Collins, 1994), 3.
12. W. G. Grewe, *The Epochs of International Law* (Berlin: Walter de Gruyter, 2000, translated and revised by M. Byers) [1984], 493.
13. A. C. Arend, and R. J. Beck, *International Law and the Use of Force* (London: Routledge, 1993), 17.

14 O. Ramsbotham and T. Woodhouse, *Humanitarian Intervention: A Reconceptualization* (Cambridge: Polity Press, 1996), 36.
15 S. Chesterman, *Just War or Just Peace? Humanitarian Intervention and International Law* (Oxford: Oxford University Press, 2001), 8.
16 M. Barnett, *Empire of Humanity: A History of Humanitarianism* (Ithaca: Cornell University Press, 2011), 76–94.
17 D. Schindler, 'International Humanitarian Law: Its Remarkable Development and Its Persistent Violation', *Journal of the History of International Law*, 5 (2003), 166.
18 H. Strebel, 'Martens's Clause', *Encyclopedia of Public International Law*, Max Planck Institute for Comparative Public Law and International Law (Amsterdam: Elsevier, 1997), 326; E. Schwelb, 'Crimes Against Humanity', *British Year Book of International Law*, 23 (1946), 178–82; Grewe, *The Epochs of International Law*, 494–5; T. Meron, *The Humanization of International Law* (Leiden: Martinus Nijhoff, 2006), 16–18. On the contribution of Russians jurists in this regard (of Martens and others) see E. Myles, '"Humanity", "Civilization" and the "International Community" in the Late Imperial Russian Mirror: Three Ideas "Topical for our Days"', *Journal of the History of International Law*, 4 (2002), 316–19.
19 A. Rougier, 'La théorie de l'intervention d'humanité', *Revue générale de droit international public*, 17 (1910), 473–8, 499–526; E. C. Stowell, *Intervention in International Law* (Washington, DC: John Byrne, 1921), 51–62; M. Ganji, *International Protection of Human Rights* (Geneva: Librairie E. Droz, 1962), 37–8; J.-P. L. Fonteyne, 'The Customary International Law Doctrine of Humanitarian Intervention: Its Current Validity Under the U.N. Charter', *California Western International Law Journal*, 4 (1973–74), 235; F. K. Abiew, *The Evolution of the Doctrine and Practice of Humanitarian Intervention* (The Hague: Kluwer Law International, 1999), 42–3; Grewe, *The Epochs of International Law*, 493.
20 We hardly claim to have discovered all the publicists involved in the debate. Our main omissions are those writing in German, Italian or Spanish and in lesser known European languages, whose works were not translated into English or French.
21 The rest of this chapter is based in part on an earlier version, for which ninety-four publicists were identified. See A. Heraclides, 'Humanitarian Intervention in International Law 1830–1939: The Debate', *Journal of the History of International Law*, 16 (2014), 26–62.
22 See Rougier, 'La théorie de l'intervention d'humanité', 490 n.3; A. Mandelstam, 'La protection des minorités', *Recueil des cours de l'Académie de droit international*, 1 (1923), 389–90.
23 Arntz's letter in G. Rolin-Jaequemyns, 'Note sur la théorie du droit d'intervention, à propos d'une lettre de M. le professeur Arntz', *Revue de droit international et de législation comparée*, 8 (1876), 673–5.
24 H. Wheaton, *Elements of International Law: With a Sketch of the History of the Science* (Philadelphia: Carey, Lea and Blanchard, 1836), 91 (emphasis added). See also H. Wheaton, *Elements of International Law* (Boston: Little, Brown and Co., 1866, 8th edition, edited by R.H. Dana) [1836], 113.
25 In G. Carnazza Amari, 'Nouvel exposé du principe de non-intervention', *Revue de droit international et de législation comparée*, 5 (1873), 376–7; and in Stowell, *Intervention in International Law*, 524.
26 N. W. Senior, 'Art.I-1. Histoire du Progrès du Droit des Gens depuis la Paix de Westphalie jusqu'au Congrès de Vienne. Par Henry Wheaton', *Edinburgh Review*, 77:156 (1843), 365.
27 Ibid., 334.

28 Cited and commented upon in Stowell, *Intervention in International Law*, 494.
29 A. W. Heffter *Le droit international de l'Europe* (Berlin: H. W. Muller and Paris: A. Cotillon et Cie, 1883, 4th French edition, translated from the German by J. Bergson) [1844], 111.
30 *Ibid.*, 113–14.
31 Quoted and translated in Stowell, *Intervention in International Law*, 525.
32 R. Phillimore, *Commentaries upon International Law* (London: Butterworth, 1879, 3rd edition) [1854], vol. I, 568 (original emphasis).
33 *Ibid.*, 568–9.
34 *Ibid.*, 622–3.
35 T. D. Woolsey, *Introduction to the Study of International Law* (London: Sampson Low, Marston, Searle and Rivington, 1879, 5th edition revised and enlarged) [1860], 44.
36 *Ibid.*, 44.
37 Quoted and translated in Stowell, *Intervention in International Law*, 472; and Rougier, 'La théorie de l'intervention d'humanité', 490 n.2 (from Berner's book, *Deutsche Staatswörterbuch*, Leipzig, 1860).
38 Count Mamiani, *Rights of Nations, or the New Law of European States Applied to the Affairs of Italy* (London: W. Jeffs, 1860, translated from the Italian by R. Acton) [1859], 177.
39 *Ibid.*, 194.
40 *Ibid.*, 140–1.
41 *Ibid.*, 197.
42 M. Bernard, *On the Principle of Non-Intervention: A Lecture Delivered in the Hall of All Souls College, December MDCCCLX* (Oxford: J. H. and J. Parker, 1860), 9, 18–20, 23.
43 *Ibid.*, 21–2.
44 *Ibid.*, 33–4.
45 H. W. Halleck, *Halleck's International Law or Rules Regulating the Intercourse of States in Peace and War* (London: Kegan Paul, Trench, Trübner, 1893, 3rd edition by S. Baker) [1861], vol. I, 101, 511.
46 Harcourt, writing under the pen-name Historicus, in *Letters by Historicus on Some Questions of International Law. Reprinted from 'The Times' with Considerable Additions* (London: Macmillan, 1863), 14.
47 *Ibid.*, 50.
48 P. Fiore, *Nouveau droit internationale public suivant les besoins de la civilization moderne* (Paris: A. Durant et Pedone-Lauriel, 1885, 2nd edition, translated from the Italian and annotated by C. Antoine) [1865], vol. I, 502.
49 *Ibid.*, 524–5.
50 P. Fiore, *International Law Codified and Its Legal Sanction or the Legal Organization of the Society of States* (New York: Baker, Voorhis and Company, 1918, translation from the 5th Italian edition with an introduction by E. M. Borchard), 269.
51 J. C. Bluntschli, *Le droit international codifié* (Paris: Librairie de Guillaumin et Cie, 1874, 2nd French edition, translated from the German by M. C. Lardy) [1868], 55, para. 5.
52 *Ibid.*, 272, para. 478.
53 Arntz quoted in Rolin-Jaequemyns, 'Note sur la théorie du droit d'intervention', 675.
54 *Ibid.*, 675.
55 *Ibid.*, 676.
56 G. Rolin-Jaequemyns, 'Le droit international et la phase actuelle de la question d'Orient', *Revue de droit international et de législation comparée*, 8 (1876), 396.
57 F. Martens, 'Étude historique sur la politique Russe dans la question d'Orient', *Revue de droit international et de législation comparée*, 9 (1877), 49.

58   F. Martens, *Sovremennoe Mezhdunarodnoe Pravo Tsivilizovannykh Narodov* (St Petersburg: Tipografiya A. Benke, 1904, 5th edition) [1883], vol. I, 310.
59   L. Komarovskiy, *Nachalo nevmeshatel'stva* (Moscow: Universitetskaja Tipografiya, 1874), 79–80. Martens refers to him as well as to Bluntschli and Phillimore, to buttress his view.
60   S. Amos (from *Lecturers on International Law*, 1874, 39–41) in Chesterman, *Just War or Just Peace?*, 37; S. Amos, *Political and Legal Remedies for War* (London: Cassel, Petter, Galpin, 1880), 79.
61   E. S. Creasy, *First Platform of International Law* (London: John van Voorst, 1876), 303–4.
62   H. Bonfils, *Manuel de droit international public (droit des gens)* (Paris: Librairie nouvelle de droit et de jurisprudence, 1905, 4th edition by Paul Fauchille) [1877], 155, para. 298.
63   T. Funck-Brentano and A. Sorel, *Précis du droit des gens* (Paris: Librairie Plon, 1887, 2nd edition) [1877], 215–16, 221, 223.
64   Carnazza Amari, 'Nouvel exposé du principe de non-intervention', 370.
65   *Ibid.*, 375.
66   *Ibid.*, 552–9.
67   L. Renault, *Introduction à l'étude du droit international* (Paris: L. Larose, 1879), 21–2.
68   *Ibid.*, 23.
69   J. Lorimer, *The Institutes of the Law of Nations: A Treatise of the Jural Relations of Separate Political Communities* (Edinburgh: William Blackwood and Sons, 1883, 1884), vol. I, 101–2; and vol. II, 51, 54.
70   É. Engelhardt, *Le droit d'intervention et la Turquie. Étude historique* (Paris: A. Cotillon et Cie, 1880), 10–11.
71   J. Hornung, 'Civilisés et barbares', *Revue de droit international et de législation comparée*, 17 (1885), 13–14.
72   According to Stowell, in Stowell, *Intervention in International Law*, 65 n.14, based on M. Kebedgy, *De l'intervention: théorie générale et étude spécial de la question d'Orient* (Paris: A. Giard, 1890).
73   W. E. Hall, *A Treatise of International Law* (Oxford: Clarendon Press, 1895, 4th edition) [1880]. The 8th edition, of 1924, was edited by A. P. Higgins.
74   See for instance the bafflement of Stowell in Stowell, *Intervention in International Law*, 60–1 n.13.
75   Hall, *A Treatise of International Law*, 302–3.
76   *Ibid.*, 304.
77   P. L. Pradier-Fodéré, *Traité de droit international public européen et américain, suivant le progrès de la science et de la pratique contemporaines* (Paris: A. Durand et Pedone-Lauriel, 1885), vol. I, 593–4.
78   *Ibid.*, 594–5.
79   *Ibid.*, 663.
80   A. Pillet, 'Le droit international public', *Revue générale de droit international public*, 1 (1894), 13, 16.
81   L. Le Fur, 'Chronique des faits internationaux', *Revue générale de droit international public*, 5 (1898), 664–5.
82   A. de Lapradelle, 'Chronique sur les affaires de Cuba', *Revue de droit publique et de science politique en France et à l'étranger*, 1 (1900), 75.
83   A. S. Hershey, 'Intervention and the Recognition of Cuban Independence', *Annals of the American Academy of Political and Social Science*, 11 (1898), 58, 77–80; A. S. Hershey, 'The Calvo and Drago Doctrines', *American Journal of International Law*, 1:1 (1907), 41–2.

International law and humanitarian intervention

84 T. S. Woolsey, *American Foreign Policy* (New York: Century, 1898), 75–6.
85 According to P. Malanczuk, *Humanitarian Intervention and the Legitimacy of the Use of Force* (Amsterdam: Het Spinhuis, 1993), 10.
86 A. de Floeckher, *De l'intervention en droit international* (Paris: A. Pedone, 1896), 5, 36–8; A. de Floeckher, 'Les conséquences de l'intervention', *Revue générale de droit international public*, 3 (1896), 329–33.
87 T. A. Walker, *The Science of International Law* (London: C. J. Clay and Sons, 1893), 151–2; T. A. Walker, *A Manual of Public International Law* (Cambridge: Cambridge University Press, 1895), 22.
88 T. J. Lawrence, *The Principles of International Law* (Boston: D. C. Heath, 1905, 3rd edition, revised) [1895], 120.
89 A. Rivier, *Principes du droit des gens* (Paris: Librairie nouvelle de droit et de jurisprudence, 1896), 403.
90 F. Despagnet, *Cours de droit international public* (Paris: L. Larose, 1894), 189.
91 A. Mérignhac, *Traité de droit public international* (Paris: Librairie générale de droit et de jurisprudence, 1905), part I, 298–9.
92 A. Cavaglieri, *L'intervento nella sua definizione guiridica* (Bologna: Luigi Betrami, 1913), 106–9.
93 W. E. Lingelbach, 'The Doctrine and Practice of Intervention in Europe', *Annals of the Academy of Political and Social Science*, 16 (1900), 17, 20, 32.
94 E. M. Borchard, 'Basic Elements of Diplomatic Protection of Citizens Abroad', *American Journal of International Law*, 7:3 (1913), 507.
95 H. G. Hodges, *The Doctrine of Intervention* (Princeton: Banner Press, 1915), 87–8, 91.
96 T. E. Holland, *Lectures on International Law* (London: Sweet and Maxwell, 1933, edited by Thomas Alfred Walker and Wyndham Legh Walker), 105, 108.
97 F. E. Smith, *International Law* (London: J. M. Dent and Sons, 1911, 4th edition, revised and enlarged by J. Wylie) [1900], 63–4.
98 According to Fonteyne, 'The Customary International Law Doctrine of Humanitarian Intervention', 217 n.42, based on K. von Gareis, *Institutionen des Völkerrechts* (2nd edition, 1901).
99 C. C. Hyde, 'Intervention in Theory and in Practice', *Illinois Law Review*, 6:1 (1911), 6–7.
100 J. Westlake, *International Law, Part I: Peace* (Cambridge: Cambridge University Press, 1904), 305–6.
101 Ibid., 306–7.
102 L. Oppenheim, *International Law: A Treatise* (London: Longmans, Green, 5th edition, edited by H. Lauterpacht, 1937) [1905], vol. I, 255, para. 137. Lauterpacht notes that he has left para. 137 unaltered from the 1905 edition.
103 Ibid., 255, para. 137 (original emphasis).
104 Rougier, 'La théorie de l'intervention d'humanité', 502.
105 Ibid., 515.
106 Ibid., 523–4.
107 Ibid., 523–5.
108 E. Nys, *Le droit international: les principes, les théories, les faits* (Brussels: M. Weissenbruch, 1912, new edition) [1906], vol. II, 223.
109 Ibid., 230–1.
110 Ibid., 232.
111 G. G. Wilson, *International Law* (New York: Silver, Burdett, 1922, 8th edition) [1901], 91.

112 P. Fauchille, *Traité de droit international public* (Paris: Rousseau et Cie, 8th updated and completely rewritten edition of Bonfils's *Manuel de droit international public (droit des gens)*, 1926) [1877], vol. I, part i, 570–1.
113 According to Hubert Thierry, Scelle introduced 'a sort of duty of interference' (*devoir d' ingérence*). See H. Thierry, 'The Thought of Georges Scelle', *European Journal of International Law*, 1 (1990), 196.
114 C. G. Fenwick, *International Law* (London: George Allen and Unwin, 1924), 154–5.
115 P. B. Potter, 'L'intervention en droit international moderne', *Recueil des cours de l'Académie de droit international*, 32 (1930), 653.
116 N. Politis, 'Le problème des limitations de la souveraineté et la théorie de l'abus des droits dans les rapports internationaux', *Recueil des cours d l'Académie de droit international*, 9 (1924), 6; N. Politis, *La morale international* (Paris: Bibliothèque Brentano's, 1944), 144.
117 S. Séfériadès, 'Principes généraux du droit international de la paix', *Recueil des cours de l'Académie de droit international*, 34 (1930), 388–9.
118 Mandelstam, 'La protection des minorités', 391.
119 Le Baron Michel Taube, 'Études sur le dévelopement historique du droit international dans l'Europe orientale', *Recueil des cours de l'Académie de droit international*, 11 (1926), 492–3.
120 P. H. Winfield, 'The Grounds of Intervention in International Law', *British Year Book of International Law*, 5 (1924), 161–2.
121 J. L. Brierly, *The Law of Nations: An Introduction to the International Law of Peace* (Oxford: Clarendon Press, 1936, 2nd edition) [1928], 248–9.
122 R. Redslob, *Traité de droit de gens* (Paris: Librairie du Recueil Sirey, 1950), 23–4.
123 K. Strupp, 'Le règles générales du droit de la paix', *Recueil des cours de l'Académie de droit international*, 47 (1934), 519–20.
124 *Ibid.*, 520.
125 A. P. Higgins, *Studies in International Law and Relations* (Cambridge: Cambridge University Press, 1928), 27.
126 *Ibid.*, 27.
127 Stowell, *Intervention in International Law*, 51–2.
128 E. C. Stowell, 'Humanitarian Intervention', *American Journal of International Law*, 33:4 (1939), 734.
129 *Ibid.*, 734. See also E. C. Stowell, 'La théorie et la pratique de l'intervention', *Recueil des cours de l'Académie de droit international*, 40 (1932), 138–48.
130 H. Lauterpacht, 'Règles générales du droit de la paix', *Recueil des cours de l'Académie de droit international*, 62 (1937), 238.
131 For the contribution of Politis to international law, see Koskenniemi, *The Gentle Civilizer of Nations*, 305–9, 314. See also R. Holsti, 'In Memoriam: Nicolas Politis, 1872–1942', *American Journal of International Law*, 36:3 (1942), 475–9.
132 Politis, *La morale international*, 144.
133 This is accepted even by Simon Chesterman, a critic of humanitarian intervention in the nineteenth century. See Chesterman, *Just War or Just Peace?*, 42.
134 See e.g. Malanczuk, *Humanitarian Intervention and the Legitimacy of the Use of Force*, 10.
135 Hornung, 'Civilisés et barbares', 14.
136 *Ibid.*, 13.
137 Fauchille, *Traité de droit international public*, vol. I, part i, 571.
138 Referred to in Stowell, *Intervention in International Law*, 65 n.14.

139 According to Bonfils, in Bonfils, *Manuel de droit international public*, 169.
140 E. DeWitt Dickinson, *The Equality of States in International Law* (Cambridge: Harvard University Press, 1920), 262–3.
141 Engelhardt, *Le droit d'intervention et la Turquie*, 61; Rolin-Jaequemyns, 'Le droit international et la phase actuelle de la question d'Orient', 295–85.
142 Phillimore, *Commentaries upon International Law*, vol. I, 621.
143 *Ibid.*, 624.
144 Pradier-Fodéré, *Traité de droit international public européen et américain*, 594–5.
145 Funck-Brentano and Sorel, *Précis du droit des gens*, 223.
146 Bonfils, *Manuel de droit international public*, 169.
147 Renault, *Introduction à l'étude du droit international*, 21–2.
148 Floeckher, *De l'intervention en droit international*, 38.
149 Winfield, 'The Grounds of Intervention in International Law', 161–2.
150 Despagnet, *Cours de droit international public*, 190 (original emphasis).
151 *Ibid.*, 190.
152 Mandelstam, 'La protection des minorités', 391; Stowell, *Intervention in International Law*, 51–62; Fonteyne, 'The Customary International Law Doctrine of Humanitarian Intervention', 223; R. B. Lillich, 'Humanitarian Intervention: A Reply to Ian Brownlie and a Plea for Constructive Alternatives', in J. N. Moore (ed.), *Law and Civil War in the Modern World* (Baltimore: Johns Hopkins University Press, 1974), 232–5; T. E. Behuniak, 'The Law of Unilateral Humanitarian Intervention by Armed Force: A Legal Survey', *Military Law Review*, 79 (1978), 166; M. Bazyler, 'Reexamining the Doctrine of Humanitarian Intervention in Light of the Atrocities in Kampuchea and Ethiopia', *Stanford Journal of International Law*, 23 (1987), 572–4; B. M. Benjamin, 'Unilateral Humanitarian Intervention: Legalizing the Use of Force to Prevent Human Rights Atrocities', *Fordham International Law Journal*, 16 (1992–93), 126; U. Beyerlin, 'Humanitarian Intervention', in *Encyclopedia of Public International Law*, Max Planck Institute for Comparative Public Law and International Law (Amsterdam: Elsevier, 1995), vol. II, 927; Abiew, *The Evolution of the Doctrine and Practice of Humanitarian Intervention*, 33, 43; C. F. Amerasinghe, 'The Conundrum of Recourse to Force – To Protect Persons', *International Organizations Law Review*, 3 (2006), 11, 23–26, 38.
153 See e.g. I. Brownlie, *International Law and the Use of Force by States* (Oxford: Clarendon Press, 1963), 338. *Contra* see Malanczuk, *Humanitarian Intervention and the Legitimacy of the Use of Force*, 11; Chesterman, *Just War or Just Peace?*, 36, 43–4.
154 As rightly pointed out by Chesterman in Chesterman, *Just War or Just Peace?*, 36.
155 Malanczuk, *Humanitarian Intervention and the Legitimacy of the Use of Force*, 10.
156 Beyerlin, 'Humanitarian Intervention', 927.
157 Oppenheim, *International Law*, vol. I, 255. See also Ganji, *International Protection of Human Rights*, 43; Grewe, *The Epochs of International Law*, 494–5; Malanczuk, *Humanitarian Intervention and the Legitimacy of the Use of Force*, 11; G. Sulyok, 'Humanitarian Intervention: A Historical and Theoretical Overview', *Acta Juridica Hungarica*, 41:1–2 (2000), 88.
158 Such as the naval blockade of Naples in 1857, the French expeditionary force sent to Lebanon and Syria in 1860–61, measures taken regarding misrule in Macedonia in 1903–08, and others.
159 P. Thornberry, *International Law and the Rights of Minorities* (Oxford: Clarendon Press, 1991), 43.
160 On Bluntschli's view on this matter, see Koskenniemi, *The Gentle Civilizer of Nations*, 77.

161 Rolin-Jaequemyns, 'Le droit international et la phase actuelle de la question d'Orient', 295–385.
162 On Westlake's view on this question, see Koskenniemi, *The Gentle Civilizer of Nations*, 49.
163 Nys regards intervention in the Eastern Question as being of a 'special character' but not as justifying intervention. See Nys, *Le droit international*, vol. II, 232.
164 According to Rougier this *lex specialis* system was set up in the Treaty of Berlin. See Rougier, 'La théorie de l'intervention d'humanité', 475.
165 N. Onuf, 'Humanitarian Intervention: The Early Years', Center for Global Peace and Conflict Studies Symposium on the Norms and Ethics of Humanitarian Intervention, University of California, Irvine, 5 May 2000, 3.

5

Intervention and non-intervention in international political theory

Contrary to international law, international political theory and political philosophy paid scant attention to the ethics of intervention in the long nineteenth century.[1] As for humanitarian intervention per se, there is nothing, apart from cursory remarks by John Stuart Mill and Giuseppe Mazzini. On the wider question of intervention and non-intervention we will refer to their views and to those of Kant, Hegel and Cobden.

Based on today's distinction between cosmopolitanism and communitarianism one would expect that cosmopolitans would be inclined towards intervention for humanitarian and other principled reasons, while communitarians would adhere to non-intervention.[2] Yet Kant, regarded as the father of modern cosmopolitanism,[3] is, prima facie, against intervention. Cobden, a cosmopolitan, is rigidly against any notion of intervention. Mazzini, a communitarian (though with a cosmopolitan bent) is a cautious supporter of intervention. J. S. Mill, arguably a communitarian,[4] places himself gingerly between non-intervention and intervention. Only Hegel, perhaps the father of the communitarian approach,[5] does not defy expectations, advocating non-intervention but inadvertently bringing military intervention in by pointing to war's positive aspects.

Kant, non-intervention and republicanism

Kant, the advocate of a cosmopolitan existence, of a cosmopolitan confederation of republican states and of universal human rights,[6] has very little to say about intervention and does not refer at all to intervention for humanitarian reasons.[7] In Preliminary Article 5 of his celebrated essay *Toward Perpetual Peace: A Philosophical Sketch* (1795),[8] it is stipulated that 'No State Shall by Force Interfere with the Constitution or Government of Another State'. And he makes two points: (1) there is a problem over who is to authorize interference, since there is no higher authority; and (2) if a state has fallen into 'evil', 'its lawlessness should serve as a warning'.[9] And he comes up with only one exception to non-intervention:[10]

if a state, through internal discord, should split into two parts, each ... laying claim to the whole; in that case a foreign state could not be charged with interfering in the constitution of another state if it gave assistance to one of them (for this is anarchy).

He cautions that prior to this critical phase, such interference would amount to 'a violation of the right of a people', making 'the autonomy of all states insecure'.[11] Only when a state has collapsed into anarchy, with rival groups claiming sovereign authority, can other states intervene to assist in bringing about an end to the anarchy.[12] Surprisingly, Kant (like Grotius) was opposed to revolution against oppression,[13] despite his great enthusiasm for the French Revolution, the American Revolution and the Irish struggle, a contradictory position that has baffled scholars ever since.[14]

Kant does not address intervention in any other work and it is clear that he does not suggest any right or duty of humanitarian intervention[15] or intervention to promote 'republicanism'.[16] His position on intervention is not unrelated to his position on war. For the German philosopher, war is 'the scourge of mankind', 'the destroyer of everything good'[17] and 'creates more evil than it destroys'.[18] Yet strictly speaking he was no pacifist.[19] He was critical of 'a long peace' in some cases[20] and regarded the historical emergence of civil society as the result of violent means and war, which unified people under a general will.[21] On the whole, a justified war was defensive: to defend one's country and repulse aggression, which could also include 'anticipatory attack'.[22] But as regards military intervention, he was more than clear: intervention even for ethical reasons introduces a right to war, with a disastrous effect on the attempt to ban war.[23]

Despite the prohibition set out in Preliminary Article 5, several scholars have tried to prove that he did not reject intervention or humanitarian intervention. There are three main positions: (1) the view that Kant upholds a rigid principle of non-intervention;[24] (2) guarded assertion that had he been faced with or contemplated massive atrocities, he would have been more open to intervention *qua* humanitarian intervention;[25] and (3) claims that he was in fact supportive of humanitarian intervention.[26]

One line of reasoning is to link Preliminary Article 5 with Kant's First Definite Article, which reads as follows: 'The Civil Constitution of Every State shall be Republican'. Republican states are peaceful internationally and base their internal policy on justice, the rule of law and respect for individual autonomy.[27] From this ambit it has been argued that, assuming that the Definitive Articles are 'more basic' (in fact this is not the case, as Kantian scholars point out), non-intervention 'does not apply to forms of intervention that might promote or defend the development or survival of republican forms of government'.[28]

John Vincent was of the view that 'Kant appeared to imply an exception to the rule of nonintervention if by intervention a republic could be established or a despotic regime crushed'.[29] Along similar lines, Fernando Tesón maintains that

Kant's 'nonintervention principle is dependent upon compliance with the First Definitive Article. Internal legitimacy based on respect for human rights and democracy is what gives states the shield of sovereignty against foreign intervention'.[30] Consequently, 'nonintervention holds *only* among liberal states'.[31] Harry van der Linden refers to Kant's concept of states as 'moral persons with autonomy' founded on 'the social contract' and 'united will'. On this basis he surmises that 'political intervention is only wrong with respect to republican states, or approximations thereof, and may be justified with regard to unjust states if it accords with the will of their people struggling for democracy'.[32]

Other Kantian scholars venture onto more controversial grounds. Thomas Hill for instance maintains that, according to Kant's logic, people in anarchy or 'a state of nature' can be forcefully made to join the legal order '*so long as it is reasonably certain that intervention is necessary and will be effective without further implications and effects that are morally unacceptable*'[33] and concludes that in Kant's ethics 'there is no absolute prohibition of humanitarian intervention in all cases'.[34] Antonio Franceschet admits that Kant has nothing explicit on humanitarian intervention,[35] but claims that one can extrapolate from his work, if it is seen from its 'ethico-political reasoning within his broad roadmap for international reform' and 'legal evolution'.[36] Accordingly, five themes provide a more comprehensive account of Kant regarding humanitarian intervention: (1) juridical pacifism; (2) institutionalization and constitutionalization; (3) the restructuring of the rights of war and peace; (4) the development of authorized coercion; and (5) cosmopolitan citizenship rights.[37]

It is hard to pass judgement on whether these authors interpret what Kant was all about or whether they present a different Kantian perspective and not Kant as such. As for Preliminary Article 5 being applicable only to republican states, in fact only the Definitive Articles refer exclusively to republican states; the Preliminary Articles refer to all states, republican or otherwise;[38] and Kant 'nowhere makes any explicit claim regarding the priority of republicanism over nonintervention'.[39] More generally, Kant wanted to deter states becoming paternalistic guardians of the well-being of other states.[40]

One is probably on safer grounds if one sticks to the letter of Kant. At least four points are worth making. First of all, Kant was guarded on intervention, not wanting to open a Pandora's box, given his views on war and peace, autonomy and morality. Secondly, he wrote *Perpetual Peace* in the wake of the French Revolution and apparently one of his main preoccupations was not to give grounds for foreign interventions against Republican France[41] (as advocated, say, by Burke). Thirdly, Kant, as a cosmopolitan, was not an advocate of conquest and colonialism, and so did not want to bring the less fortunate non-Europeans into the European fold.[42] Fourthly, even scholars critical of the extrapolations of others are prepared to offer a small opening for Kant's advocacy of intervention in extreme humanitarian instances. Pierre Laberge for instance has argued that '[s]ince genocide is an idea that can scarcely have occurred to him, to hold that he would prohibit intervention even in such extreme circumstances is surely to be guilty of an anachronism'.[43] Georg Cavallar is prepared to entertain that 'Kant might have favoured intervention to stop dramatic violations of human rights (for example genocide)'.[44] Franceschet is predictably more forthright: 'The idea that a state that would commit or allow genocide or would otherwise deny its population their basic moral rights or humanity is not only inconceivable but conceptually impossible for Kant'.[45] Howard Williams acknowledges the opening that may arise from Kant's support for universal human rights and 'a moral responsibility to be concerned about how citizens in other states are treated by their governments',[46] but asserts that this does not lead to the 'active involvement of our government in attempting to redress or punish wrongs in other states'.[47] His conclusion is that only 'the breakdown of order' tantamount to civil war, with no sovereign power in control, permits intervention, provided that intervention has been requested by one of the warring sides, notably 'the party that would bring the disputed territory into the peaceful federation'.[48]

Hegel, non-intervention and war

For Hegel, states, like persons, are autonomous in the moral sense and 'realize their nature in the choice and pursuit of ends'.[49] The state is 'ethical', 'the actuality of the ethical idea'.[50] According to Hegel: 'The nation as state is mind in its substantive rationality and immediate actuality and is thus the absolute power on earth. It follows that every state is sovereign and autonomous against its neighbors'.[51]

Tesón has called this reification of the state the 'Hegelian myth': that the state is 'a moral being, capable of making moral choices' and, as in the case of persons, whose moral choices deserve respect from others, 'state choices deserve respect from foreigners', hence '[f]oreign intervention is a violation of that autonomy, even when it is undertaken for benign purposes'.[52] Moreover, according to Tesón and others before him, such as Karl Popper, Hegel glorified war and even aggressive war in the name of 'vitality'.[53] He regarded war as one of the means 'by which the ethical character of the state is preserved'.[54] According to Steven Smith, Hegel arrives at this conclusion on the basis of the following syllogism: 'The state is an ethical unity. 2) States frequently engage in war to preserve their unity. 3) Therefore war is a "moment" in the ethical life of the state'.[55]

For Hegel, war is outside the domain of ethics and not 'a matter of right meeting wrong, but rather a clash between two subjectively perceived rights'.[56] As he put it: 'Each party claims to have right on its side; and both parties are right. It is just the rights themselves which have come into contradiction with one another'.[57] Hegel, anticipating the thinking of present-day conflict research, claims that disputes arise not as a result of 'real grievances as on subjective perception of an alleged threat posed'.[58]

These are valid points and hardly a glorification of war or militarism. But several other passages by Hegel are more extreme, such as the following: 'War is the moral health of peoples in their struggle against petrification.... Just as the breeze saves the sea from foulness, which is the result of continued complacency, so does war for people'.[59] He also refers to the heroic and sacrifice aspects of war, to courage, honour and internal cooperation and regards perpetual peace *à la* Kant as an illusion.[60]

Hegel's glorification of war and presumed militarism have been challenged, starting with John Plamenatz and Schlomo Avineri, who present him as more nuanced and not an advocate of aggressive war.[61] As is often the case with scholarly controversies, a fairer depiction is somewhere in the middle or is reached via another vantage point that makes the polar opposites less convincing.[62] Apparently, several of Hegel's extreme statements were motivated by the German predicament of his time, characterized by fragmentation and lack of unity.[63] And it is worth noting that wars were then quite different, with fewer casualties than the battles and wars that were to follow Hegel's death.[64]

Cobden, peace, free trade and non-intervention

Moving from the two great philosophers, Kant and Hegel, to Cobden may appear odd, but it is worth stressing that Cobden, though not a political philosopher, is regarded an important liberal thinker in his own right and one of the earliest exponents of the liberal internationalism in international relations. He is also regarded as a precursor of the theories of functionalism and interdependence.[65]

Cobden, the 'international man',[66] as he was called during his lifetime, was as absolute as Hegel in his stance against intervention, though not for the same reasons, and he was more consistent, not bringing intervention in through the back door by presenting the positive functions of war.

For Cobden, freedom of commerce was essential for peace, a view shared by his close associate, John Bright. He was convinced that 'unfettered commerce would create such a powerful incentive for peace that men would prevent their governments from using war as the chosen instrument for serving their interests'.[67] However, he was not an advocate of peace for the sake of free trade.[68] If free trade conflicted with peace, as in the case of trade in armaments or loans for armament, he was against it ('No free trade in cutting throats', as he put it).[69] As a committed exponent of progress brought about by industrialization and trade, he was strongly opposed to militarism, arms expenditures, colonial expansion and imperialism.[70]

It is within this context that Cobden was an advocate of 'an absolute policy of nonintervention'.[71] As he put it: 'I am against any interference by the government of any country in the affairs of another nation, even if it is confined to moral suasion'.[72] Non-intervention was 'a necessary, if not sufficient condition for international peace',[73] and could be more readily associated with interests than with a vague vision of future peace. He scathingly criticized great power intervention, even for noble goals.[74] The regeneration of a people could come about only by the 'force and virtue of native elements, and without assistance of any kind'.[75] Anticipating J. S. Mill (see below) he maintained that a 'people which wants a saviour' and 'which does not possess an earnest and pledge of freedom in its own heart, is not yet ready to be free'.[76]

According to Vincent's reading of Cobden, 'intervention was doubly inappropriate as a means of promoting liberalism abroad; outside assistance could not promote a necessarily mature growth, and if such assistance were requested by a people, that very request was evidence of its immaturity and inability to benefit from intervention'.[77] Cobden could accept counter-intervention only as a means of upholding the principle of non-intervention, and the only sanctions he could accept were 'the power of opinion and moral force'.[78] His condemnation of intervention had as its primary target British foreign policy under the sway of Palmerston, whose interventionism, according to Cobden, was against the interests of the British people.[79] The fact that the 'international man' was also a pacifist activist[80] made his absolute principle of non-intervention more convincing.[81] Moreover, Cobden was consistent in his anti-interventionism cum anti-imperialism, contrary to other British liberals who were 'more selective',[82] as in the case of James Mill and John Stuart Mill.[83]

Mazzini, nationality and non-intervention/intervention

Mazzini, like Cobden, was not a political philosopher, but a politician and activist. He is known today as the 'Beating Heart of Italy', the foremost inspirer of Italian unification. But in his lifetime he was one of the most respected theorists of democracy and of the principle of nationality (national self-determination), with considerable international influence.

Mazzini's views on nationalism were moderate and liberal, and though famous as a prophet of nationalism, 'humanity' is his keyword rather than 'nationality'.[84] For Mazzini, the starting point is the individual. Individuals fulfil themselves in the nation and the nation fulfils itself in humanity, while the idea of cosmopolitanism left out this essential middle link (i.e. the nation).[85] As in the case of Herder, he regarded all European nations as equal, each with its own mission in the world. He was basically a democratic patriot and not a nationalist, and sincerely believed that independent democratic nations (states corresponding to a nation) would be peaceful in their relations. Thus Mazzini can be seen as an advocate of 'democratic peace' on a par with Kant (democracies are peaceful at the inter-state level) and, as with Cobden, as one of the pioneers of liberal internationalism.[86]

As did both Cobden and J. S. Mill, Mazzini maintained that foreign intervention was not warranted in domestic political struggles for democratic rule and national liberation. But certain factors made him temper his views and part ways with Cobden, bringing him much closer to Mill (see below), with whom he was personally acquainted (and they respected each other's views).

Mazzini's views on intervention appear mainly in a succinct essay entitled 'On Nonintervention', written in 1851, mostly for a British audience (Mazzini lived in London for more than thirty years).[87] He argued that adherence to non-intervention had to apply if two preconditions were met. Firstly, it was applicable if it was adhered to absolutely by all states. But this was hardly ever the case, as despotic states intervened to help other despotic states threatened by revolutions or national liberation movements, contradicting the original purpose of non-intervention, which was avoiding war and conquest.[88] As he put it, this was 'Intervention on the wrong side; Intervention by all who chose, and are strong enough, to put down free movements of peoples against corrupt governments. It means cooperation of despots against peoples'.[89] Secondly, non-intervention was applicable only if all states were distinct nations, in which case 'the government must deal directly and alone with its people', with no foreign interference.[90] But most states were not nations, and empires trampled on nations aspiring to freedom.

These two factors did not lead Mazzini to advocate military intervention. He allowed only for two exceptions to non-intervention: (1) to offset a previous intervention in support of despots, that is, counter-intervention;[91] and (2) to intervene to stop massacres ('massacres of Christians').[92] In the first case he advocated mainly 'moral support' and a credible threat of counter-intervention by a powerful liberal nation in the hope that it would be sufficient to deter a despot from intervening.[93]

On intervention, including humanitarian intervention, he followed a middle path among Italians in the course of the long nineteenth century, between strict non-intervention, as advocated by jurists Mamiani, Pierantoni, Carnazza Amari and Cimbali,[94] and collective intervention in humanitarian plights, as argued by Fiore and Cavaglieri (see chapter 4). He also followed another well known tendency of the Italian school of international law: advocacy of intervention to free an oppressed nation.

J. S. Mill, non-intervention and intervention

John Stuart Mill is classified today as a communitarian, especially given his stance on nationalism.[95] But if one takes into consideration other aspects of Mill's approach to international relations, such as his emphasis on 'the general prosperity of mankind' or international law as the protector of the weak,[96] he appears more of a cosmopolitan or simply defies classification.[97]

Mill in discussing intervention made no reference to contemporary jurists, probably given his aloofness towards international law based on Austin's views (see chapter 4).[98] The international lawyers for their part returned the compliment by not mentioning Mill at all on intervention or non-intervention, with very rare exceptions, such as Bernard as regards intervention[99] and a few others with regard to intervening in 'barbarous' regions.

Mill's main work on intervention is his 1859 essay 'A Few Words on Non-Intervention',[100] in which he makes a very strong case for non-intervention but an equally convincing case for intervention in several circumstances. This has led to confusion as to where he really stands and he has been criticized as 'ambivalent',[101] and 'not at his most convincing'[102] regarding the principle (non-intervention) he presumably, judging from the title, set out to defend.

References to non-intervention and intervention were also made by Mill in an earlier essay, 'The French Revolution of 1848 and Its Assailants' (1849), and in a forgotten article, 'The Spanish Question', published in 1837, which he had written together with a former army officer.[103]

The main rule of thumb to grasp Mill's overall position on non-intervention/intervention is whether a movement striving for freedom is seeking independence from 'a foreign yoke' or is seeking to overthrow a 'native tyrant' and establish liberal democratic rule. In the first instance he advocates external intervention (starkly or hesitantly), while in the second he advocates strict non-intervention.[104]

Let us start with non-intervention. Mill was opposed to intervention in support of liberty, for a people will be better served if they 'are left to work out their own salvation'.[105] At least five arguments can be identified in buttressing non-intervention.[106]

The first argument is uncertainty as to the outcome of intervention: 'there can seldom be anything approaching to assurance that intervention, even if successful, would be for the good of the people themselves'.[107] The second argument is the readiness to wage a struggle despite the grave dangers involved. As he puts it: 'The only test possessing any real value, of a people's having become fit for popular institutions, is that they ... are willing to brave labour and danger for their liberation'.[108] This is related to the argument of authenticity.[109] He asserts 'if they have not sufficient love of liberty to be able to wrest it from merely domestic oppressors, the liberty which is bestowed on them by other hands than their own, will have nothing real, nothing permanent'.[110] In 'The Spanish Question' he puts it thus: 'The attempt to establish freedom by foreign bayonets is a solecism in terms. A government which requires the support of foreign armies cannot be a free government'.[111] This leads us to a fourth argument: the danger of reversion to tyranny again, linked to one's own fighting. He argues that '[i]f a people ... does not value it [freedom] sufficiently to fight for it, and maintain it against any force which can be mustered ... it is only a question in how few years or months that people will be enslaved'.[112] A related fifth point is that the virtues and feelings needed 'for maintaining freedom' spring up only 'during an arduous struggle to become free by their own efforts'.[113] In this context he makes a telling point: 'Men become attached to that which they have long fought for and made sacrifices for; they learn to appreciate that on which their thoughts have been much engaged'.[114] This considerable insight on the part of the utilitarian philosopher (which Cobden, as we have seen, had also touched upon) tallies with the findings of today's cognitive psychology. As Leon Festinger has put it: 'Rats and people come to love the things for which they have suffered'.[115] According to Morton Deutsch, presumably they do so 'in order to reduce the dissonance induced by the suffering, and their method of dissonance reduction is to enhance the attractiveness of the choice which led to their suffering: only if what one chose was really worthwhile would all of the associated suffering be tolerable'.[116]

The emphasis of Mill on a people's ability to use force successfully for liberation has been criticized as a social Darwinian (actually crude Spencerian[117]) 'survival of the fittest',[118] although Mill was not a social Darwinist. Walzer claims that this accusation, though not wide of the mark, is unfair to Mill, 'for it was precisely Mill's point that force could not prevail, unless it was reinforced from the outside over a people ready "to brave labor and danger"'.[119] Anthony Ellis attributes Mill's stance to his belief 'that a people will be hard to oppress for long, once they have set their minds on freedom'.[120]

Now let us present the other side of the coin, intervention. Commentators have identified various exceptions, ranging from only two (Walzer) to as many as seven (Doyle). From Mill's at times convoluted presentation, we have identified five instances where Mill's non-intervention principle can be overcome in favour of its opposite, intervention: (1) in relations with 'barbarians', (2) in order to offset a previous counter-revolution by an external party against a people fighting against foreign rule, (3) in a struggle against a foreign yoke, (4) in protracted civil wars and (5), subsumed under civil war, stopping 'severities repugnant to humanity'.

Regarding the first instance, Mill subscribed to the nineteenth-century distinction between 'civilized' and 'barbarous' peoples (see chapter 3) and claimed that '[d]espotism is a legitimate mode of government in dealing with barbarians, provided the end be their improvement'.[121] According to Mill, 'barbarians will not reciprocate. They cannot be depended on for observing any rules'[122] and 'it is likely to be for their benefit that they should be conquered and held in subjection by foreigners'.[123]

Mill, like the great majority of his European contemporaries, was an apologist for conquest and colonialism, an example of 'imperial liberalism',[124] and indeed perhaps presenting 'the most well-known liberal justification of empire'.[125] But terms such as 'benign colonialism'[126] or 'tolerant imperialism'[127] are probably more appropriate for Mill and in this way one also avoids retrospective thinking. Mill criticized harsh colonial measures in India (and, nearer home, in Ireland) and advocated the participation of Indians at the highest levels of administration.[128] Moreover, for him cultural differences were not innate but a result of upbringing and circumstances, which could be remedied by education, and he was criticized by racists for not adhering to their views.[129]

The second exception is counter-intervention against a struggle for freedom from foreign rule. As Mill puts it:[130]

> Intervention to enforce non-intervention is always rightful, always moral, if not always prudent.... It might not have been right for England (even apart from the question of prudence) to have taken part with Hungary in its noble struggle against Austria; although the Austrian Government in Hungary was in some sense a foreign yoke. But when ... the Russian despot interposed, and ... delivered back the Hungarians, bound hand and foot, to their exasperated oppressors, it would have been an honourable and virtuous act on the part of England to have declared that this should not be, and that if Russia gave assistance to the wrong side, England would aid the right.

With this we arrive at another exception, assistance to a national liberation movement if it is 'unable to contend successfully ... against the military strength of another nation much more powerful'.[131] But, as we have seen, he hesitated when faced with the Hungarian uprising.[132]

Here one is faced with a dilemma. If 'A Few Words' is to be regarded as his last and definite word on this question, then one is left with his hesitation and could agree with Walzer's first reading of Mill: that the two go together, assistance to the secessionist movement cum counter-intervention[133] and that intervention is warranted only when counter-revolution by an external party has taken place.[134] Another option is not to prioritize 'A Few Words' but to take it together with 'Vindication', where he calls for intervention in support of those fighting, to prevent them 'from being crushed and trampled' by foreign conquerors.[135]

In 1865, when campaigning for elections, he gave the clear impression that he supported intervention even without counter-intervention.[136] Mill's overall thrust regarding nationality and national self-determination[137] can also be brought in to buttress intervention in support of independence movements. Mill (like Mazzini) believed that democracy can function properly only in national states. This was the very opposite of the position taken by Lord Acton, who was of the view that national states lead to absolutism and discrimination against minorities within.[138]

It is also worth referring to what was understood at the time by the readers of and commentators on 'A Few Words'. As Georgios Varouxakis points out, all understood Mill to mean that intervention should be used only in exceptional circumstances and that one assists a liberation moment if another state has intervened to suppress its efforts; and Mill was content with this interpretation of his views.[139]

The fourth exception, protracted civil war, includes within it a fifth, our subject matter: humanitarian intervention. According to Mill in 'A Few Words':[140]

> A case requiring consideration is that of a protracted civil war, in which the contending parties are so equally balanced that there is no probability of a speedy

issue; or if there is, the victorious side cannot hope to keep down the vanquished but by *severities repugnant to humanity, and injurious to the permanent welfare of the country*. In this exceptional case it seems now to be an admitted doctrine, that the neighbouring nations, or one powerful neighbour with the acquiescence of the rest, are warranted in demanding that the contest shall cease, and a reconciliation take place on equitable terms of compromise.

In 'A Few Words' it is not clear whether he means military intervention or mediation. But the examples he provides are suggestive, such as the Battle of Navarino by the three powers during the Greek War of Independence. Mill is clearer in 'Vindication': if attempts at accommodation by third parties are not accepted, then they may intervene by force.[141]

Humanitarian reasons, even though subsumed under civil war, can be seen as one of the reasons for intervening.[142] As for the non-intervention/intervention nexus, it would seem that Mill, in his two earlier works, was more in support of intervention. But by 1859, as an older and more prudent man, he had his doubts; thus his views come out as they do, perplexing and tentative. But perhaps it is better this way and shows the agonizing dilemma involved until this very day: a very convincing case against intervening can be made, as well as an equally convincing case for intervening in humanitarian plights or internal wars.

Notes

1   P. Laberge, 'Humanitarian Intervention: Three Ethical Positions', *Ethics and International Affairs*, 9 (1995), 15.
2   M. Hoffman, 'Normative International Theory: Approaches and Issues', in A. J. R. Groom and M. Light (eds), *Contemporary International Relations: A Guide to Theory* (London: Pinter, 1994), 33.
3   For Kant's cosmopolitanism in the international relations literature, see H. Bull, *The Anarchical Society: A Study of Order in World Politics* (New York: Columbia University Press, 1977), 25–6; M. Wight, 'An Anatomy of International Thought', *Review of International Studies*, 13:3 (1987), 223–4; T. Donaldson, 'Kant's Global Rationalism', in T. Nardin and D. R. Mapel (eds), *Traditions of International Ethics* (Cambridge: Cambridge University Press, 1992), 143–4; T. Mertens, 'Cosmopolitanism and Citizenship: Kant Against Habermans', *European Journal of Philosophy*, 4:3 (1996), 329–34.
4   For Mill as a communitarian, see C. Brown, *International Relations Theory: New Normative Approaches* (London: Harvester Wheatsheaf, 1992), 71; Hoffman, 'Normative International Theory', 33.
5   Brown, *International Relations Theory*, 65.
6   For a more nuanced view regarding Kant's cosmopolitanism see F. H. Hinsley, *Power and the Pursuit of Peace* (Cambridge: Cambridge University Press, 1963), 62–80; A. Hurrell, 'Kant and the Kantian Paradigm in International Relations', *Review of International Studies*, 16:3 (1990), 183–205.
7   A. Franceschet, 'Kant, International Law, and the Problem of Humanitarian Intervention', *Journal of International Political Theory*, 6:1 (2010), 3–4.

8 For a succinct presentation of the points raised by Kant in *Perpetual Peace*, see H. L. Williams, 'Back from the USSR: Kant, Kaliningrad and World Peace', *International Relations*, 20:1 (2006), 27–48.
9 I. Kant, 'Toward Perpetual Peace', in I. Kant, *Practical Philosophy* (Cambridge: Cambridge University Press, 1996), 319.
10 Ibid., 319–20.
11 Ibid., 319–20.
12 Williams, 'Back from the USSR', 37.
13 F. R. Tesón, 'The Kantian Theory of International Law', *Columbia Law Review*, 92:1 (1992), 67–8; Laberge, 'Humanitarian Intervention', 18.
14 See S. Axinn, 'Kant, Authority, and the French Revolution', *Journal of the History of Ideas*, 32:3 (1971), 179–92; L. W. Beck, 'Kant and the Right of Revolution', *Journal of the History of Ideas*, 32:3 (1971), 411–22; H. S. Reiss, 'Kant and the Right of Rebellion', *Journal of the History of Ideas*, 17:2 (1956), 179–92.
15 T. Mertens, 'War and International Order in Kant's Legal Thought', *Ratio Juris*, 8:3 (1995), 31 n.14; H. van der Linden, 'Kant: The Duty to Promote International Peace and Political Intervention', in *Proceedings of the Eighth International Kant Congress, Memphis 1995* (Milwaukee: Marquette University Press, 1995), vol. II, 73; Franceschet, 'Kant, International Law, and the Problem of Humanitarian Intervention', 8; Williams, 'Back from the USSR', 31, 37–8.
16 Laberge, 'Humanitarian Intervention', 18.
17 All quoted in B. Orend, 'Kant's Ethics of War and Peace', *Journal of Military Ethics*, 3:2 (2004), 163.
18 Quoted in Hurrell, 'Kant and the Kantian Paradigm in International Relations', 201.
19 For Kant's complex position on war, see B. Orend, 'Kant's Just War Theory', *Journal of the History of Philosophy*, 37:2 (1999), 323–53; Orend, 'Kant's Ethics of War and Peace', 161–97; A. Pagden, *The Enlightenment and Why It Still Matters* (New York: Random House, 2013), 348–9. For Kant as a pacifist, see Mertens, 'War and International Order in Kant's Legal Thought', 296–314.
20 Axinn, 'Kant, Authority, and the French Revolution', 425.
21 Mertens, 'War and International Order in Kant's Legal Thought', 304; R. Tuck, *The Rights of War and Peace: Political Thought and the International Order from Grotius to Kant* (Oxford: Oxford University Press, 1999), 217–18.
22 Orend, 'Kant's Ethics of War and Peace', 167–9.
23 Mertens, 'War and International Order in Kant's Legal Thought', 311; T. Mertens, 'Kant's Cosmopolitan Values and Supreme Emergencies', *Journal of Social Philosophy*, 38:2 (2007), 227; Hurrell, 'Kant and the Kantian Paradigm in International Relations', 200–2; H. Williams, *Kant and the End of War: A Critique of Just War Theory* (Basingstoke: Palgrave Macmillan, 2012), 32, 130, 135.
24 Mertens, 'Kant's Cosmopolitan Values and Supreme Emergencies', 225–7; G. Reichberg, 'Just War or Perpetual Peace?', *Journal of Military Ethics*, 1:1 (2002), 30 and 30 fn.25; Hurrell, 'Kant and the Kantian Paradigm in International Relations', 200–2; Orend, 'Kant's Ethics of War and Peace', 169.
25 G. Cavallar, 'Commentary on Susan Meld Shell's "Kant on Just War and 'Unjust Enemies': Reflections on a 'Pleonasm'"', *Kantian Review*, 11 (2006), 117–24; van der Linden, 'Kant', 73–4.
26 See notes 32–7 below and the following: C. Bagnoli, 'Humanitarian Intervention as a Perfect Duty: A Kantian Argument', *Nomos*, 47 (2004), 1–29; S. M. Shell, 'Kant on Just

War and "Unjust Enemies": Reflections on a "Pleonasm"', *Kantian Review*, 10 (2005), 82–111; A. R. Bernstein, 'Kant on Rights and Coercion in International Law: Implications for Humanitarian Intervention', *Jahrbuch für Recht und Ethik/Annual Review of Law and Ethics*, 16 (2008), 57–100.
27 Tesón, 'The Kantian Theory of International Law', 54, 60–2, 67, 69–70.
28 C. R. Beitz, *Political Theory and International Relations* (Princeton: Princeton University Press, 1979), 82. This point had been made in the 1940s by K. Loewenstein and C. J. Friedrich. See *ibid.*, 82 n.35.
29 R. J. Vincent, *Nonintervention and International Order* (Princeton: Princeton University Press, 1974), 57.
30 Tesón, 'The Kantian Theory of International Law', 92.
31 *Ibid.*, 93 (original emphasis). See also R. B. Lillich, 'Kant and the Current Debate over Humanitarian Intervention', *Journal of Transnational Law and Policy*, 6 (1997), 397.
32 Van der Linden, 'Kant', 73–4.
33 T. Hill, 'Kant and Humanitarian Intervention', *Philosophical Perspectives*, 23 (2009), 229 (original emphasis).
34 *Ibid.*, 236.
35 Franceschet, 'Kant, International Law, and the Problem of Humanitarian Intervention', 4.
36 *Ibid.*, 8.
37 *Ibid.*, 8–18.
38 See on this basic point Laberge, 'Humanitarian Intervention', 18.
39 Beitz, *Political Theory and International Relations*, 82 n.35.
40 Williams, *Kant and the End of War*, 118.
41 Laberge, 'Humanitarian Intervention', 18.
42 A. Pagden, 'Stoicism, Cosmopolitanism, and the Legacy of European Imperialism', *Constellations*, 7:1 (2000), 18.
43 Laberge, 'Humanitarian Intervention', 18.
44 Cavallar, 'Commentary on Susan Meld Shell's "Kant on Just War and Unjust Enemies"', 121.
45 Franceschet, 'Kant, International Law, and the Problem of Humanitarian Intervention', 11.
46 Williams, *Kant and the End of War*, 140. See on this point also Donaldson, 'Kant's Global Rationalism', 142–6.
47 Williams, *Kant and the End of War*, 130.
48 *Ibid.*, 131, 133.
49 Beitz, *Political Theory and International Relations*, 76.
50 S. Avineri, *Hegel's Theory of the Modern State* (Cambridge: Cambridge University Press, 1972), 178.
51 Quoted in S. Avineri, 'The Problem of War in Hegel's Thought', *Journal of the History of Ideas*, 22:4 (1961), 468.
52 F. Tesón, *Humanitarian Intervention: An Inquiry into Law and Morality* (New York: Transnational Publishers, 1997) [1988], 55.
53 Tesón, *Humanitarian Intervention*, 59; K. R. Popper, *The Open Society and Its Enemies, Volume II. The High Tide of Prophesy: Hegel, Marx, and the Aftermath* (London: Routledge and Kegan Paul, 1945), 259.
54 S. B. Smith, 'Hegel's Views on War, the State, and International Relations', *American Political Science Review*, 77:3 (1983), 627.

55 *Ibid.*, 627.
56 F. Parkinson, *The Philosophy of International Relations: A Study in the History of Thought* (Beverly Hills: Sage, 1977), 78.
57 Quoted in *ibid.*, 78.
58 *Ibid.*, 79.
59 Quoted in Avineri, 'The Problem of War in Hegel's Thought', 464.
60 Smith, 'Hegel's Views on War, the State, and International Relations', 629–31; Popper, *The Open Society and Its Enemies*, 65, 69–70.
61 See H. G. ten Bruggencate, 'Hegel's Views on War', *Philosophical Quarterly*, 1 (1950), 58–60; Avineri, 'The Problem of War in Hegel's Thought', 463–74; Avineri, *Hegel's Theory of the Modern State*, 194–207; C. I. Smith, 'Hegel and War', *Journal of the History of Ideas*, 26:2 (1965), 282–5.
62 See Smith, 'Hegel's Views on War, the State, and International Relations', 624–32.
63 *Ibid.*, 628–9.
64 For this insight we thank the Greek Hegel scholar Georges Faraklas.
65 Parkinson, *The Philosophy of International Relations*, 95, 97, 145; W. Olson and A. J. R. Groom, *International Relations Then and Now* (London: Routledge, 1991), 30; M. J. Smith, 'Liberalism and International Reform', in Nardin and Mapel (eds), *Traditions of International Ethics*, 205–6; S. Burchill, 'Liberal Internationalism', in S. Burchill and A. Linklater (eds), *Theories of International Relations* (Basingstoke: Macmillan, 1995), 36, 39; T. Dunne, 'Liberalism', in J. Baylis and S. Smith (eds), *The Globalization of World Politics: An Introduction to International Relations* (Oxford: Oxford University Press, 2001, 2nd edition) [1997], 166–7.
66 J. A. Hobson, *Richard Cobden: The International Man* (London: T. F. Unwin, 1919).
67 Olson and Groom, *International Relations Then and Now*, 30.
68 Hinsley, *Power and the Pursuit of Peace*, 96.
69 *Ibid.*, 97.
70 C. Holbraad, *The Concert of Europe: A Study in German and British International Theory 1815–1914* (London: Longman, 1970), 155; Smith, 'Liberalism and International Reform', 205–6.
71 Vincent, *Nonintervention and International Order*, 46.
72 Quoted in *ibid.*, 46.
73 *Ibid.*, 47.
74 Holbraad, *The Concert of Europe*, 156.
75 Quoted in Vincent, *Nonintervention and International Order*, 53.
76 Quoted in *ibid.*, 53.
77 *Ibid.*, 53.
78 *Ibid.*, 53.
79 Parkinson, *The Philosophy of International Relations*, 97; Brown, *International Relations Theory*, 605.
80 M. Ceadel, 'Cobden and Peace', in A. Howe and S. Morgan (eds), *Rethinking Nineteenth-Century Liberalism: Richard Cobden Bicentenary Essays* (Aldershot: Ashgate, 2006), 189–207.
81 Holbraad, *The Concert of Europe*, 155–6; A. Howe, 'Introduction', in Howe and Morgan (eds), *Rethinking Nineteenth-Century Liberalism*, 2–5, 14–16.
82 C. Brown, 'Human Rights', in Baylis and Smith (eds), *The Globalization of World Politics*, 605.
83 J. Pitts, *A Turn to Empire: The Rise of Imperial Liberalism in Britain and France* (Princeton: Princeton University Press, 2005), 124–62.

84 M. Wight, 'Mazzini', in M. Wight and B. Porter (eds), *Four Seminal Thinkers in International Theory: Machiavelli, Grotius, Kant and Mazzini* (Oxford: Oxford University Press, 2005), 102.
85 *Ibid.*, 100–3; S. Recchia and N. Urbinati, 'Introduction', in S. Recchia and N. Urbinati (eds), *A Cosmopolitanism of Nations: Giuseppe Mazzini's Writing on Democracy, Nation Building and International Relations* (Princeton: Princeton University Press, 2009), 2.
86 *Ibid.*, 21.
87 G. Mazzini, 'On Nonintervention (1851)', in Recchia and Urbinati (eds), *A Cosmopolitanism of Nations*, 213–18.
88 Vincent, *Nonintervention and International Order*, 59–60.
89 Mazzini, 'On Nonintervention', 214, 217.
90 *Ibid.*, 214–15.
91 *Ibid.*, 216.
92 *Ibid.*, 216–17.
93 Recchia and Urbinati, 'Introduction', 27. See also G. Mazzini, 'The European Question: Foreign Intervention and National Self-Determination', in Recchia and Urbinati (eds), *A Cosmopolitanism of Nations*, 195.
94 On Eduardo Cimbali, see E. Stowell, *Intervention in International Law* (Washington, DC: John Byrne and Co., 1921), 477.
95 Brown, *International Relations Theory*, 71, 73–5; Hoffman, 'Normative International Theory', 33.
96 See K. E. Miller, 'John Stuart Mill's Theory of International Relations', *Journal of the History of Ideas*, 22:4 (1961), 499–501, 504.
97 Varouxakis regards Mill as an advocate of 'cosmopolitan patriotism', as he calls it. See G. Varouxakis, 'Cosmopolitan Patriotism in J. S. Mill's Political Thought and Action', in N. Urbinati and A. Zakaras (eds), *J. S. Mill's Political Thought: A Bicentennial Reassessment* (Cambridge: Cambridge University Press, 2007), 277–97.
98 See his comments in J. S. Mill, 'The French Revolution of 1848 and Its Assailants', *Westminster and Foreign Quarterly Review*, 51 (April 1849), 28. Reprinted as 'Vindication of the French Revolution of February 1848, in Reply to Lord Brougham and Others', in J. S. Mill, *Dissertations and Discussions* (London: Longmans, Green, Reader and Dyer, 1867), vol. II, 335–410 (henceforth 'Vindication').
99 M. Bernard, *On the Principle of Non-Intervention. A Lecture Delivered in the Hall of All Souls College, December MDCCCLX* (Oxford: J. H. and J. Parker, 1860), 3.
100 J. S. Mill, 'A Few Words on Non-Intervention', *Fraser's Magazine*, 60 (December 1859), reprinted in Mill, *Dissertations and Discussions*, vol. III, 153–78 (henceforth 'A Few Words').
101 A. Ellis, 'Utilitarianism and International Ethics', in Nardin and Mapel (eds), *Traditions of International Ethics*, 166.
102 M. Levin, *J. S. Mill on Civilization and Barbarism* (London: Routledge, 2004), 49.
103 J. S. Mill, 'The Spanish Question', *London and Westminster Review*, 5 (July 1837), 165–94. We thank Georgios Varouxakis for this information. Mill wrote the theoretical parts of this article, which dovetail with his statements on non-intervention and intervention in the other two essays.
104 M. Walzer, 'Mill's "A Few Words on Non-Intervention": A Commentary', in Urbinati and Zakaras (eds), *J. S. Mill's Political Thought*, 352.
105 Beitz, *Political Theory and International Relations*, 84–6; M. Walzer, 'The Rights of Political Communities', in C. R. Beitz et al. (eds), *International Ethics* (Princeton: Princeton University Press, 1985), 178–9; Ellis, 'Utilitarianism and International Ethics', 166–7.

106 Michael Doyle, in a perceptive article on Mill and Walzer, has come up with five points and we have taken on board three of them. See M. W. Doyle, 'A Few Words on Mill, Walzer, and Nonintervention', *Ethics and International Affairs*, 23 (2009), 352–5.
107 Mill, 'A Few Words', 173.
108 *Ibid.*, 173.
109 See Doyle, 'A Few Words on Mill, Walzer, and Nonintervention', 352–3.
110 Mill, 'A Few Words', 174.
111 Mill, 'The Spanish Question', 179.
112 Mill, 'A Few Words', 174.
113 *Ibid.*, 175.
114 *Ibid.*, 175.
115 Quoted in M. Deutsch, *The Resolution of Conflict* (New Haven: Yale University Press, 1973), 357.
116 *Ibid.*, 357.
117 J. A. Rogers, 'Darwinism and Social Darwinism', *Journal of the History of Ideas*, 33:2 (1972), 265–8, 276–80.
118 J. N. Moore, 'International Law and the United States' Role in Vietnam: A Reply', in R. Falk (ed.), *The Vietnam War and International Law* (Princeton: Princeton University Press, 1968), 431.
119 Walzer, 'The Rights of Political Communities', 179.
120 Ellis, 'Utilitarianism and International Ethics', 167.
121 Quoted in M. Tunick, 'Tolerant Imperialism: John Stuart Mill's Defense of British Rule in India', *Review of Politics*, 68:4 (2006), 595.
122 Mill, 'A Few Words', 167.
123 *Ibid.*, 167.
124 Pitts, *A Turn to Empire*, 126–52; S. Holmes, 'Making Sense of Liberal Imperialism', in Urbinati and Zakaras (eds), *J. S. Mill's Political Thought*, 319–46.
125 K. Mantena, 'The Crisis of Liberal Imperialism', in D. Bell (ed.), *Victorian Visions of Global Order: Empire and International Relations in Nineteenth-Century Political Thought* (Cambridge: Cambridge University Press, 2007), 118. See also E. P. Sullivan, 'Liberalism and Imperialism: J. S. Mill's Defense of the British Empire', *Journal of the History of Ideas*, 44 (1983), 599, 605–17; B. Jahn, 'Barbarian Thoughts: Imperialism in the Philosophy of John Stuart Mill', *Review of International Studies*, 31 (2005), 599–618.
126 Doyle, 'A Few Words on Mill, Walzer, and Nonintervention', 356, 363–5.
127 Tunick, 'Tolerant Imperialism', 586.
128 Sullivan, 'Liberalism and Imperialism', 611; Levin, *J. S. Mill on Civilization and Barbarism*, 41.
129 Sullivan, 'Liberalism and Imperialism', 610; G. Varouxakis, 'John Stuart Mill on Race', *Utilitas*, 10:1 (1998), 18–32.
130 Mill, 'A Few Words', 176–7.
131 *Ibid.*, 176.
132 For this hesitation on the part of Mill, see: Walzer, *Just and Unjust Wars* (New York: Basic Books, 1977), 93; Laberge, 'Humanitarian Intervention', 23; Varouxakis, 'John Stuart Mill on Intervention and Non-Intervention', *Millennium: Journal of International Studies*, 16:1 (1997), 70–1.
133 Walzer, *Just and Unjust Wars*, 90.
134 G. Varouxakis, *Liberty Abroad: J. S. Mill and International Relations* (Oxford: Oxford University Press, 2013). 90.

135 Mill, 'Vindication', 29.
136 Varouxakis, *Liberty Abroad*, 97.
137 See S. Grader, 'John Stuart Mill's Theory of Nationality: A Liberal Dilemma in the Field of International Relations', *Millennium: Journal of International Studies*, 14:2 (1985), 207–16; Georgios Varouxakis, *Mill on Nationality* (London: Routledge, 2002).
138 Grader, 'John Stuart Mill's Theory of Nationality', 211.
139 Varouxakis, *Liberty Abroad*, 92–4.
140 Mill, 'A Few Words', 172 (emphasis added).
141 Mill, 'Vindication', 29.
142 See Miller, 'John Stuart Mill's Theory of International Relations', 505, 507, 510; Holbraad, *The Concert of Europe*, 164–6; Vincent, *Nonintervention and International Order*, 55–6; Varouxakis, 'John Stuart Mill on Intervention and Non-Intervention', 59–60, 68–75; C. A. L. Prager, 'Intervention and Empire: John Stuart Mill and International Relations', *Political Studies*, 53:3 (2005), 629–30; Doyle, 'A Few Words on Mill, Walzer, and Non-intervention', 355–64; B. Jahn, 'Humanitarian Intervention – What's in a Name?', *International Politics*, 49:1 (2012), 51–2.

Part II

Practice

Introduction

Our criteria for selecting the *armed* humanitarian interventions of the nineteenth century are the following (which conform with the understanding in the long nineteenth century, as elucidated in chapters 4 and 5): (1) governmental onslaught against unarmed people or atrocities by both sides in a protracted internal war; (2) humanitarian concern, that is, stopping the 'effusion of blood', as one of the main reasons and official justifications for intervening; (3) military intervention, ranging from 'peacekeeping' (in today's parlance) to hostilities or a full-scale war; and (4) intervention opposed or reluctantly condoned by the incumbent.

A clarification is in order as regards the second criterion, motivation, which harks back to the 'right intention' of the 'just war' doctrine (see chapter 2). One view is that pure humanitarian motives are of the essence, 'altruism writ large'.[1]

A more pragmatic line is that there is always a mix, for, as Rougier had put it, with the nineteenth-century experience in mind, 'it is practically impossible to separate the humanitarian motives of intervention from the political motives and assure that the intervening parties are absolutely disinterested'.[2] Thus several authors yesterday and today are prepared to regard a case as humanitarian if there is a combination of motives and the humanitarian motives are no sham.[3]

A third line is that since even the best of motives or intentions[4] may turn out disastrously in the field, the crux is a positive humanitarian outcome irrespective of the real motives,[5] but this is probably going too far.

On this basis of the above four criteria we will examine four cases. The case of Crete, which appears in some discussions on humanitarian interventions in the nineteenth century, will not be included. In fact Crete presents two cases, in 1866–68 and again in 1896–98. The former witnessed reports of massacres while in fact the Ottoman authorities tried to be restrained in subduing the Cretan uprising so as not to allow foreign intervention on humanitarian grounds. Apart from diplomatic support for the Greeks from Russia, great power involvement was limited to the sending of warships to gather fleeing Greek Cretans. As for 1896–98, the six European powers were requested by the Porte to curb Greek aid to yet another Cretan uprising and the powers actually intervened as peacekeepers in Crete (with warships and troops) on behalf of the Ottomans. Other cases that happen to be included in some lists of humanitarian interventions, such as the Armenians or the situation in Macedonia in the Ottoman Empire at the turn of the century, did not involve military operations but diplomatic pressure.

Humanitarian reasons have also been referred to by some commentators with regard to the outbreak of the First Balkan War. In fact the official humanitarian justification at the time was bogus. The aim of the coordinated acts of aggression by Greece, Bulgaria, Serbia and Montenegro was to oust the Ottomans and annex as much of Macedonia as they could, a process which had begun in the 1890s with guerrilla warfare by rival Greek and Bulgarian volunteers supported by their respective governments.[6] Ottoman rule had its flaws, in particular under Abdulhamid, and especially in the case of the Armenians, but the Ottoman Empire, following the 1908 Young Turk Revolution (which was heralded by the minorities and by neighbouring states), had become an imperial republic, with a parliament representing most of the minorities. Ironically (and tragically), when the four states launched their attack in October 1912, the Ottoman government was under the firm grip of liberal elder statesmen bent on curbing the influence of the nationalist Young Turks.[7] Moreover, in the course of the 1912 war, Greece, Bulgaria and Serbia acted in a manner that was hardly within the confines of humanitarian law, committing a series of atrocities against unarmed Muslims.[8]

At this juncture an additional point is worth making with a bearing on the presentation of the case studies. The field of international relations as conceived by the traditional realist paradigm (which dominated the scene from 1945 until the mid-1970s and is hardly a spent force today) is statist: it regards states as the key units of analysis, seen as unitary actors, akin to billiard balls[9] whose outer shells (diplomats, foreign ministers, prime ministers and heads of state) are in contact. Further, a clear distinction is made between domestic politics and international politics, with the former being seen as having little impact on the latter save as regards aspects of power (power inputs).[10]

Such views may seem today *passé* and social constructions by recalcitrant realist scholars, but they are a fairly accurate depiction of the state of play in the nineteenth century, the golden age of traditional diplomacy, with the making of foreign policy in the hands of a small elite circle of foreign ministers, ambassadors (and other professional diplomats), monarchs, presidents (in the US case) and prime ministers, and a limited number of figures inside and outside government. This small circle shaped foreign policy and kept it away from the 'prying eyes' of an increasingly vocal public. As Richard Pipes points out, foreign policy relations 'proved to be that area of politics which was resisted most successfully the encroachments of democratic control'.[11] There was also the implicit assumption that responsible governments and diplomats knew how best to promote national interest and *raisons d'état*, away from the passions, sentimentalism or jingoism of

Introduction

the public. These few individuals played a key role in foreign policy and, despite the 'unspoken assumptions'[12] of a state's foreign policy, they at times held divergent views within the same decision-making milieu, views that are well worth referring to, and show that foreign policy was then hardly as uniform and coordinated as is often assumed.[13] This divergence of opinion within the same decision-making body was also symptomatic of the acute dilemmas posed by humanitarian plights.

On the basis of all of the above, the presentation of the four case studies will for the most part be traditional, with emphasis on diplomatic history and the views of key individuals.

Notes

1   R. B. Miller, 'Humanitarian Intervention, Altruism, and the Limits of Casuistry', *Journal of Religious Ethics*, 28:3 (2000), 4, 16. See also on this question A. Krieg, *Motivations for Humanitarian Intervention: Theoretical and Empirical Considerations* (Dordrecht: Springer, 2013), 37–55.
2   A. Rougier, 'La théorie de l'intervention d'humanité', *Revue générale de droit international public*, 17 (1910), 525.
3   It has been argued that 'concern with interests can help to give humanitarian war the kind of political anchorage that it may require in order to remain limited. As long as the interests in question are neither illegitimate nor preponderant, their presence need not subvert the justice of the war'. See A. Coates, 'Humanitarian Intervention: A Conflict of Traditions', in T. Nardin and M. S. Williams (eds), *Humanitarian Intervention* (New York: New York University Press, 2006), 77.
4   Some authors distinguish between intentions and motives, pointing out that what matter are intentions (namely the intention to save people from massacre) and not motives, which are almost by definition bound to be mixed (they include instrumental motives) and hardly purely humanitarian. See on this point in particular F. R. Tesón, 'Humanitarian Intervention: Loose Ends', *Journal of Military Ethics*, 10:3 (2011), 200–6.
5   N. J. Wheeler, *Saving Strangers: Humanitarian Intervention in International Society* (Oxford: Oxford University Press, 2000), 9, 24, 29–30, 37–40.
6   D. Dakin, *The Greek Struggle in Macedonia, 1897–1913* (Thessaloniki: Institute of Balkan Studies, 1966).
7   See F. Ahmad, *The Making of Modern Turkey* (London: Routledge, 1993), 6.
8   Carnegie Endowment for International Peace (1914), *Report of the International Commission to Inquire into the Causes and Conduct of the Balkan War* (Washington, DC: Carnegie Endowment for International Peace, 1914).
9   A. Wolfers, *Discord and Collaboration* (Baltimore: Johns Hopkins University Press, 1962).
10 K. J. Holsti, *The Divided Discipline: Hegemony and Diversity in International Theory* (Boston: Allen and Unwin, 1985), 22–3; J. A. Vasquez, *The Power of Power Politics: A Critique* (London: Frances Pinter, 1983), 18; P. R. Viotti and M. V. Kauppi, *International Relations Theory: Realism, Pluralism, Globalism* (New York: Macmillan, 1993), 5–6.
11 R. E. Pipes, 'Domestic Politics and Foreign Affairs', in I. S. Lederer (ed.), *Russian Foreign Policy* (New Haven: Yale University Press, 1967), 146.
12 K. Neilson, *Britain and the Last Tsar: British Policy and Russia, 1894–1917* (Oxford: Clarendon Press, 1995), xii.

13 J. Mayal, 'Introduction', in P. Sharp and G. Wiseman (eds), *The Diplomatic Corps as an Institution of International Society* (Basingstoke: Palgrave Macmillan, 2007), 1; K. Hamilton and R. Langhorne, *The Practice of Diplomacy: Its Evolution, Theory and Administration* (London: Routledge, 1995), 89–135; G. R. Berridge, *Diplomacy: Theory and Practice* (Basingstoke: Palgrave Macmillan, 2010), 7; Neilson, *Britain and the Last Tsar*, xii, 3–4.

6

Intervention in the Greek War of Independence, 1821–32

On intervention

The intervention of Britain, Russia and France in the Greek War of Independence is regarded as the first armed intervention on humanitarian grounds in world history (as depicted by publicists from Wheaton onwards) and it took place prior to the appearance of the new concept of humanitarian intervention. As such it was pace-setting.

From the Congress of Vienna (1814–15) until the outbreak of the Greek War of Independence, there were three views on intervention at the diplomatic level.

Metternich and his close adviser Friedrich Gentz held that the great powers could take counter-revolutionary measures and intervene to suppress uprisings against legitimate rule.[1] This doctrine was shared by Tsar Alexander I, and his brainchild, the Holy Alliance (Russia, Austria and Prussia), and was endorsed by the great power Congress system at the Congresses of Aix La Chapelle (November 1818) and Troppau (November 1820).[2]

The second view came from Britain's Foreign Secretary, Castlereagh, who stated in a famous circular (dated 19 January 1821) that states retained the right to interfere 'where their own immediate security or essential interest are seriously endangered by the internal transactions of another State' and not as 'a general and indiscriminate application to all revolutionary movements'.[3]

The third approach was peaceful involvement, mainly mediation attempts. This can be discerned in the foreign policy initiatives of the two main rivals of Metternich on the European scene, Ioannis Capodistrias[4] (co-Foreign Minister of Russia, with Nesselrode) and George Canning as British Foreign Secretary.[5]

A major concern (then and now) was finding the most propitious international reaction in instances of protracted internal wars. One approach was the *cordon sanitaire*, the sealing off of a country experiencing civil war and thus avoiding getting into a messy situation, with unpredictable results.[6] But absolute non-involvement or an arms embargo could inadvertently amount to supporting the militarily more powerful party in an internal conflict (as seen in the 1990s with the Bosnian tragedy). To remember the famous Talleyrand adage: 'non-intervention est un mot diplomatique et énigmatique, qui signifie à peu près la même chose qu'intervention'.[7]

In the nineteenth century, the concept of 'belligerency' was applicable in internal wars: another state could recognize insurgents as 'belligerents' provided the armed conflict met certain criteria, the so-called 'factual test' (protracted armed conflict, insurgents administering a large portion of a state's territory, insurgents headed by a responsible authority and so on).[8] Recognition of belligerency did not imply diplomatic support for the insurgents[9] but such recognition was more often than not seen as an unfriendly act by the incumbent government, as seen in the Greek–Ottoman case.

The uprising and international reaction

The uprising in the making

The spark that ignited the fuse leading to the 'Greek Revolution' (as it is called in Greece) was the French Revolution and its Enlightenment principles.[10] It was then that the 'Neo-Hellenic Enlightenment' was spawned, which came to see Ottoman rule as unacceptable and the Greeks as being 'in chains', even though the educated *Romioi* (Orthodox Greek-speakers or Hellenized inhabitants of the Balkans) were prospering in the Ottoman Empire, with the Phanariots (their quasi-aristocracy in Constantinople) holding high state positions, despite being a subject people, the *Rum millet* (the Orthodox Christian community).[11]

The uprising was put on course with the founding in Odessa of a clandestine organization named Philiki Hetairia (Friendly Society) in September 1814, whose aim was Greek independence with Russian support.[12] The Hetairia approached Capodistrias, who was influential throughout Europe (as the main opponent of Metternich's ultra-conservative European system[13]) and offered him the leadership. Capodistrias was seen as the only figure capable of steering the Greeks 'safe through the hurricane',[14] given his position and friendship with Tsar Alexander I. But he declined the offer and advised against the uprising, which he regarded a folly (and duly reported the incident to the Tsar).[15] The leadership of the Hetairia was then bestowed on Alexander Ypsilantis (a young Phanariot major general in the Russian army and aide-de-camp of the Tsar) in April 1820.[16]

At the time, the international landscape 'could hardly have been more unfavourable'[17] for the Greek uprising, with the Congress system and the Holy Alliance poised to subdue revolts.[18] As regards a *national* uprising by a numerical minority, on the basis of the principle of nationalities it was 'almost unheard-of'[19] and equally condemnable by the great powers.[20]

Given this state of affairs, Capodistrias and the most revered figure of the Neo-Hellenic Enlightenment, scholar Adamantios Korais (who lived in Paris), advised against taking up arms, and called instead for the regeneration of the Greeks through education.[21] Moreover, the urge for Greek freedom was not sweeping, with the Orthodox Patriarchate, most Phanariots and many primates in the southern Balkans against it, given their privileges and affluence.[22]

The uprising and the Ottoman and international reaction

Despite the bad omens, Ypsilantis launched the Greek independence struggle on 21 February 1821 from Russian soil and crossed the River Prut, in the prospect of Russian assistance. In Russian army uniform, he arrived in Jassy (Moldavia) delivering a proclamation with Enlightenment rhetoric and romantic overtones, calling for a fight for the faith and the fatherland, stressing the 'natural right to freedom' and calling the Greeks to imitate the example of European peoples who had risen up in arms to foster 'freedom and happiness'. Ypsilantis referred to 'a Mighty Empire' ready to 'defend our rights', and in a letter to the Tsar wrote: 'Will you, Sire, abandon the Greeks to their fate, when a single word from you can deliver them from the most monstrous tyranny and save them of the horrors of a long and terrible struggle?'[23]

The Tsar ordered Ypsilantis to lay down his arms and dismissed him from the Russian army. The Orthodox Patriarch, Gregorios V, excommunicated him and issued an anathema against the Hetairia. Ypsilantis's behaviour in the principalities was a disaster, marked by 'a mixture of vanity, brutality, and incompetence'.[24] By June, the Ottoman army quelled the ill-prepared Greek rebellion in Moldavia.[25]

The uprising that was to succeed was in Peloponnese from March 1821 onwards, a rugged area suited to hit-and-run warfare, with an overwhelming Christian majority, and Greek dominance in the sea due to the many ships of the nearby islands of Hydra and Spetses. Moreover, the war between the Ottomans and Ali Pasha, the powerful governor of Yannina, stranded the elite Ottoman forces, providing a unique opportunity for the Greeks to take up arms.[26]

The Laibach Congress was taken by surprise upon hearing of the Greek uprising. The Tsar was convinced that it had been masterminded by a sinister 'central governing committee' based in Paris.[27] Metternich regarded the Ottomans and Greeks 'beyond the pale of civilization' and hoped that the rebellion would 'burn itself out'.[28] Castlereagh, like France and Prussia,[29] opted for strict neutrality. The Congress made sure to denounce the uprising.[30]

For the Ottomans, the revolt was unexpected. They were unaware that an upheaval was in the making or perhaps were 'too proud to be easily alarmed'.[31] Sultan Mahmud II jumped to the conclusion that it was led by the Russians and clung to this view until the end (a self-fulfilling prophecy, as it turned out), regarding himself vindicated when Russia intervened in 1827–29. With news of massacres of Muslims, the view prevailed that the *Rum* were out to kill all the Muslims. Thus they were longer treated as *dhimmi* (protected minorities) but *harbi* (anti-Islamic warring groups) and the *zimmet* pact (loyalty in return for protection) ceased to apply.[32]

In the first months of the uprising 15,000 to 20,000 Muslims in the Peloponnese 'were murdered without mercy or remorse',[33] a tragedy barely noticed in Europe.[34] Mahmud, unable to punish the perpetrators, vented his fury on the *Rum* nearer at hand, ordering the execution of more than fifty prominent Phanariots and allowing Muslim mobs to slaughter several thousand innocent people in the capital and other cities, and to burn hundreds of churches, acts which left Europe aghast.[35]

Another act of the Sultan stunned Europe even more: the hanging on the dawn of Easter Day (22 April 1821) of the octogenarian Patriarch Gregorios (and several senior bishops), held responsible for the behaviour of his flock though he was obviously innocent. The Austrian Emperor was as shocked as if the Pope had been executed. The Russian population, including the Tsar, were so incensed that a Russo-Ottoman war seemed likely.[36]

The Russian ambassador to the Porte, Stroganov, delivered two strongly worded protestations (drafted by Capodistrias) stating that Christians had been exterminated and demanding an end to the horrors. The Reis Effendi (foreign minister) told Stroganov that they had recriminating evidence against the Patriarch, who had been aware of the plot of the Hetairia, and that the Ottoman reaction was not meant as an all-out war against the Christians.[37] Stroganov, not satisfied with the answer, left Constantinople. The British ambassador, Strangford (who was pro-Ottoman), was instructed by Castlereagh to 'bring the Porte back to reason' and to demand that the Ottoman authorities distinguish between innocent and guilty so as to restore Christian trust to the state.[38]

Russia, nearer to the scene and attached to its co-religionists, was in a quandary. For Alexander and the Russians, Orthodoxy and historical tradition justified coming to the support of the Greeks, as fellow Orthodox Christians. On the other hand, the Congress system and the Holy Alliance stood for the support of legitimate authority against rebels and the Tsar, for all his sympathy for the Greeks, was against their independence.[39] In Russia a war party took shape and clamoured for intervention.[40] It comprised many high-ranking Russian officials, including ambassadors Stroganov, Lieven (in London) and Pozzo di Borgo (in Paris), and famous commanders from the Napoleonic wars, such as generals Kiselev, Ermolov and Diebitsch. Capodistrias was the natural leader of the war party and tried to convince the Tsar to take military steps against the Ottomans. There was also a small anti-war party, headed by Nesselrode, which feared that Greek emancipation would lead to similar calls on the part of Poles, Ukrainians and other subject peoples in Russia.[41]

Metternich and Castlereagh put pressure on the Tsar by addressing his worst fears. Castlereagh wrote him a personal letter, in which he acknowledged that the atrocities committed by 'the Turks' 'made humanity shudder', but that the Greeks

Intervention in the Greek War of Independence

were in effect *Carbonari* representing the spirit of insurrection and threatening the whole of Europe.[42] The Tsar, finding no support for war outside Russia, concluded, in the interests of European stability, not to go to war for the Greek cause. As he put it to Capodistrias in August 1821: 'If we reply to the Turks with war ... the Paris directing committee will triumph and no government will be left standing.... At all costs we must find means to avoid war with Turkey'.[43] Capodistrias did his best to make him change his mind and went as far as suggesting the expulsion of the Ottomans from the Danubian principalities.[44] Realizing that Alexander was unflinching, he left the Russian service a year later (August 1822), though his resignation was not accepted (he went on indefinite leave and settled in Geneva).[45]

In the latter part of 1821 and first part of 1822, two appalling events took place within seven months. The first was the conquest of Tripolis (5–6 October 1821) by the Greeks, amidst carnage that defies description, with the indiscriminate massacring of 8,000 to 15,000 unarmed people of all ages. It was then that many philhellenes left the region in disgust, including Colonel Thomas Gordon (the later historian of the Greek uprising). News of this horrifying deed trickled abroad but there was no condemnation. The standard line was that the exaggerated Greek reaction was due to the centuries-old 'Turkish yoke'.[46]

The European response was very different in April 1822 when the Ottomans laid waste the affluent island of Chios. Gordon likened it to the carnage of Tripolis, with 'the victors butchering indiscriminately all who came in their way'.[47] According to Strangford, Ottoman ferocity had been carried 'to a pitch which makes humanity shudder'.[48] Some 25,000 were killed and 45,000 enslaved. The European uproar was even greater than in 1821. Delacroix painted *Scenes of the Massacre of Chios*, causing a sensation when it was unveiled in Paris.[49]

Castlereagh instructed Strangford to tell the Porte that 'a repetition of such deeds of blood' and 'ferocious and hateful barbarism' would not be tolerated and would lead to the withdrawal of diplomatic missions.[50] The British ambassador lectured Sadiq-Effendi (the Reis Effendi) about 'the duties of humanity which existed in all civilized countries', which 'obliged the Powers not to remain indifferent observers of the atrocities of this war, of the only war in the entire world'.[51] Sadiq-Effendi stated that events in Chios had 'deeply pained the Sultan' but that the Chiots had started it all by massacring Muslims, adding pointedly that reference had never been made to the massacres of Muslims in Tripolis, Navarino, Corinth and Athens.[52]

The philhellenes

Contrary to the aloofness of the powers, bar Russia, European and American public opinion had been on the Greek side almost from the beginning. What made the difference with the uprising of the Serbs in previous decades and the more recent rebellions for political rights in Spain, Portugal, Naples, Sicily, Piedmont and Sardinia (1820–21) was that the Greek uprising had become a *cause célèbre*, giving rise to an impressive wave of what came to be known as 'philhellenism'. Greek committees sprung up in various parts of Europe and the US, starting with Spain and Switzerland, concluding with the London Greek Committee (1823) and the Paris Greek Committee (1825), all of which were engaged in fund-raising, writing pamphlets, securing funds, foodstuffs, medicine, arms and ammunition, as well as paying ransom to free enslaved Greeks (a Russian prerogative). Over a thousand 'philhellenes', Italians, French, English, Scots, Irish, Germans, Swiss, Poles, Scandinavians, Americans, Spaniards, Portuguese, Dutch, Hungarians and others (but not Russians, much to Capodistrias's chagrin[53]) came to assist the Greeks in their struggle, including a unique celebrity, Lord Byron, with some of his greatest romantic poems referring to the Greek cause (*Childe Harold, Don Juan* and others).[54]

The philhellenes were convinced of the righteousness of the Greek cause and of the barbarity of the 'Turks'. Thus the atrocities and other barbarous acts committed by the Greeks – the few that were reported – were wished away and had little impact in stemming the enthusiasm. There was strong public pressure from elite circles in Britain (apart from Byron, Shelley, Bentham, Ricardo, Lord Erskine, Lord Russell and others), Russia (a string of poets, including Pushkin), France (Chateaubriand, Hugo, Constant, Delacroix, Berlioz, Villemain, Firmin Didot), Switzerland (banker-philanthropist Eynard) and the US (Hellenist Professor Everett, three ex-Presidents, Jefferson, Adams and Madison, and future President Harrison) to assist the beleaguered Greeks. Ludwig I of Bavaria and US President Monroe contemplated recognition of statehood (Madison suggested reference to the Greek cause in the Monroe Doctrine of December 1823) but Secretary of State (and future President) John Quincy Adams, a pragmatist, put an end to any such ventures.[55]

European and American identification with the Greeks was also due to the fact that they were regarded as the descendants of the ancient Greeks (with ancient Greece regarded as 'the cradle of European civilization'). Shelley's words in the preface of his poem *Hellas* captured the overall mood: 'We are all Greeks. Our laws, our literature, our religion [sic], our art have their roots in Greece. But for Greece … we might still have been savages and idolators.… The Modern Greek is the descendant of those glorious beings'.[56] It was a great advantage to the Greek cause that Europe and America were then under the spell of classicism, which venerated the ancient Greeks, as well as romanticism, making the uprising appear a most romantic episode.[57]

For the Russians, the Greeks striving for freedom were the descendants of the venerated Byzantines (to whom they owed Christianity, the alphabet and iconography) as well as the ancient Greeks. Co-religionism brought the support of the Russian Church and wide public support, even in rural areas, among the illiterate strata and peasants, something unique in Europe in those days. Furthermore,

Greeks were very much present in Russia as prosperous merchants, educators and high-ranking civil servants, diplomats, military personnel and members of the aristocracy, several of them close to the Tsar and court, a case in point being Capodistrias, senior officials Sturdza and Destounis and the Ypsilantis family.[58]

There is also an intriguing dimension to the Russian–Greek link, little known outside a small circle of Soviet and Russian researchers: the impact it had and the interplay it created between the Greek would-be insurgents in Moldavia (in February–March 1821) and the Russian would-be Decembrists (in December 1825).[59] This characteristic example of 'entangled histories' can be seen in: (1) the contacts between Ypsilantis and other aristocratic officers of the Russian army (most of them liberals and future Decembrists) in various salons and Masonic lodges, where they discussed and planned their respective uprisings (the liberation of the Greeks and the liberation of Russia from absolutism); (2) the assistance given by individual officers (most of them future Decembrists) to Ypsilantis in his Danubian endeavour, without the approval of the central government or army; and (3) the impact Ypsilantis's uprising had in Russia, among the future Decembrists, officers and lay people, including more than a dozen philhellene poets. Ironically for them, as in the case of Alexander's conspiracy theory (the 'Paris committee'), the Greek uprising would provide the spark, together with the uprisings in the Italian and Iberian peninsulas, for a wider European conflagration, which would overthrow absolutist rule, including absolutism in Russia.[60]

1823–25: Canning, Russia, Byron, Ibrahim and barbarization

Canning, Russia, Byron

When Canning succeeded Castlereagh (following his suicide) in September 1822 he followed his predecessor's neutral policy. Canning had 'no regard for the Turks as such, but he did not mean to excite the millions of Mohammedans in India by a display of partiality'[61] and 'did not share the illusions of the Philhellenes about the modern Greeks',[62] regarding them 'a most rascally set'.[63] He stood for the maintenance of the Ottoman Empire and 'he held that, if war occurred, Russia would gobble Greece at one mouthful and Turkey at the next'.[64] Yet, having in the meantime become renowned as the defender of oppressed peoples in Latin America and Europe, he came to regard the Greek cause more favourably, vindicating those Greeks who from the start regarded him as a philhellene.[65]

The goals of Canning's Greek policy from 1824 can be summarized as follows: (1) to further British interests in the region; (2) not to allow Russia to take undue advantage of the Greek case; (3) to limit French influence and not to permit a Franco-Russian alliance;[66] (4) not to permit the collapse of the Ottoman Empire; and (5) to bring about an autonomous or independent Greece leaning towards Britain.[67]

Canning recognized the Greeks as belligerents in March 1823. The act as such was not pro-Greek but aimed to protect British commerce from piracy and to hold the Greeks accountable for such actions.[68] Sadiq-Effendi did not miss the opportunity to ask Strangford whether Canning was now prepared to 'allow the right of America to recognise Irish rebels as belligerents'.[69] When Metternich complained, Canning's reaction was that the Greeks had acquired 'a certain degree of force and consistency' and 'monstrous consequences' would follow from treating them as pirates, adding '[c]an it be necessary to suggest the advantage to humanity of bringing within the regulated limits of civilised war, a contest which was marked on its outset on both sides, with disgusting barbarities?'[70]

The Greeks, in spite of their poor organization and vicious infighting, were able to hold their own even after the Ottomans had quelled Ali Pasha in Yannina and had sent abundant forces to the south. Thus, in January 1824 the Sultan took 'a bold but desperate step'[71] and summoned the semi-independent Muhammad Ali Pasha, the governor of Egypt, to subdue the Greeks. He agreed to send his son, Ibrahim Pasha, as head of an army and navy. The move, though successful militarily, was to prove a grave mistake.

In the same month (January 1824), Russia took the initiative with a *mémoire* proposing the establishment of three autonomous Greek principalities. The proposal was discussed in two conferences at St Petersburg (June 1824–March 1825). Britain chose not to participate, hoping that the Russian proposal would not fly. The Russian scheme fell short of the Greek demand for independence but provided more territory than the Greeks would have been able to secure though their own efforts.[72]

The Porte did not accept the Russian proposal and Mavrokordatos (the Anglophile acting as Greek Foreign Minister) sent a letter to Canning rejecting it and appealing for British support. Canning replied (in December 1824) reiterating British neutrality but hinted that Britain might mediate in the future and would not be party to an agreement unacceptable to the Greeks.[73]

Meanwhile, a unique event was to create a sensation, reviving the waning international public interest in the Greek cause. Byron, the idol of literary Europe and America, had arrived in Messolonghi in January 1824, inspiring romantic Byronists across Europe to join him. The Porte had asked Canning to shelve Byron's arrival but he had turned a deaf ear.[74] After a perilous journey by ship from the Ionian Islands, Byron, in scarlet military uniform, set foot in Messolonghi to a hero's welcome by an enthusiastic crowd and was made head of the Greek and philhellene army in western Greece, known as the Byron Brigade. His motley brigade saw no military action but his mere presence 'electrified' the Greeks[75] and acted as a 'talisman'[76] internationally. Byron, while in Messolonghi, displayed practical spirit and assisted the Greek cause both financially and organizationally. The Byron magic was to reach its apogee a hundred days later when he 'died immortally'[77] from illness (19 April 1824). His death assured the Greek cause

Ibrahim and the barbarization rumour

Ibrahim landed in the Peloponnese on 24 February 1825 and embarked upon a campaign of conquest and devastation (though initially he refrained from indiscriminate killings[79]) with the Greeks no match for his military acumen and small but well disciplined army.[80] By the end of the year there were only some pockets of resistance left. Only great power intervention could save the Greeks. Indeed, they 'were to be rescued, though in an unplanned and even reluctant way, by the great powers'.[81]

The Greeks, in desperation, placed themselves in 1825, by an 'Act of Submission', under the protection in turn of Britain, France and Russia, none of which accepted it. A Greek delegation met Canning (29 September 1825), who dismissed the protectorate idea but said that 'there might be a point in the contest when Great Britain would promote a fair and safe compromise'.[82] The Greek deputies' reaction was 'independence or death'.[83]

The idea of British mediation matured in the mind of Canning, preferably Britain on its own but if that proved impossible then together with Russia. He sent his cousin, Stratford Canning, to be the new ambassador to Constantinople,[84] with instructions to convince the Porte of the need for British mediation.[85]

At this juncture an ugly hearsay gave rise to a sense of urgency: that Ibrahim intended to depopulate the Peloponnese and re-people it with Muslims.[86] The Russian ambassador in London, Christopher Lieven, and his formidable wife, Dorothea Lieven, told Canning at a meeting in Seaford (25 October 1825) that the 'Court of Russia, had positive information that ... an agreement was entered into by the Porte with the Pasha of Egypt ... to remove the whole Greek population, carrying them off into slavery in Egypt or elsewhere, and to re-people the country with Egyptians and others of the Mohammedan religion'.[87]

The 'barbarization project' was almost certainly smoke without a fire but it was crucial in spurring eventual military intervention. Canning could hardly treat such a monstrosity lightly. As he put it, 'supposing the fact to be true' it would not be possible 'to justify to the country a continued abstinence from interposition'.[88] According to Granville Stapleton, Canning's secretary and confidant, it was then that he opted for the use of force 'if necessary to prevent the consummation of this atrocious design'.[89]

Canning asked Stratford to see whether there was truth in the rumour and 'to declare in the most distinct terms to the Porte that Great Britain would not permit the execution of a system of depopulation'.[90] The British admiral in the Mediterranean was instructed to meet Ibrahim and to demand 'an explicit disavowal ... or a formal renunciation of it, if ever entertained'.[91] Otherwise 'effectual means will be taken' by the British navy to prevent 'the accomplishment of so unwarrantable a project'.[92] Ibrahim denied any such design[93] and so did the Reis-Effendi, who referred to it to Stratford as 'imbecility'.[94] But the pro-Greek Stratford wrote to the Foreign Office to say that Ibrahim 'acted on a system little short of extermination … and there was room to apprehend that many of his prisoners had been sent into Egypt as slaves, the children, it was asserted, being made to embrace the Mahommedan Faith'.[95]

International agreements in St Petersburg and London

The St Petersburg Protocol and its aftermath

In the last months of 1825 Alexander contemplated war to save the Greeks.[96] But he died unexpectedly (in December 1825) and was succeeded by his younger brother, Nicholas I, who took over in the midst of the Decembrist revolt.

The new Tsar tried to use the Greek question to Russia's advantage and, if need be, he intended to act alone, even though he despised the Greeks as rebels against legitimate authority.[97] Under the circumstances, Canning decided to act quickly, jointly with Russia.[98] He persuaded the Duke of Wellington to undertake a delicate mission to St Petersburg with two objectives: to avert a war by smoothing Russo-Ottoman differences; and to arrive at a common line of action on the Greek question. Ibrahim's atrocities and the barbarization project were to be the justification for their common action.[99]

Wellington succeeded in his second task (the Greek question) but not in the first. Nicholas appeared to be on a war footing in relation to the Ottoman Empire and unconcerned with the Greek question. But agreement began to take shape when Lieven arrived and acted as the main protagonist on the Russian side. The final text was ready and signed on 4 April 1826 by Wellington and by both Nesselrode and Lieven.[100]

The St Petersburg Protocol offered mediation to the Porte, which, if accepted, would to lead to an autonomous Greece tributary to the Sultan. If the Porte did not agree, mediation and autonomy were to remain on the table. A self-denying clause was included, renouncing any 'augmentation of territory, any exclusive influence' or commercial advantage. There was also mention of 'intervention whether jointly or separately between the Porte and the Greeks', a Russian clause, if mediation failed.[101]

In the meantime, Messolonghi fell to the Egyptians and Ottomans. The conquest of a town famous due to Byron created a stir across Europe, with an array of poems, musical plays, essays and sermons. Victor Hugo wrote a macabre poem, 'The Seraglio Heads', in which Ibrahim is presented as sending to the Sultan 6,000 severed heads. Delacroix painted his famous *Grèce sur les ruines de Missolonghi*, and the next year the Paris Salon exhibited twenty-one paintings with Greek themes. Ibrahim may have conquered the town, but Messolonghi had become a symbol for European public opinion, and more pressure was put on governments to rescue the Greeks.[102]

Messolonghi's impact was great in France, which until then had followed an equivocal policy. Despite sympathy among the educated public for the Greeks, the French government had followed a policy of neutrality but in fact provided assistance to Egypt, with which links had existed for decades (French officers and advisers had modernized Egypt's army and navy). France, through Egypt, was influential in the Levant at the expense of Britain and Russia.

In 1825 the French philhellenic spirit became intense, bringing together the various bitter divisions of Restoration France: Liberals, Bonapartists as well as ultra-Royalists and Royalists, such as Chateaubriand, the ex-Foreign Minister. The conservatives were mainly motivated by the suffering of Christians, the liberals by the call for national liberation. Chateaubriand, in his influential *Note en Grèce* (1825), urged the French King and other monarchs: 'Will our century watch hordes of savages extinguish civilization at its rebirth on the tomb of a people who civilized the world? Will Christendom calmly allow Turks to strangle Christians?'[103] In the Comité grec de Paris, set up in 1825, one sees major figures apart from Chateaubriand and men of arts and letters: Lafayette, the dukes de Broglie, de Dalberg, de Laborde and other members of the higher French aristocracy, generals Sébastiani (Foreign Minister 1830–32), Gérard, Mathieu and Dumas, and bankers and industrialists Laffitte, Ternaux and Casimir-Périer. Eventually France withdrew its assistance to the Egyptians and remained neutral until the end of 1827. More generally the Greek case, as previously with the Spanish crisis of 1823, provided the opportunity for France to re-enter the scene as a great power.[104]

Ibrahim had almost total control of the Peloponnese and of the north of the Gulf of Corinth, having captured Athens after a long siege. But the Greeks remained dominant in the sea now with the assistance of the legendary Lord Cochrane, the ex-British officer Captain Hastings with the *Karteria* (one of the first steamships to engage in combat), Captain Hamilton with the British warship the *Cambrian* and the French Rear Admiral de Rigny, who supported the Greeks to the extent permitted by France's neutrality. Soon the British Vice Admiral Codrington was to arrive on the scene, whose role was to prove decisive.[105]

Ambassadors Stratford and Ribeaupierre (Russia) put pressure on the new Ottoman Foreign Minister, Pertev-Effendi (a hard-liner who had replaced moderate Saida-Effendi in March 1826[106]), to accept the mediation offered by the Protocol. Pertev-Effendi rejected it, adding that it was unacceptable on Muslim religious grounds as well.[107]

Canning proposed to the Tsar common action: 'to seize the first occasion of recognizing as an independent State such portion of her [Greece's] territory as should have freed itself from Turkish dominion',[108] but that was too radical for

Nicholas to accept.[109] The pressure on the Porte produced the Convention of Akkermann (October 1826), with the Porte giving in to various Russian demands unrelated to the Greek question.[110]

The Treaty of London

Meanwhile, efforts were being made to convince the other three powers to accede to the Protocol but only France (King Charles X, Premier de Villèle) agreed to join, and then only provided the Protocol was turned into a treaty.[111] Canning (who had been privately in Paris for weeks to lobby the French) readily accepted and so did Lieven. Wellington was decidedly against this course of action, however.[112] Canning wrote to Lieven to say 'a contest so ferocious ... so intolerable to civilized Europe, justifies extraordinary intervention, and renders lawful any expedients short of positive hostility'.[113]

The negotiations started with France tabling the first draft of the Treaty, which did not include means of enforcement (January 1827). A Russian draft (March) envisaged a naval blockade if the Porte was unyielding and it implied the use of armed force. British Prime Minister Liverpool was taken ill with paralysis; after a brief tussle between Wellington and Canning, the latter become Prime Minister. On 6 July 1827 the Treaty of London was signed, after six months of acrimonious deliberations between Dudley, the new British Foreign Secretary, Lieven and Polignac (the French ambassador in London). The Treaty followed the lines of the Protocol.[114]

The official justification of the Treaty was stated in the preamble: 'putting an end to the sanguinary struggle' which has led to 'the disorders of anarchy'; 'fresh impediments to the commerce of the States of Europe and gives opportunity for acts of Piracy'; 'putting a stop to the effusion of blood'; 're-establish peace between the contending parties by means of an arrangement called for, no less by sentiments of humanity, than by interests for the tranquillity of Europe'.[115] Although stopping the effusion of blood was not the only justification, it is probably the first time in history that such concern was invoked *expressis verbis* as 'a justification for intervention'.[116]

The Treaty offered three-power mediation, called for an immediate armistice and provided for the creation of Greece as 'a dependency of Turkey'. If one of the contending parties or both declined, the powers 'will, nevertheless, continue to pursue the work of pacification'.[117]

The Treaty included a secret clause (leaked to *The Times*) to the effect that the three powers 'will jointly exert all their efforts to accomplish the object of such armistice, without, however, taking any part in the hostilities between the two contending parties'.[118] In the text, the various instructions to the three admirals boiled down to the following: if the Ottomans refused an armistice, they were to 'observe extreme care to prevent the measures which you shall adopt against the

Ottoman marine from degenerating into hostilities' and 'not to make use of that force unless the Turks persist in forcing the passages which they [the admirals] have intercepted'.[119]

How could the admirals accomplish their task without hostilities? According to Marriott, '[e]ither the matter had not been clearly thought out, or there was a deliberate intention to leave the Gordian knot to be cut by the Executive Officers of the Powers', that is, the three admirals in the Levant.[120] As wryly put by Woodhouse: 'This directive [to the admirals], covering all contingencies and none, bears the stigmata of official drafting by men who had shut their eyes to facts and hoped for the best. It shifted all ill-defined responsibility to the Admirals, and left to them the glory and the blame'.[121] The lack of clarity is probably due to the fact that the Treaty was 'a compromise between a strictly impartial mediation and an open intervention on behalf of the Greeks'.[122]

The *Realpolitik* reasons for the Treaty were for France to keep Britain and Russia in check; Britain to restrain Russia from going to war and gaining advantage from the situation; and Russia to avail itself of the opportunity to gain advantages. As Crawley has put it, 'the mutual suspicion of the Powers was the Greeks' best security: no one of them was concerned to make Greece an independent State (Canning himself gave no clear indication of it) but each was driven in that direction by the fear of allowing the other an excuse for further interference'.[123]

By July 1827, when the Treaty was signed, 'the war was as good as won' by the Ottomans and Egyptians, but, as Turkish scholars have argued, the victory 'was snatched out' of their hands.[124]

The Greeks wisely accepted the armistice and mediation, though in practice they did not adhere to the armistice, with the justification that Ibrahim continued to ravage the country.[125] The provisional Greek government nominated two Britons to head the Greek forces: Cochrane the navy, and ex-general Church the army. Cochrane and Church, together with Blanquière and Hamilton, were instrumental in convincing the rival Greeks factions (and even the pro-British Mavrokordatos) that the wisest option was to nominate Capodistrias as President.[126]

The ambassadors of the three powers, Stratford, Ribeaupierre and Guilleminot (France), tried to convince Foreign Minister Pertev-Effendi to accept a cease-fire and mediation, and on 12 August 1827 gave only fourteen days to the Porte to come up with an answer. On the fourteenth day the reaction of the Porte was negative. The ambassadors sent a verbal note to Pertev-Effendi making it clear that their governments intended to implement the armistice even without the approval of the Porte, but nothing came of this.[127]

Metternich, realizing that the Ottomans were in a quandary, offered mediation to save them, which was enthusiastically accepted by the Divan (Ottoman cabinet) and the Sultan, on 23 October 1827. But unfortunately for the Ottomans, the Battle of Navarino had taken place a few days earlier.[128]

Navarino and the years 1828–32

Navarino and its aftermath

Let us see what had transpired. Following the Porte's rejection, the admirals were instructed by the Constantinople ambassadors to enforce the armistice.[129] The immediate concern of the admirals was to use their ships effectively to prevent the arrival of fresh Egyptian troops and supplies, and to do so without provoking hostilities.[130] Codrington asked Stratford for clarification, whose reply (1 September) was that 'the prevention of supplies is ultimately to be enforced, if necessary, and when all other means are exhausted, by cannon shot'.[131]

Codrington and de Rigny met Ibrahim at Navarino (on 25 September 1827) and he seemed forthcoming regarding an armistice[132] but he continued his devastating campaign against the Greeks by land, which was now even more destructive than before.[133] Following the arrival of the Russian squadron under Rear Admiral Heiden, the three admirals agreed to enter the bay 'without effusion of blood and without hostilities, but simply by the imposing presence of the squadrons', as the only way to fulfil their mandate, enforce an armistice and halt Ibrahim's onslaught.[134]

The three squadrons (first the British, followed by the French and Russian) entered Navarino on 20 October 1827, outnumbered by 1,298 to 2,000 Ottoman guns and with half the number of ships of the Egyptian and Ottoman fleets. The first shot was fired by their opponents, apparently without instructions. The outcome is well known: the annihilation of the Egyptian and Ottoman fleets.[135] Navarino, the last major naval battle fought under sail, in eighteenth-century battle conditions, has passed into legend, not least in the lore of humanitarian intervention. Navarino is retrospectively regarded as the first instance of use of force for humanitarian purposes as we understand it today,[136] but a sound case could be made that its humanitarian rationale is unconvincing.[137] Retrospective or not, convincing or not, as early as the end of the 1820s the intervention of Navarino was labelled '*d'humanité*' in several official documents.[138]

Undoubtedly the battle had come about 'by accident rather than design'[139] but it 'strengthened enormously the position of the Greeks'.[140] In fact the battle itself brought no immediate relief to the Greeks: Ibrahim remained entrenched in the Peloponnese for more than a year. The real effect of Navarino in delivering the Greeks took time to materialize, but one thing is certain: it made it almost impossible for the three powers to change track, even if they wanted to, as did Britain under Wellington.[141]

The news of the battle was received with amazement in Europe. The French public were delighted, though not the government, the Russians were jubilant, the Austrians appalled and the British uneasy. The Ottomans called it a 'revolting outrage' and denounced the Convention of Akkermann.[142] For Metternich it was a 'frightful catastrophe'.[143] Foreign Secretary Dudley addressed ten queries to Codrington regarding the battle and whether he had followed instructions, to which the admiral answered point by point.[144] When Wellington formed his government in January 1828, the speech from the throne (which he had drafted) used the famous words 'untoward event'.[145] The speech was greeted with uproar in both Houses, with most speakers praising Codrington. Wellington tried to explain away the phrase by claiming he meant 'unexpected' or 'unfortunate'.[146]

The Ottoman government demanded condemnation of the 'tragic episode' as unintended, compensation and the three powers to allow the Porte to treat the matter for what it was, an internal affair. The three ambassadors replied that the battle had indeed been unintended but the Ottomans had first opened fire; their states desired friendly relations with the Porte, provided there was an armistice and mediation; and the London Treaty was aimed at European peace and was to the benefit of the Ottoman Empire.[147]

Pertev-Effendi's reaction was that only the submission of the *Rum* would resolve the question; upon their submission they would be pardoned, despite their crimes of treason and rebellion. 'Greece', he asserted, does not exist, the *Rum* are simply a *millet* headed by their patriarch. When Guilleminot questioned whether one can speak of submission after such a long struggle, Pertev-Effendi retorted that 'it is well known what has kept the rebellion alive', implying foreign encouragement.[148]

Mahmud for his part made the following concessions (as he saw them): he would drop his demand for the rebels to pay compensation for the costs of the war, and, after their submission, he would relieve them of paying capital taxes for a year. The ambassadors made a last-ditch attempt at compromise, calling for abandonment of warfare and the acceptance of the autonomy status of the Greeks as provided by the London Treaty, but the Divan remained adamant and the three ambassadors left the Ottoman capital (December 1827).[149]

Events of 1828–32

By the end of 1827 the fate of Greece was sealed, or so it seems with the benefit of hindsight, in view of the intrusive London Treaty, Navarino, Ottoman intransigence, Russia's willingness to go to war, unremitting pressure from France on its two allies to allow France to send an expeditionary force to expel Ibrahim, and Capodistrias in charge, with his great diplomatic skills and international links. Only two things remained unresolved: whether Greece was to be autonomous or independent, and its geographical limits. Yet it took three more gruelling years to make the Greek dream and the Ottoman nightmare a reality. If one absence was deeply felt in the Greek camp it was that of Canning, especially from the moment Wellington took over.

Indeed, the Iron Duke did his best to undo the consequences of the London Treaty and Navarino. His hostility was based on his conviction that Greece was destined to become a maritime state and from this he mistakenly surmised that the new state was bound to be antagonistic towards Britain and to become 'a Russian dependency'.[150] His fear of Russia made Britain openly pro-Ottoman and this encouraged the Sultan to remain defiant.[151] Thus all the dividends of years of incremental diplomacy by Canning were thrown overboard and thereafter Britain played second fiddle to Russia and France in the Greek affair.[152]

With Russia and France standing firm, the Sultan opted for war with Russia instead of accepting the inevitable, namely Greek autonomy. Had Mahmud acted with restraint and bent with the wind after Navarino – even though Navarino was admittedly 'rather provoking'[153] – the Ottomans would have avoided an unwinnable war with Russia. Actually, moderation had been advised in a memorandum to the Sultan from a group of senior officials, headed by the eminent poet Izzet Mollâ and Hamid Bey (a former Reis-Effendi). The reasoning of the peace lobby was countered by the war lobby under Pertev-Effendi, which advocated intransigence in a memorandum that was endorsed by the Sultan.[154]

Metternich, in a last attempt to avoid a war that was bound to go Russia's way, proposed (15 March 1828) to 'invite the Porte to recognise the autonomy of Peloponnese and Islands only' and on refusal 'to recognise their entire independence'.[155] The Tsar was indignant with this Austrian proposal. As he put it, 'I detest, I abhor the Greeks, I consider them as revolted subjects and I do not desire their independence; Austria has abandoned her principles'.[156]

Meanwhile, France was able to obtain Wellington's reluctant consent for the sending of a French expeditionary force in the name of the three allies. The force of some 14,000 under General Nicolas Maison arrived in the Peloponnese in September 1828. Maison's mission, to expel Ibrahim's forces, was achieved almost without firing a shot, with only some mock sieges and momentary resistance in only two cases.[157]

The reconvened London Conference instructed the three former ambassadors to the Porte to suggest frontiers for Greece and an ambassadors' conference was convened on the island of Poros (September–December 1828), urged along by President Capodistrias. The ambassadors' report (12 December 1828) recommended the frontier run from the Gulf of Volos (in the east) to the Gulf of Arta (in the west), incorporating the large island of Euboea. The faraway islands of Samos and Crete were also suggested for inclusion. The report was not accepted as such but instead as a basis for negotiations (22 March 1829), with Samos and Crete not included. Stratford resigned his embassy in disgust.[158]

The Russo-Ottoman war which had started in April 1828 raged on much longer than had been anticipated, due to stiff resistance by the Ottomans. When the victorious Russian army entered Adrianople in August 1829 a committee under the head of the Russian Council of Ministers reached the conclusion that 'the advantages of the preservation of the Ottoman Empire outweigh its disadvantages', but if the Empire collapsed in the future Russia must take 'the most energetic measures to ensure that the exit from the Black Sea is not seized by any other power whatsoever'.¹⁵⁹ The committee also considered but did not adopt a previous plan by Capodistrias for the creation of a Balkan confederation of five independent states (Dacia, Serbia, Macedonia, Epirus and Greece).¹⁶⁰

The Treaty of Adrianople (14 September 1829) made the Porte accept an autonomous Greece. This time it was the turn of Capodistrias to reject the tributary status. Now Metternich and Wellington opted for an independent Greece, for they feared that Russian influence would be greater with Greek autonomy. The new British government of Lord Grey, with Lord Palmerston as Foreign Secretary, was more favourable to the Greeks.¹⁶¹

On 3 February 1930, at the London Conference, a protocol was signed making Greece independent. Another London protocol (8 April 1830) referred to the 'frightful calamities to humanity', which made the internationalization of the problem inevitable.¹⁶² Following the assassination of Capodistrias in 1831, Greece became a kingdom under Otto, the son of Ludwig of Bavaria. In 7 May 1832 a treaty was signed by the three powers and Bavaria which fixed the frontier as proposed – between the Gulf of Volos and the Gulf of Arta. Finally, Greek independence and its frontiers were accepted by the Porte in a convention signed in Constantinople (21 July 1832).¹⁶³

Motives for intervention and views of publicists

As we have seen, one of the official justifications for the three-power intervention concerned humanitarian factors. And had it not been for the humanitarian plight and identification with the Greeks among the educated publics in Britain, Russia and France, none of the three states would have contemplated intervening. As the war dragged on and the Greeks held their own, strategic, balance-of-power and economic concerns came to the fore, above all not to allow any of three powers to gain advantage from the Greek case. The crisis, the gravest until then of the so-called Eastern Question, namely the fate of the Ottoman Empire in decline, could not but be a key concern of the great powers. For Russia it was also a question of preserving its prestige and influence among the Balkan Christians.¹⁶⁴

Among publicists the pace was set by Wheaton as early as 1836, who asserted that this intervention was 'more justifiable' than other cases for it rescued 'a whole nation, not merely from religious persecution, but from the cruel alternative of being transported from their native land, or exterminated by their merciless oppressors'.¹⁶⁵ His conclusion is worth stressing: 'The interference of the Christian powers, to put an end to this bloody contest might, therefore, have been safely rested upon this ground alone [i.e. the ground of what he calls "the right of human nature"] without appealing to the interests of commerce and of the repose of Europe, which, as well as the interests of humanity, are alluded to in the treaty'.¹⁶⁶ Similarly Rougier pointed out that '[i]t is reasons of humanity in the widest sense of the word ... and of moral dignity which dictated this intervention of the powers ... in the general interest of Europe and civilisation. But the reasons of humanity were not yet regarded in that epoch as a just cause for intervention, thus the Treaty of London mentions it timidly'.[167]

On the whole, from the 1830s until the 1930s publicists who were advocates of humanitarian intervention referred approvingly to this intervention (we have identified twenty such publicists) as motivated solely or mainly by humanitarian reasons (this is the majority view) or at least partly by humanitarian reasons (the minority view).[168] John Stuart Mill also referred approvingly to intervention on behalf of the Greeks on humanitarian grounds (see chapter 5).

Surprisingly, in the nineteenth century even some of the jurists opposed to humanitarian intervention condone this one case on humanitarian or moral grounds (at least eight of them).[169] For instance, Calvo stated (in 1870) that 'the intervention in favour of Greece was dictated by moral and political considerations of the highest and most respectable order'.[170] Even more surprising is the view expressed by Senior, one of the earliest opponents of humanitarian intervention, put forward eleven years after the independence of Greece:[171]

> The treaty of 1827 ... was ... the most disinterested interference of sovereigns in behalf [sic] of a people that has occurred in modern times.... The long duration of the contest – the ferocity with which it was carried on by the Turks – the apparent success of Greece against her gigantic enemy until she was crushed by the invasion from Egypt – the fear of having to witness the utter extirpation of a Christian population by Mohametans, that Christian population being the descendants of those to whom the world owes its civilization; – all these were motives which it would have been hard to withstand, even if the interference had been a matter of difficulty or danger.

In Senior's assertion one sees almost all the grounds of the publicists (from the 1830s until the 1930s) justifying the humanitarian intervention (HI). They are as follows: (1) protracted barbarous war, the culprits being the 'Turks' and Egyptians (claimed by eleven pro-HI publicists and four anti-HI); (2) relative disinterestedness on the part of the three intervening states, the predominant aim being to stop the 'effusion of blood' (claimed by fourteen pro-HI and five anti-HI); (3) the barbarization project and danger of annihilation of the Greeks (claimed by two pro-HI and two anti-HI); (4) 'Turkish' despotism, oppression and religious persecution (claimed by six pro-HI and one anti-HI); and (5) debt of Europe and humankind to the ancestors of the Greeks (claimed by three pro-HI and one anti-HI).

The views of two well known supporters of humanitarian intervention are worth referring to. According to Harcourt:[172]

> The Battle of Navarino may have been an 'untoward event,' but it was the natural and almost inevitable consequence of a forcible intervention to prevent the Turkish

Government from reducing its subjects to submission. The emancipation of Greece, effected by Europe, was a high act of policy above and beyond the domain of law. As an act of policy, it may have been, and probably was, justifiable.

According to Lawrence:[173]

> The contest between them [the Greeks] and their Turkish oppressors had gone on for many years, and had been marked throughout by the most horrible barbarities. It seemed as if it would end in the extermination of the whole Greek race. The intervention of the three powers preserved a people to whom civilization owned so much and laid the foundations of a new order in Southeastern Europe, which, with all its defects, is infinitely preferable to the chaos of weltering barbarism that immediately preceded it.

The view of a prominent opponent of humanitarian intervention is also worth mentioning. Thomas Alfred Walker, writing in the 1890s, criticized intervening on the 'dictates of humanity' as opening 'a wide door to outrage'[174] but added:[175]

> On the other hand, the cause of humanity was undoubtedly really served by that intervention of the Powers which led to the establishment of the modern kingdom of Greece. It was not until after several years of singularly bloody struggle and the enactment of a long series of frightful scenes of horror, when it became evident that the alternative offered to Europe was the independence or the annihilation of the Greeks, that Great Britain, France and Russia agreed to combine their efforts.

After 1945 the jurists supportive of humanitarian intervention also tend to refer to the Greek case as the first such instance.[176] But those opposed, contrary to before, do not regard it as humanitarian. Ian Brownlie, for instance, argues that the collective intervention in Greece is an example of 'ex post factoism', for '[t]he governments of the time did not use a legal justification' for intervening, as no such right existed then.[177] For others, their reading of the official stance on intervention leads them to the conclusion that humanitarian reasons were non-existent or secondary.[178]

Concluding remarks

The Greek case, apart from being regarded as the first case of humanitarian intervention, providing the springboard for the emergence of the new concept, has a bearing on the evolution of international norms and rules of conduct in instances of humanitarian plights in a number of ways.

First is the exceptional overruling of the *grundnorms* of sovereignty and non-intervention in instances of 'effusion of blood' that shake the moral consciousness of humankind.

Second is the multilateral character of the intervention, in this case an 'alliance of the willing', of three of the five powers.

Third, in this first case one sees most of the repertoire of international involvement on humanitarian grounds: consultation of the powers, peremptory demands made of the guilty state (to halt barbarities and distinguish between guilty and innocent), formal great power agreements, calls for a cease-fire, mediation attempts, a peace conference, an important battle, a peacekeeping force and, at the end, an all-out war by one of the powers condoned by the rest.

Fourth is the reticence or hostility of the powers on instrumental *Realpolitik* grounds, and when the need for intervention becomes more evident, a mixture of humanitarian and instrumental motives. Moreover, there is a deliberate attempt to check abuse by including self-denying clauses in the relevant texts.

Fifth, it is a clear manifestation of the civilized–barbarians binary that was to dominate the scene until 1914: the 'civilized Christians' as opposed to the Muslim 'barbarian Other', with the latter prone to committing slaughters and atrocities. The massacres of Muslims were swept under the carpet, as if the Muslim victims of the Christians were less human.[179]

Last but not least is the role played by civil society across Europe and in North America in spurring intervention on humanitarian and other ethical grounds, in this case of members of the elite, politicians, thinkers, writers, poets and artists (including celebrities), which was unprecedented and a sign of things to come.

Notes

1   J. R. Vincent, *Nonintervention and International Order* (Princeton: Princeton University Press, 1974), 74.
2   Ibid., 73, 74, 80; C. Holbraad, *The Concert of Europe: A Study in German and British International Theory 1815–1914* (London: Longman, 1970), 22–34; W. G. Grewe, *The Epochs of International Law* (Berlin: Walter de Gruyter, 2000, translated and revised by M. Byers), 488.
3   Quoted in M. Wight, 'Western Values in International Relations', in H. Butterfield and M. Wight (eds), *Diplomatic Investigations: Essays in the Theory of International Politics* (London: Allen and Unwin, 1966), 118. For Castlereagh's approach regarding nonintervention, see Vincent, *Nonintervention and International Order*, 73–83.
4   P. K. Grimsted, *The Foreign Ministers of Alexander I: Political Attitudes and the Conduct of Russian Diplomacy, 1801–1825* (Berkeley: University of California Press, 1969), 247–8.
5   H. Temperley, *The Foreign Policy of Canning 1822–1827* (London: Frank Cass, 1966) [1925].
6   R. Little, *Intervention: External Involvement in Civil Wars* (London: Martin Robertson, 1975), 18, 23–4.
7   'Non-intervention is a diplomatic and enigmatic word which means more or less the same thing as intervention'. In Granville Stapleton, *Intervention and Non-Intervention or the Foreign Policy of Great Britain from 1790 to 1865* (London: John Murray, 1866), 15. For a slightly different version, with the words *métaphysique et politique* (metaphysical and political), see Wight, 'Western Values in International Relations', 115.
8   J. W. Garner. 'Recognition of Belligerency', *American Journal of International Law*, 32:1 (1938), 106–13; R. A. Falk, 'Janus Tormented: The International Law of Internal Law', in

J. N. Rosenau (ed.), *International Aspects of Civil Strife* (Princeton: Princeton University Press, 1964), 194–209.
9   Garner, 'Recognition of Belligerency', 111–13.
10 G. Finlay, *History of the Greek Revolution* (London: William Blackwood and Sons, 1861), vol. I, 20, 119–20; L. S. Stavrianos, *The Balkans Since 1453* (London: Hurst, 2000) [1958], 211–12, 278.
11 Stavrianos, *The Balkans Since 1453*, 269–76; R. Clogg, *A Concise History of Greece* (Cambridge: Cambridge University Press, 1992), 21–30.
12 T. Gordon, *History of the Greek Revolution* (Edinburgh: William Blackwood, 1844, 2nd edition) [1832], vol. I, 40–8, 50; Finlay, *History of the Greek Revolution*, vol. I, 120; T. C. Prousis, *Russian Society and the Greek Revolution* (DeKalb: Northern Illinois University Press, 1994), 18–23; D. Brewer, *The Greek War of Independence: The Struggle for Freedom from Ottoman Oppression and the Birth of the Modern Greek Nation* (Woodstock: Overlook Press, 2001), 26–7; B. Jelavich, *Russia's Balkan Entanglements 1806–1914* (Cambridge: Cambridge University Press, 1991), 51.
13 P. K. Grimsted, 'Capodistrias and a "New Order" for Restoration Europe: The "Liberal Ideas" of a Russian Foreign Minister', *Journal of Modern History*, 40:2 (1968), 170–3, 180–5, 190–2; Grimsted, *The Foreign Ministers of Alexander I*, 226, 229, 233–5, 238; C. M. Woodhouse, *Capodistria: The Founder of Greek Independence* (London: Oxford University Press, 1973), 149–52, 185–6, 189.
14 Finlay, *History of the Greek Revolution*, vol. I, 135.
15 'Zapiska Grafa Ioanna Kapodistria o ego sluzhebnoj dejatel'nosti', Geneva, 12/24 December 1826 [Memorandum of Count Ioannis Capodistrias on his official activity], *Sbornik Russkogo Istoricheskogo Obshchestvo* [Collection of the Russian Historical Society], vol. III (St Petersburg, 1868), 215–20 (henceforth 'Capodistrias Memorandum').
16 Woodhouse, *Capodistria*, 164–6, 169, 180, 218–30; Finlay, *History of the Greek Revolution*, vol. I, 135–7; M. S. Anderson, *The Eastern Question, 1774–1923: A Study in International Relations* (London: Macmillan, 1966), 51–2; Brewer, *The Greek War of Independence*, 31–5; Prousis, *Russian Society and the Greek Revolution*, 20–3.
17 C. M. Woodhouse, *The Greek War of Independence* (London: Hutchinson's University Library, 1952), 45.
18 Ibid., 45, 54; R. B. Mowat, *A History of European Diplomacy, 1815–1914* (London: Edward Arnold, 1922), 32; J. A. R. Marriott, *George Canning and His Times: A Political Study* (London: John Murray, 1903), 83; H. Nicolson, *The Congress of Vienna: A Study in Allied Unity, 1812–1822* (London: Methuen, 1946), 259–63, 270.
19 Woodhouse, *The Greek War of Independence*, 54.
20 J. A. R. Marriott, *The Eastern Question: An Historical Study in European Diplomacy* (Oxford: Clarendon Press, 1918), 194.
21 Capodistrias Memorandum, 215–20, 224–6, 228–9, 239–42, 256–7; Woodhouse, *Capodistria*, 163, 174, 180, 191, 198, 201; D. C. Fleming, *John Capodistrias and the Conference of London (1828–1831)* (Thessaloniki: Institute for Balkan Studies, 1970), 6.
22 Stavrianos, *The Balkans Since 1453*, 149–50, 280–1.
23 Quoted in Woodhouse, *Capodistria*, 252.
24 Marriott, *The Eastern Question*, 197.
25 Gordon, *History of the Greek Revolution*, vol. I, 96–124, 132–3; Finlay, *History of the Greek Revolution*, vol. I, 140–70; W. A. Phillips, *The War of Greek Independence* (London: Smith, Elder and Co., 1897), 32–43; Prousis, *Russian Society and the Greek Revolution*, 26–8; Brewer, *The Greek War of Independence*, 51–61.

26 Gordon, *History of the Greek Revolution*, vol. I, 57–8, 77, 86; D. Dakin, *The Greek Struggle for Independence, 1821–1833* (London: B. T. Batsford, 1973), 27–8; Anderson, *The Eastern Question*, 53–4; Clogg, *A Concise History of Greece*, 33.
27 Woodhouse, *Capodistria*, 234, 241, 245; Jelavich, *Russia's Balkan Entanglements*, 53; A. Zorin, '"Star of the East": The Holy Alliance and European Mysticism', *Kritika: Explorations in Russian and Eurasian History*, 4:2 (2003), 338.
28 R. Albrecht-Carrié, *A Diplomatic History of Europe Since the Congress of Vienna* (London: Methuen, 1958), 40.
29 According to a Prussian *mémoire* (whose author was the historian Ancillon) the Sultan's despotism was a travesty of government and no duty existed to obey it by the Greeks. See A. von Prokesch-Osten, *Istoria tis epanastaseos ton Ellinon kata tou Othomanikou kratous en etei 1821* (Athens: Athinas, 1868, translated from the German by G. E. Antoniades), vol. I, 155–6, n*. See also H. A. Kissinger, *A World Restored* (Gloucester: Peter Smith, 1973), 290, 296; C. Webster, *The Foreign Policy of Castlereagh 1815–1822* (London: G. Bell and Sons, 1963), 363.
30 *Ibid.*, 360–1; Marriott, *The Eastern Question*, 206; G. D. Clayton, *Britain and the Eastern Question: Missolonghi to Gallipoli* (London: Lion Library, 1971), 45; Nicolson, *The Congress of Vienna*, 271; C. W. Crawley, *The Question of Greek Independence: A Study of British Policy in the Near East, 1821–1933* (New York: Howard Fertig, 1973) [1930], 18–20.
31 Gordon, *History of the Greek Revolution*, vol. I, 39.
32 H. Erdem, '"Do Not Think of the Greeks as Agricultural Labourers": Ottoman Responses to the Greek War of Independence', in F. Birtek and T. Dragonas (eds), *Citizenship and the Nation-State in Greece and Turkey* (London: Routledge, 2005), 67–9, 76–7; H. Ş. Ilicak, 'The Revolt of Alexandros Ipsilantis and the Fate of the Fanariots in Ottoman Documents', in P. Pizanias (ed.), *I Elliniki Epanastasi tou 1821: ena evropaiko gegonos* (Athens: Kedros, 2009), 321–5, 328–30; Temperley, *The Foreign Policy of Canning*, 322–3.
33 Finlay, *History of the Greek Revolution*, vol. I, 172.
34 *Ibid.*, vol. I, 172, 181–8, 261–3; Phillips, *The War of Greek Independence*, 48, 55–61, 66–7; W. St Clair, *That Greece Might Still Be Free: The Philhellenes in the War of Independence* (Cambridge: Open Book, 2008) [1973], 1–2, 7, 12; D. Rodogno, *Against Massacre: Humanitarian Intervention in the Ottoman Empire, 1815–1914. The Emergence of a European Concept and International Practice* (Princeton: Princeton University Press, 2012), 65–6.
35 Finlay, *History of the Greek Revolution*, vol. I, 226–8, 38; Gordon, *History of the Greek Revolution*, vol. I, 185–90; Prokesch-Osten, *Istoria*, vol. I, 73, 85; Woodhouse, *The Greek War of Independence*, 51.
36 Finlay, *History of the Greek Revolution*, vol. I, 229–31, 238; Gordon, *History of the Greek Revolution*, vol. I, 185–8, 196; Prokesch-Osten, *Istoria*, vol. I, 77; Phillips, *The War of Greek Independence*, 77–8.
37 Prokesch-Osten, *Istoria*, vol. I, 85, 88–9.
38 Webster, *The Foreign Policy of Castlereagh*, 362; Woodhouse, *Capodistria*, 263–4; Dakin, *The Greek Struggle for Independence*, 142–3, 145; Jelavich, *Russia's Balkan Entanglements*, 57, 59; V. J. Puryear, *France and the Levant: From the Bourbon Restoration to the Peace of Kutiah* (Hamden: Archon Books, 1968), 28–9.
39 Prousis, *Russian Society and the Greek Revolution*, 26; Prokesch-Osten, *Istoria*, vol. I, 74–5, 81–2, 226, 245; Marriott, *The Eastern Question*, 206; Woodhouse, *Capodistria*, 17, 260–3, 269–78; Jelavich, *Russia's Balkan Entanglements*, 49–50, 53, 58, 64; D. MacKenzie, *Imperial Dreams, Harsh Realities: Tsarist Russian Foreign Policy, 1815–1917* (Forth Worth: Harcourt Brace College Publishers, 1994), 41.

40   Prousis, *Russian Society and the Greek Revolution*, 26.
41   Ibid., 30–2; Jelavich, *Russia's Balkan Entanglements*, 62, 64–5; Woodhouse, *Capodistria*, 260–78.
42   Webster, *The Foreign Policy of Castlereagh*, 360–1, 364.
43   Quoted in Capodistrias Memorandum, 269.
44   Ibid., 269–72.
45   Ibid., 285–6; Marriott, *The Eastern Question*, 205–7; Crawley, *The Question of Greek Independence*, 17–23; Woodhouse, *Capodistria*, 290–1; Prousis, *Russian Society and the Greek Revolution*, 33.
46   Gordon, *History of the Greek Revolution*, vol. I, 243–7; Finlay, *History of the Greek Revolution*, vol. I, 264–70; Phillips, *The War of Greek Independence*, 56, 60–1; St Clair, *That Greece Might Still Be Free*, 44–6; Brewer, *The Greek War of Independence*, 119–23; G. J. Bass, *Freedom's Battle: The Origins of Humanitarian Intervention* (New York: Vintage Books, 2009), 64–5.
47   Gordon, *History of the Greek Revolution*, vol. I, 358.
48   Quoted in Rodogno, *Against Massacre*, 69.
49   Gordon, *History of the Greek Revolution*, vol. I, 350–60; Finlay, *History of the Greek Revolution*, vol. I, 306–15; Woodhouse, *The Greek War of Independence*, 87–8; St Clair, *That Greece Might Still Be Free*, 78–82; Bass, *Freedom's Battle*, 67–75; Brewer, *The Greek War of Independence*, 154–67.
50   Ibid., 167.
51   Quoted in Prokesch-Osten, *Istoria*, vol. I, 186–7.
52   Ibid., 188–9.
53   Woodhouse, *Capodistria*, 299.
54   Finlay, *History of the Greek Revolution*, vol. II, 3–4; St Clair, *That Greece Might Still Be Free*, 13–91, 119–49, 263–76, 297–304; Woodhouse, *The Greek War of Independence*, 52–3, 89; C. M. Woodhouse, *The Philhellenes* (London: Doric, 1977); Marriott, *The Eastern Question*, 209–10; Mowat, *A History of European Diplomacy*, 46–7; Clayton, *Britain and the Eastern Question*, 46–7; Brewer, *The Greek War of Independence*, 137–53; Bass, *Freedom's Battle*, 52–5, 57–8, 60–3, 76–110.
55   See references above (note 54). For the stance of the Americans see details in Bass, *Freedom's Battle*, 88–99.
56   Quoted in St Clair, *That Greece Might Still Be Free*, 54.
57   Ibid., 13–22, 51–65; Marriott, *The Eastern Question*, 194, 204–5, 209–10; Albrecht-Carrié, *A Diplomatic History of Europe Since the Congress of Vienna*, 44.
58   Prousis, *Russian Society and the Greek Revolution*, xiii–ix, 3, 8–24, 30, 56, 84–158; T. C. Prousis, 'Russian Philorthodox Relief During the Greek War of Independence', University of North Florida, History Faculty Publications, Paper 17 (1985), 31–62 (http://digitalcommons.unf.edu/ahis_facpub/17); S. Ghervas, 'Le philhellénisme russe: union d' amour ou d' intérêt?', in C. Montandon (ed.), *Regards sur le philhellénisme* (Geneva: Permanent Mission of Greece to the United Nations, 2008), 33–41.
59   G. L. Ars, *Eteristskoe dvizhenie v Rossii. Osvoboditelnaya bor'ba gretseskogo naroda v natsale 19ogo veka i russkogrecheskye svyazy* (Moscow: Nauka, 1970), ch. 8; G. L. Ars, 'Aleksandr Ipsilanti i ego vzaimootnosheniya s pravitel'stvom Rossii (novye arkhivnye dannye', in I. S. Dostyan (ed.), *Rossiya i Balkany. Iz istorii obshchestvenno-politicheskikh kul'turnykh svyazey XVIIIv–1878* (Moscow: no publisher stated, 1995), 208–40; O. Orlik, *Dekabritsy I evropeiskoe osvoboditel'noe dvizhenie* (Moscow: Mysl', 1975), 114–18, 124; V. E. Syroechkovskii, 'Balkanskaya problema v politicheskikh planakh dekabristov', in

V. E. Syroechkovskii, *Iz Istorii dvizheniya dekabristov* (Moscow: no publisher stated, 1969), http://decemb.hobby.ru/index.shtml?article/bp, 216–303.
60 A. Dialla, 'Entangled Histories: Russian Decembrists and Greek Revolutionaries in the 1820s', in A. Dialla and N. Maroniti (eds), *State, Economy, Society (19th–20th Centuries): Essays in Honor of Emeritus Professor George B. Dertilis* (Athens: Metaixmio, 2013), 87–105.
61 Temperley, *The Foreign Policy of Canning*, 329.
62 W. Hinde, *George Canning* (London: Collins, 1973), 384.
63 Ibid., 384; Temperley, *The Foreign Policy of Canning*, 329.
64 Ibid., 329.
65 Hinde, *George Canning*, 384–5; Marriott, *George Canning and His Times*, 118; Nicolson, *The Congress of Vienna*, 274–5; Clayton, *Britain and the Eastern Question*, 46.
66 For the possibility of such an alliance see Dakin, *The Greek Struggle for Independence*, 177; Puryear, *France and the Levant*, 21–2.
67 Marriott, *George Canning and His Times*, 118; Clayton, *Britain and the Eastern Question*, 47; Dakin, *The Greek Struggle for Independence*, 152; Bass, *Freedom's Battle*, 113–16; J. Bew, '"From Empire to Competitor": Castlereagh, Canning and the Issue of International Intervention in the Wake of the Napoleonic Wars', in B. Simms and D. J. B. Trim (eds), *Humanitarian Intervention: A History* (Cambridge: Cambridge University Press, 2011), 131–2.
68 Marriott, *The Eastern Question*, 209; Temperley, *The Foreign Policy of Canning*, 326–7; Anderson, *The Eastern Question*, 58; Clayton, *Britain and the Eastern Question*, 46; Brewer, *The Greek War of Independence*, 251.
69 Crawley, *The Question of Greek Independence*, 27.
70 Quoted in Hinde, *George Canning*, 385.
71 Marriott, *The Eastern Question*, 210.
72 Prokesch-Osten, *Istoria*, vol. I, 353, 368–77; Temperley, *The Foreign Policy of Canning*, 330–6; Crawley, *The Question of Greek Independence*, 32, 36–41; Jelavich, *Russia's Balkan Entanglements*, 69–71; Brewer, *The Greek War of Independence*, 249–50, 252–3.
73 Finlay, *History of the Greek Revolution*, vol. II, 165–7; Dakin, *The Greek Struggle for Independence*, 153–5; Woodhouse, *The Greek War of Independence*, 105.
74 Bass, *Freedom's Battle*, 102.
75 Ibid., 106.
76 Blanquière (the driving force in the London Greek Committee) had with the talisman argument convinced Byron to leave Genoa and join the Greeks. See St Clair, *That Greece Might Still Be Free*, 150–2; Brewer, *The Greek War of Independence*, 196–8.
77 C. M. Woodhouse, *The Battle of Navarino* (London: Hodder and Stoughton, 1965), 19.
78 Finlay, *History of the Greek Revolution*, vol. II, 24–8; Phillips, *The War of Greek Independence*, 145; St Clair, *That Greece Might Still Be Free*, 150–4, 166–84; Bass, *Freedom's Battle*, 109–10.
79 Brewer, *The Greek War of Independence*, 238, 241.
80 Gordon, *History of the Greek Revolution*, vol. II, 54, 62–82; Finlay, *History of the Greek Revolution*, vol. II, 113–14, 128; St Clair, *That Greece Might Still Be Free*, 233–7.
81 Anderson, *The Eastern Question*, 57.
82 Quoted in Crawley, *The Question of Greek Independence*, 46–7.
83 Dakin, *The Greek Struggle for Independence*, 161–5, 175.
84 Stratford, unlike Strangford (who was send to St Petersburg), was a philhellene. As he put it at the time: 'as a matter of humanity, I wish with all my soul that the Greeks were put in possession of their whole patrimony, and that the Sultan were driven bag and

baggage into the heart of Asia'. Quoted in Crawley, *The Question of Greek Independence*, 48 n.14.
85 Temperley, *The Foreign Policy of Canning*, 341–4; Dakin, *The Greek Struggle for Independence*, 175–7.
86 Dakin, *The Greek Struggle for Independence*, 176; Bass, *Freedom's Battle*, 123–4.
87 Quoted in Temperley, *The Foreign Policy of Canning*, 349.
88 Ibid., 353.
89 Stapleton, *Intervention and Non-Intervention or the Foreign Policy of Great Britain*, 32.
90 Quoted in Marriott, *The Eastern Question*, 214.
91 Quoted in Woodhouse, *The Battle of Navarino*, 36.
92 Quoted *ibid.*, 36.
93 Crawley, *The Question of Greek Independence*, 56; Woodhouse, *The Battle of Navarino*, 37.
94 Prokesch-Osten, *Istoria*, vol. II, 17–18, 82; Crawley, *The Question of Greek Independence*, 56.
95 Quoted in Marriott, *The Eastern Question*, 214.
96 Grimsted, *The Foreign Ministers of Alexander I*, 284–5.
97 MacKenzie, *Imperial Dreams, Harsh Realities*, 44; Prousis, *Russian Society and the Greek Revolution*, 53.
98 Clayton, *Britain and the Eastern Question*, 49; Marriott, *The Eastern Question*, 212; Crawley, *The Question of Greek Independence*, 52–3.
99 Temperley, *The Foreign Policy of Canning*, 352–3; Clayton, *Britain and the Eastern Question*, 49–50; Crawley, *The Question of Greek Independence*, 54–5.
100 Temperley, *The Foreign Policy of Canning*, 353–5; Crawley, *The Question of Greek Independence*, 58–9; Marriott, *The Eastern Question*, 214; Mowat, *A History of European Diplomacy*, 48; Clayton, *Britain and the Eastern Question*, 50.
101 Crawley, *The Question of Greek Independence*, 59–61; Marriott, *The Eastern Question*, 215; Temperley, *The Foreign Policy of Canning*, 390–92; Anderson, *The Eastern Question*, 64–5.
102 Bass, *Freedom's Battle*, 127–8; Brewer, *The Greek War of Independence*, 286–7; St Clair, *That Greece Might Still Be Free*, 243.
103 Quoted in St Clair, *That Greece Might Still Be Free*, 270.
104 Ibid., 269–71, 273–6; D. Barau, 'Le movement philhellène en France à travers les listes de souscription du comité grec de Paris', in E. Chrysos and C. Farnaud (eds), *La France et la Grèce au XIX siècle. Actes du Colloque franco-hellénique* (Athens: Fondation du Parlement Hellénique pour le Parlementarisme et la Démocratie, 2011), 277–89; C. Farnaud, '1821: Que dissent les consuls français?', in Chrysos and Farnaud (eds), *La France et la Grèce au XIX siècle*, 21–2; Brewer, *The Greek War of Independence*, 316–17.
105 Woodhouse, *The Battle of Navarino*, 25–7; Crawley, *The Question of Greek Independence*, 71.
106 Prokesch-Osten, *Istoria*, vol. II, 125.
107 Ibid., vol. II, 168.
108 Marriott, *The Eastern Question*, 217.
109 Hinde, *George Canning*, 457.
110 Crawley, *The Question of Greek Independence*, 65; Anderson, *The Eastern Question*, 65.
111 Marriott, *The Eastern Question*, 218; Temperley, *The Foreign Policy of Canning*, 394–6; Crawley, *The Question of Greek Independence*, 64, 72.
112 Crawley, *The Question of Greek Independence*, 70; Dakin, *The Greek Struggle for Independence*, 182.
113 Quoted in Marriott, *The Eastern Question*, 218.

114 Temperley, *The Foreign Policy of Canning*, 397–400; Dakin, *The Greek Struggle for Independence*, 182–3; Crawley, *The Question of Greek Independence*, 75–6; Jelavich, *Russia's Balkan Entanglements*, 81–2; Hinde, *George Canning*, 456–7.
115 Treaty of London, in Modern History Sourcebook, http://www.fordham.edu/Halsall/mod/1827gktreaty.asp.
116 J.-P. L. Fonteyne, 'The Customary International Law Doctrine of Humanitarian Intervention: Its Current Validity Under the U.N. Charter', *California Western International Law Journal*, 4 (1973–74), 208.
117 Treaty of London.
118 Quoted in Woodhouse, *The Greek War of Independence*, 122.
119 Quoted in *ibid.*, 123.
120 Marriot, *The Eastern Question*, 219.
121 Woodhouse, *The Greek War of Independence*, 123.
122 Crawley, *The Question of Greek Independence*, 77.
123 *Ibid.*, 77.
124 Woodhouse, *The Greek War of Independence*, 121.
125 Anderson, *The Eastern Question*, 67.
126 Finlay, *History of the Greek Revolution*, vol. II, 138–9; Dakin, *The Greek Struggle for Independence*, 220–1; Woodhouse, *Capodistria*, 322–5; St Clair, *That Greece Might Still Be Free*, 325–7.
127 Woodhouse, *The Battle of Navarino*, 60; Prokesch-Osten, *Istoria*, vol. II, 172.
128 *Ibid.*, vol. II, 183–4.
129 Woodhouse, *The Battle of Navarino*, 60.
130 Hinde, *George Canning*, 457; Anderson, *The Eastern Question*, 67.
131 Quoted in Marriott, *George Canning and His Times*, 130.
132 Woodhouse, *The Battle of Navarino*, 77–80.
133 *Ibid.*, 95, 105.
134 *Ibid.*, 106.
135 Finlay, *History of the Greek Revolution*, vol. II, 181–3; Woodhouse, *The Battle of Navarino*, 29, 120–40.
136 Bass, *Freedom's Battle*, 137–51.
137 Rodogno, *Against Massacre*, 88.
138 *Ibid.*, 88.
139 Albrecht-Carrié, *A Diplomatic History of Europe Since the Congress of Vienna*, 39.
140 Anderson, *The Eastern Question*, 67.
141 Crawley, *The Question of Greek Independence*, 97; Finlay, *History of the Greek Revolution*, vol. II, 183–4.
142 Marriott, *The Eastern Question*, 221; Crawley, *The Question of Greek Independence*, 92.
143 Clayton, *Britain and the Eastern Question*, 54; Woodhouse, *The Battle of Navarino*, 162.
144 *Ibid.*, 154–60.
145 *Ibid.*, 163.
146 *Ibid.*, 163.
147 Prokesch-Osten, *Istoria*, vol. II, 199–205, 211–13; Crawley, *The Question of Greek Independence*, 92.
148 Prokesch-Osten, *Istoria*, vol. II, 208–9.
149 *Ibid.*, vol. II, 215–17.
150 Fleming, *John Capodistrias and the Conference of London*, 14.
151 Clayton, *Britain and the Eastern Question*, 54.

152 Marriott, *The Eastern Question*, 221.
153 Mowat, *A History of European Diplomacy*, 51.
154 V. Sheremet, 'The Greek Revolution of 1821: A New Look at Old Problems', *Modern Greek Studies Yearbook*, 8 (1992), 44–53.
155 Crawley, *The Question of Greek Independence*, 104.
156 Quoted in *ibid.*, 104–5.
157 Fleming, *John Capodistrias and the Conference of London*, 49–56; Puryear, *France and the Levant*, 52, 54–7.
158 Crawley, *The Question of Greek Independence*, 143–8, 153–5; Woodhouse, *The Greek War of Independence*, 130–2; Fleming, *John Capodistrias and the Conference of London*, 58–63; Dakin, *The Greek Struggle for Independence*, 259–61.
159 Quoted in Anderson, *The Eastern Question*, 71.
160 *Ibid.*, 71.
161 Crawley, *The Question of Greek Independence*, 119–20, 171; Anderson, *The Eastern Question*, 274–5; Woodhouse, *The Greek War of Independence*, 139–41; Jelavich, *Russia's Balkan Entanglements*, 85–6.
162 Rodogno, *Against Massacre*, 88.
163 Mowat, *A History of European Diplomacy*, 52–3; Jelavich, *Russia's Balkan Entanglements*, 87.
164 Marriott, *George Canning and His Times*, 118; Crawley, *The Question of Greek Independence*, 77; Clayton, *Britain and the Eastern Question*, 47; Dakin, *The Greek Struggle for Independence*, 152; Prousis, *Russian Society and the Greek Revolution*, 53; Bass, *Freedom's Battle*, 113–16; Bew, 'From Empire to Competitor', 131–2; M. Finnemore, 'Constructing Norms of Humanitarian Intervention', in P. J. Katzenstein (ed.), *The Culture of National Security* (New York: Columbia University Press, 1996), 163.
165 H. Wheaton, *Elements of International Law* (Boston: Little, Brown, 1866, 8th edition, edited by R. H. Dana) [1836], 115.
166 *Ibid.*, 115–16.
167 A. Rougier, 'La théorie de l'intervention d'humanité', *Revue générale de droit international public*, 17 (1910), 473.
168 Apart from Wheaton and Rougier, see the following: A. G. Heffter, *Le droit international de l'Europe* (Berlin: H. W. Muller; Paris: A. Cotillon et Cie, 1883, 4th French edition translated from the German by J. Bergson) [1844], 114; R. Phillimore, *Commentaries upon International Law* (London: Butterworth, 1879, 3rd edition) [1854], vol. I, 569; T. D. Woolsey, *Introduction to the Study of International Law* (London: Sampson Low, Marston, Searle and Rivington, 1879, 5th edition revised and enlarged) [1860], 60; M. Bernard, *On the Principle of Non-Intervention. A Lecture Delivered in the Hall of All Souls College, December MDCCCLX* (Oxford: J. H. and J. Parker, 1860), 22; W. V. Harcourt, as Historicus, in *Letters by Historicus on Some Questions of International Law. Reprinted from 'The Times' with Considerable Additions* (London: Macmillan, 1863), 6; E. S. Creasy, *First Platform of International Law* (London: John van Voorst, 1876), 300; F. Martens, 'Étude historique sur la politique Russe dans la question d'Orient', *Revue du droit international et de législation comparée*, 9 (1877), 55, 58; Bluntschli, 'Le Congrès de Berlin et sa portée au point de vue du droit international', Premier Article, *Revue de droit international et de législation comparée*, 11 (1879), 5; S. Amos, *Lectures on International Law* (London: Stevens and Sons, 1874), 40; G. Rolin-Jaequemyns, 'Chronique du droit international', *Revue de droit international et de législation comparée*, vol. 10 (1878), 19; T. J. Lawrence, *The Principles of International Law* (Boston: D. C. Heath, 1905, 3rd edition, revised) [1895], 132; W. E.

Lingelbach, 'The Doctrine and Practice of Intervention in Europe', *Annals of the Academy of Political and Social Science*, 16 (July 1900), 19–20; L. Oppenheim, *International Law: A Treatise* (London: Longmans, Greene, 5th edition, edited by H. Lauterpacht, 1937) [1905], vol. I, 255, para. 137; J. B. Moore, *A Digest of International Law* (Washington, DC: Government Printing Office,, 1906), vol. VI, 5; A. S. Hershey, 'The Calvo and Drago Doctrines', *American Journal of International Law*, 1:1 (1907), 42; E. C. Stowell, *Intervention in International Law* (Washington, DC: John Byrne, 1921), 126–7; A. Mandelstam, 'La protection des minorités', *Recueil des cours de l'Académie de droit international*, 1 (1923), 374–5; S. Séfériadès, 'Principes généraux du droit international de la paix', *Recueil des cours de l'Académie de droit international*, 34 (1930), 389.

169 J. Kent, *Kent's Commentary on International Law* (Cambridge: Deighton, Bell, 1878, 2nd edition, edited by J. T. Abdy), 47–50; N. W. Senior, 'Art.I-1. Histoire du Progrès du Droit des Gens depuis la Paix de Westphalies jusqu'au Congrès de Vienne. Par Henry Wheaton', *Edinburgh Review*, 77:156 (1843), 345; H. W. Halleck, *Halleck's International Law or Rules Regulating the Intercourse of States in Peace and War* (London: Kegan Paul, Trench, Trubner, 1893, 3rd edition, edited by S. Baker) [1861], vol. I., 511; C. Calvo, *Le droit internationale: théorie et pratique* (Paris: Guillaumin et Cie, G. Pedone-Lauriel, 1880, 3rd edition) [1870], 264, para. 167; H. Strauch, *Zur Interventionslehere: eine völkerrechtliche Studie* (Heidelberg, 1879), 277; F. Despagnet, *Cours de droit international public* (Paris: L. Larose, 1894), 198; T. A. Walker, *A Manual of Public International Law* (Cambridge: Cambridge University Press, 1895), 22–3; G. G. Wilson, *International Law* (New York: Silver, Burdett, 1922, 8th edition) [1901], 91–2.

170 Calvo, *Le droit international*, 264, para. 167.

171 Senior, 'Art. I-1', 345.

172 Harcourt, *Letters by Historicus on Some Questions of International Law*, 6.

173 Lawrence, *The Principles of International Law*, 132.

174 Walker, *A Manual of Public International Law*, 22.

175 *Ibid.*, 22–3.

176 C. G. Fenwick, 'Intervention: Individual and Collective', *American Journal of International Law*, 39: 4 (1945), 650; M. Ganji, *International Protection of Human Rights* (Geneva: University of Geneva, 1962), 22–4; W. M. Reisman with M. McDougal, 'Humanitarian Intervention to Protect the Ibos', in R. B. Lillich (ed.), *Humanitarian Intervention and the United Nations* (Charlottesville: University Press of Virginia, 1973), 179–80; R. Lillich, 'Humanitarian Intervention: A Reply to Ian Brownlie and a Plea for Constructive Alternatives', in J. N. Moore (ed.), *Law and Civil War in the Modern World* (Baltimore: Johns Hopkins University Press, 1974), 233; Fonteyne, 'The Customary International Law Doctrine of Humanitarian Intervention', 207–8; M. J. Bazyler, 'Reexamining the Doctrine of Humanitarian Intervention in Light of the Atrocities in Kampuchea and Ethiopia', *Stanford Journal of International Law*, 23 (1987), 582–3; B. M. Benjamin, 'Unilateral Humanitarian Intervention: Legalizing the Use of Force to Prevent Human Rights Atrocities', *Fordham International Law Journal*, 16 (1992–93), 128–9; F. K. Abiew, *The Evolution of the Doctrine and Practice of Humanitarian Intervention* (The Hague: Kluwer Law International, 1999), 48–9.

177 I. Brownlie, 'Humanitarian Intervention', in Moore (ed.), *Law and Civil War in the Modern World*, 220–1.

178 T. M. Franck and N. S. Rodley, 'After Bangladesh: The Law of Humanitarian Intervention by Military Force', *American Journal of International Law*, 67:2 (1973), 280; S. Chesterman, *Just War or Just Peace? Humanitarian Intervention and International Law* (Oxford: Oxford

University Press, 2001), 29, 32. This is also the view of Charles de Visscher, a supporter of humanitarian intervention. See C. de Visscher, *Théories et réalités en droit international public* (Paris: Editions A. P. Pedone, 1960, 3rd edition), 159.
179 For this aspect see Finnemore, 'Constructing Norms of Humanitarian Intervention', 163.

7

Intervention in Lebanon and Syria, 1860–61

On intervention

The second intervention in the nineteenth century on humanitarian grounds is regarded the great power intervention in Lebanon and Syria, headed by France.[1] Both were at the time provinces of Greater Syria, within the Ottoman Empire, which included today's Lebanon, Syria, Jordan, Israel, the West Bank and Gaza.

When the intervention in Lebanon and Syria took place in 1860–61, the debate among publicists on humanitarian intervention that had started in the 1830s was almost thirty years old, with a slight majority favourable to such interventions, which included major jurists of the time (see chapter 4), and there were also the recent contributions of Cobden, against intervening, and Mazzini and Mill in support of counter-intervention and intervention in humanitarian plights (see chapter 5).

France, the main initiator of the intervention, did not yet have thinkers participating in the debate for or against *intervention d'humanité*.[2] As for intervention in general, the leaders of the French Revolution had come out in favour of both non-intervention and intervention. Condorcet, for instance, asserted in 1792 that it is an inalienable right of a people for their state to have a Constitution and no outside power could intervene in this domain[3] and non-intervention was adopted by the French National Assembly in 1790 and in the 1793 French Constitution.[4] The French Revolution can also be credited with the right to intervene in order to lend diplomatic and even military support 'to all peoples who shall wish to recover their liberty' (Declaration of 19 November 1792).[5]

In 1823, Chateaubriand, as French Foreign Minister, stated that 'no Government has a right to interfere in the affairs of another Government, except in the case where the security and immediate interests of the first Government are compromised'.[6] Two decades later, during the July Monarchy (1830–48), the historian François Guizot, as French Foreign Minister, maintained that '[n]o State has the right to intervene in the affairs and government of another State so long as its interest and proper security do not render this intervention indispensable'.[7]

The opposite, intervention to assist liberation movements, resurfaced in the early days of the July Monarchy with Lafayette and Armand Carrel,[8] and in the wake of the February 1848 French Revolution by writer Alphonse de Lamartine, as French Foreign Minister (whose stance was then defended in Britain by J. S. Mill).

Consequently, if one can speak of a French approach to intervention from 1789 until 1860, it could be summarized it as: (1) non-intervention in a state's political system; (2) intervention if French interests are at stake; and (3) assistance to liberation movements under foreign domination. A new dimension to be seen in 1860–61 was intervention for the sake of humanity, as evoked by French officials and mostly by Foreign Minister Édouard Antoine de Thouvenel. Napoleon III, then in power, had a contradictory record of having militarily intervened in 1849 against the Roman Republic, much to the disappointment of Mazzini (the head of the governing triumvirate of the Republic), upon the Pope's invitation to restore the Papal States, and ten years later having sent the French army to support the Italians fighting against Austria–Hungary for Italian unification.

Britain was then under Palmerston as Prime Minister, who, contrary to Castlereagh's non-intervention stance (see chapter 6) and as an admirer of Canning, 'drew the outer limits of permissible conduct for Britain as the champion of liberalism as well as an opponent of the European despots'.[9] But he was careful not to upset the European balance of power or British interests for ideological reasons, by being too supportive of national self-determination and constitutional government. He thus earned the criticism of non-interventionists, such as Cobden, as well as interventionists in support of liberty, such as J. S. Mill. Palmerston was also well aware of the downside of intervention in civil wars, noting that 'they who in quarrels interpose, will often get a bloody nose'[10] and used non-intervention as a 'ring-holding device'.[11]

In the years 1830–60, British jurists had been at the forefront of the ongoing debate together with their German, Italian and American colleagues, and were evenly split among opponents and supporters of humanitarian intervention, though by far the most authoritative and recent contributions were by two influential publicists within the British establishment, Phillimore (in 1854) and Bernard (in 1860), both guarded supporters of moral grounds for intervention (see chapter 4).

The landscape

Among the Arab-speaking communities, the Maronites (Eastern Catholics linked to the Roman Catholic Church), the largest community in Lebanon, and the Druzes (an offshoot of the Ismaili branch of Shia Islam), one of the smaller communities, lived in Lebanon in two self-governing districts headed by an Ottoman governor.[12] From 1840 until the events of 1860, there was tension between them that was accentuated by European influence and commercial, religious and other interests in the region. More generally, European intrusion in the region and the traditional Ottoman policy of keeping religious communities apart (the *millet* system) hardly provided the ground for integration between the Arab communities of Lebanon (Arab nationalism as pan-Arabism was to arrive at the start of the twentieth century, with Christian Arabs at the forefront[13]).[14]

The Maronites sought the support of France and Paris was keen to oblige, a support deeply resented by the Druzes. French involvement had its origins in the first capitulations of 1536 and 1569, under the reigns of Sultans Suleiman the Magnificent and Selim II.[15] The end result was that the French regarded themselves as the defenders of the Maronites of Lebanon, their agents and protégés in the Levant. The British played almost the same role with the Druzes and for a while Palmerston toyed with the idea of a 'special relationship' with the Druzes (the missionaries went even further in the belief that they could convert the Druzes to Protestantism).[16] The French and British consuls as well as the consuls of other powers, especially Russia (as regards the Lebanese Greek Orthodox community), became routinely involved in various aspects of Lebanese life.[17]

European interest in the region had also another dimension worth referring to. As Davide Rodogno points out, Syria and especially Lebanon were presented by romantic writers, such as Lamartine, and Orientalist painters, such as David Roberts and Edward Lear, as an 'Eden on earth', 'a timeless biblical land' in need of 'cultural redemption and religious salvation' so as to be reconnected with the evolutionary 'stream of Time' from which it had been severed due to the Ottoman conquest and tyranny.[18]

The Muslims in the region (Sunni, Shia and Druzes) strongly objected to the emancipation of the Christian subjects of the Empire initiated with the Tanzimat reforms, from 1839 onwards, which made the Christians, in law, equal to the Muslims. Equality before the law, despite far from strict adherence to it by the Ottomans in Greater Syria (or elsewhere in the Empire), benefited the Christians, who were generally better educated and made the most of new opportunities for economic and social ascendency: entry into the civil service, representation in provincial councils and prosperity, taking advantage of the European economic presence and protection in the region. The Maronites made their new-found freedoms as conspicuous as possible, building churches, establishing community schools and so on, at times with a show of superiority, or so it seemed to the Muslims, who became increasingly resentful. Another aspect of the Tanzimat was the adoption of a code which permitted Europeans and their protégés to buy agricultural land and real estate, the outcome being that property was bought from impoverished Muslim notables in Damascus and elsewhere.[19] The Muslims became increasingly frustrated with this turn of events, dreading that their dominant role was slipping away for good. In this, the Christian powers had a hand, with their aid to the Christians and calls for the full implementation of the sweeping 1856 Reform Edict.[20]

On the Maronite side there was a rise in expectations. They learned French and were inspired by the principles of the French Revolution; they increasingly felt themselves to be an alien island in a Muslim ocean and began to dream of the creation of an independent Maronite Lebanon, or at least a French protectorate.[21]

The massacres and the Ottoman authorities

The 'massacres of '60' (*madhabih al-sittin*), as they are known in Lebanon and Syria, which started in April and continued until July, were premeditated[22] in the sense that the Maronites were planning an all-out attack against the Druzes, the aim being the creation of a Maronite protectorate under France.[23] The Maronites had been mobilized by their notables and clerics, headed by 'Awn, the Maronite bishop of Beirut, and prepared themselves with arms in units under a commanding officer, poised to assail the Druzes. The Druzes took wind of it and organized themselves for the worst.[24]

Sporadic violent clashes began in April 1860, with Maronites raiding a Druze village. The well prepared Druzes retaliated ferociously, burning villages (within a few weeks more than sixty villages were in ashes), sacking churches and monasteries and massacring 10,000 to 15,000 Christians (not even sparing the Greek Orthodox Arabs, with whom they were on good terms), in what was the bloodiest ethno-religious confrontation in the history of sectarian strife in Lebanon (the number of Druzes killed is unknown).[25]

The acts of arson and atrocities continued, culminating in an appalling massacre in Damascus (9–11 July 1860) of 5,000 to 10,000 Christians. The Russian, French, Austrian and US consulates were sacked and part of the famous city was ablaze, with the governor doing nothing to stop the carnage.[26] Apparently the underlying cause of the onslaught was the aforementioned Muslim resentment at the rising Western influence and the economic prosperity of the Christians.[27]

The role of the Ottomans in the region from April to July 1860 has been a subject of controversy: were they inefficient, callously indifferent, or had they colluded with the Druzes? The key Ottoman officials in charge were the two governors, Khurshid Pasha in Lebanon and *müşir* (field-marshal) Ahmed Pasha in Damascus, an able soldier who had distinguished himself in the Crimean War.

The view of prominent French international lawyers until the First World War, such Despagnet and Rougier, was that there was 'complicity' on the part of the Ottoman authorities in having allowed the massacre of 'six thousand' people to take place.[28] The American Stowell was of the view that the Druzes 'had massacred six thousand Christian Maronites without any efforts on the part of the Porte to fulfill its obligations to protect the victims'.[29] But let us see what the specialists of the region have to say.

Ottomanists tend to absolve the local Ottoman authorities of any responsibility. The Shaws also claim that the British had sent arms to the Druzes so as to counter

French influence with the Maronites.[30] Most Arab and other Middle East specialists attribute responsibility of one kind or another to the Ottomans, ranging from ineffectiveness and indifference to actual participation in the onslaught. According to Hitti, the Ottoman regulars did nothing to stop the fighting and the irregulars (*bashibazouk*) 'maltreated and pillaged refugees fleeing to Damascus or Beirut'.[31] Salibi points out that when the European consuls in Beirut urged Khurshid to act, he was in no position to do so or 'stood by and watched'.[32] According to Akarli, the Ottoman authorities were ineffective in protecting the Maronites and other Christians due to a shortage of armed personnel, mismanagement and unwillingness to fight fellow Muslims to protect Christians.[33] Ma'oz puts most of the blame on Ahmed Pasha[34] and suggests there was 'a concealed alliance' between him and local leaders 'to punish the Christians for their disobedience' by 'secretly instigating or at least tacitly directing the fatal course of events'.[35]

Among Middle East scholars Tibawi is almost alone in absolving the Ottoman authorities of responsibility. He maintains that the accusations of conspiracy with the Druzes 'have never been judiciously investigated by any historian'[36] and that Khurshid could do little, due to lack of adequate forces.[37] Abraham takes the opposite line, pointing to Ottoman collusion on the part of both governors, while blaming the onslaught and even the instigation on the Druzes.[38]

In the most detailed study of the Maronite–Druze clash, by Farah, the picture that emerges is that the data do not confirm the Maronite view and French press reports of Druzes chiefs spoiling for a fight in 1860. In fact, Sa'îd Janblât, the senior Druze leader, had urged both communities to show restraint, but to no avail. The decision to initiate an all-out ethnic war was taken by the Maronite leadership in Beirut with the approval of Bishop 'Awn.[39]

As to the possibility of the Porte being somehow involved, no documentary evidence has surfaced to prove such a scenario.[40] Plausibly, the anti-Tanzimat circles may have encouraged ethnic strife so as to bring about a crisis that would overthrow reformist Sultan Abdulmecid in favour of his conservative brother, Abdulaziz, but this hypothesis has also not found documentary evidence.[41]

European and Ottoman reaction

The news of the gruesome events reached the Ottoman capital only after a delay of some two months (on 7 June 1860), via the Izmir telegraph station. The European consuls in Beirut gave a slanted pro-Maronite account of the events, especially the French consul-general, Bentivoglio, who referred mainly to the massacres of Christians, portraying them as innocent victims, the Druzes as barbarians and alluding to the complicity of the local Ottoman authorities.[42] Lavalette, the French ambassador at the Porte, cabled his Foreign Minister, Thouvenel, referring to 'the interest of humanity' and suggesting a military operation against the Druzes and local Ottoman authorities, whom he regarded as accomplices.[43]

Thouvenel, who was familiar with the region (he had served as ambassador to the Porte in 1855–59), sent the chilling dispatch to his British counterpart, Lord Russell. He appealed to the other four great powers for a unanimous response, because, he said, this was 'a question of humanity, and does not comprise any difference of opinion between cabinets'.[44] Thouvenel told the Prussian ambassador that France wanted to maintain the Ottoman Empire, 'but to maintain it in conditions which can be reconciled with the rights of humanity and of civilization'.[45]

On the Russian side, Alexander Gorchakov, the Russian Foreign Minister, suggested joint Franco-Russian action. France called for the convening of a conference of the powers, but British Prime Minister Palmerston was uneasy with France's motives and was reluctant to give his approval.[46]

The Porte condemned the atrocities at the highest level – that of Sultan Abdulmecid. The anger of the Sultan and of his two senior officials (both enlightened reformists), Grand Vizier Ali Pasha and Fuad Pasha, the Foreign Minister, with the behaviour of the regional authorities was genuine; it was seen as a disgrace to the Ottoman army. The Sultan took the unusual step of sending Fuad with 15,000 soldiers and extraordinary emergency powers to oversee the operation (he named him Commissioner Extraordinary of the Porte and personally handed him the seal of authority, by Ottoman ritual a sign of considerable commitment) and thus gave few pretexts for European meddling in the Empire's internal affairs. Abdulmecid sent letters to Napoleon III and Queen Victoria expressing his grief at the massacres, promising the re-establishment of order, punishment of the guilty and assuring justice for all.[47]

The Damascus massacre was a turning point. European and in particular French public opinion was horrified. The Ottomans were accused, especially by the French press, of deliberately staging the massacres and there were calls for military intervention. Thouvenel stated that '[i]n the face of these massacres, reproducing from city to city and everywhere where Christians live, it is impossible not to recognize that humanity commands the Powers to interpose their action'.[48] The British press and public were in favour of intervention for humanitarian reasons and supported the French initiatives. Russell conceded, fearing a Russo-French alliance that would isolate Britain, and endorsed the sending of European troops in the name of humanity if it was sealed by an official agreement between the five powers and the Porte.[49]

Upon Thouvenel's invitation, the five powers and the Ottoman Empire convened an ambassadors' conference in Paris (26 July–3 August 1860). The Porte was represented by its Paris ambassador, the worldly Vefik Effendi, whose instructions were to stall and try to divide the other powers, but to give in if the five were united.[50] Two Paris protocols were adopted (3 August 1860). The first justified 'active cooperation' by referring to the Paris Peace Treaty of 1856 (article IX), which guaranteed the rights of Ottoman Christians.[51] The second provided for 12,000 soldiers to be sent, 6,000 of them French, together with sufficient naval forces from various European countries and commissioners from the great powers. A disinterestedness proviso was inserted: not to seek 'any territorial advantage, any exclusive influence, or any commercial concession'.[52] The period of foreign troop presence was to be limited to six months (at British insistence). A declaration by Abdulmecid was included in the second protocol, stating that his aim was 'to stop by prompt and efficacious measures, the effusion of blood in Syria'.[53]

Clearly, the operation was intended to be a 'rescue mission' and not a punitive one.[54] Napoleon's message to the French force as it left Toulon (6 August 1860) was 'to aid the Sultan recall to their allegiance subjects blinded by an antiquated fanaticism'.[55] The French contingent was headed by General de Beaufort d'Hautpoul, with instructions that the expedition was not to be 'an occupation of some duration'; the mission was 'essentially restorative, temporary ... assuming the character of an act of justice and humanity'.[56]

Fuad was informed of the Damascus massacres while his ships were refuelling in Cyprus. Exasperated, he arrived in Beirut on 17 July and hastened to Damascus to re-establish order and give little excuse for French presence in the city.[57] His 'justice was swift and harsh'.[58] He was able to re-established order prior to the arrival of the French troops, who landed on 16 August 1860; he assisted the Christians and arrested offenders, hundreds of whom were put to death or imprisoned following summary trials. Ahmed Pasha (a friend of Fuad) and some sixty Ottoman officials were hanged, while Khurshid and his officers were imprisoned. Fuad wanted to demonstrate that the Ottoman government was in no way responsible for the massacres, which were, as he put it, against 'the principles of civilization current in the world'.[59] In order not to provide grounds for the French to render their presence a real occupation, the Pasha did not punish the Maronite instigators.[60]

In record time no less than twenty-eight warships from the powers and also from small states (such as Greece and Sardinia) arrived on the coastline of Lebanon to monitor the situation. Fuad's troops, together with the French contingent under Beaufort and the five commissioners of the great powers, were able to keep the peace. The French troops were no menace to the Ottoman authorities and did not engage in any major military activity. The French acted as peacekeepers and not as peacemakers (to use present parlance), since Fuad had already pacified the region. The French soldiers were engaged mainly in humanitarian activities. Indeed, they 'beat their swords into plough-shares and their spears into pruning-hooks',[61] burying the dead, cleaning streets, and rebuilding houses, villages and farms.[62]

The six-month limit was extended upon French request (with Russian support) to three more months, after which the French forces duly left, having gained acclaim inside and outside Lebanon for their conduct.[63]

Final agreement

Fuad was able to dominate the scene and control the other commissioners, with the support of Lord Dufferin, the British commissioner.[64] The mandate of the commission was to punish the guilty, secure reparations for the Christian losses and suggest reforms that would ensure order and security.[65] Deliberations, with Fuad chairing, started on 5 October 1860 with the aim of arriving at a new arrangement for Lebanon. The French tried to set up a Maronite Lebanon under a native Christian governor. The Austrian and Prussian commissioners aligned with the French, but Fuad, with Dufferin's support and help from the Russian commissioner Novikov, was able to shelve the French idea. Finally, after eight months of talks, the six commissioners were able to reach agreement (May 1861) on a draft statute for Lebanon.[66]

The draft was revised at a meeting of the ambassadors of the six powers at the Porte under the chairmanship of the Grand Vizier, which concluded with the signing of the Beyoglu Protocol (9 June 1861). A new system of autonomy was adopted, the *Règlement Organique*, known in Lebanon as the *Mustasarrifiyya* (Governorate). Lebanon became a separate administrative region (*sanjak*) from Syria. The six Lebanese communities (Maronites, Druzes, Greek Orthodox, Greek Catholic, Sunni and Shia) participated in a twelve-person Administrative Council based on their percentage. The *Mustasarrifiyya* was to be headed by a Christian governor from outside Lebanon, with the consent of the great powers. The first governor was Daud Pasha, a Roman Catholic Armenian by birth, which proved an excellent choice, for he was one of the most capable officials of the Empire. In effect, Lebanon, though part of the Ottoman Empire, now came under the collective tutelage of the powers and remained so until the First World War.[67]

Assessment

Humanitarian and other motives

Humanitarian concern on the part of the French government was not insincere, as seen in the French internal correspondence from Napoleon III, Thouvenel and other French officials regarding the plight of the Maronites.[68] The dismal fate of the Christians 'constituted an affront to the conscience of Europe and to the specific susceptibilities of the French, who had long prided themselves on their traditional role as champion of the Roman Catholic peoples in the Near East'.[69]

However, instrumental motives were also prevalent. Thouvenel had realized that in this case humanitarian concerns were compatible with *Realpolitik*.[70] With the intervention, France sought to enhance its influence at the expense of Britain and place a marker for the future, should 'the Sick Man' dissolve: namely, to acquire Syria as a protectorate. Moreover, Napoleon wanted to project himself as a resolute leader, to be respected internationally, to divert the attention of the

French public and, by the same token, to enhance his waning popularity at home, especially with the clerical party and Catholic public opinion, which was incensed by his recent stance in support of Italian unification (one of the outcomes being the dissolution of the Papal States).[71]

More generally, Syria and Lebanon were at the centre of an arc between the British route to India and the Straits route to the Black Sea, a region of French–British rivalry for most of the century, though the rivalry was kept within reasonable bounds.[72] Britain's motives were humanitarian and it opted for collective intervention so as to keep a close eye on France. London's support for the Druzes was motivated by a sense of justice (after all, the Maronites had started it) and as a counter-weight to French support for the Maronites.[73]

The overall verdict

All the international lawyers who have referred to this episode, from those days until today, regard it as 'motivated substantially, if not entirely, by humanitarian considerations'.[74]

Jooris, a contemporary French jurist, had claimed that the intervention was not only humanitarian but also due to the fact that European flags had been insulted and Europeans living in Syria had been killed and their properties destroyed.[75] Lawrence asserted that as 'the Great Powers intervened to put a stop to the persecution and massacre of Christians in the district of Mount Lebanon, their proceedings were worthy of commendation'.[76] Rougier regarded it as 'a very clear application of the idea of intervention for humanity', not least because it was 'disinterested'.[77] Stowell referred to it as 'an incident typical of humanitarian intervention'[78] and 'one in which the states were actuated by motives of humanity to prevent religious persecutions which took the form of massacres of the Christian Maronites'.[79]

This was also the assessment from 1945 onwards.[80] Even opponents of humanitarian intervention, such as Brownlie, have claimed that: 'No genuine case of humanitarian intervention has occurred [in the nineteenth century] with the possible exception of the occupation of Syria in 1860 and 1861'.[81] Franck and Rodley do not concur on various grounds (especially on the role of the Maronites in starting the mayhem) but praise the operation for being a multilateral one.[82]

But three factors make this case questionable as a *stricto sensu* humanitarian intervention. One is that the Ottomans were not overtly averse to the operation. Secondly, Fuad had the situation well under control before the arrival of the French troops and French activity hardly amounted to a military intervention. Thirdly, those to blame for the initial aggression were the Maronites, making them less worthy to be singled out for intervention, although they suffered immensely.[83]

We will limit ourselves to the first issue. Bluntschli claimed that the acquiescence of the Sultan was sought in order to 'save appearances' and so that 'the

Porte's hand was forced'.[84] Equally, Rougier regarded the consent of the Ottoman Empire as 'a fiction' sought 'in courtesy towards the Sultan'.[85] Stowell put it thus: '[a]lthough the Sultan gave his official consent to this occupation, it was none the less a measure to which he only consented through constraint and a desire to avoid worse'.[86]

Be this as it may, there was by and large 'relative disinterestedness' on the part of the five powers, and their humanitarian concern seems 'genuine'.[87] As for the French, as Gary Bass points out, they acted on the basis of treaty obligations; worked alongside Fuad's mission; 'forswore any imperial or commercial gains from its mission'; 'participated without reservations in the international commission' set up there; 'allowed the Concert to dictate the parameters of the expedition; and accepted European restrictions on the size and duration of the French occupation'.[88]

The outcome in Lebanon was almost idyllic. Apart from disorder in 1864–67, the 1861 Lebanese settlement proved resilient, with the region enjoying peace, known as 'the long peace', until the eve of the First World War.[89]

Concluding remarks

In the Lebanon case one sees several elements that appeared in the Greek case (Christian humanitarian plight, mixture of motives, multilateral character, agreements, self-denying clause, peacekeeping force, calls to end hostilities, role of public opinion). The new features with a bearing on the evolution of humanitarian intervention are the following: (1) co-optation of the state on whose territory the outrages had taken place, (2) an overseeing committee comprising commissioners of all the great powers, and (3) the setting up of a new political-administrative arrangement which placed a region of a state under the collective tutelage of the great powers, limiting that state's control over its sovereign territory.

Notes

1   See S. Kloepfer, 'The Syrian Crisis, 1860–61: A Case Study of Classic Humanitarian Intervention', *Canadian Yearbook of International Law*, 23 (1985), 246–59; I. Pogany, 'Humanitarian Intervention in International Law: The French Intervention in Syria Re-examined', *International and Comparative Law Quarterly*, 35 (1986), 182–90.

2   The only exception was Pellegrino Rossi (a naturalized French citizen and close friend of François Guizot, French Foreign Minister), who advocated non-intervention (see chapter 4).

3   W. G. Grewe, *The Epochs of International Law* (Berlin: Walter de Gruyter, 2000, translated and revised by M. Byers), 416–17.

4   M. Schröder, 'Non-intervention, Principle of', in *Encyclopedia of Public International Law*, Max Planck Institute for Comparative Public Law and International Law (Amsterdam: Elsevier, 1997), vol. III, 620.

5   Ibid., 620; R. J. Vincent, *Nonintervention and International Order* (Princeton: Princeton University Press, 1974), 67.
6   Quoted in H. W. Halleck, *Halleck's International Law or Rules Regulating the Intercourse of States in Peace and War* (London: Kegan Paul, Trench, Trubner and Co., 1893, 3rd edition, edited by S. Baker) [1861], vol. I, 97.
7   Quoted in G. Carnazza Amari, 'Nouvel exposé du principe de non-intervention', *Revue du droit international et de législation comparée*, 5 (1873), 363.
8   J. Jennings, 'Nationalist Ideas in the Early Years of the July Monarchy: Armand Carrel and Le National', *History of Political Thought*, 7:3 (1991), 497–8, 507–8.
9   Vincent, *Nonintervention and International Order*, 90.
10 Quoted in R. Little, *Intervention: External Involvement in Civil Wars* (London: Martin Robertson, 1975), 23, 110.
11 Vincent, *Nonintervention and International Order*, 90–101.
12 P. K. Hitti, *Lebanon in History* (London: Macmillan, 1967), 436; E. D. Akarli, *The Long Peace: Ottoman Lebanon, 1861–1920* (London: I. B. Tauris, 1993), 28; A. J. Abraham, *Lebanon in Modern Times* (Lanham: University Press of America, 2008), 63.
13 See G. Antonius, *The Arab Awakening* (Beirut: Khayats, 1939); B. Tibi, *Arab Nationalism: A Critical Inquiry* (London: Macmillan, 1971).
14 A. L. Tibawi, *A Modern History of Syria Including Lebanon and Palestine* (London: Macmillan, 1969), 103–14; M. Ma'oz, *Ottoman Reform in Geographical Syria and Palestine, 1840–1861: The Impact of the Tanzimat on Politics and Society* (Oxford: Clarendon Press, 1968), 210–20.
15 H. Inalcik, *The Ottoman Empire: The Classical Age, 1300–1600* (London: Phoenix, 2000) [1973], 137.
16 D. Rodogno, 'The "Principles of Humanity" and the European Powers' Intervention in Ottoman Lebanon and Syria in 1860–1861', in B. Simms and D. J. B. Trim (eds), *Humanitarian Intervention: A History* (Cambridge: Cambridge University Press, 2011), 165.
17 Ibid., 164; Ma'oz, *Ottoman Reform in Geographical Syria and Palestine*, 214; Akarli, *The Long Peace*, 28; Y. M. Choueri, 'Ottoman Reform and Lebanese Patriotism', in N. Shehadi and D. H. Mills (eds), *Lebanon: A History of Conflict and Consensus* (London: I. B. Tauris, 1988), 70–4.
18 Rodogno, 'The "Principles of Humanity"', 165–6.
19 C. E. Farah, *The Politics of Interventionism in Ottoman Lebanon, 1830–1861* (London: Centre for Lebanese Studies in association with I. B. Tauris, 2000), 527; Rodogno, 'The "Principles of Humanity"', 165.
20 Tibawi, *A Modern History of Syria Including Lebanon and Palestine*, 101, 112–20, 128; Ma'oz, *Ottoman Reform in Geographical Syria and Palestine*, 200–5, 221, 226, 231–2; Akarli, *The Long Peace*, 29–30; Choueri, 'Ottoman Reform and Lebanese Patriotism', 68–74.
21 Z. M. Zeine, *Arab–Turkish Relations and the Emergence of Arab Nationalism* (Beirut: Khayat's, 1958), 38–9.
22 Hitti, *Lebanon in History*, 437.
23 Zeine, *Arab–Turkish Relations and the Emergence of Arab Nationalism*, 38–9.
24 K. S. Salibi, *The Modern History of Lebanon* (New York: Frederick A. Praeger, 1965), 88–90; Tibawi, *A Modern History of Syria Including Lebanon and Palestine*, 123–4; Akarli, *The Long Peace*, 29.
25 Hitti, *Lebanon in History*, 437–8; Akarli, *The Long Peace*, 30; S. Khalaf, *Civil and Uncivil Violence in Lebanon* (New York: Columbia University Press, 2002), 95–7; G. J. Bass,

Freedom's Battle: The Origins of Humanitarian Intervention (New York: Vintage Books, 2009), 163-9; Rodogno, 'The "Principles of Humanity"', 167.
26 Hitti, *Lebanon in History*, 438-9; Tibawi, *A Modern History of Syria Including Lebanon and Palestine*, 127-8; Ma'oz, *Ottoman Reform in Geographical Syria and Palestine*, 234-38; Bass, *Freedom's Battle*, 174-5.
27 J. P. Spagnolo, *France and Ottoman Lebanon 1861-1914* (London: Ithaca Press, 1977), 32; Ma'oz, *Ottoman Reform in Geographical Syria and Palestine*, 232; Farah, *The Politics of Interventionism in Ottoman Lebanon*, 587.
28 F. Despagnet, *Cours de droit international public* (Paris: L. Larose, 1894), 201; A. Rougier, 'La théorie de l'intervention d'humanité', *Revue générale de droit international public*, 17 (1910), 473-4.
29 E. C. Stowell, *Intervention in International Law* (Washington, DC: John Byrne, 1921), 63.
30 S. J. Shaw and E. K. Shaw, *History of the Ottoman Empire and Modern Turkey* (Cambridge: Cambridge University Press, 1977), vol. II, 143.
31 Hitti, *Lebanon in History*, 437.
32 Salibi, *The Modern History of Lebanon*, 93-5.
33 Akarli, *The Long Peace*, 30.
34 Ahmed was reported to have said that 'there were two great evils in Syria, the Christians and the Druzes and that the massacre of either party was a gain' for the Ottoman government. Quoted in Ma'oz, *Ottoman Reform in Geographical Syria and Palestine*, 235.
35 *Ibid.*, 235, 238.
36 Tibawi, *A Modern History of Syria Including Lebanon and Palestine*, 125.
37 *Ibid.*, 126-7.
38 Abraham, *Lebanon in Modern Times*, 64-5, 67.
39 For details see Farah, *The Politics of Interventionism in Ottoman Lebanon*, 557-93.
40 Ma'oz, *Ottoman Reform in Geographical Syria and Palestine*, 239; Spagnolo, *France and Ottoman Lebanon*, 31.
41 Ma'oz, *Ottoman Reform in Geographical Syria and Palestine*, 239.
42 Bass, *Freedom's Battle*, 163; Rodogno, 'The "Principles of Humanity"', 166-9.
43 Bass, *Freedom's Battle*, 169.
44 Quoted *ibid.*, 170.
45 Quoted in W. E. Echard, *Napoleon III and the Concert of Europe* (Baton Rouge: Louisiana State University Press, 1983), 130.
46 Spagnolo, *France and Ottoman Lebanon*, 34; M. S. Anderson, *The Eastern Question, 1774-1923: A Study in International Relations* (London: Macmillan, 1966), 156-7; Echard, *Napoleon III and the Concert of Europe*, 129-31; Stowell, *Intervention in International Law*, 63-5; Bass, *Freedom's Battle*, 163-86.
47 Farah, *The Politics of Interventionism in Ottoman Lebanon*, 604-5; Bass, *Freedom's Battle*, 173.
48 Quoted in Bass, *Freedom's Battle*, 175.
49 Echard, *Napoleon III and the Concert of Europe*, 130-2; Rodogno, 'The "Principles of Humanity"', 170-4; Bass, *Freedom's Battle*, 175-6; Farah, *The Politics of Interventionism in Ottoman Lebanon*, 606-8; Spagnolo, *France and Ottoman Lebanon*, 33-4.
50 Bass, *Freedom's Battle*, 186.
51 *Ibid.*, 188.
52 Quoted in Stowell, *Intervention in International Law*, 64-5.
53 Bass, *Freedom's Battle*, 186-9; Farah, *The Politics of Interventionism in Ottoman Lebanon*, 647-8; Stowell, *Intervention in International Law*, 64-6; Rodogno, 'The "Principles of Humanity"', 174-5.

54 Spagnolo, *France and Ottoman Lebanon*, 35.
55 Quoted *ibid.*, 35.
56 Quoted in O. Forcade, 'Les missions humanitaires et d'interposition devant l'histoire', *Toqueville Review*, 8:1 (1996), 41.
57 Salibi, *The Modern History of Lebanon*, 107–8.
58 Akarli, *The Long Peace*, 30.
59 Quoted in Rodogno, 'The "Principles of Humanity"', 178.
60 For details see Farah, *The Politics of Interventionism in Ottoman Lebanon*, 605, 608–15, 623–9. See also: Tibawi, *A Modern History of Syria Including Lebanon and Palestine*, 130–1; Hitti, *Lebanon in History*, 439; Salibi, *The Modern History of Lebanon*, 108–9.
61 Tibawi, *A Modern History of Syria Including Lebanon and Palestine*, 131.
62 *Ibid.*, 131; Rodogno, 'The "Principles of Humanity"', 175–6.
63 Anderson, *The Eastern Question*, 156–8; Stowell, *Intervention in International Law*, 66.
64 Hitti, *Lebanon in History*, 439; Bass, *Freedom's Battle*, 190.
65 Bass, *Freedom's Battle*, 190.
66 Salibi, *The Modern History of Lebanon*, 109–10; Hitti, *Lebanon in History*, 439–40; Abraham, *Lebanon in Modern Times*, 78; Spagnolo, *France and Ottoman Lebanon*, 35–9.
67 Salibi, *The Modern History of Lebanon*, 109–12; Hitti, *Lebanon in History*, 441–5; Akarli, *The Long Peace*, 30–3; Choueri, 'Ottoman Reform and Lebanese Patriotism', 74; Spagnolo, *France and Ottoman Lebanon*, 41–7; Farah, *The Politics of Interventionism in Ottoman Lebanon*, 677–94; Abraham, *Lebanon in Modern Times*, 78–81; Anderson, *The Eastern Question*, 158.
68 Echard, *Napoleon III and the Concert of Europe*, 131–2; Bass, *Freedom's Battle*, 231.
69 Echard, *Napoleon III and the Concert of Europe*, 129.
70 Rodongo, 'The "Principles of Humanity"', 181; Echard, *Napoleon III and the Concert of Europe*, 131.
71 Echard, *Napoleon III and the Concert of Europe*, 130–1; Anderson, *The Eastern Question*, 156–7; Forcade, 'Les missions humanitaires et d'interposition devant l'histoire', 41; Bass, *Freedom's Battle*, 231; Rodogno, 'The "Principles of Humanity"', 179–80; Pogany, 'Humanitarian Intervention in International Law', 188.
72 J. Spagnolo, 'Franco–British Rivalry in the Middle East and Its Operation in the Lebanese Problem', in N. Shehadi and D. Mills (eds), *Lebanon: A History of Conflict and Consensus* (London: I. B. Tauris, 1988), 101–10; Forcade, 'Les missions humanitaires et d'interposition devant l'histoire', 41.
73 Rodogno, 'The "Principles of Humanity"', 181.
74 Kloepfer, 'The Syrian Crisis', 255.
75 J. Jooris, 'La question du Liban', *Revue du droit international et de législation comparée*, 15 (1883), 248.
76 T. J. Lawrence, *The Principles of International Law* (Boston: D. C. Heath, 1905, 3rd edition, revised) [1895], 132.
77 Rougier, 'La théorie de l'intervention d'humanité', 474.
78 Stowell, *Intervention in International Law*, 63.
79 *Ibid.*, 66.
80 M. Ganji, *International Protection of Human Rights* (Geneva: Librairie E. Droz, 1962), 24–6; J.-P. L. Fonteyne, 'The Customary International Law Doctrine of Humanitarian Intervention: Its Current Validity Under the U.N. Charter', *California Western International Law Journal* (1973–74), 208–9; M. Finnemore, 'Constructing Norms of Humanitarian Intervention', in P. J. Katzenstein (ed.), *The Culture of National Security*

(New York: Columbia University Press, 1996), 165; Bass, *Freedoms' Battle*, 159–232; Rodogno, 'The "Principles of Humanity"', 181.

81 I. Brownlie, *International Law and the Use of Force by States* (Oxford: Oxford University Press, 1963), 340. See also S. Chesterman, *Just War or Just Peace? Humanitarian Intervention and International Law* (Oxford: Oxford University Press, 2001), 33.

82 T. M. Franck and N. S. Rodley, 'After Bangladesh: The Law of Humanitarian Intervention by Military Force', *American Journal of International Law*, 67:2 (1973), 281–3.

83 *Ibid.*, 281–2; Pogany, 'Humanitarian Intervention in International Law', 186–90; Chesterman, *Just War or Just Peace?*, 33.

84 Bluntschli, 'Le Congrès de Berlin et sa portée au point de vue du droit international', *Revue de droit international et de législation comparée*, 11 (1879), 13.

85 Rougier, 'La théorie de l'intervention d'humanité', 474.

86 Stowell, *Intervention in International Law*, 66.

87 Chesterman, *Just War or Just Peace?*, 33.

88 Bass, *Freedom's Battle*, 231.

89 Anderson, *The Eastern Question*, 158; Akarli, *The Long Peace*.

8

The Bulgarian atrocities: a bird's eye view of intervention with emphasis on Britain, 1875–78

On intervention

The great power involvement triggered by the Bulgarian atrocities was part of a wider international reaction to uprisings in the Balkans known as the Great Eastern Crisis of 1875–78, which was to change the map of the Balkans. Events began with the Serbs of Herzegovina (July 1875), followed a little later by Bosnia, the Bulgarians (April–May 1876) and the war of the autonomous principalities of Serbia and Montenegro against the Ottoman Empire (June–July 1876).

By the mid-1870s the debate over humanitarian intervention was in full swing, with over forty publicists participating, among whom a two-thirds majority supported intervention. The 1850s and 1860s had seen some of the seminal advocacies of the new doctrine: those by Phillimore, Fiore and Bluntschli. In the 1870s (before and during the Balkan crisis) there followed those by Arntz, Rolin-Jaequemyns and Martens. The 1870s had also seen three of the main rejections, by Carnazza Amari, Bonfils and Renault (see chapter 4).

Advocates argued that intervention should preferably be collective and in instances of outrages against humanity; remaining an apathetic bystander was unacceptable. Opponents pointed that interventions when a state's proper interests were not at stake were unacceptable and would play havoc with state sovereignty and independence and were open to abuse.

Diplomatic initiatives, the Bulgarians and the Serbs

Great power diplomacy

The uprisings in Herzegovina and Bosnia against Ottoman rule were a source of major concern, especially for Vienna, which feared the creation of a large Slav state bordering Dalmatia and Croatia and thus toyed with the idea of annexing the region.[1] Russia called for three-state mediation in the crisis (Russia,

The Bulgarian atrocities

Austria–Hungary and Germany) within the confines of the *Dreikaiserbund* (the League of Three Emperors, created in 1873)[2] and for autonomy, making Gyula Andrassy, the Foreign Minister of Austria–Hungary, suspicious of the Russian motives. The British Prime Minister Benjamin Disraeli was incensed with the autonomy idea in a region whose majority were Muslims (that is, loyal to the Sultan) and likened the situation to Ireland.[3] Andrassy came out with what is known as the Andrassy Note (December 1875), which called for modest reforms in Herzegovina and Bosnia.[4]

The Note was well received by the other powers, but Disraeli, who detested the *Dreikaiserbund* (he believed that it wanted to isolate Britain and resolve the Eastern Question in its favour) and suspected ulterior motives on the part of Andrassy, was not supportive. But when the Porte asked for British assent, Disraeli had no choice than to acquiesce (as he put it, 'We can't be more Turkish than the Sultan'[5]).[6]

The Andrassy Note bore no fruit, due to the Porte's evasiveness. Thus Tsar Alexander II and Otto von Bismarck, the German Chancellor, took the initiative, although the latter was known for his lack of interest in the Balkans (as he had famously put it, it was not worth the bones of a Pomeranian grenadier[7]).[8] Bismarck's blunt *Realpolitik* approach was that a Balkan crisis could be forestalled provided there were territorial gains on the part of the great powers in the Ottoman Empire, but his scheme was not endorsed by the other powers.[9]

Bismarck, Andrassy and Alexander Mikhailovich Gorchakov, concurrently Foreign Minister and Chancellor of Russia, held a meeting in Berlin that produced the Berlin Memorandum (13 May 1876), mainly the work of Andrassy. The Porte was to accept a cease-fire, implement reforms, supply food for the refugees and rebuild houses and churches. The other powers were asked to be signatories to the Memorandum. Italy and France were forthcoming, but not Britain, which sent a squadron to Besika Bay on the mouth of the Dardanelles (sent there, as Disraeli put it, not to repeat the 'bloody blunder' of Navarino,[10] but to support the Ottomans against the Russians). The stance of Britain emboldened the Porte not to accept the Memorandum and made a collective great power involvement impossible.[11]

Lord Derby, the Foreign Secretary, told Pyotr Shuvalov, the Russian ambassador in London, that the Memorandum could exacerbate the situation by giving the impression to the rebels that they were backed by the great powers. Disraeli believed that behind the Memorandum was a masked conspiracy by Russia and Austria–Hungary to partition the Ottoman Empire.[12]

The rejection of the Berlin Memorandum was criticized in Britain by Odo Russell (the British ambassador in Berlin), Edmund Hammond (permanent under-secretary at the Foreign Office from 1854 to 1873) and the respected octogenarian Stratford Canning (now Stratford de Redcliffe). Even Queen Victoria was unhappy about this collusion with 'Turkey'.[13]

The Bulgarian uprising

Meanwhile, an event unknown in Europe had taken place: an uprising by the Bulgarians in the Ottoman province of Rumelia, culminating in what came to be known as the 'Bulgarian atrocities'.

Since the mid-nineteenth century, what is known as the 'Bulgarian Revival' (*vŭzrazhdane*)[14] had taken place. The first major Bulgarian political revolutionary was Georgi Rakowski, who died of tuberculosis in 1867, but not before he put on course the idea of overthrowing Ottoman rule. He was followed by journalist Lyuben Karavelov, poet Christo Botev and the main organizer, Vasil Levski (the 'Apostle of Freedom').[15]

Karavelov, Botev and Levski, as expatriates in Bucharest, formed the Bulgarian Revolutionary Central Committee (BRCK). Levski organized a network of committees in the Bulgarian-inhabited regions, but was arrested by the Ottomans and hanged in Sofia in 1873, a major blow to the Bulgarian cause. Following his death the BRCK was split, with Karavelov opposed to an uprising and Botev advocating it. New figures came to the fore, such as Georgi Benkovsky, Stefan Stambulov (a future Bulgarian Prime Minister and regent) and Zakhari Stoyanov (the later historian of the April Uprising). The BRCK felt that the Herzegovina and Bosnia uprisings provided a good opportunity and decided to take up arms in April or May 1876. The revolt commenced prematurely, on 20 April 1876, for fear that the Ottomans would get wind of it, but it was limited to a few mountain towns; it was headed by Stambulov, Benkovsky and Stoyanov. Botev crossed the border between the principalities and with a number of armed men, to join the rebels, but was killed in a skirmish.[16]

The April Uprising (*Aprilsko vastanie*), as it is known in the Bulgarian narrative, was badly organized and ended in disaster.[17] The whole endeavour was bound to fail; indeed, it has been entertained by Bulgarian historians that it was deliberately staged that way to provoke Ottoman retaliations and bring about external intervention on their behalf by the powers, which raises the agonizing question of whether 'the organizers consciously led the people into massacre'.[18]

The Ottomans, short of money and regular troops (they were preoccupied with Bosnia and Herzegovina), brought in irregular Bashibazouks and Circassians (refugees from Russia) to quell the uprising and terrorize the Bulgarian population into submission.[19] The official Ottoman justification was that these were reprisals for the wanton attacks on Muslim civilians (apparently a few outrages had been committed by the Bulgarians[20]). The onslaught of the irregulars was ghastly: a trail of mayhem with some sixty towns and villages in ashes and a staggering number of massacred women and children, which came to be known in Europe as the 'Bulgarian atrocities'. Reasonable estimates of dead vary from 12,000 to 30,000. The first figure was suggested in the report by the British consul Walter Baring (who had been sent from Constantinople to assess the situation), who, though pro-Ottoman, came out with a scathing indictment of the behaviour of the irregulars.[21] US consul Eugene Schuyler and a compatriot, the noted war correspondent Januarius MacGahan, estimated the dead at 15,000 in a joint on-the-spot investigation. The Bulgarians have claimed 30,000 to as many as 100,000 dead, the Ottomans 2,000 to 3,000. The best-known instance of massacres was in the village of Batak, which was burned to the ground, with 5,000 people killed, including women and children.[22]

The spread of the Balkan crisis

Meanwhile, the revolts in Bosnia and Herzegovina had not been quelled and now Serbia and Montenegro confronted the Porte. In June 1876 the two autonomous principalities of Serbia and Montenegro, under pressure from their respective publics, declared war, in search of independence and territorial gains.[23]

The Serbian and Montenegrin uprisings produced a wave of support in Russian society, led by the Slavophiles. More than 500 soldiers and officers left the Russian army to come as volunteers to the assistance of the Serbs. Much to the dismay of the Tsar, the Serbian army was led by Victor Cherniaev, a former major general of the Tsarist army and hero of Russia's Asian wars. The Montenegrins 'marched from victory to victory', while the Serbs 'went from defeat to defeat',[24] failing miserably under their Russian general. Russia called for a cease-fire (threatening the severance of diplomatic relations if none was forthcoming) to save the Serbs and the Ottoman government agreed to a two-month cease-fire.[25]

In the meantime, a preliminary secret agreement was reached at Reichstadt in Bohemia between Austria–Hungary and Russia, hammered out by Andrassy and the Russian ambassador in Vienna, Novikov (who, like Shuvalov in London, was anti-Pan-Slav), concluding with a more comprehensive agreement between Andrassy and Gorchakov (8 July 1876). In the event of a Russo-Ottoman war, Austria–Hungary would annex Bosnia and Herzegovina; Russia would annex Bessarabia, which it had lost with the 1856 Paris Treaty; Bulgaria, Rumelia and Albania were to become autonomous states; and Thessaly and Crete would be annexed by Greece. If the Ottoman Empire collapsed, Constantinople was to become a free city.[26]

Disraeli, Gladstone and the British public

Apart from apprehension about Russia, another reason for Britain's aloofness was that Henry Elliot, the pro-Ottoman ambassador of Britain in Constantinople, had not drawn attention to the scale of the massacres, downplaying the scale of the massacres, claiming that they had been grossly exaggerated and that there were Bulgarian atrocities against innocent Muslims.[27] Reports in the British press were delayed by two months. But when the news did appear in Britain, especially in the

London *Daily News* (23 June 1876), in an article by Edwin Pears (who had visited the region) with gruesome details, it created a stir. In the following eighteen months no fewer than 3,000 articles appeared in Britain and elsewhere in Europe denouncing the atrocities.[28] Disraeli tried to convince Parliament and Queen Victoria (who was also disturbed by the reports) that the events were exaggerated by the press. Derby, however, instructed Elliot to tell the Ottomans that 'any renewal of the outrages would be more fatal to the Porte than the loss of a battle'[29] and to demand that the crimes stop and the Ottomans rectify the damage.[30]

On 26 June Disraeli dismissed, in Parliament, the *Daily News* story of atrocities and on 10 July denied that torture had been practised 'on a great scale'. 'Oriental people', he added, 'seldom, I believe, resort to torture, but generally terminate their connection with culprits in a more expeditious manner'[31] (laughter was heard, much to Disraeli's annoyance). It was then that his popularity fell and allusions were made to his Jewish origins, implying that this was the reason for his apparent callous indifference to the suffering Balkan Christians.[32]

When William Gladstone (the greatest Liberal British politician of the nineteenth century) told the House that it had been unwise to reject the Berlin Memorandum, Disraeli retorted acidly that the British government could not accept 'coffee-house babble brought by an anonymous Bulgarian to a consul' (he meant Baring) – another phrase that stuck.[33] But Disraeli complained to Derby that he had not been given accurate information.[34]

The person responsible for the lack of adequate information was Elliot, who believed that the insurgents themselves were guilty of 'revolting barbarities'[35] and was convinced that all the insurgencies were Russian plots orchestrated by his arch-rival in Constantinople, the Russian ambassador Nikolay Ignatiev, a well known Pan-Slavist.[36]

Derby, who, unlike Disraeli, was shocked by the atrocities, wrote to Elliot (22 August and 5 September 1876) to say that the sympathy felt in England for the Ottoman Empire 'has been completely destroyed by the lamentable occurrences in Bulgaria', that it had given rise to 'indignation in all classes of English society' and that, 'in the extreme case of Russia declaring war against Turkey, Her Majesty's Government would find it practically impossible to interfere in defence of the Ottoman Empire'.[37]

For Disraeli, any move which could lead to the break-up the Ottoman Empire was to be curbed. Disraeli (as well as the Queen) believed that Russia's aim was the destruction of the Ottoman Empire, and the seizure of the Straits and Constantinople and possibly even territory extending as far British India. Only a credible British threat to intervene on the side of the Ottomans could deter the Russians.[38]

Shuvalov assured Disraeli and Derby that his government had no such outlandish agendas in mind.[39] But given the well known Pan-Slav current in Russia (see chapter 9), it was not totally unreasonable for Disraeli to have adopted a worst-case analysis. Even though Shuvalov and Gorchakov were sincere (though it is not clear whether Disraeli was convinced of their sincerity), the Pan-Slav view could still prevail with the Tsar.[40] Moreover, Disraeli found the oppressors more agreeable than the oppressed Christians. An antipathy for the Balkan Christians and a fascination with the 'Turks' (as aristocrats and fellow conservatives, like the Tories)[41] were ingrained in Disraeli's thinking and originated in his grand tour of the East in 1830 (ironically inspired by Byron's grand tour of 1809). As he had put it then: 'I find the habits of this calm and luxurious people [the Ottomans] entirely agree with my own preconceived opinions of property and enjoyment, and detest the Greeks more than ever'.[42]

In Britain the anti-Ottoman sentiment covered a wider spectrum of opinion than in the Greek case in the 1820s.[43] In those days, 'Victorian religious and ethical sensibility was at its apogee'.[44] According to Richard Shannon, two aspects of Victorian moral sensibility contributed markedly to the domestic agitation over the Bulgarian atrocities: 'the vision of progress and the veiling and exaltation of sexuality'.[45]

The atrocities were seen as a flagrant anachronism. The politician and economist George Campbell (Duke of Argyle) was shocked at the spectacle of the horrors of 'African warfare' and the cruelties of Genghis Khan 'in the days of Queen Victoria'.[46] Thomas Carlyle referred to the 'unspeakable Turk'.[47] The historian Edward Augustus Freeman (a virulent anti-Turk), in his pamphlet 'The Turks in Europe', noted that progress had been achieved in the last twenty years – abolition of slavery, Italy and Germany united, France rid of Bonapartism, Hungary no longer oppressed, Irish no longer bondsmen on their own soil – but 'Turkey remained the last great blot on the face of Europe, a persistent and outrageous challenge to all that nineteenth-century civilisation stood for'.[48]

The dishonouring of chastity and the debauching of the conjugal union touched on the most sensitive of Victorian nerves.[49] William Stead, the famous journalist, editor of the daily *Northern Echo*, saw the outrages perpetrated against Bulgarian women as if they had been committed against his mother. Freeman referred to the Turkish reputation for pederasty.[50]

Soon none other than Gladstone, the undisputed leader of British popular liberalism,[51] chose to abandon his retirement and join the fray. He began with careful speeches in Parliament and upon receiving no satisfactory answers from Disraeli he decided to write a pamphlet. *Bulgarian Horrors and the Question of the East*, written within three days while he was in bed with lumbago, sold more than 200,000 copies within less than a month. This fiery pamphlet 'did more than any other publication of the century to destroy pro-Turkish feeling in Britain'.[52]

Curiously, Gladstone had not come on board from the beginning. As Shannon has put it, this was 'far less a case of Gladstone exciting passion than of popular passion exciting Gladstone'.[53] Three fellow Oxonians played a considerable role in his conversion, all three his friends: Freeman, the theologian James Fraser, and

Henry Liddon, Professor of Theology at Oxford University. A fourth Oxonian should be mentioned who was close to Gladstone and was an authority on matters of international law, Robert Phillimore.[54] Stratford was the first to bring the atrocities to Gladstone's attention. Mention should also be made of a formidable Russian lady residing in London, Madame Olga Kireeva Novikova (see chapter 9), the Duke of Argyle, Stead, the Reverent William Denton and Canon Malcolm MacColl.[55]

In retrospect, it is difficult to imagine Gladstone indifferent on a matter that 'ignited the moral passion of the great section of the British public on an issue which engaged every element of his politico-religious existence – his Catholic Christianity, his European sense, his Liberalism, his democratic sympathies'.[56]

Gladstone in his pamphlet painted a bleak picture of the situation and of Ottoman culpability and added: 'I entreat my countrymen ... to require and to insist that our Government ... shall apply all its vigour to concur with the other States of Europe in obtaining the extinction of the Turkish executive power in Bulgaria'.[57] He famously continued:[58]

> Let the Turks now carry away their abuses in the only possible manner, namely by carrying off themselves. Their Zaptiehs and their Mudirs, their Bimbashis and their Yuzbashis, their Kaimakams and their Pashas, one and all, bag and baggage, shall, I hope, clear out of the province they have desolated and profaned.

The expression 'bag and baggage' was Stratford's from the 1820s and Gladstone did not mean that the Ottomans should leave Europe, but only Bulgaria.[59] In a previous passage (as well as in Parliament[60]) he referred to upholding the 'territorial integrity of Turkey', though he added that there were 'higher objects of policy', such as 'humanity, rationally understood' and 'justice'.[61]

Disraeli was furious with the pamphlet and regarded it 'vindictive and ill-written', and 'of all the Bulgarian horrors the greatest'.[62]

Three days later, at a rally in Blackheath (9 September 1876), 10,000 to 15,000 people, in pouring rain, listened enthralled to Gladstone's captivating speech. He repeated the argumentation of his pamphlet, accusing the Ottomans of misgovernment, repression and massacres, and pointed to the Tory government's complicity by withholding information from the British public and supporting the Sultan. His proposal, however, was moderate: Bulgarian autonomy under Ottoman suzerainty.[63]

A national convention was organized by Stead and the Liberals, which took place at St James Hall in Piccadilly, London (8 December 1876), with the participation of a wide spectrum of leading personalities. Gladstone's speech at the meeting was a sensation. At the close of the meeting he offered his arm to Madame Novikova and escorted her from the platform to the door.[64]

Gladstone's overall stance during this period had several effects, according to Gerald Clayton: it completed the estrangement between himself and Disraeli

The Bulgarian atrocities

(and the Queen); it made it impossible for Disraeli to resort to war on behalf of the Ottoman Empire; it introduced a note of bitterness into public life that divided the country; and it encouraged the consideration of moral values as an important aspect of foreign policy.[65]

The Disraeli–Gladstone clash over the Bulgarian atrocities was also a discord between realism and idealistic liberalism in international politics. For Disraeli it was inconceivable that *Realpolitik* should give way to 'a moral crusade' and that the 'interests of humanity' should prevail over 'the permanent and important interests of England'.[66] For Gladstone, the very opposite was the case: moral and humanitarian concerns had to override narrow national interests. As he put it: 'What is to be the consequence to civilisation and humanity, to public order, if British interests are to be the rule for British agents all over the world, and are to be for them the measure of right or wrong?'[67] No doubt had Gladstone and not Disraeli been the Prime Minister, then British policy during the Balkan crisis would have been different. As Blake has put it: 'That Disraeli of all people should have been Prime Minister at this particular moment seems indeed an irony of history'.[68]

For the next two years the country was divided between 'Turks', Turcophiles, 'home-Turks' or Russophobes, and 'Bulgarians', 'Russians', Russophiles, Turcophobes or 'Muscovites'.[69] The latter, the so-called 'atrocitarians', were in a great majority in the north of England, in the south-east and in Wales, but not in the rest of England and negligible in Scotland and Ireland, and generally among Catholics (probably due to the fact that the Bulgarians were Orthodox Christians). The Church of England was also for the most part anti-atrocitarian, as were the army, navy, high financial circles, top bankers and most of the nobility.[70]

In addition to an array of prominent Liberal politicians, such as Lord John Russell, William Harcourt, the Duke of Argyll and John Bright, an impressive number of thinkers and academics, the 'high Victorian intelligentsia', condemned the atrocities and called for British involvement on behalf of the Bulgarians. They were personalities of different ideological hues, who on other matters were at loggerheads. Apart from Freeman and Liddon, they included Charles Darwin, Herbert Spencer and Thomas Carlyle, philosophers Henry Sidgwick and Thomas Hill Green, the blind economist Henry Fawcett, the Oxford jurist and Liberal politician James Bryce, political theorist William Lecky, historian and social critic Goldwin Smith, art critic and polymath John Ruskin, poet Robert Browning, artist and writer William Morris, and novelists Antony Trollope, James Anthony Froude and Thomas Hughes. The intellectuals against were fewer but included an equally odd assortment, such as theologian Benjamin Jowett, judge Fitzjames Stephen, essayist Walter Bagehot, socialist writer Henry Hyndman, the exiled Karl Marx[71] and poets Matthew Arnold, Lord Tennyson and Algernon Charles Swinburne (who pointed out that the 'Turks' were no worse than the British and other oppressors across the world).[72]

The Balkan crisis gave rise to another intriguing phenomenon, British humanitarian aid, which went both ways, including wounded Ottomans during the Russo-Ottoman War of 1877–78, which is quite striking, given the well known European bias against 'the Turks' (see chapter 3). The bulk of assistance was provided by trained medical personnel, that is, nurses, medical doctors and surgeons, but there were also some former military supporting the Serbs.

There were three variants of humanitarianism by voluntary groups. There were those supporting the Balkan nationalist struggles that assisted the sick and wounded Balkan Slavs. The main spokespersons of this trend were Freeman, Lindon, James Lewis Farley and the medical doctor Humphrey Sandwith, based in Belgrade. In this context we see the activities of the League in Aid of the Christian *Rayahs* in Turkey, the Bulgarian Peasants Relief Fund and the Sick and Wounded Russian Soldiers' Relief Fund. There were those who wanted to remain equidistant (along the standards set by International Commission of the Red Cross) and were thus prepared to assist all victims of the wars. They were headed by Lady Strangford, Vincent Barrington-Kennett and Colonel Robert Loyd Lindsay, and this line was obvious in the activity of the Eastern War Sick and Wounded Fund, the National Aid Society and the Red Cross Society. There was also a smaller group providing humanitarian aid to the wounded Ottoman soldiers in both the Balkan and Caucasus war theatres. The main figures in this endeavour were Lady Burdett-Coutts and the Duke of Sutherland (Lady Strangford and Barrington-Kennett also contributed), and its main organizations were the Turkish Compassionate Fund and in particular the Stanford House Committee.[73]

The Conference of Constantinople and the prelude to war

Derby, upon the suggestion of Gorchakov, called (on 4 November) for a conference to be held in Constantinople to settle the Balkan crisis, but a few days later Disraeli delivered a bellicose veiled anti-Russian speech at a dinner at Guildhall, London (see chapter 9). The powers agreed to take part in the conference, as did a reluctant Porte. Derby urged that, in the conference, no power was to gain territorial advantages and called for autonomy for Bosnia and Herzegovina, status quo in generous terms for Serbia and Montenegro and nothing for the Bulgarians.[74]

Lord Salisbury (the Minister for India) was appointed by Disraeli to head the British delegation. In his visits before the conference, to Paris, Berlin (Bismarck), Vienna (Andrassy) and Rome, he got the impression that the integrity of the Ottoman Empire could not be upheld.[75] As he reported to Derby, 'In the course of my travels I have not succeeded in finding the friend of the Turk. He does not exist. Most believe his hour has come'.[76] Bismarck tried to dispel British suspicions of Russia and Salisbury found him indifferent to the possibility of a Russo-Ottoman war, but ready to do everything possible to avert an Austro-Russian or Anglo-Russian clash.[77]

The Bulgarian atrocities

In the Constantinople Conference (11 December 1876–20 January 1897) the main figures were Salisbury and Ignatiev, the latter chairing the conference. The most fruitful period of the deliberations was the preliminary phase, in December, in which the Porte was not allowed to participate. The humanitarian aspect loomed large in the discussions. According to the minutes of the first meeting of the conference (11 December) they were dealing with a collective, European question 'which does not interest Russia alone, but the whole of Europe, the general prosperity, humanity, and Christian civilization. May the peace of Europe and the well-being of the Christian populations of Turkey serve as a recompense for the troubles and difficulties connected with the undertaking [of the conference]'.[78]

Surprisingly, confidence developed between Salisbury and Ignatiev. Their ability to work closely was due – apart from Ignatiev's adroitness and charm – to the fact that Salisbury, unlike Elliot (who participated in the conference), had no illusions about the Ottoman Empire; he accepted the idea of eventual independence of the Balkan peoples and was not obsessed by the Russian bogey. Ignatiev and Salisbury agreed to the formation of two autonomous Bulgarian entities (see chapter 9). Ignatiev favoured a short-term European collective humanitarian intervention[79] and Salisbury was not completely averse to some kind of short-term military occupation. The powers agreed that some coercive measure would be indispensable to enforce the reforms and to ensure that such massacres were not repeated. Serbia was to retain the status quo, Montenegro was to gain an outlet to the sea, Bulgaria was to be divided into two parts and Bosnia and Herzegovina were to be united.[80]

When the Ottoman representative, Erdem Pasha, was admitted to the conference (24 December), he referred to Ottoman sovereign rights and told the representatives that a modern Constitution was to be adopted, a two-chamber Parliament was to be elected and substantial reforms were to be made by the Ottoman state anyway, and thus the proposals of the conference were redundant and overtaken by events.[81]

Indeed, a Constitution was promulgated, elections were duly held (January–March 1877) and the first Ottoman Parliament emerged, with all major communities represented, making the measures suggested by the powers seemingly irrelevant. But when the conference ended its work inconclusively (20 January 1877), the new Sultan, Abdulhamid II, sacked Grand Vizier Midhat Pasha (5 February), the main initiator of the liberalization process, though the Parliament was allowed to function for some ten months.[82]

The conference's failure was ostensibly due to the Ottoman posture. But it has been argued that the failure of the conference was due to Britain, because it spoke with two voices, with Elliot, at daggers drawn with Ignatiev, regarded – not least by the Ottomans – to be the true representative of the British Prime Minister.[83] Characteristically, Derby wired Salisbury on 22 December asking him to tell the Porte 'that England will not assent to, or assist in, coercive measures, military or naval, against the Porte'.[84] In April 1877 (on the eve of the Russo-Ottoman War) Elliot was replaced by Austen Henry Layard (a former archaeologist of Mesopotamia), who was pro-Ottoman, like Elliot, and a close friend of Disraeli, a clear sign that the British favourable stance towards the Porte had not changed.[85]

In the meantime, exploratory talks had commenced in secrecy from November 1876 onwards between Russia and Austria–Hungary, and secret agreements were signed (15 January and 18 March 1877) that in the event of a Russo-Ottoman war, Vienna would adopt a benevolent neutrality and 'occupy' (and not 'annex', as the Austrians wanted) Bosnia and Herzegovina. If the Ottoman Empire collapsed, Constantinople was to become a free city, no great Slav state was to be created in the Balkans and the two parties were to lend each other assistance at the diplomatic level in reaching a final settlement that would be favourable to both of them.[86]

Following the failure of the Constantinople Conference, Gorchakov sent Ignatiev to the European courts in a last-ditch attempt to establish a united front. An ambassadors' conference was held in London, which adopted the London Protocol (31 March 1877), a watered-down version of what Ignatiev had proposed, mainly the work of Derby and Shuvalov. The Protocol called upon the Ottomans to demobilize and introduce reforms. Were such reforms to fail, the powers reserved the right to consider what common measures to adopt.[87]

Gorchakov was unhappy with the Protocol and it remains unclear whether the Russians desired it, for if accepted by the Porte it would have tied their hands. The Tsar was initially against resorting to war but told the British, via Shuvalov, that he desired peace, although not at any price.[88]

Abdulhamid made the fatal mistake of rejecting even this mild Protocol, on the grounds that it violated the 1856 Treaty of Paris (which guaranteed Ottoman territorial integrity)[89] and that it amounted to 'humiliating tutelage by Europe';[90] his rejection permitted Russia to take matters into its own hands, and it declared war (24 April 1877). Russia justified its aggression by its traditional role as protector of the Christians of the Ottoman Empire and on humanitarian grounds (see chapter 9).

Given how things had transpired, with the Porte the obstructing party, the other parties (bar Britain) were hardly at odds with Russia's resort to war. Russia entered the war in favourable international circumstances, having an arrangement with Austria–Hungary and having been assured of benevolent neutrality on the part of Germany, France and Italy. As for Britain, it could scarcely act without at least one ally, and no such ally was forthcoming.[91]

The British divided over the war

The Russian forces advanced on two fronts against the Ottomans, in the Balkans directed towards the Bulgarian regions and in the southern Caucasus towards the Armenian-inhabited regions. Upon the start of the war Derby sent a note to

The Bulgarian atrocities

Russia through Shuvalov (6 May 1877) referring to the danger to British interests in Suez, Egypt, the Persian Gulf and Constantinople.[92] The reply was that Russia would not touch Suez and Egypt, and as for Constantinople, Gorchakov could give only one assurance: that there would be no annexation, specifying that a pledge against temporary occupation would, if it became known, only encourage the 'Turks' in their obstinacy. Shuvalov told Derby that once the British realized that Russia did not want Constantinople they could put pressure on the Porte and save them from the need to occupy the city. Derby believed that the Russians were sincere but Disraeli was convinced that the Russians sought to take over Constantinople and dictate their terms to Europe on that basis.[93]

At this juncture Gorchakov wrote to Shuvalov: *'The English find it hard to understand a war of religious and national sentiment, and being incapable of one themselves, they consequently look for* arrières pensées'.[94]

Throughout the hostilities and its aftermath, the British were bitterly divided as supporters or foes of Russia as never before on a matter of foreign policy, or at least since the French Revolution.[95] The issue was so acute that personal relationships were severed, families clashed, and Tories and Liberals were divided even among themselves. As for the animosity between the two great statesmen, Disraeli (since June 1876 Earl of Beaconsfield, a gift of the Queen) and Gladstone, it now reached its peak.[96] As Harcourt put it to Charles Dilke: 'Gladstone and Dizzy [Disraeli] seem to cap one another in folly and imprudence, and I do not know which has made the greatest ass of himself'.[97] Gladstone became very unpopular in fashionable circles, was hissed in public, hooted at the lobby of the House of Commons and had the windows of his house smashed (he was derided by the Tory press as a Russian agent, especially in view of the Novikova connection[98]). Gladstone was deeply hurt but told the House (on 14 May 1877) that if the Russians, who were 'capable of noble spirits as any people in Europe', succeeded in the war, 'as an Englishman I shall hide my head, but as a man I shall rejoice'.[99]

The mood grasped the public as well. According to a popular music hall song:[100] 'We don't want to fight but by Jingo if we do / We've got the ships, we've got the men, we've got the money too / We've fought the Bear before, and while we're Britons true / The Russians shall not have Constantinople'. It was from this mention of 'Jingo' (apparently meant as a minced oath, to avoid saying Jesus) that the contemporary radical thinker George Holyoake coined the term 'jingoism'[101] to mean extreme and aggressive nationalism.[102]

The Queen in jingoist pitch sent an avalanche of letters and telegrams to Disraeli. As he put it: 'The Faery [Victoria] writes every day and telegrams every hour: this is almost literally the case' and a little later he added, 'it rains telegrams morn, noon and night'.[103] She wrote that if the Russians reached Constantinople 'the Queen would be so humiliated that she thinks that she will abdicate at once'.[104] In January 1878, when the Russians had won the war, she was beside herself with rage, writing to Disraeli that '[s]he feels she cannot …

remain the sovereign of *a country that is letting itself down to kiss the feet of the great barbarians*, the retarders of all liberty and civilization that exists'. And added: '*Oh, if the Queen were a man, she would like to go and give those Russians*, whose word one cannot believe, *such a beating*! We shall never be friends again till we have it out'.[105]

The cabinet remained divided between those espousing a vigorous response, headed by Disraeli, and those calling for restraint and the avoidance of war, headed by Derby, Carnarvon, the Colonial Secretary, and Salisbury, 'the three Lords' as they were known.[106] Derby in his attempt to avoid a war with Russia went as far as revealing to Shuvalov – directly or through his wife, Lady Derby, who was on close terms with the Russian ambassador[107] – the lack of unity in the cabinet for going to war. Derby was convinced that the Russians meant what they said, that they sought reforms in the Balkans and not Constantinople, and he feared that war could come about as a result of the bellicosity of Disraeli, which could provoke the Tsar to do exactly what Britain did not want him to do.[108]

In spite of the differences in the British government, Disraeli was able to extract a unanimous decision from the cabinet to declare war if Russia occupied Constantinople without arranging for the immediate retirement from the city, and the British fleet under Admiral Hornby was send to the Dardanelles.[109]

From San Stefano to Berlin

The Russian army, after initial success, faced tough resistance from the modernized Ottoman army, notably in the fortress of Plevna in northern Bulgaria. The war on two fronts dragged on for ten months and the previously confident Russians had to ask for the military assistance of Serbia, Montenegro and Romania, as well as Greece (the first three entered the war). Finally the Russians took Plevna (11 December), and then entered Sofia (in 4 January 1878) and Adrianople (20 January 1878).

An armistice was concluded on very severe Russian terms (27 January 1878), a development that, incidentally, gave Abdulhamid the excuse to dissolve Parliament (14 February) and assert his own brand of reactionary despotism and Muslim conservatism.[110]

Ignatiev and the Ottoman Foreign Minister signed the Treaty of San Stefano (3 March 1878), which provided for a large autonomous Bulgaria, from the Aegean Sea to the Danube, far larger than present-day Bulgaria, with a considerable Aegean coastline, covering even areas in which Bulgarians were not the majority population (Skopje, Prizren, Monastir, the lakes of Prespa and Ohrid) – areas that could have gone, on the basis of ethnic composition (if the Muslims were not taken into consideration), to Serbia, Greece or a future Albania.[111]

San Stefano was obviously a major mistake on the part of Russia, however, for it upset the power balance in the Balkans and showed no consideration for the interests of other states, especially Austria–Hungary, disregarding the two secret agreements with Andrassy.[112]

The terms of San Stefano brought Britain and Austria–Hungary 'to the verge of open rupture' with Russia.[113] London and Vienna called for a fundamental revision of San Stefano and threatened war.[114] From February 1878 onwards, and for some ten weeks, an Anglo-Russian war seemed likely.[115] As Disraeli put it, 'We are drifting into war', but he added 'If we are bold and determined we shall secure peace, and dictate its conditions to Europe'.[116] Clearly, war was not what he really wanted but his threat at this stage was no bluff. Russia seemed impressed by British stance and, with its forces depleted by battle and disease and with its finances strained, was keen to avoid a war with Britain.[117]

Derby resigned as Foreign Secretary, to be replaced by Salisbury, who presented the British views for a settlement in a letter he sent to the other great powers, known as the 'Salisbury circular'. Shuvalov, after some initial hesitation, was able to meet Salisbury eye to eye, when the latter made it clear that the views of the two governments were not far apart; that the main aim of Britain was a much smaller Bulgaria; and that, for its part, Britain wanted to acquire an outpost that would safeguard its Asiatic interests (Cyprus was to be that outpost, though it was not mentioned). A secret protocol between Salisbury and Shuvalov was signed (30 May), whose terms included drastic modification of the Bulgarian boundaries, no Bulgarian opening to the Aegean Sea, Ottoman troops not to be allowed in the Bulgarian province (a Russian *sine qua non*), Greece to have a voice in the future of Thessaly and Epirus (a British desire), Bessarabia to revert to Russia and Batoum, Ardahan and Kars to be annexed by Russia.[118]

The Congress of Berlin was held at the highest level, with the participation of Bismarck and Bülow (the German Foreign Minister), Disraeli and Salisbury, Gorchakov and Shuvalov, and Andrassy as the main protagonists, with Italy under Corti and France under Waddington in the background. Ironically, the Ottoman Empire was represented by two non-ethnic Turks, the Ottoman Greek Karatheodori Pasha (the Foreign Minister) and Mehmed Ali Pasha, a renegade Prussian, both of whom were snubbed and side-lined, not least by Bismarck. Bismarck was made president of the Congress and proved a very effective one at that. Yet even though previous understandings had been reached as to the general outline of the forthcoming treaty, there was considerable wrangling, especially over the limits of Bulgaria, with Disraeli threatening to leave the conference and Shuvalov being as accommodating as possible.[119]

According to the Treaty of Berlin, Romania, Serbia and Montenegro, with some additions to their territories, were to become fully independent states. The Bulgarian-inhabited region was split into two: a vassal state of Bulgaria with Sofia as its capital; and a semi-autonomous Eastern Rumelia. Russia acquired Bessarabia and Kars, Ardahan and Batum from the Ottoman Empire, Britain got Cyprus (under Ottoman suzerainty) and Austria–Hungary was to occupy

Bosnia and Herzegovina as well as the Sanjak of Novipazar. The Berlin Treaty also referred to the treatment and protection of the Armenians in the Ottoman Empire and to the well-being of the Christians.[120]

The Berlin Treaty holds a special place in the history of humanitarian intervention. It was agreed that 'intervention for humanity becomes a basis of a special public law in the relations between Europe and the Porte', whereby the Porte was henceforth 'under the permanent control of the Concert of Europe regarding internal administrative acts'.[121] The Treaty allowed for a right of intervention on the part of the signatory states 'in all the cases in order to guarantee a minimum of rights of the inhabitants of Turkey in Europe and in particular to assure religious liberty'.[122]

Assessment

A basic characteristic of this case was the unprecedented role played by public opinion,[123] especially in Russia (see chapter 9) and Britain. The 1877 war was at the time not regarded as humanitarian by European policy-makers,[124] the obvious exception being Russian policy-makers and commentators (see chapter 9). However, it was not seen unsympathetically. According to the authoritative Bluntschli for instance (writing in 1879), Russia was motivated by its honour and 'sentiments of sympathy for the oppressed Christians', which led it 'to force Turkey to abide by its duties'.[125]

More generally, according to Rodogno the European powers regarded intervention against massacre in the Ottoman Empire conceivable but in the end their security priorities prevailed, which did not make a collective humanitarian intervention possible. For Britain in particular 'humanity' was given up in the name of 'balance of power' interests.[126] Rodogno argues that this was a case of 'non-intervention' on humanitarian grounds, though the plan of the Constantinople Conference of 1876 'was quite close to a humanitarian intervention for it encompassed coercive measures to enforce the reforms aimed at avoiding the repetition of massacre in the future'.[127]

But, over time, an increasing number of scholars have come to regard it as a case of collective humanitarian involvement, which, in view of the Ottoman intransigence, led to Russian military intervention, amounting to a full-scale war within a humanitarian rationale, as seen by the stance of publicists such as Rougier[128] and Stowell,[129] apart from Russian publicists such as Martens[130] and Mandelstam.[131] More recently, a number of international lawyers have regarded it as a case of military humanitarian intervention by Russia with the support of the other powers bar Britain. They include Ganji,[132] Fonteyne,[133] Behuniak,[134] Bazyler,[135] Abiew[136] and Grewe,[137] and, more circumspectly, Fenwick,[138] and among international relations scholars dealing with humanitarian intervention, Finnemore,[139] Bass[140] and Knudsen.[141]

Concluding remarks

In the Bulgarian case one sees a similar pattern with the previous two cases (saving Christians, great power consultations, conferences in Constantinople and London, agreements and so on). The main new features in dealing with humanitarian plight are the following: final whole-sale military intervention (war), unilateral this time, but with benevolent neutrality by the other great powers, save Britain; the far greater role of the press and public opinion, especially in Britain and Russia, in the former case putting a lid on the British government's pro-Ottoman behaviour and in the latter spurring intervention; and a final high-level peace conference, the Congress of Berlin, which drastically altered the situation in the Balkans (new borders, three new independent states and two tributary states) and also addressed the well-being of religious minorities in the Ottoman Empire. On the downside there were four problems: (1) deviation from previous agreements by one great power (Russia in San Stefano), (2) a real danger of war between great powers (in this case Russia and Britain), (3) bitter internal split in one of the great powers, Britain, over the question; and (4) the aggressive stance of many influential Russians based on pan-nationalist grounds, namely Pan-Slavism, triggered by the humanitarian plight.

Notes

1. R. Albrecht-Carrié, *A Diplomatic History of Europe Since the Congress of Vienna* (London: Methuen, 1958), 168; R. Millman, *Britain and the Eastern Question 1875–1878* (Oxford: Clarendon Press, 1979), 31; A. L. Macfie, *The Eastern Question, 1774–1923* (London: Longman, 1996) [1989], 36; M. Ković, *Disraeli and the Eastern Question* (Oxford: Oxford University Press, 2011), 97–8.
2. For the League of Three Emperors see R. B. Mowat, *The Concert of Europe* (London: Macmillan, 1930), 48–9.
3. Ković, *Disraeli and the Eastern Question*, 91–2.
4. B. H. Sumner, *Russia and the Balkans, 1870–1880* (Oxford: Clarendon Press, 1937), 152–3; R. W. Seton-Watson, *Disraeli, Gladstone and the Eastern Question* (London: Frank Cass, 1962) [1935], 27–8; M. D. Stojanovic, *The Great Powers and the Balkans, 1875–1878* (Cambridge: Cambridge University Press, 1939), 22–5, 28–43–4; Ković, *Disraeli and the Eastern Question*, 97–101.
5. Quoted in R. B. Mowat, *A History of European Diplomacy, 1815–1914* (London: Edward Arnold, 1922), 224.
6. Ibid., 224; Ković, *Disraeli and the Eastern Question*, 84–5, 99–101; G. D. Clayton, *Britain and the Eastern Question: Missolonghi to Gallipoli* (London: Lion Library, 1971), 127, 132; Albrecht-Carrié, *A Diplomatic History of Europe Since the Congress of Vienna*, 169; Seton-Watson, *Disraeli, Gladstone and the Eastern Question*, 28–9; Stojanovic, *The Great Powers and the Balkans*, 48–9.
7. Albrecht-Carrié, *A Diplomatic History of Europe Since the Congress of Vienna*, 167.
8. Seton-Watson, *Disraeli, Gladstone and the Eastern Question*, 32; Mowat, *A History of European Diplomacy*, 224.

9   Stojanovic, *The Great Powers and the Balkans*, 44–5, 61; L. S. Stavrianos, *The Balkans Since 1453* (London: Hurst, 2000) [1958], 407.
10 Ković, *Disraeli and the Eastern Question*, 112.
11 Seton-Watson, *Disraeli, Gladstone and the Eastern Question*, 32–5; Sumner, *Russia and the Balkans*, 161–5; Stavrianos, *The Balkans*, 400–1; M. S. Anderson, *The Eastern Question, 1774–1923: A Study in International Relations* (London: Macmillan, 1966), 183; B. Jelavich, *A Century of Russian Foreign Policy* (Philadelphia: J. B. Lippincott, 1964), 177; Millman, *Britain and the Eastern Question*, 87–9; D. Rodogno, *Against Massacre: Humanitarian Intervention in the Ottoman Empire, 1815–1914. The Emergence of a European Concept and International Practice* (Princeton: Princeton University Press, 2012), 145–6.
12 Macfie, *The Eastern Question*, 37–8; Seton-Watson, *Disraeli, Gladstone and the Eastern Question*, 38–9;Ković, *Disraeli and the Eastern Question*, 107–12; R. Blake, *Disraeli* (London: Methuen, 1966), 588.
13 Seton-Watson, *Disraeli, Gladstone and the Eastern Question*, 34; Clayton, *Britain and the Eastern Question*, 152; Millman, *Britain and the Eastern Question*, 95.
14 R. Daskalov, *The Making of a Nation in the Balkans: Historiography of the Bulgarian Revival* (Budapest: Central European University Press, 2004), 1.
15 Ibid., 176–90; see also M. Glenny, *The Balkans 1804–1999: Nationalism, War and the Great Powers* (London: Granta Books, 1999), 119–20.
16 R. J. Crampton, *A Concise History of Bulgaria* (Cambridge: Cambridge University Press, 2005, 2nd edition) [1997], 78; H. Temperley, 'The Bulgarian and Other Atrocities, 1875–8, in the Light of Historical Criticism', *Proceedings of the British Academy*, 17 (1931), 8, 11; D. Harris, *Britain and the Bulgarian Horrors of 1876* (Chicago: University of Chicago Press, 1939), 9–18; Stavrianos, *The Balkans*, 378–9; B. Jelavich, *History of the Balkans: Eighteenth and Nineteenth Centuries* (Cambridge: Cambridge University Press, 1983), 346–7.
17 Jelavich, *History of the Balkans*, 347; Stavrianos, *The Balkans*, 379–80; Crampton, *A Concise History of Bulgaria*, 80; Daskalov, *The Making of a Nation in the Balkans*, 199, 201; Glenny, *The Balkans*, 107–8.
18 Daskalov, *The Making of a Nation in the Balkans*, 195, 197, 199, 201.
19 Clayton, *Britain and the Eastern Question*, 135; Crampton, *A Concise History of Bulgaria*, 80; S. K. Pavlowitch, *A History of the Balkans, 1804–1945* (London: Longman, 1999), 109.
20 Temperley, 'The Bulgarian and Other Atrocities', 92; R. J. Crampton, *Bulgaria* (Oxford: Oxford University Press, 2007), 92; Stavrianos, *The Balkans*, 379; Glenny, *The Balkans*, 107–110; Rodogno, *Against Massacre*, 147.
21 Rodogno, *Against Massacre*, 148–9.
22 Temperley, 'The Bulgarian and Other Atrocities', 21–5; Harris, *Britain and the Bulgarian Horrors*, 20–3; Pavlowitch, *A History of the Balkans*, 109–10; Stavrianos, *The Balkans*, 380; Glenny, *The Balkans*, 108–10; G. J. Bass, *Freedom's Battle: The Origins of Humanitarian Intervention* (New York: Vintage Books, 2009), 235–7, 256–7.
23 Stavrianos, *The Balkans*, 401–2; D. MacKenzie, *Imperial Dreams, Harsh Realities: Tsarist Russian Foreign Policy, 1815–1917* (Fort Worth: Harcourt Brace College Publishers, 1994), 74; Jelavich, *A Century of Russian Foreign Policy*, 178.
24 Temperley, 'The Bulgarian and Other Atrocities', 8.
25 Ković, *Disraeli and the Eastern Question*, 166.
26 Seton-Watson, *Disraeli, Gladstone and the Eastern Question*, 46–8; Sumner, *Russia and the Balkans*, 173–6; Stojanovic, *The Great Powers and the Balkans*, 74–7; Jelavich, *A Century of Russian Foreign Policy*, 179; Macfie, *The Eastern Question*, 38–9.

27 Harris, *Britain and the Bulgarian Horrors*, 27–32. However, Rodogno claims that Elliot *had* duly reported the disturbance to his government but that Lord Tenterden, the permanent under-secretary at the Foreign Office, had censored the documents in question. Rodogno, *Against Massacre*, 147.
28 Glenny, *The Balkans*, 109.
29 Quote in Macfie, *The Eastern Question*, 38.
30 Anderson, *The Eastern Question*, 184; Blake, *Disraeli*, 592; Bass, *Freedom's Battle*, 258–79; Rodogno, *Against Massacre*, 147–51.
31 Quoted in Harris, *Britain and the Bulgarian Horrors*, 53; Blake, *Disraeli*, 593.
32 Ković, *Disraeli and the Eastern Question*, 130, 147–8.
33 Blake, *Disraeli*, 593, 593.
34 Seton-Watson, *Disraeli, Gladstone and the Eastern Question*, 54–5; Blake, *Disraeli*, 593; Clayton, *Britain and the Eastern Question*, 154;Ković, *Disraeli and the Eastern Question*, 130–1.
35 Temperley, 'The Bulgarian and Other Atrocities', 9; Millman, *Britain and the Eastern Question*, 125–6.
36 Harris, *Britain and the Bulgarian Horrors*, 26–7, 29, 31; Seton-Watson, *Disraeli, Gladstone and the Eastern Question*, 64–7.
37 Quoted in Seton-Watson, *Disraeli, Gladstone and the Eastern Question*, 62.
38 Blake, *Disraeli*, 571, 578, 608.
39 *Ibid.*, 577.
40 *Ibid.*, 610.
41 Ković, *Disraeli and the Eastern Question*, 25.
42 Quoted *ibid.*, 23. For details of his grand tour and identification with the Ottomans, see *ibid.*, 9–28.
43 R. Shannon, *Gladstone and the Bulgarian Agitation 1876* (London: Thomas Nelson and Sons, 1963); Harris, *Britain and the Bulgarian Horrors*, 61–253.
44 Blake, *Disraeli*, 600.
45 Shannon, *Gladstone and the Bulgarian Agitation*, 30.
46 Quoted *ibid.*, 31.
47 Quoted in Rodogno, *Against Massacre*, 156.
48 Quoted in Shannon, *Gladstone and the Bulgarian Agitation*, 31.
49 *Ibid.*, 33.
50 *Ibid.*, 34.
51 For British popular liberalism and Gladstone, see E. F. Biagini, *Liberty, Retrenchment and Reform: Popular Liberalism in the Age of Gladstone, 1860–1880* (Cambridge: Cambridge University Press, 1992).
52 Anderson, *The Eastern Question*, 184.
53 Shannon, *Gladstone and the Bulgarian Agitation*, 110.
54 See C. Sylvest, 'International Law in Nineteenth Century Britain', *British Year Book of International Law*, 75 (2004), 27 and 27 n.87.
55 Shannon, *Gladstone and the Bulgarian Agitation*, 49, 93, 99; Rodogno, *Against Massacre*, 153, 157.
56 Shannon, *Gladstone and the Bulgarian Agitation*, 89.
57 Right Hon. W. E. Gladstone, M.P., *Bulgarian Horrors and the Question of the East* (London: John Murray, 1876), 61.
58 *Ibid.*, 61–2.
59 Clayton, *Britain and the Eastern Question*, 155. Gladstone in a letter to *The Times* stated

that he meant the Ottomans leaving Bulgaria and not the Balkans. See Rodogno, *Against Massacre*, 155.
60 Ković, *Disraeli and the Eastern Question*, 134–5.
61 Gladstone, *Bulgarian Horrors and the Question of the East*, 50.
62 Quoted in Blake, *Disraeli*, 602.
63 Biagini, *Liberty, Retrenchment and Reform*, 388; Rodogno, *Against Massacre*, 155.
64 Seton-Watson, *Disraeli, Gladstone and the Eastern Question*, 110–12; Rodogno, *Against Massacre*, 156.
65 Clayton, *Britain and the Eastern Question*, 153–4, 155.
66 Blake, *Disraeli*, 605.
67 Quoted in Seton-Watson, *Disraeli, Gladstone and the Eastern Question*, 69.
68 Blake, *Disraeli*, 600.
69 D. Anderson, *The Balkan Volunteers* (London: Hutchinson, 1968), 5–6; Blake, *Disraeli*, 603–4.
70 Shannon, *Gladstone and the Bulgarian Agitation*, 150–61.
71 Marx detested imperial Russia and hoped that the 'gallant Turks' would defeat the Russians and provoke a revolution in Russia. See *ibid.*, 237.
72 See for the motives and rationale of each one of them, *ibid.*, 203–38. See also V. Goldsworthy, *Inventing Ruritania: The Imperialism of the Imagination* (New Haven: Yale University Press, 1998), 31, 36–41; Rodogno, *Against Massacre*, 156–7.
73 Anderson, *The Balkan Volunteers*. For an account of the activities of the Stanford House Committee, see *Report and Record of the Relief and Sick and Wounded Turkish Soldiers* (Chairman the Duke of Sutherland), *Russo-Turkish War, 1877–78* (London: Spottiswoode, 1879). See also R. Gill, *Calculating Compassion: Humanitarianism and Relief in War, Britain 1870–1914* (Manchester: Manchester University Press, 2013), 96–123.
74 Sumner, *Russia and the Balkans*, 232–3; Blake, *Disraeli*, 611; Millman, *Britain and the Eastern Question*, 195; Ković, *Disraeli and the Eastern Question*, 168–70.
75 Sumner, *Russia and the Balkans*, 237.
76 Quoted in Seton-Watson, *Disraeli, Gladstone and the Eastern Question*, 108.
77 *Ibid.*, 107–8.
78 Quoted in Rodogno, *Against Massacre*, 161.
79 Bluntschli, 'Le Congrès de Berlin et sa portée au point de vue du droit international', *Revue de droit international et de législation comparée*, 11 (1879), 18.
80 Clayton, *Britain and the Eastern Question*, 137; Seton-Watson, *Disraeli, Gladstone and the Eastern Question*, 121, 127, 137; Ković, *Disraeli and the Eastern Question*, 177–8; Rodogno, *Against Massacre*, 162, 169. See also Bluntschli, 'Le Congrès de Berlin et sa portée au point de vue du droit international', 18.
81 Mowat, *The Concert of Europe*, 51; Stavrianos, *The Balkans*, 405.
82 For developments in the Ottoman Empire in 1877 see B. Lewis, *The Emergence of Modern Turkey* (London: Oxford University Press, 1968) [1961], 160–74.
83 Seton-Watson, *Disraeli, Gladstone and the Eastern Question*, 135; Sumner, *Russia and the Balkans*, 236.
84 Quoted in Seton-Watson, *Disraeli, Gladstone and the Eastern Question*, 135.
85 Layard had direct personal correspondence with the British Prime Minister and was able to influence his decisions. See Ković, *Disraeli and the Eastern Question*, 204.
86 Seton-Watson, *Disraeli, Gladstone and the Eastern Question*, 142–4; Sumner, *Russia and the Balkans*, 274–98; Mowat, *The Concert of Europe*, 50; Stavrianos, *The Balkans*, 406; Macfie, *The Eastern Question*, 40; Jelavich, *A Century of Russian Foreign Policy*, 180.

The Bulgarian atrocities

87 Sumner, *Russia and the Balkans*, 260–7; Anderson, *The Eastern Question*, 193–4; Bass, *Freedom's Battle*, 295–6.
88 Sumner, *Russia and the Balkans*, 260–3, 266.
89 Seton-Watson, *Disraeli, Gladstone and the Eastern Question*, 406.
90 A. Mandelstam, 'La protection des minorités', *Recueil des Cours de l'Académie de droit international*, 1 (1923), 376. See also M. Ganji, *International Protection of Human Rights* (Geneva: Librairie E. Droz, 1962), 32.
91 Seton-Watson, *Disraeli, Gladstone and the Eastern Question*, 170; Stavrianos, *The Balkans*, 406.
92 Seton-Watson, *Disraeli, Gladstone and the Eastern Question*, 173.
93 *Ibid.*, 193; Mowat, *A History of European Diplomacy*, 229; Ković, *Disraeli and the Eastern Question*, 210–12.
94 Quoted in Seton-Watson, *Disraeli, Gladstone and the Eastern Question*, 194 (original emphasis).
95 P. Magnus, *Gladstone: A Biography* (London: John Murray, 1954), 246.
96 Seton-Watson, *Disraeli, Gladstone and the Eastern Question*, 175.
97 Quoted *ibid.*, 176.
98 See J. O. Baylen, 'Madame Olga Novikov, Propagandist', *American Slavic and East European Review*, 10:4 (1951), 261–2, 264–70.
99 Quoted in Magnus, *Gladstone*, 248.
100 The song was written by G. W. Hunt and sung by the popular singer G. H. Macdermott.
101 The term was coined by Holyoake in the *Daily News* (13 March 1878). See M. Ceadel, *Semi-Detached Idealists: The British Peace Movement and International Relations* (Oxford: Oxford University Press, 2000), 105.
102 In 1901 John A. Hobson defined jingoism as 'inverted patriotism whereby the love of one's nation is transformed into the hatred of another nation and the fierce craving to destroy the individual members of that other nation'. See J. A. Hobson, *The Psychology of Jingoism* (London: G. Richards, 1901), 1.
103 Quoted in Seton-Watson, *Disraeli, Gladstone and the Eastern Question*, 198.
104 Quoted *ibid.*, 198.
105 Quoted *ibid.*, 267 (original emphasis).
106 Macfie, *The Eastern Question*, 41; Clayton, *Britain and the Eastern Question*, 141; Blake, *Disraeli*, 622–3. According to Disraeli in an entertaining note he sent to the Queen (3 November 1877) the cabinet was split into some seven groups. See Seton-Watson, *Disraeli, Gladstone and the Eastern Question*, 236.
107 Millman, *Britain and the Eastern Question*, 10–11, 211, 213; Ković, *Disraeli and the Eastern Question*, 203.
108 Blake, *Disraeli*, 623, 625.
109 Seton-Watson, *Disraeli, Gladstone and the Eastern Question*, 217, 229–30.
110 On Abdulhamid's regime, which lasted until 1908, see E. J. Zürcher, *Turkey: A Modern History* (London: I. B. Tauris, 1993), 80–90; M. Ş. Hanioğlu, *A Brief History of the Late Ottoman Empire* (Princeton: Princeton University Press, 2008), 123–49.
111 Mowat, *The Concert of Europe*, 54–5; Albrecht-Carrié, *A Diplomatic History of Europe Since the Congress of Vienna*, 172; Seton-Watson, *Disraeli, Gladstone and the Eastern Question*, 334, 408–9.
112 Mowat, *The Concert of Europe*, 54–5; Albrecht-Carrié, *A Diplomatic History of Europe Since the Congress of Vienna*, 172; Jelavich, *A Century of Russian Foreign Policy*, 182.
113 Sumner, *Russia and the Balkans*, 419.

114 Ibid., 460; Clayton, *Britain and the Eastern Question*, 144; Macfie, *The Eastern Question*, 42.
115 Blake, *Disraeli*, 639;Ković, *Disraeli and the Eastern Question*, 242–6.
116 Quoted in Mowat, *A History of European Diplomacy*, 231.
117 Ibid., 231–2.
118 Seton-Watson, *Disraeli, Gladstone and the Eastern Question*, 379–81, 408–19; Sumner, *Russia and the Balkans*, 473–96; Clayton, *Britain and the Eastern Question*, 144–5;Ković, *Disraeli and the Eastern Question*, 258–9, 262–6.
119 For the deliberations in Berlin, see Seton-Watson, *Disraeli, Gladstone and the Eastern Question*, 431–59; Sumner, *Russia and the Balkans*, 501–53; W. N. Medlikott, *The Congress of Berlin and After* (London: Frank Cass, 1963), 36–146;Ković, *Disraeli and the Eastern Question*, 269–77.
120 Seton-Watson, *Disraeli, Gladstone and the Eastern Question*, 460–2; Stavrianos, *The Balkans*, 410–12; Anderson, *The Eastern Question*, 205–14.
121 A. Rougier, 'La théorie de l'intervention d'humanité', *Revue générale de droit international public*, 17 (1910), 475.
122 Ibid., 475; C. Calvo, *Le droit internationale: théorie et pratique* (Paris: Guillaumin et Cie, G. Pedone-Lauriel, 1880, 3rd edition) [1870], 278.
123 Rodogno, *Against Massacre*, 141.
124 Ibid., 141.
125 Bluntschli, 'Le Congrès de Berlin et sa portée au point de vue du droit international', 19.
126 Rodogno, *Against Massacre*, 141, 168–9.
127 Ibid., 169.
128 Rougier, 'La théorie de l'intervention d'humanité', 469.
129 E. C. Stowell, *Intervention in International Law* (Washington, DC: John Byrne, 1921), 131–2.
130 F. Martens, 'Étude historique sur la politique Russe dans la question d'Orient', *Revue du droit international et de législation comparée*, 9 (1877), 49–50.
131 Mandelstam, 'La protection des minorités', 376–7.
132 Ganji, *International Protection of Human Rights*, 29–33.
133 J.-P. L. Fonteyne, 'The Customary International Law Doctrine of Humanitarian Intervention: Its Current Validity Under the U.N. Charter', *California Western International Law Journal* (1973–74), 211–12.
134 T. E. Behuniak, 'The Law of Unilateral Humanitarian Intervention by Armed Force: A Legal Survey', *Military Law Review*, 79 (1978), 161–2.
135 M. J. Bazyler, 'Reexamining the Doctrine of Humanitarian Intervention in Light of the Atrocities in Kampuchea and Ethiopia', *Stanford Journal of International Law*, 23 (1987), 582–3.
136 F. K. Abiew, *The Evolution of the Doctrine and Practice of Humanitarian Intervention* (The Hague: Kluwer Law International, 1999), 51–3.
137 W. G. Grewe, *The Epochs of International Law* (Berlin: Walter de Gruyter, 2000, translated and revised by M. Byers), 491–2.
138 C. G. Fenwick, 'Intervention: Individual and Collective', *American Journal of International Law*, 39:4 (1945), 650.
139 M. Finnemore, 'Constructing Norms of Humanitarian Intervention', in P. J. Katzenstein (ed.), *The Culture of National Security* (New York: Columbia University Press, 1996), 161–8.
140 Bass, *Freedom's Battle*, 235–312.
141 T. B. Knudsen, 'The History of Humanitarian Intervention: The Rule or the Exception?', 50th ISA Annual Convention, New York, 15–18 February 2009, 24–8.

9

The Balkan crisis of 1875–78 and Russia: between humanitarianism and pragmatism

In this chapter our focus will be wider. It will include other aspects of humanitarian intervention and not only diplomatic exchanges and the views of major protagonists. We will attempt to pinpoint the elements of a rising Russian and European sense of identification and empathy with the suffering. Moreover, we will trace the links and vehicles through which the suffering of 'strangers' in the unknown Balkans (the 'Christian East' of the Asian Department of the Russian Foreign Ministry) were brought to the attention of the wider Russian public and not only to elite circles. We will also include the contemporary critique of Russia's policy and the questioning of whether its humanitarian motives were pure.

Russian foreign policy and the Eastern Question, 1856–78

The overall picture

The 'geo-schizophrenia'[1] of Russia, situated between Europe and Asia, created in the nineteenth century an 'uncertainty' as to the place of the Russians within the 'civilized' (read 'European') world. Russian educated society pondered whether Russia was European, Eurasian or basically Slavic and Orthodox, that is, in a special category of its own civilization-wise.

Nineteenth-century Russian foreign policy was based on European international norms, the balance-of-power system, geopolitical and economic considerations and the limitation of costs for the Russian Empire. Most Russian diplomats and other high-ranking officials, most of them aristocrats, though not immune to the ideological, political and cultural differences within Russian society, were attuned to the reigning spirit and culture of Europe. Thus they upheld the concept of legitimacy, diplomatic dialogue and limited war as a last resort in order to resolve outstanding conflicts that could not be settled by concord.[2]

Despite the overall Russian conformity with the European *modus operandi*, the other European states regarded Russia as bent on expansion and world domination. This often led to recurring bouts of Russophobia, buttressed by semi-Orientalist stereotypes which placed Russia, as well as the emerging Slavic Orthodox states in the Balkans, between civilization and semi-civilization, in the twilight zone between Europe and Asia. The fact that the Russians were Orthodox, hence 'schismatic' according to Catholicism, was also a factor in downgrading them. The wars of Russia with the Ottoman Empire did little to lessen these fears, as they were seen as an effort to dissolve the 'Turkish Empire', with Constantinople and the Straits as the ultimate prize. The expansion of Russia in the Caucasus and central Asia did little to allay these suspicions.[3]

In fact, the eventual dissolution of the Ottoman Empire was not solely a Russian interest but was widely discussed among the great powers, especially by Austria–Hungary. Russian policy was aimed at the survival of its weakening neighbour, in which Russian influence would be constant and intrusive. Russian decision-makers were aware that the balance of power was at no time so favourable as to give them full freedom of action and permit them to control Constantinople (which many Russians coveted), and that a unilateral move by Russia in the region would lead to a European war.[4]

Russia – like France in northern Africa or Britain in India – was also, partially, a Muslim power, as the imperial state expanded in the Caucasus and central Asia, thereby creating porous frontier zones with the Muslim Ottoman Empire. A 'Christian war' against the Ottomans could lead to the estrangement of Russia's Muslims, with repercussions in its frontier regions. The Orthodox Christians of the Ottoman Empire could side with Russia, but there was also the danger of Russian Muslims creating a fifth column within Russia.[5] In particular, the conquest of the Caucasus, a process which lasted half a century, led to the exodus of many Turkic Muslims, and the expulsion of the Circassians, who settled in the Ottoman Empire.

The 1875–76 uprisings in the Balkans were a great headache for Russian leaders and especially for Tsar Alexander II and Chancellor/Foreign Minister Gorchakov. In Europe, however, the primary focus was on the personality and activities of Ambassador Nikolay Ignatiev in Constantinople, who was bent on achieving Russian prominence in the region through the Orthodox Slavic population in the Balkans.

When the Balkan crisis erupted in 1875–76, various publications appeared in Europe, translated into several languages (including Greek), all pointing to Russian expansionism on Pan-Slavic grounds. Among the best-known was *Russian Intrigues: Secret Dispatches of General Ignatieff and Consular of the Great Panslavic Societies*, which included Ignatiev's correspondence as well as the minutes of the famous Slavic benevolent societies. The text in question and other such texts were forgeries, written in all probability by the Porte to throw the blame for the alleged strategy of destroying the Ottoman Empire on Ignatiev and the Russian Pan-Slavists. Yet at the time they were regarded as genuine and later,

The Balkan crisis

as Mathias Schulz has pointed out, they formed the basis for several biased studies on Russian foreign policy.[6]

'Vice Sultan' Ignatiev versus the European Russian Gorchakov

Ignatiev was regarded by his contemporaries as a person of great ability and diplomatic skill but also controversial and untrustworthy. Within the Russian Foreign Ministry he had made his mark as head of the Asian Department and was regarded the foremost expert on the 'Ottoman East'. Gorchakov's lack of interest in anything related to the Ottoman East left ample room for Ignatiev to try to forge his own vision of Russian foreign policy in the region.[7] His various diplomatic successes in Constantinople, where he served from 1864 until 1877, and his good relations with Sultan Abdulaziz and various grand viziers, made him the most powerful European diplomat at the Porte, hence the nickname Vice Sultan.

Ignatiev was convinced that the vital interests of Russia lay in the 'Christian East', particularly in the Balkans, where Russia could expand its influence by leading the Slavic Balkan people to statehood.[8] His active participation in the Slavic benevolent societies made his name synonymous with Pan-Slavism. As pointed out by his colleague A. N. Kartsov, his approach was not dissimilar to the *politique des nationalités* of France under Napoleon III; it was also in accord with the liberal tendencies of educated Russian society in the age of reforms.[9] Ignatiev, like many nationalists in Europe, called for greater Russian independence and put into question the European Concert. Clearly, this approach was at odds with the Russian Foreign Ministry, which advocated a prudent foreign policy.[10]

Alexander Mikhailovich Gorchakov, who in his youth was a classmate of Russia's national poet, Pushkin, was an astute European diplomat, moderate and fairly liberal, at least by Russian standards. He represented a new type of Russian official, one devoted primarily to the state and secondarily to the Tsar. Gorchakov, 'the European Russian diplomat', regarded the Eastern Question as a European issue. From this perspective, any unilateral Russian initiative against the status quo related to the Eastern Question was mistaken or downright foolish.[11] Two factors reinforced this view: the traumatic experience of the Crimean War, and the need for international stability to allow time for the consolidation of Russia's Great Reforms initiated under the reign of Alexander II. Hence until the 1875–78 Balkan crisis, Russia followed a policy of *recueillement*, the main emphasis being on domestic rather than foreign affairs.[12]

However, Gorchakov was not impervious to the 'racial and religious' links of Russia with the Christians of the East. As he put it: 'As regards the East, apart from our immediate and vital interests, there are also traditions and national sympathies that influence our policy'.[13] A constant theme was that Russia, having brought Greece to life, had a 'historical duty' to liberate the rest of the Balkan peoples. Obviously, this 'duty' ran counter to the pledge of Russia in the 1856 Paris Treaty, namely to abide by the territorial integrity of the Ottoman Empire.[14] Hence the constant advice to their Orthodox co-religionists in the Balkans to remain peaceful until the time when Russia would be in a position to assist them without running the risk of a great power coalition against it.[15]

Gorchakov's reluctance to endorse Balkan nationalism was also based on his appraisal that the Balkan peoples were not mature enough to establish responsible states. Thus his instructions to Ignatiev were not to encourage irresponsible nationalist activities.[16] The ageing Foreign Minister could not understand, let alone appreciate, the fascination of the Balkan peoples with the 'cosmopolitan revolutionary spirit' of Italy, which they tried to emulate.[17] This overall line was tempered somewhat by his great dislike of the 'Turkish Empire'.

Peaceful intervention

When the Serbian rebellion in Herzegovina erupted, Ignatiev foresaw other rebellions in the Balkans.[18] For him, Russia should come to their support, given Slav affinity and the fact that only Russia's intervention would be selfless. He hoped that his cordial relations with the Sultan and the Grand Vizier would permit the settlement of the problem on a bilateral basis, without European involvement.[19] He therefore suggested a plan of broad reforms, including autonomy, a Christian police force, tax reductions and the handing over of the provinces that had revolted to the principality of Montenegro.[20] But Andrassy reacted to the Russian suggestion with his own plan (the Andrassy Note). Gorchakov's acceptance of the Berlin Memorandum expressed the willingness of St Petersburg (against the wishes of Ignatiev) to settle the conflict *à trois*.[21]

The Bulgarian leaders based in Bucharest were leftists (Karavelov, Levski and Botev) and thus beyond Russian control, as they 'espoused doctrines dangerous to the Russian state'.[22] Ignatiev urged the Porte to send regular troops to the Bulgarian regions to restore order and advised punishing the guilty and not the innocent; the officials in the Russian Foreign Ministry remained apprehensive but non-committal, as did their European counterparts.[23]

It was mainly European and Russian public opinion that brought the matter onto the European agenda, following detailed reports of the atrocities. A case in point was the report of MacGahan in the London *Daily News* on the Bulgarian atrocities. MacGahan was well known in Russian society (he was married to Varvara Nikolaeva Elagina, who, after her husband's death, became a correspondent in Russia of various US newspapers) and was a friend of General Skobelev (of central Asian fame and later head of the Russian army in the 1877–78 Russo-Ottoman War).

Contrary to their lack of information regarding the Bulgarians, the Russian officials were aware of the upcoming Serbian and Montenegrin war against the

Ottomans. St Petersburg instructed Kartsov, the Russian consul in Belgrade, to restrain them and to warn the Serbs that if they resorted to war they would be on their own, without Russian support. Privately, however, Kartsov advised Prince Milan of Serbia not to heed the warning. It seems that the consul was trying to strike a balance between instructions from St Petersburg and rival instructions from his immediate boss, Ignatiev. Following a visit to the Russian capital, he got the impression that Russia's official stance was not crystal clear on the Serbian question, as pointed out to him by Alexander Jomini (the son of the famous Swiss strategist), the third in command at the Foreign Ministry after Gorchakov and Assistant Foreign Minister Nikolay Giers.[24]

When the Serbs and Montenegrins were prepared to declare war, the Russian Pan-Slavs and liberals called for Russian support. Ex-general Cherniaev, editor of the Pan-Slav newspaper *Ruskii mir*, predicted that the Serbs would win and liberate themselves and the other Balkan Christians. The liberal *Viesnik Evropy* urged moral support for the Serbian cause. But other leading Russian newspapers backed the official Russian policy of not becoming involved. Alexander forbade Cherniaev to recruit volunteers and leave for the Balkans, which of course he did not heed. The Tsar could not stomach a former Russian general becoming the head of 'those thieves' as he called the Serbs.[25] When Cherniaev and the other volunteers arrived in Belgrade (28 April 1876), openly advocating an independent and enlarged Serbia under the Obrenovic dynasty and implying that Russia would come to their aid, he was made a Serbian citizen and commander of its eastern army. In Russia the undisputed leader of the Russian Pan-Slav movement was Ivan Aksakov, chairman of the Moscow Slav Committee, who urged greater Russian involvement and was in contact with Cherniaev.[26]

Alexander ordered Kartsov to sever all ties with Cherniaev and prevent Serbia from going to war.[27] But Gorchakov was equivocal. As he put it to Kartsov: 'Do not forget that although the Tsar is opposed to war, his son, the heir to the throne, stands as the head of the Slav movement'.[28] Indeed, the Tsar's heir as well as the Tsar's wife pressed Alexander for a dynamic intervention in the name of the Slavic cause.[29] St Petersburg did not want the Serbs to start a war but being irresolute, known to sympathize with the Serb cause and having sent contradictory signals, it prompted the Serbs and Montenegrins to resort to war on 18 June (old-style Julian calendar) or 30 June (new-style Gregorian calendar) 1876.[30] In private even the Tsar and Gorchakov sympathized with the Serbians and, under pressure from public opinion, allowed Russian military personnel to resign from the army and join as volunteers. Jomini told a member of the St Petersburg Slavophile Committee, 'Do anything you like provided we do not know anything about it officially'.[31]

But throughout the Serb-Ottoman war the main concern of the Tsar was to avoid a wider conflagration which could involve the other powers. As Gorchakov put it in desperation to Miliutin (the Minister of War): 'Let us leave everything to chance. Let the arms decide which party wins and which party is destroyed'.[32] Even Ignatiev had second thoughts and was not supportive of Russian military intervention, although he did endorse the use of diplomacy and, if possible, a European conference that would stop the bloodshed and settle the conflict.[33]

The careful policy of Russia throughout 1876 did not allay the fears of Vienna and London, despite the attempts of ambassadors Novikov and Shuvalov, respectively. Novikov was a distinguished Slav specialist but as a diplomat he was anti-Pan-Slav. Shuvalov, a diehard conservative, had previously served in various posts related to internal security, including the Third Department of the Imperial Chancellery, in charge of suppressing revolutionary movement within the Russian Empire. He had become so powerful that he came to be known as Pyotr IV. The two ambassadors had gained the confidence of Andrassy and Derby, respectively, and played a considerable role in not allowing bilateral relations to deteriorate. But the fact that they were known to be anti-Pan-Slav and against war with the Ottoman Empire – more resolutely so than either the Tsar or Gorchakov on both counts – limited their credibility as true representatives of the 'real Russia'.

Disraeli made a bellicose speech at a banquet held by the Lord Mayor of London, in Guildhall (28 October/9 November 1876), where the following words made their mark: 'Peace is especially an English policy.... She covets no cities and no provinces.... But although the policy of England is peace, there is no country so well prepared for war as our own. If she enters into conflict in a righteous cause ... her resources, I feel, are inexhaustible'.[34]

Two days later (30 October/11 November) Alexander, travelling from Livadia (in the Crimea) to St Petersburg, broke his journey to make a speech, addressing the Moscow nobility and civic authorities, in what seemed like a reply to Disraeli.[35] He stated: 'As you know Turkey submitted to my demand for immediate ending of the hostilities, to put an end to the aimless slaughtering in Serbia and Montenegro'.[36] And he concluded thus:[37]

> I know that all Russia joins with me in taking the deepest interest in the sufferings of our brothers by faith and by origin; but for me the true interests of Russia are dearer than everything, and I would do my utmost to spare precious Russian blood being shed. That is why I have striven and am continuing to strive to achieve by peaceful means a real improvement in the life of all the Christian inhabitants of the Balkan peninsula. Deliberations between the representatives of the six great powers are shortly to be begun at Constantinople ... I much desire that we shall reach a general agreement. If this is not attained and if I see that we are not gaining such guarantees as would assure the execution if our just demands upon the Porte, then I firmly intend to act independently and I am convinced that in such an eventuality all Russia will respond to my appeal, when I count it necessary and the honour of Russia requires it.

Alexander's aim was to publicly clarify Russian policy and to show to the excited Russian public that he was on the same wavelength, while indicating his preference

The Balkan crisis

for peace and for a wider international consensus for the adequate protection of the insurgents. According to Richard Wortman, Alexander in his speech sought 'to show himself acting in concert with his people and taking account of public opinion'.[38] Aksakov's wife, Anna Aksakova (daughter of the famous poet and diplomat Tyuchev), wrote in her diary that the Tsar was clearly moved by what he said and this was also the case with his wife and his son (the future Alexander III), who were present. Many of the listeners shed tears according to Aksakova.[39]

The very next day, mobilization was announced. According to General Nikolay Obruchev, who was put in charge of setting out a plan for a war with the Ottoman Empire, 'The aim of the war is to extract from the Sultan's authority that Christian country [Bulgaria] where the Turks had committed atrocities and to put an end to every crisis of the Eastern Question'.[40]

When the Constantinople Conference was convened in December 1876, Ignatiev presented a maximum and a minimum proposal. Tsereteliev, who had experience as consul in various Balkan posts, and the US diplomat Eugene Schuyler (who had travelled to Batak together with MacGahan and had written a detailed account of the atrocities, which had been published as a booklet) were given the task of preparing the maximum plan. It provided for a large autonomous Bulgaria headed by a Christian administrator, a security force comprising locals, and other measures. Ignatiev prepared the minimal plan, to be put forward if Britain objected to the maximum approach. This divided Bulgaria into two parts, which included most of the Bulgarian-inhabited regions. When Salisbury accepted the minimum plan with some minor changes, Ignatiev was able to make some small territorial changes in favour of Serbia and Montenegro and recommend a level of autonomy for Bosnia and Herzegovina. With agreement reached, Ignatiev was satisfied to have made Russian aims the official goals of the great powers and hoped that, in the future, the two parts of Bulgaria would be united (an aspiration which in fact came about).[41]

The overall Russian aim was to bring about great power pressure for Ottoman reforms that would defuse the situation. Alexander, Miliutin, Reutern (the Economics Minister) and Gorchakov were averse to war and regarded the Bulgarian and other uprisings of Slavic peoples in the Balkans with deep suspicion, viewing the activists as socialists, radicals and atheists, the 'worst possible revolutionaries', and were fearful that the Balkan rebellions would send shockwaves within Russia itself, triggering insubordination against the imperial order.[42] The various reforms that had commenced in the army and elsewhere, the considerable economic difficulties facing the country (in 1874 there was a major famine), the lack of funds, the limited industrial and military hardware as well as the lack of infrastructure and transportation (railways towards the south or adequate roads), called for caution and not for a military adventure.[43]

It is within this spirit that Ignatiev was sent to the European capitals, though the choice of envoy was hardly ideal in that it created great nervousness, especially in London. The final outcome was of course the watered-down London Protocol. When Disraeli, following the Protocol, called for the demobilization of the Russian army, Alexander mused: 'They forgot the subject of the amelioration of the life of the Christians and they are only interested in disarming Russia'.[44]

The Russo-Ottoman War: 'a generous crusade'

As Seton-Watson has argued, the correspondence before the war between Ignatiev and Shuvalov and of both to Gorchakov, 'leave[s] no possible room for doubt as to the pacific intentions of the Tsar and his Government', whose aim was limited to obtaining an agreement with Britain to protect the Christians 'against Turkish misrule'.[45]

Following the failure of the Constantinople Conference, Russia presented the crisis not as 'a Russo-Turkish or Slav question, but one of humanity and Christendom' (the very words of the Tsar).[46] The Tsar was in a dilemma: 'pacific though he was, he could not abandon the cause of Christian kith and kin without alienating those upon whose support his throne rested'.[47]

As pointed out by Alfred Rieber: 'Officially Alexander opposed the grandiose designs of the Pan-Slavs, but his moral commitment to Orthodoxy as a kind of substitute for national unity left him helpless to resist their pressure at the decisive moment'.[48] His assessment is that by 1877 the Tsar had reached the point 'where he had unwittingly staked his own honor and that of the empire upon saving the rebellious Christian population of the Ottoman Empire from their legitimate sovereign'.[49]

Above all, it was a matter of prestige and honour for Alexander to implement Russia's will, if necessary by force. Within the imperial ideology and mentality, the Tsar was sensitive to the need to be seen to maintain an 'ethical authority' in policy matters, which in this case was keeping his promise to save the Christian Balkan peoples.[50] He was of the belief that, by now, the prospect of war had been justified in the eyes of Europe as humanitarian, as a reaction to the extreme violence against the Christians and to Ottoman intransigence. He also had in mind the precedent fifty years previously, when the three powers had saved the Greeks.[51]

By now not only the Tsar, but even Gorchakov and Miliutin, who had been opposed to war, had given in. The only minister to oppose war until the end (for it would upset fiscal stability) was the Economics Minister, Reutern, who resigned.[52] The moderate Jomini saw it as the best opportunity to crush the Ottomans. The war planner Obruchev estimated that the Russian army would be within reach of Constantinople within three months.[53]

Miliutin saw the prospect of war as 'a sad but inevitable reality'[54] in view of the stance of the European powers, which were prepared 'to sacrifice the fate of the Balkan peoples to Turkish barbarity'. '[E]nvy towards us has made Europe abandon its dignity in the deep belief that any bolstering of the Turkish Porte would be a blow to our traditional policy'. He concluded that the goal of war was 'a real peace, a dignified peace ... that would protect the existence of the Balkan Christians from all bestiality and violence'.[55]

When the war started, Professor F. F. Martens, the legal adviser to the Russian Foreign Ministry, wrote that 'Russia was obliged to draw the sword, in order to safeguard the interests recognized worthy of sympathy by all civilized nations. Russia could not consent to the abandonment at the mercy of the Bashibazouks the life and honour of the Christians'.[56] He called the Ottoman regime 'an outrage to human nature' and asserted that 'Russia declared war against Turkey in the name of the interests of humanity ... to put an end to a state of affairs that revolted the most respectable sentiments of the Russian people'.[57]

In his proclamation to the army in Kishinev, where the official declaration of war was made on 12/24 April 1877, Alexander pointed out that the war was waged for high moral reasons: for the honour of Russia, to save the Christian population from the wrath of the Turks, to bring about necessary reforms and to establish a lasting peace. War was rendered a necessity in view of the intransigence of the Porte. Moreover, the self-definition of Russian dignity at the time made the war inevitable and necessary.[58]

In the proclamation for the Bulgarians, the Tsar stressed 'the sympathies of Russia for her coreligionists in the East', 'the sacred rights of your nationality' gained not by 'armed resistance, but at the cost of centuries of suffering, and the cost of blood of martyrs with which you and your ancestors have soaked the soil of your country'.[59] However, humanitarian motives, including safeguarding the moral integrity and prestige of Russia, were not unrelated to political objectives, namely acquiring greater influence in the Balkans by saving its Slav Orthodox peoples.

It was made abundantly clear that Russia had no intention of dissolving the Ottoman Empire; it had 'neither the interest to do so, nor the desire or the means'. If Constantinople was to be occupied, this would be provisional and only for short-term military purposes. Any final arrangement would involve all the Europeans.[60] When the Russian army did in fact reach the outskirts of Constantinople, Alexander did not permit its seizure, despite the strong pressure to do so by a segment of the military, by his brother Grand Prince Nicholas (after his army entered Adrianople) and by the nationalist and Pan-Slav circles headed by Aksakov.[61]

Alexander also made it a point to be present as the army advanced. Wortman, who has studied the symbolism of ceremonies in the Russian Empire, points out that 'Alexander's presence at the theater of war was widely publicized and dramatized his personal leadership' and eyewitnesses presented him as 'a sentimental hero, acting purely out of the altruism that inspired his people', 'a military leader and a moral one', who had 'the ability and compassion for suffering'.[62] In the conservative national discourse of the time, these were regarded as the virtues of the Russian people – love for the stranger, emotion for the suffering of others – thus the Balkan cause was one of altruism, sacrifice for the high goal of liberating the Balkans from the Muslim yoke, and all this without an inkling of national ambition or insatiable appetite for gains.

Interestingly, the war has been presented as humanitarian even by foreign witnesses hardly associated with Russian expansionism or Pan-Slavism, as seen in the case of Francis Greene, a lieutenant in the US army who covered the war from the Russian ranks. He assured his readers that Alexander's attempt was to 'free his co-religionists from the intolerable oppression of the Turks. No more generous or holy crusade was ever been undertaken on the part of a strong race to befriend a weak one'.[63]

The victory of the Russian army brought Ignatiev to the highest point of his career. Now was his chance to remodel the Ottoman Empire according to his taste.[64] An imperial council was convened and Ignatiev presented (as at Constantinople earlier) a maximum and minimum proposal. The first suggested the creation of a large independent Bulgaria with an extended outlet to the Aegean Sea, including Salonica (where a large segment of the population were Sephardic Jews) as well as major gains for Serbia, Montenegro and Greece. The minimum plan was accepted, which limited the gains to Montenegro and the Bulgarians (the climate was not favourable to Serbia). Independence for Bulgaria, including Salonica, were not accepted, but a large Bulgaria with an extended Aegean outlet was endorsed. Ignatiev left for Constantinople triumphant and regarded as the most likely successor of the ageing and almost senile Gorchakov.[65]

The Treaty of San Stefano was seen as a worthy reward for the war and the sacrifices of the Russian people but it could not be implemented due to the resistance of Europe, which regarded Great Bulgaria as a Russian satellite that brought Russian power and influence to the Aegean and not far from the Straits and Constantinople.[66] According to Shuvalov, San Stefano was 'the greatest act of stupidity we could have committed', adding that 'Ignatiev's Bulgaria is nonsense'.[67] As regards San Stefano, apart from the Ignatiev factor and the clamouring of the Pan-Slavists and the Russian press, it seems that the Russians were momentarily carried away by their victory and now wanted gains commensurate with their difficult victory (the war had cost Russia more men and money than defeat in the Crimean War[68]). There were the territorial demands of the Balkan states to reckon with, not least for reasons of Russian credibility and prestige. Moreover, it seems that Gorchakov wanted to confront the other powers with a maximum number of *faits accomplis*[69] or, put differently, 'they took more than they expected to keep in order to have some surplus for bargaining'.[70]

Ignatiev was sent to Andrassy to convince him of the need to retain the essence of San Stefano but the demands of the latter were so excessive that, in effect, Vienna would have made the greatest gains without having fired a single shot.[71]

The Berlin Congress, when Russia was obliged to back down from San Stefano, was seen as 'a black page' in Russian diplomacy. Gorchakov, who avoided sessions in Berlin when Russia had to yield (and thus was able to throw the onus as well as the blame for yielding on Shuvalov), wrote: 'I only regret having had my signature to such a transaction' and told Alexander that 'I consider the Berlin treaty the darkest page of my life', to which Tsar's answer was 'and in mine too'.[72]

Ignatiev used the following words: 'My whole soul rebelled against destroying with my own hands my ... work of fifteen years, killing all the hopes of the Slavs and strengthening Vienna's predominance in the east ... I considered granting Bosnia and Herzegovina to Austria to be a crime against the Slav population and shameful to Russia'.[73]

But not all Russian officials felt this way. Shuvalov regarded the compromise as inevitable, since Russia was in no position to wage another war, this time against Europeans.[74] Giers was optimistic. He wrote to Jomini during the Berlin Congress to say that the results were satisfactory, pointing to the independence of three principalities and the creation of two Bulgarian entities, and that everything was done with the 'sanction of Europe'.[75]

Three years later, Alexander II was assassinated (1/13 March 1881) by a member of a revolutionary organization named Narodnaya Volya (People's Will). Alexander III, who as heir to the throne had been a supporter of war on behalf of the Bulgarians and Serbs on Pan-Slav grounds, changed his mind following the Berlin Congress. In 1885, when relations with Bulgaria were worse than ever, following an uprising in Eastern Rumelia, which declared union with Bulgaria, he was not prepared to spend even a coin for them.[76] Similar views were held by Giers, the successor of Gorchakov to the Foreign Ministry. As he told the British ambassador in 1885: 'a lesson we can never forget and one which is most wholesome for us – Never again to go forth making moral conquests with our blood and money but to think of ourselves and our interests only'.[77]

San Stefano, Ignatiev's brainchild,[78] can be seen as 'the fullest practical expression ever given in Russian foreign policy to the Panslav ideal'.[79] But the Russian government (with the exception of Ignatiev and the consuls under his command) did not adopt the Pan-Slav agenda.[80] However, Alexander II had every reason to bow to public opinion and to the rhetoric of protection of life, and to present it as the justification for war, a war that could also serve Russian influence and prestige in the region, as both had faced a severe blow with defeat in the Crimean War.[81] War had the added advantage of silencing internal divisions and redirecting interest to external matters.

As we have seen in the 1875–78 Balkan crisis, Pan-Slavism looms large and was seen by European Russophobes as the bogey. Thus a brief discussion of Pan-Slavism is in order.

Russian Pan-Slavism

Pan-Slavism (an offshoot of Slavophilism) was an assortment of contrasting narratives. It was not merely the terrain of right-wing conservatives and nationalists, but represented an array of ideologies across the political spectrum. Adherents included: conservative intellectuals such as Mikhail P. Pogodin, Aleksey S. Khomyakov, the brothers Konstantin S. and Ivan S. Aksakov, Juriy F. Samarin and Nikolay Yakovlevich Danilevskiy; liberals such as Aleksander Pypin; radicals and socialists such as Aleksander Gertsen, N. I. Kostomarov, M. P. Drahomanov and others; and even anarchists such as M. Bakunin.[82]

The Pan-Slav discourse was developed by different Slavic peoples who lived in the three continental empires, Austria–Hungary, the Russian Empire and the Ottoman Empire. The common elements were Slavic ancestry (actually a perceived common ancestry based on language) from which the need for Slavic solidarity arose and the principle of nationalities. The whole discourse put into question the basis of legitimacy of the three empires and was linked in part to the famous Eastern Question.

In Russian society this narrative came to the fore following the traumatic Crimean War. The Slavic idea was part and parcel of the discussion of the national question in Russia and the creation of Russian national identity. There were no fewer than three versions of Russian identity: ethnically or culturally *russkiy*, racially Slav or state *rossiskiy*.

The Crimean War – the European 'invasion' into Russia's 'soft underbelly' – coupled with Europe's Russophobia and the dogma of the integrity of the Ottoman Empire, convinced an increasing number of Russian intellectuals that Western Europe's object of enmity and hatred was no longer Islam and the 'Turk' but Russia and the Slavic world. Thus some conservative Pan-Slavs, such as Nikolay Danilevskiy and General Fadeev, jumped to the conclusion that Europe was not only different but also the 'absolute Enemy'.[83] The Slavophiles and other conservatives argued that the Western European model of historical evolution was not the only way forward and far from ideal. However, the majority of Russian intellectuals of various ideological hues came to perceive the difference between Europe and Russia as an intra-European family affair rather than a clash between Europe as a whole and Russia. The Slavophiles, particularly those of the second generation, though anti-European, defined Europe as part of their world, of their own 'Christian world', with common Indo-European roots.[84]

The Russian Slavophiles felt a greater affinity for the southern Slavs, who were Orthodox. The issue of the relationship of Russia to Europe soon became the relationship of the Slavic world as a whole towards Europe. The situation was conceived as one of exclusion of the Slavic world from the rest of Europe. In the words of M. Pogodin: 'The Slavs are forgotten by history, they are forgotten by geography, by diplomacy and by politics'.[85] The Slavs were 'the plebeians of history' according to Orest Miller. However, this predicament had a positive twist: these very plebeians had historical time on their side, as youthful nations; they were in a process of revival and political struggle. Thus, according to Miller, the future belonged to these very plebeians.[86] For second-generation Slavophiles such as Ivan Aksakov, V. I. Lamanskiy or Orest Miller, Russia's historical mission in the East (and with regard to the Eastern Question) derived not only from its Christian Orthodox faith but also from its Slavic credentials. The Slavic question overlapped and was interlinked with the Eastern Question and the ultimate fate of the 'Sick Man'. Hence the Eastern Question was perceived largely as 'the narration of the gradual emancipation of the Slavs'.[87]

The Slavophiles tried to reorient the foreign (and internal) policy of Russia. Russia should go ahead and play a leading role in liberating the Slavic peoples, and in so doing follow an unfettered foreign policy not wedded to the traditional Russian line of trying to forge a common great power policy towards the unwieldy Eastern Question.[88]

The conservative version of Pan-Slavism went hand in hand with Russian state imperialism and Russian nationalism. Conservative Pan-Slavs, such as Fadeev, Danilevskiy and Ivan Aksakov, sought Russian dominance of the Slavs, with Russia functioning as the Slavic Piedmont for a future union of all the Slavs. Others, such as Miller, put emphasis on two prerequisites: on the principle of nationalities, which should apply to the Slavic peoples as well as to all the nations of Europe; and on selflessness on the part of Russia, which, in helping its Slav brothers, should not aim to gain territory from the Ottoman Empire when the Eastern Question was resolved.[89]

For the liberals, the Slav nations were European nations that had to follow the road of European civilization and progress. A case in point among the liberal Slavophiles was Pypin, who, in his long academic carrier and through the liberal journal *Vesntik Evropy*, studied Slav solidarity. For Pypin, Russia should participate in a Pan-Slav federation of equal members, provided that it had shed absolutism and become a modern democratic society. He criticized the repressive Russian policies against the Slavs within Russia, as in the case of the Poles and Ukrainians, and endorsed the Ukrainian cultural movement, although without endorsing its separatist ideas.[90] As Alexei Miller points out, he shared the idea of the all-Russian nation but opposed forced assimilation.[91]

Radical and socialist Slavophiles, such as Gertzen, Chernisevsky and Bakunin, claimed that Pan-Slavism and nationalism could be democratic and lead to the liberation of suppressed Slavic peoples in a confederation of equal independent states.[92]

Ukrainian Slavophiles, such as Kostomarov and Drahomanov, supported the Ukrainian renaissance but not secessionism, provided Russia became a modern democratic state. Their approach had intellectual links with the Decembrists, notably with Pavel Pestel, and with the Society of Saints Cyril and Methodius, which envisaged the creation of a large Slavic union, a federation, comprising Russians, Ukrainians, Byelorussians, Poles, Czechs, Slovaks, Lusitians, Illyrian Serbs, Serbs, Croatians and Bulgarians.[93]

Public opinion in Russian and Russian–British–American entanglements

Russian society was transformed in the 1860s and 1870s as a result of Alexander's reforms; new social strata and an array of social organizations came to the fore calling for the 'common good', 'public duty' and effective participation and greater change than that provided by the reforms. From the 1860s onwards a new political and social conscience crystallized with novel notions, such as *obshchestvennost'*, a complex term which refers to public space, educated society engaged in the common good and progress, and a sense of public duty, implying a civil society and citizenship. The concept of intelligentsia also came with the Narodnics, as people equipped with critical thought, independent of the state, who acted on the basis of high ideals and aiming at human progress.[94]

The daily and weekly press multiplied. The printed press was of great importance in the absence of institutionalized political dialogue. The role of publishers was also of importance.[95] New forms of contact and information flourished, such as letters, distributed handwritten manuscripts, and trips abroad, all of which contributed to the exchange of ideas like running water, with information and views across frontiers as never before in the history of Russia.

When the Balkan uprisings occurred, various currents in Russia's educated society supported them in the hope that liberty would arrive at home as well.[96] Educated society increasingly criticized absolutism, which it regarded as responsible for the backwardness and other problems of the country in comparison with most of Europe. There was a widening gap between the authoritarian state and 'unruly' society.

Khevrolina, who has studied the archives of the police and the Imperial Third Department, found that following the defeat of the Serbs in the autumn of 1876, there was revolutionary ferment, indeed, a real danger of a revolution, especially among young students. If the state did not take measures in support of the Balkan Slavs, the prospect of revolution in Russia along Pan-Slav lines could become real.[97]

The Russian press had had since the 1860s a good information network regarding Balkan affairs, due to southern Slavic emigration to Russia. A case in point was the daily *Golos*, which had correspondents in various Balkan cities, and published articles on the Slavic and Eastern questions by progressive radicals from the Balkans, such as the Serb Zhivoin Zhuevich and the Bulgarian Karavelov, who wrote on Ottoman misrule and independent statehood for Serbia and Bulgaria as the only way out of their predicament.[98]

When the Bulgarian April Uprising took place there were constant reports in the Russian press from its network in the Balkans, in Cherniaev's newspaper

Russkiy Mir, and in the newspapers *Moskovskoe Vedomosti* and *Novoe Vremya*, which painted a grim picture of the suffering of the Bulgarians as martyrs at the hands of the atrocious 'Turks'.[99]

When the first report by Pears appeared in the *Daily News* it was immediately translated into Russian, as was a booklet by MacGahan (*Turkish Atrocities in Bulgaria*), who was fluent in Russian. MacGahan was close to Schuyler, the US diplomat, who also knew Russian (he had translated into English Tolstoy and Turgenev, whom he knew personally), who wrote the preface to the booklet.

Gladstone was highly regarded in Russia. His *Bulgarian Horrors* was immediately translated as a booklet and it was introduced in *Vsemirnaya Illiustratsiya*, with an engraving of him speaking in the pouring rain at Blackheath, with fist raised. The publication noted that Gladstone recognized the selfless aims of the Russians and supported a common policy for the two European states. Jomini noted that even the British accepted the Russian demands for Bulgarian autonomy under Ottoman suzerainty.[100] The money raised from Gladstone's pamphlet was handed to the relatives of the Bulgarian victims.[101]

The anarchist Kropotkin, in exile outside Russia, remembered that his anarchist friends, among them the radical intellectuals Stepnyak and Clements, after having read the *Daily News*, went to volunteer for the Bulgarian cause as soldiers or hospital assistants.[102]

Pears, MacGahan, Schuyler and their views were constantly referred to, as were those of Stead, who supported Gladstone and was considered the prime Russophile journalist in Britain. Stead stressed the need for a crusade in the name of outraged humanity – blurring the boundaries between the medieval crusade and a nineteenth-century humanitarian crusade against the Turks.[103] The entry of Reed's diary for 14 January 1877 makes it clear: 'The honour of Bulgarian virgins is in the custody of the English voter. And what is true of Bulgaria is true of larger things.'[104] It also won him the compliments of two of his heroes: Gladstone and Carlyle. He became a key figure in the British journalistic landscape and was invited to the London salons of the expatriate Russian propagandist Olga Kireeva Novikova (Novikoff in her English writings), where he first met Gladstone, Carlyle and Froude, among others. Stead was one of the three Englishmen, alongside Gladstone and the liberal journalist Peter Clayden, the editor of the *Daily News*, to receive a vote of thanks from the first Bulgarian National Assembly in 1878 for their role in the Bulgarian agitation movement in Britain.[105]

Novikova had cultivated Gladstone since 1873, when they were introduced by the Russian ambassador in London, and they were united by their common interest in religious questions. Novikova, of aristocratic background, while in Russia was part of an intellectual circle comprising Turgenev, Dostoevsky, Tolstoy, Tiuchev and others. After her divorce from the brother of ambassador Novikov, she passed from 1866 onwards her winters in London, surrounded by a circle of like-minded people in her salon at Claridge's Hotel. Following the death of her brother, Nicholas Kireev, in Serbia, she started writing to her many British friends, including Napier, Froude, Kinglake, Freeman, Villiers, Harcourt and of course Gladstone. To her surprise and grief Gladstone was one of the few who did not answer. But he did something more worthwhile: a little later he sent her a copy of his famous pamphlet.[106] During the crisis Aksakov kept her well informed on Russian foreign policy and she in her turn wrote many articles in Stead's *Northern Echo*, where she translated the views of Aksakov and his speeches to the Slavic Committee of Moscow. At the same time she wrote a column 'News from England' in the conservative *Moskovkye Vedomosty* of Katkov. Among her best-known articles are the following, with characteristic titles: 'Is Russia Wrong?' (1878), 'Friends or Foes' (1879), 'Russia and England, a Protest and an Appeal' (1880), which Gladstone appreciated very much, and 'Skobelev and the Slavonic Cause' (1884).[107]

Russian society's sympathy for the Slavs

In the years preceding the Balkan crisis there had been considerable advances in literacy in Russia, among the peasants and workers.[108] 'Once the farmers learned to read they covered all the news of the paper', especially events in the Balkans, the head of police in Siberia wrote in a report.[109] Though this may have been an overstatement, it is a fact that far more than in the Greek case half a century previously, members of the lower classes who could now read joined in the pro-Balkans call. The elaborate Pan-Slavist argumentations of Pagodin, Miller or Lamanski may have been very difficult to understand but there were also the sermons in the churches which referred to the agony of the Slavs at the hands of the 'barbaric Muslims'.

The publishers of the daily press reacted accordingly to this rising literacy, trying to augment the circulation of their newspapers. There were also the so-called *lubki*, cheap publications with many illustrations accompanied by short texts. The events of 1875–78 led to a great rise in demand for such publications. As put by Ivan Dmitrievich Sytin, a successful publisher of *lubki*, I 'hired the best graphic artists and first class printers, did not bargain with them over wages, but demanded high quality work; finally, I followed the market and with the greatest effort studied people's preferences'.[110] There were also new periodicals with wide circulation which included evocative illustrations, such as the weakly *Niva*, intended for reading by families, and the popular scientific *Vsemirnaya Illiustratsiya* (*World Illustration*), whose target audiences were the middle strata. Contrary to the elitist 'thick journals', the periodicals, especially *Vsemirnaya Illiustratsiya*, presented a visual form of narration easily understood by simple folk. The Bulgarian horrors and other atrocities in the Balkans were presented by dramatic illustrations that depicted all kinds of barbarities, arson, pillage, rape (the raping of semi-nude women was one of the most common images), sodomy, torture, people in chains,

The Balkan crisis

priests in chains, the slaughtering of women, children, the elderly and priests, with various symbols of Christianity wrecked or downtrodden, such as the cross, the Bible, icons, church bells and so on. The image of the Turks (usually presented as very dark-skinned) was of ferocious men equipped with an array of daggers and swords. The captions were also very suggestive: 'Turkish barbarities', 'Brutalities', 'The Balkan drama', 'Bulgarian village robbed by the Bashibazouks and the Circassians'. Noted artists also joined in, such as Konstantin Makovskiy, with his 1877 painting *The Bulgarian Martyresses*, which depicted the rape of two women (one of whom is killed) within a church by two African-looking Bashibazouks (a year later the painting appeared in France as part of the Russian contribution to the Paris Art Exhibition).

The same publications also had articles and illustrations of peaceful events in the secure, civilized world, such as the 1876 World Fair in Philadelphia, and advertisements for beauty lotions for ladies. These made a stark contrast between 'civilization' and 'barbarity', peace and tragedy. Readers might have felt a sense of shame for doing little for the Slavs.

Turgenev, the liberal writer who lived in Paris and often travelled to Britain (where he was widely acclaimed), was so moved by the news of the horrors that he wanted to go to the Balkans as a volunteer, as was the case with Tolstoy (both of them were dissuaded from going due to their old age). Turgenev, while travelling by train from Moscow to St Petersburg, wrote a satirical poem entitled 'Croquet at Windsor', whose first version in English (a prose version from the French translation) runs thus:[111]

> The Queen is sitting in her forest of Windsor, around her the ladies of her court play at a game which not long since came into fashion – a game called croquet.... The Queen looks on and laughs; but suddenly she stops; her face grows deathly pale.
>
> It seems to her that, instead of shapely balls driven by the lightly-tapping mallet, there are hundreds of heads rolling along, all smeared with blood. Heads of women, of young girls, of children: faces with marks of dreadful tortures and bestial outrages, of the claws of beasts, and all the horror of death-pangs....
>
> 'My doctor, quick, quick, let him come to me!' And she tells him her terrible vision. But he then answers: 'It doesn't surprise me; reading the newspapers has disturbed you. The *Times* explains to us so well how the Bulgarians have deserved the wrath of the Turks....

The Russian newspapers did not publish the poem (it was circulated by hand), in order not to offend Queen Victoria, and this was also the case in Britain. But it was translated into French, German and Bulgarian, and into English first by Henry James (the above prose version), who was an admirer and friend of Turgenev, and published in the American journal *The Nation*. James explained why he liked the poem: 'At any rate the cynical, brutal barbarous pro-Turkish attitudes of an immense mass of people here (I am no fanatic for Russia, but I think the Emperor of Russia might have been treated like a gentleman!) has thrown into vivid relief the most discreditable side of the English character'.[112]

The events also moved Pyotr Ilyich Tchaikovsky, who was commissioned by the Russian Musical Society to write an orchestral piece for a concert in aid of the Red Cross Society, for the benefit of wounded Serbian veterans. He initially called the piece the 'Serbo-Russian March' but when it was performed in Moscow in November 1876 (conducted by his close friend Nikolai Rubinstein) it was named 'Slave March' (Slavonic March).

Art and literature, as an aesthetic experience, are connected to perceptions and the emotions connected to perceptions are another way to make sense of international politics. Emotions have a social character and can construct communities of understandings and like-mindedness and in this way can play an important role in political events. In this case sentiment for those suffering was the basis for the construction of a community of saviours of the Balkan Slavs, stirred by images of martyrdom and torture, not least represented by the frail but alluring bodies of women. As one Russian volunteer put it in a letter back home, 'I have joined to defend freedom, the human rights of my brothers and the disgraced honour of their wives and daughters'.[113]

According to reports of the police forwarded to the Third Department, sympathy of all the social classes for war was sweeping the country, as was the belief that the Tsar should save and liberate the Balkan Slavs.[114] Andrey Zhelyabov (who set up in Odessa 'The People Will', a secret revolutionary organization, which organized Alexander's assassination in 1881) wrote that '[t]here was much discussion about the various efforts for collecting monetary contributions for the Serbian refugees. The humanitarian concerns were widespread, in particular among the little people and the peasantry: they were all ready to sacrifice their own lives and families fortunes for the cause that they considered sacred'.[115]

The patriotic enthusiasm expressed itself in different ways. The Slavic benevolent societies were especially active, led by Ivan Aksakov, gathering money for the cause, an activity initially prohibited by the Tsar (he later accepted the contribution if they were for the benefit of victims).[116] The Russian Red Cross Society worked in Serbia with its doctors and nurses, with the Russians helping their Serbian colleagues, who were generally ill-trained as medical doctors. Several hundred thousand volunteers left for the unknown Balkans from various social strata and backgrounds. The Southern Russian Union of Workers and the Odessa Railroad Workers were among the first to announce their solidarity with the Balkan insurgents. Half of the several thousand volunteers to Serbia were Ukrainians.[117] Members of the Young Latvians, involved in planning the Latvian national revival, became volunteers, such as the romantic writer Andreis Pumpurs (he met Aksakov, who sent him to the volunteers).[118] Among the volunteers were radical friends of Kropotkin as well as monarchists, such as the brother of Novikova, one of the main organizers of the volunteers.

Rethinking the 'noble cause'

Russian solidarity with the Slavs in the Balkans has been characterized as a spontaneous democratic movement and compared with the great Patriotic War of 1812 (against Napoleon's invasion).[119] In fact, the movement had lost much of its allure and enthusiasm once the first defeats of the Serbs became known and the volunteers themselves found that their Serbian 'brothers' were not particularly enthusiastic about their 'saviours' who had come to shed their blood for the Serbian cause.

The writer and prominent Narodnik Gleb Uspensky, who had gone to Serbia, sent reports in the form of letters. The gist of these is that the volunteers had gone there above all for the experience and in order to leave behind the various dead-ends of Russian life. It was, he said, 'in order to live at a thousand different levels' that the volunteers left for Serbia.[120]

But best known is the controversy between Dostoevsky and Tolstoy, as a result of the eighth and last chapter of *Anna Karenina* (Russian novels at the time were serially published in journals before being released in book form). In a scene where various positive as well as negative views are presented regarding the volunteer body sent to Serbia, the main protagonist of the novel, Levin, expresses the conviction that Russian society did not associate itself with the southern Slavs and, worse, did not even understand their national movements. Levin went even further, questioning the size and mass character of the pro-Serbian movement.

Tolstoy's doctrine of non-resistance to evil and strict pacifism (which later impressed Gandhi, who corresponded with Tolstoy) put into question the possibility of a 'just war', which he regarded as unattainable, however noble the goal. He questioned how one could ever be certain what the general good is. The central hero of *Anna Karenina* contemplated that the achievement of this general good was possible with strict adherence to the law of goodness, which is inherent in every person, and as a result he could not desire war or propagate it for general aims.

Dostoyevsky, from the pages of *A Writer' Diary*, voiced his strong disagreement with Tolstoy. Dostoyevsky's discourse of Slavophile and romantic nationalism is founded on the belief that 'Russia's psyche' is imbued with a unique blend of universal humanism and selflessness which empathizes with alien pain. Thus the Russian people could not but participate in the Balkan quest for freedom, equipped as they were 'with an inherent and well-developed historical instinct'. In this endeavour the Russian people were also putting into effect what was no less than God's will. From a humanistic perspective, the Russian people had the moral duty to afford support to their suppressed Slav Orthodox brethren. Furthermore, by pursuing a foreign policy aimed at saving the southern Slavs, Russia was accelerating the process of Slavic national emancipation, which would eventually lead to Slavic unity, which was a godly end.[121]

When the Russo-Ottoman War was declared, Dostoyevsky stated in 'The Dream of a Ridiculous Man' (April 1877) that this step gave the Russian people the opportunity to create a new Christian order. In an article entitled 'The Paradoxalist', referring to the Christian ethical belief that war brings only blood and violence (and obviously intended for Tolstoy's pacifism), he retorts that wars take place because humanity cannot live without noble ideas, and he underlines that 'I suspect that humanity loves war precisely because it wants to be part of a noble idea'.[122]

A few months later, in October 1877, Vsevolod Garshin, one of the most talented authors of his generation (who committed suicide at the age of thirty-three), wrote his acclaimed first short story, 'Four Days', a statement on modern war, in the Narodnik journal *Otechestvennye Zapiski*, based on a real incident from his experience as a volunteer in the 1877–78 Russo-Ottoman War, in which he had fought bravely and was wounded. The hero of the story, Ivanov, goes to war in the belief that he is serving a noble cause. He is wounded and taken for dead, is left on the battleground for four days, face to face with the corpse of the Ottoman soldier he had killed. The story is a basically a monologue by the wounded Russian soldier, who asks himself 'why did I kill him?' He ponders about the duty of an intellectual when faced with the horror of killing another human being.[123]

There was also the question of Russia itself, which, immersed in the war, had left many of its own daunting problems unresolved. As put in the pages of *Otechestvennye Zapiski*, 'In view of the fate of the Slavs Russia has forgotten that it exists in the world ... it has all transformed itself into a society of self-sacrifice ... in fact we also need help no less than the [Balkan] Slavs'.[124] As acidly put by Jomini to Giers in September 1877, while the war was still raging:[125]

> I continue to think that instead of pursuing these Slavic fantasies, we should have done better to have taken care of our own Christian Slavs. If the emperor wished to descend from official heights and splendors and play Haroum al Rashid, if he wished to visit incognito the suburbs of Bucharest and his own capital, he would be convinced of all that there was to do to civilize, organize and develop his own country and he would be convinced that a crusade against drunkenness and syphilis was more necessary and profitable to Russia than the ruinous crusade against the Turks for the profit of the Bulgarians.

Criticism came on other grounds as well. The Ukrainian academic Drahomanov questioned the humanistic motives of the Tsar. For one, the war started late, when all the uprisings had been quelled and a great number of Serbs, Bulgarians and Russian (the volunteers) had been killed. He argued that the Tsar had in fact started a war not in order to save human beings but for his honour and fame, not as the representative of the Slavs but as the leader of a great European power poised to show resolve and power; in other words, the humanitarian rhetoric was simply a smoke-screen for political and other tangible interests. In a series of articles with characteristic titles such as 'Internal and External Turks', 'Clean Cases Need Clean Hands' and 'Internal Slavery and the War of Liberation', he pointed to the hypocrisy of Russia's 'humanitarian intervention' against the Turks in support of the Slavs, while the Russian state suppressed a number of Slav nations in its midst. He also pointed to the contradiction of, on the one hand, the so-called historical Russian mission to liberate the Slavs and, on the other, having 'Turkish structures' and absolutism within the Russian Empire. And he referred to discrimination against many ethnic groups, including the Jews, and the use of violence by the Russian state in the Caucasus and against the Poles, the Ukrainians and others, violating the right to life which it supposedly wanted to defend in the Balkans.[126] He called for the creation of a democratic federal Russia, for Russia was not 'Turkey', with its innate inability to join the 'civilized' states.

The east of the semi-east

In 1876 an important international scientific event took place in St Petersburg, the conference of Orientalists, little noticed by educated society, which was absorbed by events in the Balkans. The introductory speech by Orientalist Grigoriev referred to events of 'religious passions' and 'one race arming against the other', but reassured his audience that they were secure in the safe embrace of science, where even rival parties can search for truth.[127] The scientific committee of the conference had set forth thirty-eight subjects to address, the twenty-sixth being whether in the history of the Arabs the motivating force was Islamic fanaticism or the thirst for plunder and booty which characterized all nomadic peoples. Note that the massacres in the Balkans were largely depicted as outbursts of religious fanaticism, which was regarded an inherent characteristic of all those who hailed from Asia.

Such Orientalist thinking was in line with the views of the young science of international law, which distinguished between civilized and semi-civilized or barbarous states (see chapter 3). In Russia, this view was set forth in the second half of the nineteenth century by international jurists Kamarowski and Martens, who asserted that between civilized states no intervention for humanitarian reasons was conceivable; this was applicable only between civilized states against barbarous states if the latter persecuted Christian communities (see chapter 4).

As pointed out by Susan Layton, the events of 1875–78 contributed to the further 'Easternization' of the Ottoman state, which, though obliged to reform and treat its Christian subject decently, was seen as unable to truly reform and act in a civilized way. In the case of Russia, the Turkic Circassians showed that the 'Turks' in the Ottoman Empire, as well as Russia, were unredeemable barbarians, on the prowl and capable of the most despicable acts of inhumanity. This was seen in popular illustrations as well as in high literature. She describes a picture which appeared in 1878 in *Niva*, entitled 'Circassians Returning from a Raid':[128]

[The illustration] shows a band of tribesmen crossing a river with captives, rustled horses, and cattle. Near the center rides a swarthy mountaineer with a blonde woman on his horse. She is naked to the waist with some cloth loosely draped about her legs. Another woman with an infant is visible on a raft in the foreground. This iconography gave even illiterate Russians access in the postwar mythology of national victory over Asian fiends.

Dostoevsky in *A Writer's Diary* referred on a number of occasions to 'a Muslim conspiracy in the interior of the empire', reacting in this way to the various calls that treating the Muslims disdainfully was inappropriate when so many millions of them lived peacefully and loyally within the confines of the Russian Empire. The *Diary* dramatizes Islamic savagery with the story of a simple soldier who was caught by the Muslims during the conquest of central Asia, and was offered his freedom and wealth if he became Muslim. He did not want to convert and suffered terrible torture as a martyr to the Christian faith.[129] And it was probably no coincidence that the Russian heroes of the Russo-Ottoman War were also previously heroes of the colonial expeditions of Russia to central Asia or the Caucuses.

This image of the Turkic peoples in the Caucasus or central Asia or in the Balkans with the Circassian onslaught against the Bulgarians served a distinct purpose: to justify Russian violence and absolve Russia of the guilt of the ethnic cleansing of the Circassians in the Caucasus in the 1860s. Needless to say, such a posture left little room for the discourse of the 'Other', of the Muslim, Turk or Turkic, while the Russian conquest was dubbed pacification and a civilizing mission. The Christian slaughters and atrocities against Muslims were not registered at all, for the Muslim as a victim was simply not visible.

The Russian (and European) image of the Balkans, as shown by the work of Maria Todorova,[130] is more complex, the presentation not only of the 'Turks' but also of all the Balkan Christians as beyond the purview of civilization, as Metternich saw it the first part of the nineteenth century and Bismarck in the 1870s. According to the journal *Otechestvennye Zapiski*:[131]

> Hearing of the violent behaviour of the Turks we should bear in mind that it is not a unique characteristic for them alone, but one of the East and of the southern Christians as well. Harshness and violence are an everyday occasion and it is used by all against all. Human life may cost little to the Ottomans but this also applies to the [Balkan] Christian peoples, who are at a low level of cultural development. Even in the present insurgency the most popular are those leaders who never give in, such as Peiko Pavlovits, who collected as his trophies human heads.

Humanitarian sentiments went hand in hand with the patronizing attitude of the 'saviour' towards the victim, another aspect of humanitarian interventions in the nineteenth century.

Notes

1 This metaphor was used by M. Bassin, 'Asia', in N. Rzhevsky (ed.), *The Cambridge Companion to Modern Russia Culture* (Cambridge: Cambridge University Press, 1998), 58.
2 H. Rogger, *Russia in the Age of Modernization and Revolution, 1881–1917* (London: Longman, 1992, 9th edition) [1983], 163.
3 I. B. Neumann, *Uses of the Other: The 'East' in European Identity Formation* (Minneapolis: University of Minnesota Press, 1999); J. Howes Gleason, *The Genesis of Russophobia in Great Britain* (Cambridge: Harvard University Press, 1950).
4 The architect of this policy was Nesselrode (a German Protestant in office as Secretary of State for Foreign Affairs from 1815 until 1856), whom the nationalists regarded as a non-Russian, an Austrian agent who headed Russian diplomacy. In contrast, Capodistrias (who held the same post with Nesselrode from 1815 until 1822) was seen as a patriot, even though he was not Russian. See L. A. Komarovskiy, *Vostochniy Vopros* (Moscow: A. A. Levenson, 1896), 12–13. The dogma of an independent 'Turkey' first appeared in 1802 and was adopted following the 1828–29 war. It was further reinforced with the Treaty of Unkiar Skelessi (1833) with which Russia's position was reinforced vis-à-vis the Ottoman state. See I. S. Kinyapina (ed.), *Bostochniy Vopros vo vneshney politike Rossii, konets XVIII– nachalo XX vv.* (Moscow: Nauka, 1978); H. N. Ingle, *Nesselrode and the Russian Rapprochement with Britain, 1836–1844* (Berkeley: University of California Press, 1976); G. H. Bolsover, 'Aspects of Russian Foreign Policy, 1815–1914', in R. Pipes and A. J. Taylor (eds), *Essays Presented to Sir Lewis Namier* (New York: Books for Libraries Press Freeport, 1956), 340–1; I. J. Lederer, 'Russia and the Balkans', in I. J. Lederer (ed.), *Russian Foreign Policy: Essays in Historical Perspective* (New Haven: Yale University Press, 1967), 422; Rogger, *Russia in the Age of Modernization and Revolution*, 162–81.
5 A. J. Rieber, 'Persistent Factors in Russian Foreign Policy: An Interpretive Essay', in H. Ragsdale and V. N. Ponomarev (eds), *Imperial Russian Foreign Policy* (New York: Woodrow Wilson Center Press and Cambridge University Press, 1993), 351.
6 M. Schulz, 'The Guarantees of Humanity: The Concert of Europe and the Origins of the Russo-Ottoman War of 1877', in B. Simms and D. J. B. Trim (eds), *Humanitarian Intervention: A History* (Cambridge: Cambridge University Press, 2011), 185.
7 This view was advanced by his younger colleague A. N. Kartsov. See Yu S. Kartsov, *Za kulisami diplomatii* (St Petersburg: Nadezhda, 1908), 4.
8 D. MacKenzie, 'Russia's Balkan Policies Under Alexander II, 1855–1881', in Ragsdale and Ponomarev (eds), *Imperial Russian Foreign Policy*, 228.
9 Kartsov, *Za kulisami diplomatii*, 5.
10 For the disagreement and contrasting approaches of Gorchakov and Ignatiev see N. P. Ignatiev, 'Poezdka grafa N.P. Ignatieva po evropeyskim stolitsam pered voinoy 1877–1878 g.g.', *Russkaya Starina*, 3 (1914), 493.
11 MacKenzie, 'Russia's Balkan Policies Under Alexander II', 227.
12 B. Jelavich, *Russia's Balkan Entanglements 1806–1914* (Cambridge: Cambridge University Press, 1991), 143–7.
13 Arkhiv Vneshney Politiki Rossiiskoy Imperii (henceforth AVPRI), Sekretniy Arkhiv, 1867, d. 9, *Doklad ministra inostrannykh del Rosii A.M. Gorchakova Aleksandru II o deyatel'nosti ministerstva c1856 po1867 g po balkanskim problemam*, l. 16–28. See also N. B. Zueva and E. M. Satokhina, 'Iz Istorii balkanskoy politiki Rossii 1856–1867gg', *Otnoshenie russkoy diplomatii k bolgarskomu natsional'no-osvoboditel'nomu dvizheniyu*, *Balkanskie Issledovaniya*, Vyp.8 (Moscow: Nauka, 1982), 167.

14 Lederer refers to this contradictory dual approach of Russian policy in the Balkans, which he regards as the main reason for its lack of success. See Lederer, 'Russia and the Balkans', 422.
15 Zueva and Satokhina, 'Iz Istorii balkanskoy politiki Rossii 1856–1867gg', 167–72. See also Jelavich, *Russia's Balkan Entanglements*, 146–7, 153.
16 During the 1866 Paris Conference on the Romanian question, Gorchakov's instructions to Ignatiev were to be restrained and careful: 'Our international situation and the great reforms that are taking place oblige us to limit our activity abroad'. AVPRI, Kantselyariya, d. 52, Gorchakov to Ignatiev, 27 February 1866, l. 97.
17 AVPRI, Kantselyariya, 'Otchet Ministra Inonstrannykh Del za 1859', l. 41 (ob).
18 I. S. Kinyapina, *Vneshnyaya politika Rossii vtoroy poloviny XIXv* (Moscow: Visshaja Shkola, 1974), 160.
19 Ignatiev, 'Poezdka grafa N.P. Ignatieva', 496; N. P. Ignatiev, 'Zapiski grafa N.P. Ignatieva', *Istoricheskiy Vestnik*, 1 (1914), 74; V. M. Khevrolina, 'Vostochniy krisis 70-kh godov XIX v.', in V. M. Khevrolina et al. (eds), *Istoriya Vneshney Politiki Rosii, Vtoraya polovina XIX veka* (Moscow: Mezhdunarodnye otnoshenija, 1997), 178.
20 Ignatiev, 'Zapiski grafa N. P. Ignatieva', 442; Khevrolina, 'Vostochniy krisis 70-kh godov XIX v.', 179.
21 Khevrolina, 'Vostochniy krisis 70-kh godov XIX v.', 180–2.
22 Jelavich, *Russia's Balkan Entanglements*, 163.
23 *Ibid.*, 169.
24 MacKenzie, 'Russia's Balkan Policies Under Alexander II', 230, 232; D. MacKenzie, *Imperial Dreams, Harsh Realities: Tsarist Russian Foreign Policy, 1815–1917* (Fort Worth: Harcourt Brace College Publishers, 1994), 74; W. E. Mosse, *Alexander II and the Modernization of Russia* (London: I. B. Tauris, 1992), 150.
25 Kartsov, *Za kulisami diplomatii*, 198; D. MacKenzie, 'Panslavism in Practice: Cherniaev in Serbia (1876)', *Journal of Modern History*, 36 (1964), 281–2.
26 MacKenzie, 'Russia's Balkan Policies Under Alexander II', 230–3, 235.
27 MacKenzie, *Imperial Dreams, Harsh Realities*, 77.
28 Quoted in MacKenzie, 'Russia's Balkan Policies Under Alexander II', 233.
29 Mosse, *Alexander II and the Modernization of Russia*, 147.
30 MacKenzie, 'Russia's Balkan Policies Under Alexander II', 233.
31 Quoted *ibid.*, 232.
32 Quoted in Khevrolina, 'Vostochniy krisis 70-kh godov XIX v.', 188.
33 Kartsov, *Za kulisami diplomatii*, 33 (N. P. Ignatiev to A. N. Kartsov, correspondence dated 17 June 1876).
34 Quoted in B. H. Sumner, *Russia and the Balkans, 1870–1880* (Oxford: Clarendon Press, 1937), 226; S. S. Tatishchev, *Imperator Aleksandr II, ego zhizn' I tsarstvovanie* (St Petersburg: Izdanie A. S. Suvorin, 1903), vol. II, 335.
35 Disraeli wrote to the Queen that the Tsar could not have known of his speech so quickly and he himself had sent it to Vienna but not to St Petersburg. See M. Ković, *Disraeli and the Eastern Question* (Oxford: Oxford University Press, 2011), 171–2.
36 Tatishchev, *Imperator Aleksandr II*, 336.
37 Quoted *ibid.*, 336; translation into English in Sumner, *Russia and the Balkans*, 227.
38 R. Wortman, *Scenarios of Power: Myth and Ceremony in Russian Monarchy* (Princeton: Princeton University Press, 1995), vol. II, 135.
39 Fragmenti dnevnikov i vospominaniy suprugi I. S. Aksakova I starshey docheri F. I. Tyucheva, 29 October 1876, online at http://az.lib.ru/a/aksakowa_a_f/text_0010.shtml.

The Balkan crisis

40 'Sobstvennorychnaya dokladnaya zapiska gen.-leit. N. N. Obrucheva ot 1 oktryabrya 1876', appendix 1 in M. Gazenkanpf, *Moj Dnevnik, 1877–1878gg* (St Petersburg: V. A. Berezovskij, 1908), 1.
41 Khevrolina, 'Vostochniy krisis 70-kh godov XIX v.', 190–1; Sumner, *Russia and the Balkans*, 240–1.
42 A. Dialla, *I Rosia apenanti sta Valkania: Ideologia kai politiki sto defter imisi tou 19ou aiona* (Athens: Alexandria, 2009), 281–2. Alexander, at the start of the crisis, had written a letter to Kaiser Wilhelm I, to try to convince him that their countries should put an end to the insurrections, whose participants were 'the worst revolutionaries of all the countries, even Garibaldists'. In AVPRI, f. Kantselyariya, d. 4, 30 August 1875, l. 2–4.
43 Ignatiev et al., *Istoriya vneshney politiki Rossii*, 175; M. S. Anderson, *The Eastern Question, 1774–1923: A Study in International Relations* (London: Macmillan, 1966), 181–2; Dialla, *I Rosia apenanti sta Valkania*, 280–1.
44 Quoted in Khevrolina, 'Vostochniy krisis 70-kh godov XIX v.', 193.
45 R. W. Seton-Watson, *Disraeli, Gladstone and the Eastern Question* (London: Frank Cass, 1962) [1935], 127.
46 Ibid., 145.
47 Ibid., 140.
48 A. J. Rieber, 'Alexander II: A Revisionist View', *Journal of Modern History*, 43:1 (1971), 57.
49 Ibid., 57.
50 For the importance of the 'ethical authority' in the imperial ideology of the Russian Empire, see the works of Jelavich, which highlight the importance of honour and duty in the enactment of Russian foreign policy. See e.g. Jelavich, *Russia's Balkan Entanglements*, 172. See also D. Geyer, *Russian Imperialism: The Interaction of Domestic and Foreign Policy, 1860–1914* (New Haven: Yale University Press, 1987), 84.
51 Schulz, 'The Guarantees of Humanity', 202.
52 Rieber, 'Alexander II', 48.
53 MacKenzie, 'Russia's Balkan Policies Under Alexander II', 236–7.
54 *Osvobozhdenie Bolgarii ot turetskogo iga* (Moscow, 1961), vol. I, document 265, 396.
55 'Zapiska voennago Ministra D. A. Miliutina ot 7 Fevralya 1877 g. Sostavlennaya N. N. Obruchevym', appendix 2 in M. Gazenkanpf, *Moy Dnevnik, 1877–1878gg*, 2, 3.
56 F. Martens, 'Étude historique sur la politique russe dans la question d'Orient', *Revue de droit international et de législation comparée*, 9 (1877), 49.
57 Ibid., 49–50.
58 *Pol'nyi Sbornik offitsial'nykh telegram vostochnoy voyny, 1877* (St Petersburg: Tipografiya Shredera, 1877), 1–2; Jelavich, *Russia's Balkan Entanglements*, 172–3.
59 Quoted in Jelavich, *Russia's Balkan Entanglements*, 172 n.37.
60 *Osvobozhdenie Bolgarii ot turetskogo iga* (Moscow: Izdatel'stvo RAN, 1962), vol. II, document 62, 88 and 61, 82.
61 MacKenzie, 'Russian Balkan Policies Under Alexander II', 239–40.
62 Wortman, *Scenarios of Power*, 138.
63 Quoted in S. N. Norris, *A War of Images: Russian Popular Prints, Wartime Culture, and National Identity, 1812–1945* (DeKalb: Northern Illinois University Press, 2006), 82 (from F. V. Greene, *Sketches of Army Life in Russia*, 1880).
64 Sumner, *Russia and the Balkans*, 399.
65 Ibid., 399–405; MacKenzie, 'Russia's Balkan Policies Under Alexander II', 240.
66 See San Stefanskiy mirnyy dogovor, 19 February/3 March 1878, online at www.hist.msu.ru/ER/Etext/Foreign/Stefano.htm; Anderson, *The Eastern Question*, 203; Kinyapina,

Vneshnyaya politika Rossii vtoroy poloviny XIXv, 173–81; I. S. Kinyapina (ed.), *Vostochniy Vopros vo vneshney politike Rossii, konets XVIII–nachalo XX vv.* (Moscow: Nauka, 1978), 222–7; Ignatiev et al., *Istoriya vneshney politiki Rossii*, 174–219.

67 See G. D. Clayton, *Britain and the Eastern Question: Missolonghi to Gallipoli* (London: Lion Library, 1971), 142, 144.
68 Rieber, 'Alexander II', 57.
69 MacKenzie, 'Russia's Balkan Policies Under Alexander II', 239–40.
70 L. S. Stavrianos, *The Balkans Since 1453* (London: Hurst, 2000) [1958], 409.
71 MacKenzie, 'Russian Balkan Policies Under Alexander II', 241.
72 For both quotes see MacKenzie, *Imperial Dreams, Harsh Realities*, 85.
73 Quoted *ibid.*, 83.
74 Jelavich, *Russia's Balkan Entanglements*, 177–8.
75 *Ibid.*, 176.
76 A. N. Kartsov, in Ju. Kartsov (ed.), *Sem' let na Blizhnem Vostoke* (St Petersburg: Economicheskaya Tipo-Litografiya, 1906), 354. See for another similar statement by Alexander III in April 1881, Jelavich, *Russia's Balkan Entanglements*, 181.
77 Quoted *ibid.*, 273.
78 B. Jelavich, *A Century of Russian Foreign Policy* (Philadelphia: J. B. Lippincott, 1964), 181.
79 Anderson, *The Eastern Question*, 203. See also Stavrianos, *The Balkans*, 408–10.
80 MacKenzie, 'Russia's Balkan Policies Under Alexander II', 236; H. Kohn, *Panlavism: Its History and Ideology* (New York: Vintage Books, 1953), 145. For the ambivalence of Russian foreign policy towards the Balkans during this period see Kartsov, *Za kulisami diplomatii*, 27.
81 S. A. Nikitin, *Slavyaskie komitety v Rossii v 1858–1876* (Moscow: Moskovskiy Universitet, 1960), 260–351. A month before the start of the Russo-Ottoman War, Ivan Aksakov announced with satisfaction the legalization of the Slavic Benevolent Society of Moscow: 'At last after 18 years of semi-legal activity we have been officially recognized by the state'. See I. S. Aksakov, *Slavjanskiy Vopros. 1860–1886* (Moscow: M. G. Volchaninov, 1886), 263.
82 For the wide range of approaches under Pan-Slavism see the works of A. Pypin in the nineteenth century. See in particular A. Pypin, *Panslavism v proshlom i nastoyashchem* (Moscow: Kolos', 1913) [1878]. More recently, for the various versions of Pan-Slavism, from the ultra-conservative to the liberal and left wing, see F. Fadner, *Seventy Years of Pan-Slavism in Russia: Karazin to Danilevskii 1800–1870* (Georgetown: Georgetown University Press, 1961); A. Dyakov, *Slavyanskiy vopros v obchshestvennoy zhizni dorevoljutsionnoy Rossii* (Moscow: Nauka, 1993).
83 R. Fadeev, *Mnenie o Vostochnom Voprose. Po povodu poslednikh retsentsii na vooruzhennye sily Rossii* (St Petersburg: Tipografiya Gogenfel'gena i Co, 1870); N. Ya. Danilevskiy, *Rossiya i Evropa. Vzglyad na kulturnye i polticheskie otnoshenija slavyanskogo mira k germano-romanskomu* (St Petersburg: Glagol, 1995) [1869, 1895]; Pypin, *Panslavism v proshlom i nastoyashchem*, 146.
84 Dialla, *I Rosia apenanti sta Valkania*, 107–8.
85 Quoted in Pypin, *Panslavism v proshlom i nastojashchem*, 102.
86 O. Miller, *Slavjanskiy vopros v nauke i v zhizni. Po povodu Obzora istorii slavyanskikh literatur A. N. Pypina i V. D. Spasovicha* (St Petersburg: no publisher stated, 1865).
87 O. K. [Olga Kireeva Novikoff], *Skobelleff and the Slavonic Cause* (London: Longmans, Green and Co., 1883), 230.
88 Fadner, *Seventy Years of Pan-Slavism in Russia*, 229.

89 V. A. Cherskaskiy, 'Dva slova po povodu Vostochnogo Voprosa', *Russkaya Beseda*, 4 (1858), 65–92; Danilevskiy, *Rossiya i Evropa*; O. Miller, 'Russko – slavyanskiy vopros i nachalo narodnosti', in *Slavyanstvo i Evropa* (Moscow: SPb, 1877), 79–113; Aksakov, *Slavyaskiy Vopros*.
90 Pypin, *Panslavism v proshlom i nastoyashchem*, 102.
91 A. Miller, *The Ukrainian Question: The Russian Empire and Nationalism in the Nineteenth Century* (Budapest: Central European University Press, 2003), 169, 177 n.72.
92 Dyakov, *Slavyanskiy vopros*, 82–101; H. S. Dzhong, *Ideya slavyanskoy integratsii v rossiyskoy obchshestvenno-politicheskoy mysli XIX veka. Avtoreferat, dissertatsii* (Moscow: Institut Rossijskoy Istoriy RAN, 1996), ch. 4; Fadner, *Seventy Years of Pan-Slavism in Russia*, 147–82; G. A. Kuznetsova, 'Voprosy voiny i mira, mezhdunarodnikh otnoshenii na stranitsakh "KOLOKOLA" v osveshenii A.I. Gertsena', in *Vneshnyaya politika Rossii i obshchestvennoe mnenie* (Moscow: no publisher stated, 1988), 90.
93 D. von Mohrenschildt, *Toward a United States of Russia: Plans and Projects of Federal Reconstruction of Russia in the Nineteenth Century* (London: Associated University Press, 1981), 43; Miller, *The Ukrainian Question*, 105; Pypin, *Panslavism v proshlom I nastojashchem*, 95–7.
94 See J. Bradley, 'Voluntary Associations, Civic Culture, and "Obshchestvennost"' in Moscow', in E. W. Clowes, S. D. Kassow and J. L. West (eds), *Between Tsar and People: Educated Society and the Quest for Public Identity in Late Imperial Russia* (Princeton: Princeton University Press, 1991), 147. More generally for the emergence of new social groups and their identity in the last decades of the nineteenth century see Clowes, Kassow and West (eds), *Between Tsar and People*; E. Kimerling Wirtschafter, *Structures and Society: Imperial Russia's 'People of Various Ranks'* (DeKalb: Northern Illinois University Press, 1994); D. Wartenweiler, *Civil Society and Academic Debate in Russia, 1905–1914* (Oxford: Clarendon Press, 1999).
95 A. Renner, 'Defining a Russian Nation: Mikhail Katkov and the "Invention" of National Politics', *Slavonic and Eastern European Review*, 81:4 (2003), 668.
96 Kartsov, *Za kulisami diplomatii*, 40, 43.
97 Khevrolina, 'Vostochniy krisis 70-kh godov XIX v.', 188.
98 A. N. Rovnyakova, *Bor'ba Yuzhnikh Slavyan za svobody i russkaya periodicheskaya pechat' (50–70e gody XIX veka). Ocherki* (Leningrad: Nauka, 1986).
99 See in particular: *Russkiy Mir*, 2 July 1876; *Moskovskie Vedomosti*, May to July, especially 16 July 1876; and *Novoe Vremya*, 13 May 1876. See also Rovnyakova, *Bor'ba Yuzhnikh Slavjan*, 214.
100 Quoted in Schulz, 'The Guarantees of Humanity', 194.
101 *Vsemirnaya Illyustratsiya*, 403 (18 September 1876), 209.
102 P. Krapotkin, *Zapiski Revoliutsionera* (Moscow: no publisher stated, 1966), 353.
103 S. Prévost, 'W. T. Stead and the Eastern Question (1875–1991)', *Interdisciplinary Studies in the Long 19th Century*, 16 (2013), 7.
104 As quoted *ibid.*, 10.
105 R. T. Shannon, *Gladstone and the Bulgarian Agitation 1876* (London: Thomas Nelson and Sons, 1963), 70.
106 *Ibid.*, 99.
107 F. A. Brokgauz and I. A. Efron, *Entsiklopedicheskiy Slovar'* (St Petersburg: no publisher or year stated); J. O. Baylen, 'Madame Olga Novikov, Propagandist', *American Slavic and East European Review*, 10:4 (1951), 255–71. See also her memoirs: O. Novikoff, *Russian Memories* (London: Herbert Jenkins, 1917, with an Introduction by Stephen Graham).

108 J. Brooks, *When Russia Learned to Read: Literacy and Popular Literature, 1861–1917* (Princeton: Princeton University Press, 1985).
109 Khevrolina, 'Vostochniy krisis 70-kh godov XIX v.', 195.
110 Quoted in Norris, *A War of Images*, 104.
111 'Croquet at Windsor', *The Nation* (5 October 1876), 213. For a more accurate translation as a poem from the original Russian, see 'The Croquet in Windsor', in P. Waddington (ed.), *Ivan Turgenev and Britain* (Oxford: Berg, 1995), 206–7 (from a 1983 article in the *New Zealand Slavonic Journal* by N. Zekulin).
112 Quoted in B. W. Tedford, 'The Attitudes of Henry James and Ivan Tyrgenev Toward the Russo-Turkish War', *Henry James Review*, 4:1 (1980), 257–61.
113 As quoted in D. Vovchenko, 'Gendering Irredentism? Self and Other in Russian Pan-Orthodoxy and Pan-Slavism (1855–1885)', *Ethnic and Racial Studies*, 34:2 (2011), 263.
114 Khevrolina, 'Vostochniy krisis 70-kh godov XIX v.', 195.
115 Quoted in J. Milojkovic-Djuric, *Panslavism and National Identity in Russia and in the Balkans 1830–1880: Images of the Self and Others* (New York: Columbia University Press, 1994), 101.
116 Nikitin, *Slavyaskie komitety v Rossii*, 272; Milojkovic-Djuric, *Panslavism and National Identity*; Khevrolina, 'Vostochnij krisis 70-kh godov XIX v.', 181.
117 Milojkovic-Djuric, *Panslavism and National Identity*, 102.
118 *Ibid.*, 103.
119 A. P[ypin], 'Neskol'ko slov po povudu yuzhno-slayanskogo voprosa', *Vestnik Evropy*, 61 (1876), 876.
120 Г-въ [Gleb Uspenskiy], 'Iz Bel'grada', *Otechestvennye Zapiski*, 12 (December 1876), part ii, 184–5.
121 F. M. Dostoevsky, *Dnevnik Pisatelya* (Moscow: Sovremennik, 1989) [1877], 466–77. See also J. Milojković-Djurić, *The Eastern Question and the Voices of Reason: Austria–Hungary, Russia, and the Balkan States 1875–1908* (Boulder: East European Monographs, 2002), 32–47.
122 Dostoevsky, *Dnevnik Pisatelya* (April 1876), 209–14.
123 V. Garshin, 'Chetire Dnya', *Otechestvennye Zapiski*, 10 (October 1877), 461–71. For details on this short story and its originality (hailed among others by Tolstoy) see P. Henry, *A Hamlet of his Time: Vsevolod Garshin. The Man, His Works, and His Milieu* (Oxford: Willem A. Meeuws, 1983), 41–54.
124 'Vnutrennoe Obozrenie', *Otechestvennye Zapiski*, 10 (October 1876), 190.
125 Quoted in Jelavich, *Russia's Balkan Entanglements*, 272.
126 M. Drahomanov, *Turki Vnutrennie i Vneshnie* (Geneva: no publisher stated, 1876).
127 'Congress Orientalistov v Peterburg', *Otechestvennye Zapisky*, 10 (December 1876), 24–5.
128 S. Layton, 'Nineteenth-Century Russian Mythologies of Caucasian Savagery', in E. J. Brower and D. R. Lazzerini (eds), *Russia's Orient: Imperial Borderlands and Peoples, 1750–1917* (Bloomington: Indiana University Press, 1997), 95. See also Brooks, *When Russia Learned to Read*, 111–14.
129 Dostoevsky, *Dnevnik Pisatelya* (January 1877), 363–8.
130 M. Todorova, *Imagining the Balkans* (New York: Oxford University Press, 1997); Vovchenko, 'Gendering Irredentism?'
131 *Otechestvennye Zapiski*, 11 (November 1875), part ii, 119.

10

The US and Cuba, 1895–98

On intervention

Among the handful of humanitarian interventions of the nineteenth century the intervention in Cuba is the most controversial, in view of the US reluctance to leave Cuba and the huge advantages it accrued, including the acquisition of even the faraway Philippines.

Any discussion of the US stance on intervention before 1914 has to take into consideration the Monroe Doctrine of 1823.[1] The Doctrine contained three principles: (1) that the Americas were 'henceforth not to be considered as subjects for future colonization' by any European power; (2) that the US would abstain from interfering in European affairs; and (3) that there will be no 'interposition' by the European powers in 'this hemisphere'.[2] Conversely, there was to be no US interference in the existing European colonies in the Americas. Thus it was not applicable to Cuba, which was held by Spain.

According to John Bassett Moore of Columbia University, the doyen among international lawyers in the US during that period, 'the most pronounced exception ever made by the United States, apart from cases arising under the Monroe Doctrine, to its policy of non-intervention, is that which was made in the case of Cuba'.[3]

As for the justification of the intervention in Cuba on humanitarian grounds, the US government was well aware of this concept and its practice as it had evolved in Europe. The US administration included acclaimed lawyers, such as Secretary of State William Day, many of them proficient in international law, such as Attorney General John Griggs, Elihu Root[4] and Moore, who served as Assistant Secretary of State in 1897–98 and was Day's main adviser on foreign affairs. Moreover, American jurists had for decades contributed to the debate on humanitarian intervention, with Kent and Halleck in earlier periods having come out against the idea; and a majority in support, namely Wheaton, Woolsey, as well as Pomeroy and Hershey prior to 1898 (see chapter 4, especially table 4.1).

More generally, the intervention in Cuba was to prove a turning point. As Charles Fenwick has put it: 'Henceforth the role of the United States was to be no longer that of a leader of the American States in opposing intervention of Europe in American affairs but was to be itself the intervening power with the other American States ranged against it'.[5] The subsequent 1903 treaty with Cuba provided the US with a right to intervene ostensibly for the good of Cuba (see below); Theodore Roosevelt's 'corollary' to the Monroe Doctrine of 1904 said that 'chronic wrongdoing' in Latin American states could lead to intervention; and the Wilson Doctrine (1913) led to US interventions in Mexico (1914), Haiti (1915) and the Dominican Republic (1916). Such blatant interventionism led to a strong reaction on the part of the Latin American states, and intervention was declared 'inadmissible' at the 1936 Buenos Aires Conference for the Maintenance of Peace.[6]

The setting

In the first part of the nineteenth century all the overseas territories of Spain's *Siglo de oro* (golden age) had gained independence save Cuba (and Puerto Rico), earning it the name 'the ever-faithful isle'. Spaniards emigrated to Cuba well into the 1880s. Of some 1.6 million inhabitants, 150,000 were *peninsulares* (first-generation immigrants), 950,000 creoles (their offspring) and 500,000 were Afro-Cubans and mulattos. Spain's imperial rule was reactionary, ensuring the *peninsulares* a privileged position.[7]

The first bid for *Cuba libre* was the Ten Years' War (1868–78), initially headed by Carlos de Céspedes, who freed his slaves and declared Cuban independence, followed by Máximo Gómez (a former colonel from Santo Domingo), Antonio Maceo (the mulatto hero of the peasants), Calixto García and others. The war ended with the Pact of Zangón (1878), after victory by the Spaniards under General Martínez de Campos. There were some meagre reforms and in 1886 the long-awaited abolition of slavery. A second independence attempt, known as the Little War (1879–80), headed by García, was also abortive.[8]

April 1892 saw the formation of the Partido revolucionario cubano, by poet and political theorist José Martí, who recruited seasoned soldiers from the previous war, Gómez, Maceo, García and others. On 24 February 1895 the Guerra de independencia was declared. Martí issued the Proclamation of Montecristi (25 March), which stated that the struggle was also for liberation from economic oppression and racial discrimination. Martí together with Gómez arrived in Cuba on 11 April, the latter becoming the overall military leader, seconded by Maceo.[9]

In Spain, Antonio Cánovas, the leader of the Conservative Party, had stated (in 1891) that Spain would fight to 'the last man and the last peso' to retain Cuba.[10] When the revolt broke out, Premier Práxedes Sagasta, the leader of the Liberal Party, blamed the uprising on external agitators and declared that '[t]he Spanish nation is disposed to sacrifice to the last peseta ... and to the last drop of blood of the last Spaniard before consenting that anyone snatch from it even one piece of its sacred territory'.[11] A few days later the Sagasta government fell and Cánovas took over, but he was even more determined to crush the rebellion.

Why the last drop of blood and the last peso? Spain in the last decades of the nineteenth century was a country whose people were disgruntled and poor and whose governments were often corrupt. Spain, in contrast to the days of its 'golden age', trailed behind the other Western countries. Yet all Spaniards were united by the memory of a glorious past, now symbolized by the possession of Cuba (the island had been claimed by Columbus for Spain in his very first voyage, of 1492). Cuba and the immense overseas empire were regarded as God's gift to Spain for the *Reconquista* (the re-conquest) of Christian Spain from the Muslims and an integral part of the Spanish nation.[12] As put by one contemporary, Cuba was 'the flesh of the flesh of Spain; it is part of the history, the glory, and the grandeur of Spain', and surrendering it would be tantamount to denying Spain's national identity and heritage.[13] Thus the Spaniards scoffed at the repeated US attempts to purchase the island and pressed on till the very end for a military solution; in the process Spain sustained 50,000 soldiers dead and 50,000 disabled by wounds and disease, out of more than 200,000 men who fought in the Cuban jungles, many of them mere teenagers, in what was the largest number of troops ever sent by Spain to the Americas.[14]

Around 100 miles to the north of Cuba lies the US, the 'Colossus of the North' as Martí called it.[15] US Secretary of State John Quincy Adams had commented (in 1823) that there 'are laws of political as well as physical gravitation' and Cuba 'can gravitate only toward the North American Union, which by the same law of nature cannot cast her off from its bosom'.[16] Similar views were voiced by an array of office-holders, from ex-President Thomas Jefferson to Secretary of State James Blaine in the early 1880s.[17] Four US Presidents, from John Quincy Adams in 1825, to James Buchanan in 1858, tried to purchase the island from Spain.[18] Here, a phrase from another country bordering the US comes to mind, attributed to the Mexican President Porfirio Díaz: 'Poor Mexico, so far from God and so close to the United States'. Cuba had become 'an object of desire' because of its fertility, commanding geographical position and proximity to the US.[19]

There is also another side to the US attitude that played its part in bringing about military intervention, which followed what Julián Juderías dubbed, a decade later, the 'black legend' regarding Spain and the Spaniards peddled in Europe and North America since the Enlightenment.[20] In US school textbooks of the nineteenth century, the image of Spain was strikingly negative, a stereotype buttressed by scholarly books.[21] Tyrannical rule, cruelty, decadence and bigotry were regarded as Spain's trademarks for centuries. When a journalist dared mention Las Casas's pithy criticism of the Spanish conquerors, the view was that even he had indicted his compatriots.[22] The influential US senator Henry Cabot Lodge called Spain 'medieval, cruel, dying', 'three hundred years behind the rest of the world'.[23] Moreover, in the racist narrative dominant in the country, the 'Anglo-Saxon race', the Americans in particular, were regarded the 'superior race', with the Africans and American Indians at the lowest scale, and Latin people, such as the Spaniards, somewhere between the two extremes. At various times during 1895–98 the Cuban insurgents were disparaged on the basis that the majority of fighters were Afro-Cubans and mulattos.[24]

US intervention: humanitarian or not?

One can discern two main versions of the 1898 Spanish–US war, the 'splendid little war' as labelled by John Hay, Secretary of State in the McKinley and Roosevelt administrations. The version which can accommodate the humanitarian dimension is that the initial overriding goal was humanitarian: colonization and imperialism were unintended and came about by chance;[25] they were a 'great aberration', as famously put by Samuel Flagg Bemis (the father of American diplomatic history);[26] it was a case of 'empire by default'.[27]

According to the other version, the switch was hardly accidental. As George Herring has put it, '[i]t was less a case of the United States coming upon greatness almost inadvertently than of it pursuing its destiny deliberately and purposefully'.[28] The uprising in Cuba and the slipping away of the Spanish overseas empire in the two great oceans provided the US with an unprecedented opportunity. From such a perspective there are no accidents in history; 'great nations' seek opportunities to symbolize their great power status and deliberately propagate greatness.[29]

As regards the first version, the head of the administration from 1897 onwards, President William McKinley, was by all accounts against resorting to war and innocent of expansionist intentions until mid-1898. When he finally decided that war was on, he did so reluctantly, and humanitarian reasons loomed large in his thinking and were no sham.[30]

Secondly, big business was against intervention until the eve of the war. This has been 'conclusively demonstrated'[31] by historian Julius Pratt (in the 1930s), who refers to the attitude of chief industrialists and bankers and the articles in leading financial journals, such as *Journal of Commerce*, *American Banker* and the *Wall Street Journal*, and, to an almost equal extent, business linked with Cuba (mainly sugar interests).[32] The upper crust of the business community initially stood firmly against intervention, men such Andrew Carnegie, John Pierpont Morgan, John Rockefeller, Alfred du Pont and Grenville Dodge.[33] Business people were so opposed that they were pilloried by the public and in the 'yellow press' (sensational ill-researched journalism) as 'soulless', 'the syndicated Judas Iscariot of Humanity' and the like.[34] The switch to interventionism on the part of big business took place a few weeks prior to the war, and was based initially on humanitarian grounds and patriotism and not on business opportunities and prospective gains.[35]

Thirdly, there was genuine sympathy for the Cuban plight among the public and on Capitol Hill, which called for US intervention on humanitarian grounds that would bring about Cuban independence.[36] Even sceptics of US intentions acknowledge that there is 'no reason to doubt the authenticity of popular perceptions'.[37]

There is also the related question of the yellow press, mainly William Randolph Hearst's *New York Journal* and Joseph Pulitzer's *New York World*, and its role in bringing about war, with its often exaggerated and sensationalized presentations of Cuban suffering.[38] Recent scholarship has convincingly contested this view and even without the yellow press, the public would have learned about the abhorrent conditions in Cuba from more reliable sources.[39]

But other factors seem to point to another direction, making humanitarian reasons appear skin deep.

First was the maturing of an older approach, held by Secretaries of State Sewell in the late 1860s and Blaine in the early 1880s: 'national extension and aggrandizement', 'the large policy'. In the last decade of the nineteenth century several influential people, who could sway foreign policy were associated with the large policy.[40] A central figure was Captain Alfred Mahan, President of the Naval War College (one of the founding fathers of the new field of geopolitics, together with the British geographer Halford Mackinder and the German geographer Friedrich Ratzel), who advocated naval strength, along the British model, as the road to great power status for the country. Mahan was close to two avowed expansionist Republican politicians, Lodge and Theodore Roosevelt (then Assistant Secretary of the Navy). Others who shared these views were the influential Republican senators William Frye, Cushman Davis, Joseph Foraker, the Democratic senators John Tyler Morgan, Whitelaw Reid (former ambassador to Paris, long-serving editor of the *New York Tribune* and Republican vice presidential nominee in 1892) and John Hay (ambassador to London and Secretary of State immediately after the war). However, when it came to Cuba, most expansionists called for intervention on humanitarian grounds and not for annexation.[41]

A rehashed 'Manifest Destiny' (the concept coined by John O'Sullivan in 1839) also entered the scene, a 'New Manifest Destiny', now infused with racism and crude social Darwinism, based on the notion of 'survival of the fittest'.[42] Two widely read authors, the historian John Fiske (who reiterated the Manifest Destiny theme and popularized the views of Darwin and Spencer on evolution) and the clergyman and Social Gospel leader Josiah Strong, presented the 'Anglo-Saxons' as the most gifted 'race', destined to civilize and lead the world in the name of progress. Such views were endorsed by the leading political scientist of the day, Professor John Burgess, of Columbia University, who called on the Teutonic races (Anglo-Saxons and Germans) to expand and civilize the world (ironically, however, Fiske, Strong as well as Burgess were against military intervention in Cuba[43]).[44]

Research has also shown that, for the 'jingoes', expanding and acquiring colonies was a reaffirmation of their manhood that had suffered a shock from the 1893 economic crisis that devastated the US.[45] In the gendered imagery of the 1890s, Cuba was presented as a feminized victim, as a voluptuous damsel in distress calling to be rescued by the manly Yankee, or an unruly female child in need of a firm father.[46]

Secondly, when Commodore George Dewey vanquished the Spanish fleet in Manila Bay (1 May 1898), business journals switched their position, pointing to the advantages of an independent Cuba. They toyed with colonies, an isthmian canal and US presence in the Pacific, the very ideas previously derided. The 'fabled China market' in particular loomed large, though some authors have disputed this.[47] The 'glut thesis' prevailed, namely that a surplus of goods was piling up in the US, which needed an outlet in Latin America and Asia. For the *American Banker* the opportunity to expand in the Pacific was 'a coincidence which has a providential air'.[48] With the turn of events, expansion and the search for new markets were presented as a necessity and doing otherwise a folly.[49]

Thirdly is what occurred in the wake of the US victory: (1) acquisition of Puerto Rico and distant Guam, (2) annexation of Hawaii, (3) holding on to Cuba and (4) acquiring the faraway Philippines.

The economic dimension is worth returning to, together with the role of President McKinley. The economic aspect, which had dominated scholarly literature in the 1920s, was discarded by Pratt's intervention in the 1930s. But in the 1960s and 1970s it resurfaced, with the works of new left historians, such as W. A. Williams, Philip Foner and Walter LaFeber.[50] The thrust of LaFeber's subtle version is not that Pratt was mistaken regarding the period up to March 1898, but that, in view of the sudden conversion to imperialism, which 'grabbed greatness with both hands', the aberration thesis is unconvincing as an explanatory paradigm.[51]

The role of McKinley is intertwined with the economic dimension, given the President's partnership with leading business people. Until the 1950s the predominant scholarly view was that the President was well meaning but weak, buckling to public opinion, Congress and the expansionists; to remember Roosevelt's phrase, McKinley had a backbone like a chocolate éclair. This assessment is evident in the works of Bemis and Pratt in the 1930s, Ernest May in the 1950s and Gerald Linderman in the 1970s. However, in recent decades the image of McKinley has been redeemed, with the twenty-fifth US President emerging as a 'master of men', able to orchestrate foreign policy, as argued by H. Wayne Morgan, Lewis Gould, Richard Hamilton, John Offner as well as LaFeber. In this sense McKinley was perhaps the first modern US President.[52]

The US and Cuba

Main events

1895–96

Martí and Gómez sought US recognition and aid but not military intervention, for fear of domination. As Martí mused, 'To change masters is not to be free'.[53] The inspiring Martí died in an ambush (19 May 1895) and Cuba declared itself independent (15 July), with Salvador Betancourt as President. The Cuban movement in the US, known as the Cuban Junta, was headed by Tomás Estrada Palma (a general in the Ten Years' War in Cuba and associate of Martí), who believed that a special relationship with the 'colossus' was inevitable and to the benefit of the Cuban people.[54] The Junta vigorously lobbied the State Department and Congress, organized demonstrations, raised funds and sent arms to Cuba via filibustering operations and fed the press with information, mostly exaggerated, of Spanish brutalities. In Cuba the overall strategy of Gómez was 'abominable devastation' aimed at rendering Cuba 'an economic desert', making the cost of Spain's retention of the island unbearable.[55]

Cánovas's reaction was to send General Campos. But the veteran soldier was reluctant to use extreme measures to stem the uprising and was replaced by General Valeriano Weyler. The energetic and ruthless Weyler (previously governor of the Philippines) as governor of Cuba initiated a brutal policy of 'reconcentration', namely building trenches 100 yards wide, equipped with barbed wire and blockhouses, to separate the governmental region from that of the rebels, burning villages and crops, killing all the cattle and herding the inhabitants (mostly peasants) into various fortified areas and towns. The result was horrendous: more than 200,000 died from malnutrition and disease.[56]

All this was widely reported, not least by the yellow press in the US and in cartoons which presented the Spaniards as barbarians.[57] Weyler came to be known as 'Butcher Weyler', for having 'turned the island into a prison', a 'wasteland of human misery'.[58] Weyler's strategy met with some initial success by slowing the insurgent advance and by killing the legendary Maceo on 7 December 1896 (he was replaced by García as second in command). Thus 1896, which had started with the prospect of victory for the Cubans, had ended with demoralization and victory as distant as ever. But the Spanish forces for their part were hardly closer to victory.[59]

The Democratic President, Grover Cleveland, feared the creation of a 'Negro republic' like Haiti and thus adopted a policy of strict neutrality. Secretary of State Richard Olney offered US mediation to Enrique Dupuy de Lôme, the Spanish Minister in Washington, stressing that the sole aim of the US administration was the pacification of the island and that it was opposed to independence, for the Cubans were not fit to govern themselves. Cánovas did not accept mediation and his Foreign Minister, the Duke of Tetuan, called for the support of the great powers in Madrid's dispute with Washington.[60]

In April 1896 a joint resolution of the two Houses deplored the situation in Cuba and called for belligerent status for the Cubans, which the President ignored.[61] The new US consul-general in Havana, Fitzhugh Lee, painted a dismal picture of the situation in Cuba and deadlock, and recommended US intervention or the purchase of the island.[62]

Cleveland, in his farewell address to the nation (7 December 1896), lamented the 'spectacle of the utter ruin of an adjoining country, by nature one of the most fertile and charming on the globe', and warned that 'the United States is not a nation to which peace is a necessity'.[63] The outgoing President in the night before the inauguration of McKinley told him that he was afraid that he had left him with a war, to which the latter answered graciously that he hoped that he could do as well as he had done to avoid it.[64]

From 1897 until the eve of the war

The new President upon taking office seemed determined to avoid going to war. As he put it to the respected independent politician Carl Schurz, a few weeks after his inauguration, 'there will be no jingo nonsense under my Administration'.[65] McKinley wanted to first establish the facts in Cuba before charting his Administration's position. He thus sent a trusted political friend, William Calhoun, to Cuba to assess the situation. Calhoun, upon returning, painted a bleak picture of Cuba as a result of reconcentration ('children with swollen limbs and extended abdomens'), and claimed that if Spain continued in its policy of seeking a military solution, the total destruction of the island and the almost total extermination of its population could not be avoided.[66]

The President sent Stewart Woodford as the US Minister to Madrid to try to iron out differences with Spain,[67] but sent a stern message to the Spanish government, stating that 'the rights of humanity exceeded the rights of states' and demanded the revocation of reconcentration 'in the name of common humanity'.[68]

Cánovas was assassinated on 8 August 1897 and the new Spanish Premier, Sagasta, promised a humane policy in Cuba. Woodford advised Cuban autonomy and was able to develop a relationship of trust with the main moderate, Professor Segismundo Moret, a distinguished politician, then Minister of Overseas Colonies. On 25 November Madrid adopted a policy of autonomy for Cuba in principle and Weyler was replaced by General Rámon Blanco, with instructions to end reconcentration.[69] McKinley in his annual message to Congress (6 December 1897) called reconcentration 'not civilized warfare' but 'extermination',[70] but referred to the autonomy scheme in favourable terms and noted that Spain 'should be given a reasonable chance to realize her expectations and to prove the asserted efficacy of the new order of things'.[71]

The autonomy offered by Spain to the Cubans was 'too little, too late, too slowly'.[72] It was unacceptable to Gómez and Estrada Palma. It was also rejected by the *peninsulares*, who embarked on anti-autonomy riots in Havana (January 1989), shouting 'death to Blanco' and blaming the US for Spain's offer of autonomy.[73] Many *peninsulares* prayed for the annexation of Cuba by the US to save them from the insurgents.[74]

At this juncture McKinley tried to purchase the island from Spain. In January Reid was charged to undertake private negotiations with Madrid to purchase Cuba but the mission failed. In March Woodford tried to convince Moret that selling the island to the US was the best way to 'part with Cuba without loss of self-respect'.[75]

A series of unfortunate events were to bring matters to a head. One concerned a personal letter by Lôme that was published by the *New York Journal* (the letter had been passed on by the Junta) on 9 February 1898 under the title 'Worst Insult to the United States in History'. The letter portrayed the President as 'weak', 'on good terms with the jingoes' and a 'wound-be politician', and implied that talks with the US and autonomy were a ruse to gain time.[76]

Six days later a prized US battleship, the USS *Maine*, at anchor in Havana, was destroyed by an explosion, killing 266 officers and men out of 354. Spain expressed its deep sorrow but, predictably, the two states' respective investigations reached different conclusions: the US report found that an external explosion, a mine or torpedo, had caused it, while the Spanish report concluded that internal combustion (an explosion within the ship) had caused it (the Spanish version is more likely).[77] But the public, even before the publication of the US report, was convinced that Spain was guilty of 'foul play'.[78] 'Remember the *Maine*, to hell with Spain' became an everyday catchphrase in 'a hysterical demand for immediate intervention'.[79] Most students of 1898 regard this episode as the single event that made war impossible to avoid.[80] McKinley, for his part, had no intention of being 'swept off his feet', as he put it, as a result of the *Maine* episode.[81]

Specialists of '1898' attach great importance to a speech made a month later by the respected Senator Redfield Proctor (a former Secretary of War), in the Senate on 17 March, following a visit to Cuba (the Republican senator was a close friend of McKinley and had seen him shortly before the speech, so it can be deduced that he had cleared it with him).[82] Proctor, speaking dispassionately presented a situation of 'desolation and distress, misery and starvation', children with 'abdomen bloated to three times the natural size'.[83] He estimated that of the 400,000 *reconsentrandos*, half had died and one-quarter could not be saved. He pointed out that the autonomy scheme had failed. Proctor's intervention had the effect of swinging towards war those in big business (Proctor was a self-made millionaire), Congress and the general public, including Protestant and Catholic organizations which until then, though sympathetic to the Cuban cause, were against armed intervention. Now the conservative press called for intervention as a duty to humanity.[84]

Proctor's speech was followed in the next days by several emotional speeches in both Houses, by others who had visited Cuba, who confirmed Proctor's findings.[85]

There were also many petitions and letters to Congress and the President, calling for Cuban independence and war with Spain.[86] In several petitions the colourful phrase 'carnival of blood' appeared, fuelled by the Junta, a phrase that had been used by Las Casas to describe the cruelties of the *conquistadores*.[87] McKinley's name was hissed in public and his effigy burned, but he hoped to avert a showdown, believing that Spain would give up Cuba to avoid a disastrous war. Apparently, several factors made McKinley switch. Firstly, the view prevailed that the war was at a stalemate and would continue with catastrophic consequences if no intervention took place. Secondly, autonomy, even if genuine, was unacceptable to the Cubans and *peninsulares* alike, and thus impossible to implement. A third factor was the switch of the business community and the nationwide support for intervention. Congress was on a war footing, Lodge, Root, Garret Hobart (the Vice President) and some fifty members of the Republican House caucus told the President that if no intervention took place the party would face the worst defeat ever in the upcoming November elections, and the formidable Speaker of the House of Representatives, Thomas Reed, told McKinley that he could not hold the House anymore – it would declare war together with the Senate.[88]

The final proposal to Spain, on 27 March 1898, was for a peaceful settlement, the end of reconcentration, an armistice, talks with the insurgents, and 'full self-government, with reasonable indemnity', which the next day was changed to 'Cuban independence'. With this final touch, it was obvious that the die was cast.[89]

Spain was in dire straits. The unintended clash with the US had raised nationalist fervour in Spain, with demonstrations rocking major cities, and crowds shouting *muerte a los Yanques*. As was the case in the US, newspapers had their share in rousing the masses (they referred to US horrors towards the Indians now cramped in reservations).[90] Madrid believed that conceding to Washington would lead to the government's fall and the overthrow of the monarchy (the bastion of stability),[91] so it tried to wriggle itself out of the situation by providing some last-minute concessions short of independence and gaining the support of the European great powers.

The Spanish government retorted that reconcentration had ceased, armistice would be implemented, provided the insurgents did the same, and autonomy was on course. The Spanish diplomatic initiative bore little fruit. Vienna, Berlin and Paris were sympathetic to the Spanish call but did not want to alienate Washington and bring about an Anglo-Saxon alliance. The British Prime Minister, Salisbury, regarded the matter a US question and supported McKinley.[92]

Mediation was offered by Pope Leo XIII, which was declined by McKinley, and a visit by the ambassadors of the six European powers to McKinley took place (6 April), in which a text was read out calling for restraint in the name of peace. The *New York World* aptly parodied the meeting as follows: 'we hope for humanity's sake you will not go to war', to which the President answered 'We hope if we go to war you will understand that it is for humanity's sake'.[93]

Apparently, Spain preferred war to the ignominy of giving in: defeat to the US with honour was better than surrender.⁹⁴ Under the circumstances, McKinley felt he had little choice but to ask Congress for the authority to wage war (11 April 1898). In his message to Congress the President pointed out that '[t]he forcible intervention of the United States as a neutral to stop the war, according to the large dictates of humanity and following many historical precedents where neighboring States have interfered to check the hopeless sacrifices of life by internecine conflicts beyond their borders, is justifiable on rational grounds'.⁹⁵ He summarized the grounds for intervention as follows: (1) 'In the cause of humanity and to put an end to the barbarities, bloodshed, starvation, and horrible miseries now existing there'; (2) to protect US citizens in Cuba; (3) to end 'the very serious injury to the commerce, trade, and business of our people'; and (4) '[t]he present condition of affairs in Cuba is a constant menace to our peace, and entails upon this Government an enormous expense'.⁹⁶ Before concluding, he declared: 'In the name of humanity, in the name of civilization, in [sic] behalf of endangered American interests which give us the right and the duty to speak and to act, the war in Cuba must stop'.⁹⁷ But McKinley 'did not exclude a peaceful settlement',⁹⁸ referring to the Spanish suspension of hostilities and calling Congress to address this aspect as well.⁹⁹

The lack of recognition of Cuban independence in McKinley's speech aroused Cuban indignation and was denounced.¹⁰⁰ It also disappointed most of the senators and congressmen when the message was read out, but they all listened in profound silence, broken only once by a wave of applause for the phrase 'in the name of humanity'.¹⁰¹ The debate in the Senate and Congress, however, largely on the question of independence, lasted a whole week. The stalemate was broken by Senator Henry Teller, who proposed a self-denying ordinance: the US would disclaim any 'intention to exercise sovereignty' over the island (the Teller Amendment). Congress empowered the President (20 April 1898), with 42 to 35 votes in the Senate and 310 to 6 in the House, to make the people of Cuba 'free and independent' and to utilize the armed forces in order to do so. Spain, upon hearing of the resolution, declared war (24 April 1898); Congress followed the next day with its own a declaration of war, which was made retroactive to 21 April.¹⁰²

The consequences of intervention: the Philippines and Cuba's predicament

The Spanish–American War (24 April–12 August 1898), as it came to be known in the US, a designation that ignores the Cubans and their role in the US victory,¹⁰³ was waged by sea and land, the decisive event being the naval Battle of Santiago de Cuba of 3 July. Puerto Rico was also occupied. Beforehand, Commodore Dewey was instructed to begin 'offensive operations' against the Spanish in the Philippines and the US Asiatic squadron entered Manila Bay and sank the Spanish Pacific squadron at anchor (1 May). This battle was the first major engagement of the war and opened the prospect of the US acquiring the Philippines, though this had not been the original goal. The Philippine theatre had been sought for military strategic reasons, to put the squeeze on Spain at little cost to the US and to shorten the war (in the Atlantic there was another contingency, but one that was not realized, in the form of the US occupying the Canary Islands).[104]

The expansionists were on the alert not to miss the opportunity of acquiring the Philippines.[105] But the anti-expansionists also came to the fore, seeking to prevent that from happening (see below).[106] McKinley remained undecided and the cabinet was split over the issue. Following French mediation, peace talks were to start in Paris, with Spain reluctantly accepting the loss of Cuba, Puerto Rico and Guam, with the fate of the Philippines open to negotiation.[107]

The President selected five commissioners for the peace talks: three expansionists, Davis, Frye and Reid, anti-expansionist Democrat Senator George Gray and Day (who resigned as Secretary of State to act as chairman of the commission and was succeeded by Hay), who was wary of acquiring the Philippines.[108] McKinley told the commission (16 September) that 'we took up arms only in obedience to the dictates of humanity and in the fulfillment of high public and moral obligation',[109] and to end Spanish colonialism in the Western hemisphere.[110] But the US approach to the Philippines was on a different basis. As he pointed out to the commission in his instructions: 'we cannot be unmindful that, without any desire or design on our part, the war has brought us new duties and responsibilities which we must meet and discharge as becomes a great nation on whose growth and career from the beginning the Ruler of Nations has plainly written the high command and pledge of civilization'.[111] He instructed the commission to secure control of Manila and extend US jurisdiction to the whole of the island of Luzon.[112]

When the Paris peace conference was in session, McKinley made a tour of the US, delivering speeches. He stressed that they had entered the war for humanitarian reasons and to help the Cubans liberate themselves and he got the clear impression that the public was elated and not averse to expansion. Thus Hay telegraphed the commissioners that the rest of the islands should not be left to Spain.[113]

The end result was that Spain ceded Puerto Rico, Guam and the Philippines (the latter with payment of $20 million to soften the blow), and relinquished sovereignty over Cuba. The war with Spain provided the momentum to resolve the pending question of Hawaii, which was annexed.[114]

As Foster Rhea Dulles has put it, many Americans 'dazzled by the vision of empire but reluctant to confess to economic or prestige motives ... found their justification for expansionist policy in the obligation of the United States to assume its share of the civilizing mission of the Anglo-Saxon race'.[115] In February 1899, Rudyard Kipling came out with his famous imperialist poem 'The White Man's Burden', which makes explicit reference to the US and the Philippines (indeed, it was first published with the subtitle 'The United States and the Philippine Islands'), much to the delight of Lodge and Roosevelt. The 'white man's burden' dovetailed with 'new manifest destiny', legitimizing US imperialism, presenting it as the 'imperialism of righteousness'.[116] Protestant clergymen went further, viewing US expansion as 'divinely inspired', as God having handed the Philippines to the 'American Christians' (forgetting that the majority of Filipinos were Christians).[117]

Regarding divine inspiration and the white man's burden, a revealing vignette is worth mentioning. A year after the crucial decision, McKinley told a Methodist delegation (the President was a Methodist) that when faced with what to do with the Philippines he asked for guidance with prayers to 'Almighty God'. 'And one night it came to me this way …: (1) That we could not give them back to Spain – that would be cowardly and dishonorable; (2) that we could not turn them over to France or Germany … that would be bad business and discreditable; (3) that we could not leave them to themselves – they were unfit for self-government …; and (4) that there was nothing left for us to do but to take them all, and to educate the Filipinos, and uplift and civilize and Christianize them, and by God's grace do the best'.[118]

One need not regard the religious touch as mere window-dressing or the epitome of hypocrisy. Apart from McKinley's genuine religious feelings,[119] bringing together the sacred with the secular, however absurd it may appear to us today, is a proclivity in US foreign policy with a long tradition.[120] In any event, similar pronouncements, though more down to earth, were made by McKinley on a number of occasions privately as well as in his public speeches in late 1898 and early 1899. It seems that he initially deemed the 'wisest course' taking a coaling station for vessels in the Philippines (early May 1898),[121] then a port in the Philippines and a coaling station in the Marianas (3 June),[122] then Manila Bay (30 June),[123] then Luzon (September) and finally all the islands. What probably did the trick, apart from feedback from the public, were the tidings of General Greene, who, after having toured the Philippines, told the President that handing the island to the insurgents would bring anarchy; Germany and Japan would grab them; and that due to the peculiar geography of the islands Luzon on its own could not be kept (the some 400 islands were so close to each other that a cannon shot from one could reach another). There were also reports that the Filipino Hispanicized elite were favourable to annexation and that Emilio Aguinaldo's self-proclaimed Republic of the Philippines was unpopular, and that his fighters had committed atrocities against Spanish captives and priests.[124]

All the statements of the President give credence to the view that it was an unintentional expansion and not calculated;[125] that the US had 'greatness thrust upon it', as it were.[126] But by the same token, the fact that McKinley had taken, however reluctantly, this major decision after considerable deliberation with US interests in mind,[127] ushering the country into a new age, undermines the 'fit of absentmindedness' thesis.[128]

The Paris Treaty (10 December 1898) had 'to run the gauntlet of the Senate'[129] for ratification, where a heated two-month debate took place, focusing mainly on the acquisition of the Philippines.

The anti-imperialists organized themselves in the Anti-Imperialist League and fought expansionism 'tooth and nail'[130] from 1898 until 1900. Their campaign included major figures, such as ex-President Cleveland and eight of his cabinet members (including Olney), ex-President Harrison and an older generation of Republicans such as Senator George Frisbie Hoar, John Sherman (McKinley's first Secretary of State) and Reed, William Jennings Bryan (the Democratic presidential nominee in 1896 and in 1900), Schurz, journalist Edwin Lawrence Godkin (founder of *The Nation* and editor-in-chief of the *New York Evening Post*), Carnegie and the major labour union leader Samuel Gompers (President of the American Federation of Labor). Included were top intellectuals, such as philosophers William James, John Dewey and Felix Adler, sociologist William Graham Sumner, medieval scholar Charles Eliot Norton, social reformer David Starr Jordan and the foremost writers of the day, including Mark Twain (see his essay 'To the Person Sitting in Darkness'), Finlay Peter Dunne, Henry Fuller and William Vaughn Moody (see his poem 'An Ode in Time of Hesitation').[131]

The anti-imperialist argument centred on political principles, above all that acquiring the Philippines was a clear break with time-honoured American republican values, as enshrined in the Declaration of Independence, Washington's farewell address and Lincoln's Gettysburg address, on which the US was created and lived by: that a government cannot rule people without the consent of the governed; and acquiring the Philippines amounted to blatant imperialism that would harm not only the Filipinos but also the US, which would find itself in league with the European colonialists and monarchies.[132]

In the Senate, the anti-imperialist approach was headed by Hoar, who argued that the US, having delivered the Cubans from political oppression, must do the same with the Filipinos and that such imperialist ventures would lead to dangerous foreign entanglements and economic ruin for the country.[133]

The expansionists, led by Lodge, argued that American rule was a blessing of civilization upon the unfortunate Filipinos, who were not prepared to rule themselves; that if the US did not step in others would do so, primarily Germany and Japan, both of them undemocratic; and that following the annexation of Hawaii, the next obvious step was the Philippines, opening the way to the China market.[134]

Given the impressive list of anti-expansionists and their arguments, it comes as a surprise that they did not carry the day. According to Robert Beisner's assessment, the most effective and articulate anti-imperialists were 'Mugwumps' (independent former Republicans) such as Schurz, James, Godkin and Norton and Republicans out of step with their party, foremost Hoar and Carnegie, with the other anti-imperialists ineffective. Another weakness of the anti-expansionists was that they were disunited and that their lofty arguments seemed old-fashioned and did not inspire the wider public.[135]

The treaty was eventually ratified by fifty-seven in favour and twenty-seven against, that is, with one vote over the two-thirds majority required for ratification (6 February 1899), which, surprisingly, included even some anti-imperialists, such as Bryan. Ironically, two days before (4 February) the Filipinos under Aguinaldo resumed fighting to gain independence, this time against the US.[136] The anti-imperialists felt vindicated, the imperialists appalled and the debate continued, becoming a central theme in the 1900 presidential elections, between McKinley and Bryan. The Filipino insurrection was to be subdued under Roosevelt's administration, though, interestingly the new President, for all his well known jingoism, was alienated from the whole affair, regarding it as 'our heel of Achilles'.[137]

But let us revert to Cuba. In 1898–1902, the worst nightmares of Martí and Gómez had come to life. As a sign of things to come, when Spain surrendered, the US general in Cuba refused to allow the Cubans under García to participate in the surrender ceremony or enter Havana. García protested in writing in a dignified manner but to no avail.[138] The US forces did not leave the island, but stayed on until 1902. When the Roosevelt administration allowed the adoption of an independence Constitution and Estrada Palma was elected President, Roosevelt withdrew US forces but secured Guantanamo Bay as a base with a lease in perpetuity. The Platt Amendment (drafted by Root, the Secretary of War, and introduced by Senator Thomas Platt)[139] was thrust upon the Cubans as a parting gift. It stated that 'the government of Cuba consents that the United States may exercise the right to intervene for the preservation of Cuban independence, the maintenance of a government adequate for the protection of life, property, and individual liberty'.[140] Washington did not fail to use the Amendment on several occasions until its abrogation in 1934, by sending troops to prop up friendly governments in power or to protect US investments.[141]

Unfettered Cuban independence was to arrive more than half a century later, in 1959, with the triumph of the Cuban Revolution under Fidel Castro. Upon taking power, Castro and other Cuban figures alluded to the 1895–98 experience, pointing out that the goals of the liberators had been dashed in 1898, with the US intervention and the hegemony that followed it, pointing out that it was more than a century later, in 1959, that the dreams of those heroic fighters had finally become a reality.[142]

Assessment

Cuba, the US, Spain

Most US and Spanish historians have claimed that the Cubans would not have been able to overwhelm the Spaniards and gain independence without US intervention. By contrast, most major Cuban historians (well before the arrival of Castro), including Emilio Roig de Leuchsenring, Herminio Portell Vilá and Fernando Ortiz, dispute this hegemonic US paradigm.[143] They argue that the Cuban forces were on the verge of winning, and that the intervention of the US was unnecessary and 'robbed them of their fruits of victory'.[144] But a minority of equally reputable Cuban historians, including Cosme de la Torriente, the father of Cuban diplomatic history, who also happened to be García's chief of staff, doubts their ability to vanquish the Spanish army without the intervention.[145] More recently, Pérez has produced evidence that Gómez was convinced that Cuban victory over the Spaniards was imminent and that this was also the assessment of US officials, including Sherman, Day, Lodge and consul general Lee from Havana.[146]

As regards the US, contemporary commentators stressed three themes: (1) the war re-united 'the nation', healing the wounds of the American Civil War; (2) crushing Spain marked the historical moment when the US emerged as a great power; and (3) the victory confirmed that the US was 'the nation of progressive civilization'.[147]

As Josiah Strong had put it: 'This race has been honored not for its own sake, but for the sake of the world. It has been made powerful, and rich, and free, and exalted-powerful'.[148] A central theme was the 'mission' to instil freedom and democracy across the world.[149] How this tallies with Washington's ugly war against Filipino independence and on the prevention of Cuban independence is another matter.

For Spain, the events in Cuba and the Philippines became known as 'the Disaster', and prompted nationwide protests and agonizing soul-searching. The proud Spaniards felt humiliated at having been defeated by the North Americans, whom they held in low esteem (as 'sausage-makers'). The Spaniards, in a state of shock, pondered why it was the case that when other states were still building empires, Spain had lost its own, which was much older. Were they, after all, a decadent nation? Whatever might be the shortcomings of *fin de siècle* Spain, was true 'regeneration' of the once great Spain possible?[150]

US motives revisited: in search of a thread

A way out as to the motives of US intervention is 'to disentangle the imperialist outcome of the war from the conflict itself',[151] or, put differently, the events from 1895 through to the consequences of the Battle of Manila.

In its bare essentials, the search for Washington's stance boils down to seven dichotomous questions: (1) humanitarian concern or quest for world power, (2) aberration or culmination, (3) action taken in response to public outrage or as part of a well-thought-out strategy, put differently, emotion or design; (4) public opinion (with or without the yellow press) or drive for markets (glut thesis),

(5) genuine support for *Cuba libre* or control of the island, (6) chocolate éclair or resolute President and (7) stalemate or imminent victory for the Cuban fighters?[152]

One can make a reasonable case by selecting evidence to support any of the above fourteen polar opposites, for there is much in abundance for all to be content.[153] Some polar opposites seem equally valid, or 'reality' lies somewhere in between. For instance, as regards humanitarian concern or quest for world power, the public and several politicians, including McKinley, were motivated by humanitarian concern, to alleviate the suffering of the Cuban people.[154] Many supporters of intervention for humanitarian reasons and in order to liberate Cuba, such as Hoar, Carnegie and Twain, were anti-expansionist and against the annexation of the Philippines.[155] But the President had tangible interests in mind as well, which he hardly concealed, and the expansionists had their own agenda. Regarding aberration or culmination, Washington may have unexpectedly found the Philippines on its lap, but it then pursued its destiny 'deliberately and purposefully'.[156] As for chocolate éclair or resolute leader, McKinley may have been more flexible, less forceful and more attuned to the voice of the people than his predecessor, Cleveland, or his successor, Roosevelt, but this hardly makes him 'a well intentioned bungler' as portrayed by Bemis and others. He was in control of the situation most of the time and when intervention seemed inevitable he went along on his own terms.[157]

Reverting to the aberration or culmination dilemma, cognitive psychology can provide a clue. Before a crucial decision is taken there is great uncertainty and angst, but when a decision is finally taken the decision-makers are unwavering, as if the decision was in the making for years. This is done in order to discard the previous agonizing dilemma and uncertainty reigning prior to the decision.

The publicists' verdict

Overall, international lawyers have failed to agree on the character of the US action in 1898.[158] Contemporary jurists such as Theodore S. Woolsey claimed that it was an 'intervention on the grounds of humanity' and the motives pure, even though they were not the only motives; the US was so deeply involved in Cuba that one can also speak in terms of self-defence.[159] Amos Hershey referred to the humanitarian plight but also to the cost of the war to US interests and the hardships of its citizens in Cuba.[160] George Grafton Wilson, an opponent of humanitarian intervention, opined that 'the United States interfered in the affairs of Cuba on the ground of humanity'.[161] Elbert Benton, on the contrary, was of the view that the civil war in Cuba 'did not present clearly and unmistakably such tyranny or cruelty as writers on international law seem to regard as justifying intervention'.[162]

Moore referred to 'the ruin of the island', to 'abhorrent conditions' and to the *Maine* episode,[163] concluding that US 'intervention rested upon the ground that there existed in Cuba conditions so injurious to the United States ... that they could no longer be endured. Its action was analogous to what is known in private law as the abatement of a nuisance'.[164] Ellery Stowell criticized the nuisance idea, maintaining that the US intervention in Cuba was '[o]ne of the most important instances of humanitarian intervention'.[165] Charles Fenwick concurred with the nuisance thesis but regarded the 'cause of humanity' as first in the list as the grounds for intervention, followed by the rest.[166]

Some contemporary European publicists rejected a US right to intervene in Cuba for it was a violation of the Monroe Doctrine, the pledge not to intervene in the existing colonies of the European states in the Americas.[167] Others, such as Le Fur,[168] Lapradelle,[169] Rougier[170] and Westlake[171] claimed that it was basically humanitarian. And there was also the nuisance approach, first introduced by Rivier.[172]

From the 1950s onwards, various international lawyers who supported the concept of humanitarian intervention regarded the US intervention as humanitarian, as in the case of Lillich,[173] McDougal and Reisman,[174] and others.[175] Brownlie regards it as an 'intervention in terms of American interests'.[176] Franck and Rodley dismiss it with the following comment: 'if the suppression of "barbarities, bloodshed, and misery" were the sole yardstick for U.S. intervention in the Latin America of that period, Washington would have been extremely busy ousting regimes, some of which it was rather active in establishing and upholding'.[177] Fonteyne, who refers approvingly to a number of humanitarian interventions in the nineteenth century, does not regard it as humanitarian.[178]

We will conclude with the views of three present scholars engaged with the wider question of humanitarian intervention. Michael Walzer in his classic *Just and Unjust Wars* is dismissive, characterizing it 'as an example of benevolent imperialism, given the "piratical times", but it is not an example of humanitarian intervention'.[179] He bases his view mainly on the fact the US intervened militarily supposedly on behalf of the oppressed but against their ends, namely true independence, as seen by the three years of military occupation, the Platt Amendment and the limited independence of Cuba for decades.[180] More recently, Gary Bass concluded that what could have been regarded as the US's first humanitarian intervention 'was sullied by imperialism', since it was not limited to driving Spain out of Cuba.[181] Tonny Brems Knudsen regards it humanitarian, given the Spanish policies and McKinley's justification to Congress (including his reference to European precedent), but also open to abuse given the instrumental motives and the lack of a collective framework for intervention.[182]

Concluding remarks

The elements in common between the US intervention in Cuba and the previous cases were the humanitarian plight, the pressure by the press and public opinion on humanitarian grounds, in this case also the pressure from Capitol Hill, the mixture of motives, the attempt to mediate in the conflict as well as the self-denying ordinance (here, the Teller Amendment). There were also bilateral consultations with European great powers (despite the Monroe Doctrine, which made that unnecessary) and the green light from most of them to go ahead. The final military intervention was an all-out war (as with Russia in 1877–78), with benevolent neutrality on the part of the European great powers. The main new features which made humanitarian intervention appear in a negative light are the following: the expansionist agenda of the imperialists, the whetting of the appetite of Washington and above all the huge benefits brought about by the intervention – colonialism and overseas empire, no real independence for Cuba itself – which made the whole venture as humanitarian seem hollow. Put differently, it brought in the abuse factor in humanitarian plights more starkly than ever before, especially when a great power is the protagonist.

Notes

1. E. Root, 'The Real Monroe Doctrine', *American Journal of International Law*, 8:3 (1914), 430.
2. R. J. Vincent, *Nonintervention and International Order* (Princeton: Princeton University Press, 1974), 110.
3. J. B. Moore, *The Principles of American Diplomacy* (New York: Harper and Brothers, 1918), 205.
4. Root, Secretary of War (under McKinley) and Secretary of State (under Roosevelt) was the first president of the American Society of International Law. For a scholarly article of his which touches upon intervention, see E. Root, 'The Basis of Protection to Citizens Residing Abroad', *American Journal of International Law*, 4:3 (1910), 517–28.
5. C. G. Fenwick, 'Intervention: Individual and Collective', *American Journal of International Law*, 39:4 (1945), 651.
6. Ibid., 652–6.
7. J. Smith, *The Spanish–American War: Conflict in the Caribbean and the Pacific, 1895–1902* (London: Longman, 1994), 2–3.
8. A. Ferrer, *Insurgent Cuba: Race, Nation, and Revolution, 1868–1898* (Chapel Hill: University of North Carolina Press, 1999), 15–89; P. T. McCartney, *Power and Progress: American National Identity, the War of 1898, and the Rise of American Imperialism* (Baton Rouge: Louisiana University Press, 2006), 88–9.
9. D. F. Trask, *The War with Spain in 1898* (New York: Macmillan, 1981), 2–3; McCartney, *Power and Progress*, 89; Smith, *The Spanish–American War*, 6–8; J. L. Offner, *An Unwanted War: The Diplomacy of the United States and Spain Over Cuba, 1895–1898* (Chapel Hill: University of North Carolina Press, 1992), 3–4; L. A. Pérez, Jr, *The War of 1898: The United States and Cuba in History and Historiography* (Chapel Hill: University of North Carolina Press, 1998), 7.
10. Quoted in Smith, *The Spanish–American War*, 6.
11. Quoted ibid., 9.
12. Trask, *The War with Spain in 1898*, 15, 44; H. W. Morgan, *America's Road to Empire: The War with Spain and Overseas Expansion* (New York: John Wiley and Sons, 1965), 2.

13 Ibid., 6, 15.
14 Ibid., 6; A. Smith and E. Dávila-Cox, '1898 and the Making of the New Twentieth-Century Order', in A. Smith and E. Dávila-Cox (eds), *The Crisis of 1989: Colonial Redistribution and Nationalist Mobilization* (Basingstoke: Macmillan, 1999), 8.
15 Smith and Dávila-Cox, '1898 and the Making of the New Twentieth-Century Order', 10.
16 Quoted in Smith, *The Spanish–American War*, 28.
17 Pérez, *The War of 1898*, 3–7.
18 B. M. Miller, *From Liberation to Conquest: The Visual and Popular Cultures of the Spanish–American War of 1898* (Amherst: University of Massachusetts Press, 2011), 6.
19 Morgan, *America's Road to Empire*, 28–9; McCartney, *Power and Progress*, 87–8, 92, 93–5; Pérez, *The War of 1898*, 1–7.
20 C. Gibson (ed.), *The Black Legend: Anti-Spanish Attitudes in the Old World and the New* (New York: Alfred A. Knupf, 1971).
21 R. L. Kagan, 'Prescott's Paradigm: American Historical Scholarship and the Decline of Spain', *American Historical Review*, 101:2 (1996), 423–46.
22 G. F. Linderman, *The Mirror of War: American Society and the Spanish–American War* (Ann Arbor: University of Michigan Press, 1974), 122.
23 Quoted ibid., 123.
24 M. Hunt, *Ideology and US Foreign Policy* (New Haven: Yale University Press, 1987), 58–60; Linderman, *The Mirror of War*, 115, 120–4; McCartney, *Power and Progress*, 87–8; J. Offner, 'United States Politics and the 1898 War Over Cuba', in Smith and Dávila-Cox (eds), *The Crisis of 1989*, 18–21; T. G. Paterson, 'United States Intervention in Cuba, 1898: Interpretations of the Spanish–American–Cuban–Filipino War', *History Teacher*, 29:3 (1996), 353–4; Kagan, 'Prescott's Paradigm', 425–40.
25 J. W. Pratt, *A History of United States Foreign Policy* (Englewood Cliffs: Prentice-Hall, 1965, 2nd edition) [1955], 201, 205, 212–16; J. A. Field, Jr, 'American Imperialism: The Worst Chapter in Almost Any Book', *American Historical Review*, 83:3 (1978), 644–68. For a rebuttal see W. LaFeber and R. Beisner, 'Comments', ibid., pp. 669–78; see also Field's 'Reply', ibid., 679–83.
26 S. F. Bemis, *A Diplomatic History of the United States* (New York: A. Holt, 1965, 5th edition) [1936], 469, 475, 503; M. T. Gilderhus, 'Founding Father: Samuel Flagg Bemis and the Study of U.S.–Latin American Relations', *Diplomatic History*, 21:1 (1997), 1.
27 I. Musicant, *Empire by Default: The Spanish–American War and the Dawn of the American Century* (New York: Henry Holt, 1998). See also J. Dobson, *Reticent Expansionism: The Foreign Policy of William McKinley* (Pittsburg: Duquesne University Press, 1988).
28 G. C. Herring, *From Colony to Superpower: U.S. Foreign Relations Since 1776* (New York: Oxford University Press, 2008), 309.
29 Paterson, 'United States Intervention in Cuba', 344–5.
30 Morgan, *America's Road to Empire*, 21, 61–2; L. L. Gould, *The Spanish–American War and President McKinley* (Lawrence: University Press of Kansas, 1982), 104, 117–19; Trask, *The War with Spain in 1898*, 31; J. L. Offner, 'McKinley and the Spanish–American War', *Presidential Studies Quarterly*, 34:1 (2004), 54–61; R. F. Hamilton, *President McKinley, War and Empire* (New Brunswick: Transaction, 2006), vol. I, 136; W. Zimmermann, *First Great Triumph: How Five Americans Made Their Country a World Power* (New York: FSG, 2002), 386–92, 494–9; M. Sewell, 'Humanitarian Intervention, Democracy, and Imperialism: The American War with Spain, 1898, and After', in B. Simms and D. J. B. Trim (eds), *Humanitarian Intervention: A History* (Cambridge: Cambridge University Press, 2011), 303, 309, 316.

31 As acknowledged even by Walter LaFeber, a critic of Pratt's approach. See W. LaFeber, 'That "Splendid Little War" in Historical Perspective', *Texas Quarterly*, 11:4 (1968), 90. However, other leftist revisionist historians are not convinced by Pratt's evidence. See e.g. N. L. O'Connor, 'The Spanish–American War: A Re-evaluation of Its Causes', *Science and Society*, 22 (1958), 129–43; P. S. Foner, 'Why the United States Went to War with Spain in 1898', *Science and Society*, 32:1 (1968), 39–65.

32 J. W. Pratt, 'American Business and the Spanish–American War', *Hispanic American Historical Review*, 14:2 (1934), 163–75; Hamilton, *President McKinley, War and Empire*, 120–35.

33 Ibid., 120–6; Paterson, 'United States Intervention in Cuba', 355.

34 Morgan, *America's Road to Empire*, 14.

35 Pratt, 'American Business and the Spanish–American War', 163–201; F. R. Dulles, *1898–1954, America's Rise to World Power* (New York: Harper and Row, 1963) [1954], 39 n.1, 41; Hamilton, *President McKinley, War and Empire*, 111–13, 119–33, 135; Offner, *An Unwanted War*, 30–1; Sewell, 'Humanitarian Intervention, Democracy, and Imperialism', 307, 310.

36 Pratt, *A History of United States Foreign Policy*, 207, 215; Morgan, *America's Road to Empire*, 13–14; Trask, *The War with Spain in 1898*, 58; McCartney, *Power and Progress*, 91; Hamilton, *President McKinley, War and Empire*, 149–65.

37 As accepted even by Louis Pérez, a scathing critic of the US administration's intentions. See Pérez, *The War of 1898*, 24.

38 Hearst was reported to have telegraphed artist Frederic Remington, whom he had sent to Cuba, 'furnish the pictures, and I'll furnish the war'. Hearst has denied this. See W. J. Campbell, 'Not Likely Sent: The Remington-Hearst "Telegrams"', *Journalism and Mass Communication Quarterly*, 77:2 (2000), 405–22.

39 Offner, *An Unwanted War*, 229–30.

40 J. W. Pratt, 'The "Large Policy" in 1898', *Mississippi Valley Historical Review*, 19:2 (1932), 220–2, 228–31, 239–42; Paterson, 'United States Intervention in Cuba', 350–1.

41 Hamilton, *President McKinley, War and Empire*, 114–15; Herring, *From Colony to Superpower*, 308–9; Zimmermann, *First Great Triumph*.

42 J. W. Pratt, 'It Was a Courant Manifest Destiny', in R. H. Miller (ed.), *American Imperialism in 1898: The Quest for National Fulfillment* (New York: John Wiley and Sons, 1970), 24–7.

43 See Field, 'American Imperialism', 647, 649–50.

44 Pratt, 'It Was a Courant Manifest Destiny', 24–30; Pratt, 'The "Large Policy" in 1898', 219–42; Pratt, *A History of United States Foreign Policy*, 202–6; Dulles, *1898–1954, America's Rise to World Power*, 30–6, 39; R. Hofstadter, *Social Darwinism in American Thought, 1860–1915* (Philadelphia: Pennsylvania University Press, 1944); Morgan, *America's Road to Empire*, 15; Herring, *From Colony to Superpower*, 299–300, 302–5; Hamilton, *President McKinley, War and Empire*, 113–15; Paterson, 'United States Intervention in Cuba', 350–2. Contra as regards social Darwinism in the US, see R. C. Bannister, '"The Survival of the Fittest in Our Doctrine": History or Histrionics', *Journal of the History of Ideas*, 31:3 (1970), 377–98.

45 Herring, *From Colony to Superpower*, 300, 302.

46 Paterson, 'United States Intervention in Cuba', 352–3; K. L. Hoganson, *Fighting for American Manhood: How Gender Politics Provoked the Spanish–American and Philippine–American Wars* (New Haven: Yale University Press, 1998), 43–5, 67–73, 85; Miller, *From Liberation to Conquest*, 25–32.

47 On the controversy see the Varg–McCormick debate: P. A. Varg, 'The Myth of the China Market, 1890–1914', *American Historical Review*, 73:3 (1968), 742–58; T. J. McCormick, 'American Expansion in China', *American Historical Review*, 75:5 (1970), 1393–6.
48 Dulles, *1898–1954, America's Rise to World Power*, 47.
49 D. M. Pletcher, 'Rhetoric and Results: A Pragmatic View of American Economic Expansion, 1865–98', *Diplomatic History*, 5:2 (1981), 95–6; LaFeber, 'That "Splendid Little War"', 90–8; Pratt, 'American Business and the Spanish–American War', 190–201.
50 See J. A. Fry, 'William McKinley and the Coming of the Spanish–American War: A Study of the Besmirching and Redemption of an Historical Image', *Diplomatic History*, 3:1 (1979), 93–5.
51 LaFeber, 'That "Splendid Little War"', 90, 92, 95–8.
52 Morgan, *America's Road to Empire*, xi; Hamilton, *President McKinley, War and Empire*, 135–6; Gould, *The Spanish–American War and President McKinley*; Offner, *An Unwanted War*, 38–9; LaFeber, 'That "Splendid Little War"', 96, 98; Fry, 'William McKinley and the Coming of the Spanish–American War', 77–97; Paterson, 'United States Intervention in Cuba', 341–61.
53 Quoted in Smith, *The Spanish–American War*, 32. For Martí's negative assessment of the US, see L. A. Pérez, Jr, *Cuba and the United States: Ties of Singular Intimacy* (Athens: University of Georgia Press, 2003), 77–81.
54 Offner, *An Unwanted War*, 3–4.
55 Trask, *The War with Spain in 1898*, 1–6; Smith, *The Spanish–American War*, 9, 15, 32–3; Hamilton, *President McKinley, War and Empire*, 105, 112, 115; Offner, *An Unwanted War*, 3–7; Pérez, *Cuba and the United States*, 82–3.
56 H. E. Flack, *Spanish–American Diplomatic Relations Preceding the War of 1898* (Baltimore: Johns Hopkins University Press, 1906), 60; E. J. Benton, *International Law and Diplomacy of the Spanish–American War* (Baltimore: Johns Hopkins University Press, 1908), 27–8; Pratt, *A History of United States Foreign Policy*, 206–7; Morgan, *America's Road to Empire*, 7–8; Trask, *The War with Spain in 1898*, 8–9; Smith, *The Spanish–American War*, 18–23.
57 Morgan, *America's Road to Empire*, 13–14; Hamilton, *President McKinley, War and Empire*, 105; Miller, *From Liberation to Conquest*, 33–6.
58 Morgan, *America's Road to Empire*, 6–8, 13; Smith, *The Spanish–American War*, 33–4; Miller, *From Liberation to Conquest*, 33–4.
59 Ferrer, *Insurgent Cuba*, 170.
60 Offner, *An Unwanted War*, 25–30; Pérez, *Cuba and the United States*, 84–6; Smith, *The Spanish–American War*, 31, 34–6.
61 Smith, *The Spanish–American War*, 34.
62 Offner, *An Unwanted War*, 26–7.
63 Quoted in Morgan, *America's Road to Empire*, 11–12.
64 Ibid., 18.
65 Quoted in R. L. Beisner, *Twelve Against Empire: The Anti-Imperialists, 1898–1900* (New York: McGraw-Hill, 1968), 24.
66 Offner, *An Unwanted War*, 46–7.
67 Benton, *International Law and Diplomacy of the Spanish–American War*, 61; Smith, *The Spanish–American War*, 38; Offner, *An Unwanted War*, 54–9.
68 Quoted in Morgan, *America's Road to Empire*, 27.
69 Offner, *An Unwanted War*, 68–76.
70 W. McKinley, 'McKinley's View of the Cuban Crisis, 6 December 1897', in Miller (ed.), *American Imperialism in 1898*, 61.

71 Ibid., 67.
72 Sewell, 'Humanitarian Intervention, Democracy, and Imperialism', 304.
73 Morgan, *America's Road to Empire*, 30–1, 40, 49; Trask, *The War with Spain in 1898*, 19–20; Linderman, *The Mirror of War*, 25–6; Pérez, *The War of 1898*, 8–11.
74 Pérez, *Cuba and the United States*, 88–9.
75 Ibid., 91–2.
76 Offner, *An Unwanted War*, 116–22; Benton, *International Law and Diplomacy of the Spanish–American War*, 74–5; Morgan, *America's Road to Empire*, 41–2.
77 Morgan, *America's Road to Empire*, 51; McCartney, *Power and Progress*, 105.
78 Offner, *An Unwanted War*, 123; Morgan, *America's Road to Empire*, 53.
79 Dulles, *1898–1954, America's Rise to World Power*, 41.
80 L. A. Pérez, Jr, 'The Meaning of the *Maine*: Causation and the Historiography of the Spanish–American War', *Pacific Historical Review*, 58:3 (1989), 293–322.
81 Flack, *Spanish–American Diplomatic Relations*, 41–7; Pratt, *A History of United States Foreign Policy*, 208–9; Morgan, *America's Road to Empire*, 45–8; Trask, *The War with Spain in 1898*, xii–xiii, 28–9; Smith, *The Spanish–American War*, 40–1; McCartney, *Power and Progress*, 98–9; Offner, *An Unwanted War*, 122–5.
82 M. B. Davis and R. W. Quimby, 'Senator Proctor's Cuban Speech: Speculations on a Cause of the Spanish–American War', *Quarterly Journal of Speech*, 55:2 (1969), 140.
83 Quoted *ibid.*, 134.
84 Ibid., 131–41; Morgan, *America's Road to Empire*, 50–1; McCartney, *Power and Progress*, 100–2; Offner, *An Unwanted War*, 130–5.
85 McCartney, *Power and Progress*, 103–6.
86 Ibid., 102–6.
87 Ibid., 91.
88 Offner, *An Unwanted War*, 15–16, 150–3, 227; Linderman, *The Mirror of War*, 26–8, 32–4; Hamilton, *President McKinley, War and Empire*, 117–18; Musicant, *Empire by Default*, 168–75.
89 Trask, *The War with Spain in 1898*, 39–41; Linderman, *The Mirror of War*, 26; Smith, *The Spanish–American War*, 43; Offner, *An Unwanted War*, 153–8.
90 Benton, *International Law and Diplomacy of the Spanish–American War*, 107; Herring, *From Colony to Superpower*, 313.
91 Morgan, *America's Road to Empire*, 51–2; Smith, *The Spanish–American War*, 43–4.
92 Flack, *Spanish–American Diplomatic Relations*, 89–92; Benton, *International Law and Diplomacy of the Spanish–American War*, 85–90; Trask, *The War with Spain in 1898*, 45–52; Offner, *An Unwanted War*, 159–76.
93 Quoted in Morgan, *America's Road to Empire*, 58.
94 Herring, *From Colony to Superpower*, 313; Morgan, *America's Road to Empire*, 32, 57; Smith, *The Spanish–American War*, 43–4; Offner, *An Unwanted War*, 121, 155, 157.
95 W. McKinley, 'The President Asks for War', in Miller (ed.), *American Imperialism in 1898*, 97.
96 Ibid., 97.
97 Ibid., 99.
98 Offner, *An Unwanted War*, 181.
99 McKinley, 'The President Asks for War', 100.
100 Pérez, *Cuba and the United States*, 95.
101 McCartney, *Power and Progress*, 129.
102 Ibid., 141; Flack, *Spanish–American Diplomatic Relations*, 38–41; Trask, *The War with Spain in 1898*, 54–6.

103 See D. C. Corbitt, 'Cuban Revisionist Interpretations of Cuba's Struggle for Independence', *Hispanic American Historical Review*, 43:3 (1963), 400; Pérez, *The War of 1898*, 81–107.
104 J. A. S. Grenville, 'American Naval Preparations for War with Spain, 1896–1898', *Journal of American Studies*, 2:1 (1968), 33–7; E. K. Smith, '"A Question From Which We Could Not Escape": William McKinley and the Decision to Acquire the Philippines', *Diplomatic History*, 9:4 (1985), 363–75.
105 Pratt, 'The "Large Policy" in 1898', 221–3, 241–2; Dulles, *1898–1954, America's Rise to World Power*, 45.
106 F. H. Harrington, 'The Anti-Imperialist Movement in the United States, 1898–1900', *Mississippi Valley Historical Review*, 22:2 (1935), 211–19; Beisner, *Twelve Against Empire*.
107 J. Offner, 'The United States and France: Ending the Spanish–American War', *Diplomatic History*, 7:1 (1983), 12–13, 17–18.
108 Pratt, *A History of United States Foreign Policy*, 215–16.
109 Quoted in Sewell, 'Humanitarian Intervention, Democracy, and Imperialism', 317.
110 Smith, *The Spanish–American War*, 196.
111 Quoted *ibid.*, 196.
112 *Ibid.*, 195.
113 Dulles, *1898–1954, America's Rise to World Power*, 50; Smith, *The Spanish–American War*, 198–9.
114 Pratt, *A History of United States Foreign Policy*, 216, 218; Dulles, *1898–1954, America's Rise to World Power*, 50; Smith, *The Spanish–American War*, 199–200.
115 Dulles, *1898–1954, America's Rise to World Power*, 48.
116 *Ibid.*, 48.
117 Offner, 'United States Politics and the 1898 War Over Cuba', 22.
118 Quoted in Dulles, *1898–1954, America's Rise to World Power*, 51.
119 Sewell, 'Humanitarian Intervention, Democracy, and Imperialism', 316, 318.
120 See A. Preston, 'Bridging the Gap Between the Sacred and the Secular in the History of American Foreign Relations', *Diplomatic History*, 30 (2006), 783–812; Sewell, 'Humanitarian Intervention, Democracy, and Imperialism', 316–20.
121 Offner, 'The United States and France', 4.
122 *Ibid.*, 5.
123 *Ibid.*, 12–13.
124 Smith, 'A Question from Which We Could Not Escape', 363–75; Offner, 'United States Politics and the 1898 War Over Cuba', 37–38; Sewell, 'Humanitarian Intervention, Democracy, and Imperialism', 313–17.
125 Offner, 'The United States and France', 3, 13, 15–16.
126 Gould, *The Spanish–American War and President McKinley*, 117–19; Smith, 'A Question from Which We Could Not Escape', 369–70.
127 Pletcher, 'Rhetoric and Results', 100; Smith, 'A Question from Which We Could Not Escape', 373.
128 Smith, 'A Question from Which We Could Not Escape', 374; E. P. Crapol, 'Coming to Terms with Empire: The Historiography of Late-Nineteenth Century American Foreign Relations', *Diplomatic History*, 16 (1992), 587–90.
129 Pratt, *A History of United States Foreign Policy*, 217.
130 Harrington, 'The Anti-Imperialist Movement in the United States', 211.
131 *Ibid.*, 211–19; Dulles, *1898–1954, America's Rise to World Power*, 52–5; Smith, *The Spanish–American War*, 201–3.

132 Harrington, 'The Anti-Imperialist Movement in the United States', 211–13.
133 Smith, *The Spanish–American War*, 202.
134 Dulles, *1898–1954, America's Rise to World Power*, 53; Smith, *The Spanish–American War*, 203.
135 Beisner, *Twelve Against Empire*.
136 For US outrages (the burning of villages, the order to 'take no prisoners', the 'water cure' torture and others) and racism during the Philippine–American War (1898–1902), see P. A. Kramer, 'Race-Making and Colonial Violence in the U.S. Empire: The Philippine-American War as Race War', *Diplomatic History*, 30:3 (2006), 169–210.
137 Dulles, *1898–1954, America's Rise to World Power*, 54–8; Pratt, *A History of United States Foreign Policy*, 218; Smith, *The Spanish–American War*, 204–5; Offner, 'United States Politics and the 1898 War Over Cuba', 36–7.
138 Linderman, *The Mirror of War*, 142.
139 'The Origin and Purpose of the Platt Amendment', *American Journal of International Law*, 8:3 (1914), 585–6.
140 Quoted *ibid.*, 589.
141 Pérez, *The War of 1898*, 32–4.
142 *Ibid.*, 126–30.
143 See Corbitt, 'Cuban Revisionist Interpretations of Cuba's Struggle for Independence', 395–404; Pérez, *The War of 1898*, 125–6.
144 Corbitt, 'Cuban Revisionist Interpretations of Cuba's Struggle for Independence', 400.
145 *Ibid.*, 402.
146 Pérez, *The War of 1898*, 11–12.
147 McCartney, *Power and Progress*, 148.
148 Quoted *ibid.*, 159.
149 *Ibid.*, 161.
150 R. Carr, 'Liberalism and Reaction, 1833–1931', in R. Carr (ed.), *Spain: A History* (Oxford: Oxford University Press, 2000), 224–5.
151 McCartney, *Power and Progress*, 87.
152 Our list is inspired by Beisner's three questions and five issues, in R. L. Beisner, 'Comments to "American Imperialism: The Worst Chapter in Almost Any Book"', *American Historical Review*, 83:3 (1976), 673.
153 See Field, 'American Imperialism', 646.
154 Morgan, *America's Road to Empire*, 21, 61; McCartney, *Power and Progress*, 87–8; 136; Trask, *The War with Spain in 1898*, 31; Zimmermann, *First Great Triumph*, 494–9.
155 Sewell, 'Humanitarian Intervention, Democracy, and Imperialism', 310.
156 Herring, *From Colony to Superpower*, 309.
157 Morgan, *America's Road to Empire*, xi; Hamilton, *President McKinley, War and Empire*, 135–6; Herring, *From Colony to Superpower*, 311–12, 314.
158 S. Chesterman, *Just War or Just Peace? Humanitarian Intervention and International Law* (Oxford: Oxford University Press, 2001), 35.
159 T. S. Woolsey, *America's Foreign Policy* (New York: Century, 1898), 75–6, 106–7.
160 A. S. Hershey, 'Intervention and the Recognition of Cuban Independence', *Annals of the American Academy of Political and Social Science*, 11 (1898), 74–80.
161 G. G. Wilson, *International Law* (New York: Silver, Burdett, 1922, 8th edition) [1901], 91–2.
162 Benton, *International Law and Diplomacy of the Spanish–American War*, 107.
163 Moore, *The Principles of American Diplomacy*, 206–8.

164 *Ibid.*, 208.
165 E. C. Stowell, *Intervention in International Law* (Washington, DC: John Byrne, 1921), 481.
166 Fenwick, 'Intervention: Individual and Collective', 651.
167 Referred to *ibid.*, 651.
168 L. Le Fur, 'Chronique sur la guerre hispano-américaine', *Revue générale de droit international public*, 5 (1898), 664–5.
169 A. de Lapradelle, 'Chronique sur les affaires de Cuba', *Revue de droit public et de la science politique en France et à l'étranger*, 1 (1900), 74.
170 A. Rougier, 'La théorie de l'intervention d'humanité', *Revue générale de droit international public*, 17 (1910), 476.
171 J. Westlake, *International Law, Part I: Peace* (Cambridge: Cambridge University Press, 1904), 307.
172 According to Moore, *The Principles of American Diplomacy*, 208.
173 R. B. Lillich, 'Humanitarian Intervention: A Reply to Ian Brownlie and a Plea for Constructive Alternatives', in J. N. Moore (ed.), *Law and Civil War in the Modern World* (Baltimore: Johns Hopkins University Press, 1974), 233–4.
174 M. McDougal and M. Reisman, 'Response', *International Lawyer*, 3 (1968–69), 439.
175 See also C. F. Amerasinghe, 'The Conundrum of Recourse to Force – To Protect Persons', *International Organizations Law Review*, 3 (2006), 26; A. V. W. Thomas and A. J. Thomas, *Non-Intervention – The Law and Its Import in the Americas* (Dallas: Southern Methodist University Press, 1956), 22; M. J. Bazyler, 'Reexamining the Doctrine of Humanitarian Intervention in Light of the Atrocities in Kampuchea and Ethiopia', *Stanford Journal of International Law*, 23 (1987), 583; F. K. Abiew, *The Evolution of the Doctrine and Practice of Humanitarian Intervention* (The Hague: Kluwer Law International, 1999), 53–4.
176 I. Brownlie, *International Law and the Use of Force by States* (Oxford: Clarendon Press, 1963), 46.
177 T. M. Franck and N. S. Rodley, 'After Bangladesh: The Law of Humanitarian Intervention by Military Force', *American Journal of International Law*, 67:2 (1973), 285.
178 J.-P. L., Fonteyne, 'The Customary International Law Doctrine of Humanitarian Intervention: Its Current Validity under the U.N. Charter', *California Western International Law Journal*, 4 (1973–74), 206.
179 M. Walzer, *Just and Unjust Wars* (New York: Basic Books, 1977), 104.
180 *Ibid.*, 104.
181 G. J. Bass, *Freedom's Battle: The Origins of Humanitarian Intervention* (New York: Vintage Books, 2009), 317.
182 T. B. Knudsen, 'The History of Humanitarian Intervention: The Rule or the Exception?', 50th ISA Annual Convention, New York, 15–18 February 2009, 30.

Part III
Conclusion

11
Assessment

Main characteristics

In the nineteenth century, a humanitarian justification was invoked by governments, press, public opinion and international jurists from the three-power intervention in the Greek War of Independence (1821–31) through to the more controversial US intervention in Cuba in 1898, but also for other instances short of the use of armed force in humanitarian plights. The doctrine of humanitarian intervention was at its zenith in international law discourse from the mid-nineteenth century until the 1930s and in particular from the 1870s onward (see chapter 4).

As regards the practice of humanitarian intervention in the nineteenth century, we will highlight a number of characteristics.[1]

Within a period of nine decades (1821–1914), there were barely four *military* interventions justified on humanitarian grounds, contrary to the 1990s, with as many as seven within a decade. Clearly, this new tendency from the 1820s onwards did not open the flood gates to constant intervention.

The interventions were taken (1) by the great powers in concert, as seen with the 1860 Paris protocols regarding Lebanon; (2) by an 'alliance of the willing', as with the three powers in the 1827 Treaty of London and its consequences (Navarino and French expeditionary force); and (3) by declaring war following several attempts at good offices and mediation (Russia in 1827 and 1877, or the US in 1898). Although some aspects of one-power intervention were criticized, there was no overall condemnation but benign neutrality, regarding Russia in 1828–29 and 1877–78 (bar Britain, with the cabinet and people divided) or the US in 1898. Moreover, the intervening states were aware of the abuse factor and thus made sure to adopt self-denying clauses or to limit the time frame for the presence of troops (bar the US in Cuba). More generally, in the cases examined one can see a repertoire of international norms and rules of conduct in instances of humanitarian plight, most of which are applicable today (see end of chapters 6, 7, 8 and 10).

Three of the four cases involved Christians suffering at the hands of Muslims, where the 'effusion of blood' and other suffering were shocking. The great powers and the rest of Europe or the Americas were blind to atrocities committed by

Christians against Muslims, which in instances of liberation wars were committed first by the Christian insurgents, who had opted for the use of violence, with the Ottomans over-reacting (in the Greek and Bulgarian cases) and then facing the wrath of 'civilized' Europe.

Military intervention was never contemplated for the excesses and barbarities of the British in Jamaica, South Africa and elsewhere in Africa, the French and Belgians in Africa, quasi-genocide in British Australia or US policy against the indigenous peoples or for acts of violence by the great powers when conquering neighbouring territories, as in the case of Russia in the Caucasus and central Asia. Such acts were not even acknowledged by the governments in question. As Mowat had put it: 'Civilized Governments do not openly acknowledge themselves to be bandits or plunderers; they can always put forward a "case" in their favour. This they do ... partly because, for political reasons, they do not wish to offend brutally the opinion of moral people in their own or other countries'.[2]

The four interventions were successful in stopping the 'effusion of blood'. They were not merely better than nothing (as in the case of Somalia today), too late (Rwanda) or leading to inordinate destruction, refugees and civilian deaths (Kosovo/Serbia).

The insurgents themselves sought foreign armed intervention to save them. With the exception of the Cubans in 1895–98, they did not seem apprehensive of future domination by the intervening parties, probably for one or more of the following reasons: because their yearning for freedom from a 'foreign yoke' obscured all other considerations and fears; confidence reigned that when independence was achieved they could neutralize their patron's influence or use it to their advantage; or the belief that even circumscribed independence was better than nothing and in due course would lead to unfettered independence.

Criticism and counter-criticism

Supporters of the nineteenth-century precedent point to many commonalities with today's landscape. As Gary Bass has argued:[3]

> All of the major themes of today's heated debates about humanitarian intervention – about undermining sovereignty ... about altruistic or veiled imperialistic motivations, about the terrible danger of taking sides in civil wars ... about multilateral and unilateral uses of force, about the moral responsibility of political leaders – were voiced loud and clear throughout the nineteenth century.

Leaving aside those who regard humanitarian intervention as inconceivable and a contradiction in terms, the practice of armed humanitarian intervention in the period under study has been criticized mainly on three grounds: the civilization–barbarian construction, the related selectivity (double-standards) factor, and abuse.

Assessment

Franck and Rodley, for instance, have claimed that the nineteenth century is 'illustrative of principles applicable to relations between unequal states in a community of law which prefers one socio-religious system over another and in which "civilized" states exercise de facto tutorial rights over "uncivilized" ones'. Therefore they 'are of little precedential value in the contemporary world'.[4] Others have also pointed to 'double standards', with the 'international community' defined as the Christian community of states, and they maintain that no useful inferences can be drawn, for this would amount to reintroducing the unacceptable imperialist ethos of bygone days.[5]

As for the selectivity factor, why support one of many cases, for instance the Greeks, the Maronites or the Bulgarians, but not intervene militarily on behalf of the Jews of Russia or the Armenians in the Ottoman Empire?[6] And why did the US intervene only in Cuba and not in, say, oppressive regimes of South America, which instead it chose to support?[7] But as even Franck and Rodley are prepared to accept, the Greek case and some others against the Ottoman Empire 'are probably not to be dismissed as bogus. At least they struck a responsive chord in Western European and Russian public opinion. But these motives were certainly neither wholly pure, nor were they consistently pursued in the absence of other power considerations'.[8]

Knudsen has reasoned that the fact that almost all of the interventions were against the Ottoman Empire 'does not make them irrelevant to the evolution of humanitarian intervention', for they sought to protect Ottoman subjects 'against outrageous treatment'; the treatment was indeed 'outrageous' and 'the humanitarian justification was important for the general European acceptance of the interventions'; and the essential goal of these humanitarian interventions, 'namely to stop or prevent large-scale massacres, was mostly accomplished'.[9]

Eurocentrism, Orientalism, binary oppositions of civilized and barbarian/savage, the standard of civilization and, not least, the negative image of the 'Turks' cast a shadow on the nineteenth-century idea of humanitarian intervention. This is reinforced by its practical application, aimed at saving Christians from 'Turkish barbarism'. But as we have seen, this obvious double standard had been a source of criticism in the long nineteenth century.

To conclude, we would argue that one is better served by avoiding throwing the baby out with the bathwater. If we try to judge 'reality' in the long nineteenth century on its own terms, as perceived then and not anachronistically (on the basis of today's more scrupulous standards of morality and justice), then the following assessment is probably more fair: that despite the obvious Christian bias, Eurocentrism, hardly disguised 'anti-Turkism', incipient racism, double standards and national interests, not to mention the unabashed 'civilizing' (read haughty imperialist) spirit reigning in those days, the overriding motive of European publics (and some in government, the bureaucracy and opposition) was indeed humanitarian, to save lives and alleviate suffering.

Tentative propositions

There is, according to Knudsen, 'plenty of evidence'[10] to support Martin Wight's claim that '[i]n the history of nineteenth century intervention, humanitarianism became increasingly the prime motive, as the balance of power was always the limiting one'.[11] This may be an overstatement, but worth making are the following observations that are also of relevance today.

As seen in the four cases examined, the initial reaction by foreign governments was one of restraint, not wanting to be involved, certainly not militarily. But as the problem could not be wished away and diplomatic pressure and mediation failed, intervention did take place, though with limited goals, save in the case of the US in 1898 with its sudden imperialist appetite.

The role of public opinion was decisive. Had it not been for the humanitarian plight and for the pressure from the press and public opinion, no great power would have intervened. After a while, these governments found it increasingly difficult to appear insensitive to a plight that moved their citizens. It is also crucial for a humanitarian or national cause to enlist the advocacy of celebrities, the Byron example (and in this sense the role of celebrities is hardly novel, as depicted by the recent literature on the role of celebrities in international relations[12]).

In humanitarian plights, the most likely supporters of intervention are the 'liberal humanitarians' (Byron, Shelley, Bentham, Pushkin, Hugo, Gladstone, Twain) or 'conservative humanitarians' (Chateaubriand, Dostoevsky), and those against intervention are pacifists (Tolstoy) and, in particular, *Realpolitik* advocates (Castlereagh, John Quincy Adams, Disraeli, Bismarck). But from a certain point onwards and as the armed clash and suffering continue unabated, some realist decision-makers may opt for intervention if geostrategic and other interests also come into play or their state's and government's prestige is on the line (Nicholas I, Palmerston, Napoleon III, Gorchakov), especially if a conflict appears unending and catastrophic, is likely to escalate or spill over into other regions, or if a rival power is likely to intervene and gain advantage.[13] For some pragmatists, instrumental considerations may go hand in hand with humanitarian concerns in a given case (Canning, Thouvenel, Alexander II, Ignatiev, McKinley).

When it comes to states, especially great powers, searching for pure humanitarian motives without an inkling of instrumental motives for intervening militarily is unrealistic. As seen in the 1990s in the case of Bosnia and Herzegovina and Kosovo prior to intervention, and at the end of the nineteenth century in the case of the Armenians, when vital interests are not at stake, there is considerable reluctance to intervene, however just a cause and shocking to the moral conscience of humankind. As Stowell had put it, '[s]tates are not generally willing to incur the burdens of the intervention, even on the appealing ground of humanity, unless they are also actuated by other and more selfish considerations'.[14] After all, there is no greater sacrifice than to go to war 'for total strangers',

Assessment

given the heavy economic cost, casualties and risks involved. Thus humanitarian intervention in the nineteenth century (and today) is not to be rejected out of hand as a mere fig-leaf for imperialist and other designs. It is rather a question of degree. If affective and instrumental motives are more or less balanced, one reinforcing and justifying the other, then a good case can be made for intervening, especially if there is a fair chance of succeeding and alleviating extreme suffering, and provided there are no advantages for the intervening party that will make a mockery of intervention.

Lastly, it may well be that motivation (or the intention but not the motivation per se[15]) is basically humanitarian. However, given the heavy costs involved in any military venture, governments have to justify their future intervention to their home publics (who may see coffins arriving back home) and can hardly do so on lofty humanitarian grounds alone – by claiming to be the world's conscience as it were – but only by invoking, perhaps fabricating, dire threats to vital national interests. Alternatively, governments or leaders may seek the moral high ground to enhance their waning international credentials, for 'humanitarian prestige',[16] to act in conformity with existing 'standards of justice',[17] to mobilize their citizens to a noble cause, or simply in order to vilify their adversary. Thus they may invoke humanitarian motives to conceal their instrumental goals. But after a while they may regard these concocted motives as equally valid, or they may use them to attain a positive self-definition and to ensure their legacy for posterity.

Notes

1 For other such attempts regarding nineteenth-century practice (though in far less detail) see M. Ganji, *International Protection of Human Rights* (Geneva: Librairie E. Droz, 1962), 37–8; W. G. Grewe, *The Epochs of International Law* (Berlin: Walter de Gruyter, 2000, translated and revised by M. Byers), 493; J.-P. L. Fonteyne, 'The Customary International Law Doctrine of Humanitarian Intervention: Its Current Validity Under the U.N. Charter', *California Western International Law Journal* (1973–74), 235; M. Finnemore, 'Constructing Norms of Humanitarian Intervention', in P. J. Katzenstein (ed.), *The Culture of National Security* (New York: Columbia University Press, 1996), 168–9; K. F. Abiew, *The Evolution of the Doctrine and Practice of Humanitarian Intervention* (The Hague: Kluwer Law International, 1999), 42–3.

2 Quoted in G. W. Keeton and G. Schwarzenberger, *Making International Law Work* (London: Stevens and Sons, 1946), 63.

3 G. J. Bass, *Freedom's Battle: The Origins of Humanitarian Intervention* (New York: Vintage Books, 2009), 5.

4 T. M. Franck and N. S. Rodley, 'After Bangladesh: The Law of Humanitarian Intervention by Military Force', *American Journal of International Law*, 67:2 (1973), 281.

5 See e.g. H. Köchler, 'Humanitarian Intervention in the Context of Modern Power Politics', *Studies in International Relations*, 26 (2001), 3–4, 6–7.

6 Franck and Rodley, 'After Bangladesh', 290–5.

7 Ibid., 285.

8   *Ibid.*, 281.
9   T. B. Knudsen, 'The History of Humanitarian Intervention: The Rule or the Exception?', 50th ISA Annual Convention, New York, 15–18 February 2009, 32.
10 *Ibid.*, 31.
11 M. Wight, 'Western Values in International Relations', in H. Butterfield and M. Wight (eds), *Diplomatic Investigations: Essays in the Theory of International Politics* (London: Allen and Unwin, 1966), 119.
12 See e.g. A. F. Cooper, *Celebrity Diplomacy* (Boulder: Paradigms Press, 2008); L. Tsaliki, C. A. Frangonikolopoulos and A. Huliaras (eds), *Transnational Celebrity Activism in Global Politics: Changing the World?* (Bristol: Intellect, 2011).
13 See the more recent cases of US involvement in Somalia and Bosnia, in J. Western, 'Sources of Humanitarian Intervention: Beliefs, Information, and Advocacy in the US Decisions on Somalia and Bosnia', *International Security*, 26:4 (2002), 117–18, 127–9, 131–2.
14 E. C. Stowell, *Intervention in International Law* (Washington, DC: John Byrne, 1921), 64 n.14.
15 For those who distinguish between intention and motives. See e.g. F. R. Tesón, 'Humanitarian Intervention: Loose Ends', *Journal of Military Ethics*, 10:3 (2011), 200–6. See also n. 4, p. 103, in the present volume.
16 T. B. Knudsen, 'Humanitarian Intervention Revisited: Post-Cold War Responses to Classic Problems', in M. Pugh (ed.), *The UN, Peace and Force* (London: Frank Cass, 1997), 154.
17 Finnemore, 'Constructing Norms of Humanitarian Intervention', 159.

Select bibliography on international law until 1945

Bernard, Mountague, *On the Principle of Non-Intervention: A Lecture Delivered in the Hall of All Souls College, December MDCCCLX* (Oxford: J. H. and J. Parker, 1860).

Bluntschli, Johann Caspar, *Le droit international codifié* (Paris: Librairie de Guillaumin et Cie, 1874, 2nd French edition, translated from the German by M. C. Lardy) [1868].

Bonfils, Henri, *Manuel de droit international public (droit des gens)* (Paris: Librairie nouvelle de droit et de jurisprudence, 1905, 4th edition by Paul Fauchille) [1894].

Borchard, Edwin M., 'Basic Elements of Diplomatic Protection of Citizens Abroad', *American Journal of International Law*, 7:3 (1913).

Brierly, J. L., *The Law of Nations: An Introduction to the International Law of Peace* (Oxford: Clarendon Press, 1936, 2nd edition) [1928].

Calvo, Charles [Carlos], *Le droit internationale: théorie et pratique* (Paris: Guillaumin et Cie, G. Pedone-Lauriel, 1880, 3rd edition) [1870].

Carnazza Amari, G. [Guiseppe], 'Nouvel exposé du principe de non-intervention', *Revue de droit international et de législation comparée*, 5 (1873).

Creasy, Sir Edward S., *First Platform of International Law* (London: John van Voorst, 1876).

Despagnet, Frantz, *Cours de droit international public* (Paris: L. Larose, 1894).

Engelhardt, Éd. [Édouard Philippe], *Le droit d'intervention et la Turquie. Étude historique* (Paris: A. Cotillon et Cie, 1880).

Fauchille, Paul, *Traité de droit international public* (Paris: Rousseau et Cie, 1926, 8th updated and rewritten edition of Bonfil's *Manuel de droit international public (droit des gens)*) [1877], vol. I, part i.

Fenwick, C. G., 'Intervention: Individual and Collective', *American Journal of International Law*, 39:4 (1945).

Fiore, Pasquale, *Nouveau droit international public suivant les besoins de la civilization moderne* (Paris: A. Durant et Pedone-Lauriel, 1885, 2nd edition, translated from the Italian and annotated by Charles Antoine) [1865], vol. I.

Floeckher [Flöcker], Adolph de, *De l'intervention en droit international* (Paris: A. Pedone, 1896).

Funck-Brentano, Théophile and Albert Sorel, *Précis du droit des gens* (Paris: Librairie Plon, 1887, 2nd edition) [1877].

Hall, William Edward, *A Treatise on International Law* (Oxford: Clarendon Press, 1895, 4th edition) [1880].

Halleck, Henry Wager, *Halleck's International Law or Rules Regulating the Intercourse of States* in *Peace and War* (London: Kegan Paul, Trench, Trubner and Co., 1893, 3rd edition by S. Baker) [1861], vol. I.

Harcourt, William Vernon [pen-name Historicus], *Letters by Historicus on Some Questions of International Law. Reprinted from 'The Times' with Considerable Additions* (London: Macmillan, 1863).

Heffter, A. W. [August Wilhelm], *Le droit international de l'Europe* (Berlin: H. W. Muller; Paris: A. Cotillon et Cie, 1883, 4th French edition, translated from the German by Jules Bergson) [1844]

Hershey, Amos S., 'The Calvo and Drago Doctrines', *American Journal of International Law*, 1:1 (1907).

Higgins, A. Pearce, *Studies in International Law and Relations* (Cambridge: Cambridge University Press, 1928).

Hodges, Henry Green, *The Doctrine of Intervention* (Princeton: Banner Press, 1915).

Holland, Thomas Erskine, *Lectures on International Law* (London: Sweet and Maxwell, 1933, edited by Thomas Alfred Walker and Wyndham Legh Walker).

Hornung, Joseph, 'Civilisés et barbares', *Revue de droit international et de législation comparée*, 17 (1885).

Hyde, Charles Cheney, 'Intervention in Theory and in Practice', *Illinois Law Review*, 6:1 (1911).

Kent, James, *Kent's Commentary on International Law* (Cambridge: Deighton, Bell, 2nd edition 1878) [1866], extracted and edited by John Thomas Abdy from James Kent, *Commentaries on American Law* (New York: O.Halsted, 1848) [1826].

Komarovskiy [Kamarowski], Count L. [Leonid], *Nachalo nevmeshatel'stva [The Principle of Non-intervention] (Moscow:* Universitetskaja Tipografiya, 1874).

Lauterpacht, H. [Hersch], 'Règles générales du droit de la paix', *Recueil des cours de l'Académie de droit international*, 62 (1937).

Lawrence, T. J. [Thomas Joseph], *The Principles of International Law* (Boston: D. C. Heath, 1905, 3rd edition, revised) [1895].

Lingelbach, W. E. [William Ezra], 'The Doctrine and Practice of Intervention in Europe', *Annals of the Academy of Political and Social Science*, 16 (1900).

Lorimer, James, *The Institutes of the Law of Nations: A Treatise of the Jural Relations of Separate Political Communities* (Edinburgh and London: William Blackwood and Sons, 1883, 1884), vols I, II.

Mamiani, Count [Terenzio], *Rights of Nations, or the New Law of European States Applied to the Affairs of Italy* (London: W. Jeffs, 1860, translated from the Italian by Roger Acton, and dedicated, by special permission, to Lord John Russell) [1859].

Mandelstam, André, 'La protection des minorités', *Recueil des cours de l'Académie de droit international*, 1 (1923).

Martens, F. F., *Sovremennoe Mezhdunarodnoe Pravo Tsivilizovannykh Narodov [The Contemporary International Law of Civilized Peoples]* (St Petersburg: Tipografiya A. Benke, 1904, 5th revised edition) [1883], vol. I.

Mérignhac, A. [Alexandre], *Traité de droit public international* (Paris: Librairie générale de droit et de jurisprudence, 1905), part i.

Moore, John Bassett, *A Digest of International Law* (Washington, DC: Government Printing Office, 1906), vol. VI.

Nys, Ernest, *Le droit international: les principles, les théories, les faits* (Brussels: M. Weissenbruch, 1912, new edition) [1906], vol. II.

Oppenheim, L. [Lassa F. L.], *International Law: A Treatise* (London: Longmans, Green and Co., 5th edition, edited by H. Lauterpacht, 1937) [1905], vol. I.

Phillimore, Sir Robert, *Commentaries upon International Law* (London: Butterworth, 1879, 3rd edition) [1854], vol. I.
Pillet, Antoine, 'Le droit international public', *Revue générale de droit international public*, 1 (1894).
Politis, Nicolas, *La morale internationale* (Paris: Bibliothèque Brentano's, 1944).
Potter, Pitman B., 'L'intervention en droit international moderne', *Recueil des cours de l'Académie de droit international*, 32 (1930).
Pradier-Fodéré, Paul Louis, *Traité de droit international public européen et américain, suivant le progrès de la science et de la pratique contemporaines* (Paris: A. Durand et Pedone-Lauriel, 1885), vol. I.
Renault, Louis, *Introduction à l'étude du droit international* (Paris: L. Larose, 1879).
Rivier, Alphonse, *Principes du droit des gens* (Paris: Librairie nouvelle de droit et de jurisprudence, 1896).
Rolin-Jaequemyns, Gustave, 'Note sur la théorie du droit d'intervention, à propos d'une lettre de M. le professeur Arntz', *Revue de droit international et de législation comparée*, 8 (1876).
Rougier, Antoine, 'La théorie de l'intervention d'humanité', *Revue générale de droit international public*, 17 (1910).
Séfériadès, Stélio, 'Principes généraux du droit international de la paix', *Recueil des cours de l'Académie de droit international*, 34 (1930).
Senior, Nassau William, 'Art.I-1. Histoire du Progrès du Droit des Gens depuis la Paix de Westphalies jusqu'au Congrès de Vienne. Par Henry Wheaton', *Edinburgh Review*, 77:156 (1843).
Stowell, Ellery C., *Intervention in International Law* (Washington, DC: John Byrne, 1921).
Strupp, Karl, 'Les règles générales du droit de la paix', *Recueil des cours de l'Académie de droit international*, 47 (1934).
Walker, Thomas Alfred, *A Manual of Public International Law* (Cambridge: Cambridge University Press, 1895).
Westlake, John, *International Law, Part I: Peace* (Cambridge: Cambridge University Press, 1904).
Wheaton, Henry, *Elements of International Law: With a Sketch of the History of the Science* (Philadelphia: Carey, Lea and Blanchard, 1836).
Wilson, George Grafton, *International Law* (New York: Silver, Burdett, 1922, 8th edition) [1901].
Winfield, P. H., 'The History of Intervention in International Law', *British Year Book of International Law*, 3 (1922–23).
Woolsey, Theodore D., *Introduction to the Study of International Law* (London: Sampson Low, Marston, Searle and Rivington, 1879, 5th edition revised and enlarged) [1860].
Woolsey, Theodore Salisbury, *American Foreign Policy* (New York: Century, 1898).

Select bibliography

Works in Russian are to be found in the notes of chapters 6 and 9.

Abiew, F. K., *The Evolution of the Doctrine and Practice of Humanitarian Intervention* (The Hague: Kluwer Law International, 1999).
Akarli, E. D., *The Long Peace: Ottoman Lebanon, 1861–1920* (London: I. B. Tauris, 1993).
Albrecht-Carrié, R., *A Diplomatic History of Europe Since the Congress of Vienna* (London: Methuen, 1958).
Alexandrowicz, C. H., 'New and Original States: The Issue of Reversion to Sovereignty', *International Affairs*, 45:3 (1969).
Anderson, D., *The Balkan Volunteers* (London: Hutchinson, 1968).
Anderson, M. S., *The Eastern Question, 1774–1923: A Study in International Relations* (London: Macmillan, 1966).
Anghie, A., *Imperialism, Sovereignty and the Making of International Law* (Cambridge: Cambridge University Press, 2004).
Arend, A. C. and R. J. Beck, *International Law and the Use of Force* (London: Routledge, 1993).
Avineri, S., *Hegel's Theory of the Modern State* (Cambridge: Cambridge University Press, 1972).
Barker, E., 'The Authorship of the *Vindiciae Contra Tyrannos*', *Cambridge Historical Journal*, 3:2 (1930).
Barnett, M., *Empire of Humanity: A History of Humanitarianism* (Ithaca: Cornell University Press, 2011).
Bass, G. J., *Freedom's Battle: The Origins of Humanitarian Intervention* (New York: Vintage Books, 2009).
Becker Lorca, A., 'Universal International Law: Nineteenth-Century Histories of Imposition and Appropriation', *Harvard International Law Journal*, 51:2 (2010).
Beisner, R. L., *Twelve Against Empire: The Anti-Imperialists, 1898–1900* (New York: McGraw-Hill, 1968).
Beitz, C. R., *Political Theory and International Relations* (Princeton: Princeton University Press, 1979).
Bell, D. (ed.), *Victorian Visions of Global Order: Empire and International Relations in Nineteenth-Century Political Thought* (Cambridge: Cambridge University Press, 2007).
Benton, E. J., *International Law and Diplomacy of the Spanish-American War* (Baltimore: Johns Hopkins University Press, 1908).
Blake, R., *Disraeli* (London: Methuen, 1966).

Select bibliography

Bodin, J., *On Sovereignty: Four Chapters from the Six Books of the Commonwealth* (Cambridge: Cambridge University Press, 1992, edited and translated by J. H. Franklin).
Brewer, D., *The Greek War of Independence: The Struggle for Freedom from Ottoman Oppression and the Birth of the Modern Greek Nation* (Woodstock: Overlook Press, 2001).
Bull, H., *The Anarchical Society: A Study of Order in World Politics* (New York: Columbia University Press, 1977).
Bull, H. (ed.), *Intervention in World Politics* (Oxford: Clarendon Press, 1984).
Cavallar, G., 'Vitoria, Grotius, Pufendorf, Wolff and Vattel: Accomplices of European Colonialism and Exploitation or True Cosmopolitans?', *Journal of the History of International Law*, 10 (2008).
Chesterman, S., *Just War or Just Peace? Humanitarian Intervention and International Law* (Oxford: Oxford University Press, 2001).
Christopher, P., *The Ethics of War and Peace* (Saddle River: Prentice Hall, 2004, 3rd edition) [1999].
Clayton, G. D., *Britain and the Eastern Question: Missolonghi to Gallipoli* (London: Lion Library, 1971).
Cobden, R., *Political Writings* (London: Routledge/Thoemmes Press, 1995), vol. I.
Crampton, R. J., *A Concise History of Modern Bulgaria* (Cambridge: Cambridge University Press, 2005, 2nd edition) [1997].
Crawley, C. W., *The Question of Greek Independence: A Study of British Policy in the Near East, 1821–1933* (New York: Howard Fertig, 1973) [1930].
Dakin, D., *The Greek Struggle for Independence, 1821–1833* (London: B. T. Batsford, 1973).
Daskalov, R., *The Making of a Nation in the Balkans: Historiography of the Bulgarian Revival* (Budapest: Central European University Press, 2004).
Dialla, A., *I Rosia apenanti sta Valkania: Ideologia kai politiki sto deftero imisi tou 19ou aiona* [Russian attitudes towards the Balkans: ideology and politics in the second half of the nineteenth century] (Athens: Alexandria, 2009).
Donnelly, J., 'Human Rights: A New Standard of Civilization?', *International Affairs*, 74:1 (1998).
Doyle, M. W., 'A Few Words on Mill, Walzer, and Nonintervention', *Ethics and International Affairs*, 23 (2009).
Dulles, F. R., *1898–1954, America's Rise to World Power* (New York: Harper and Row, 1963) [1954].
Echard, W. E., *Napoleon III and the Concert of Europe* (Baton Rouge: Louisiana State University Press, 1983).
Edwards, C., 'The Law of War in the Thought of Hugo Grotius', *Journal of Public Law*, 19 (1970).
Elbe, J. von, 'The Evolution of the Concept of the Just War in International Law', *American Journal of International Law*, 33:4 (1939).
Ellis, A., 'Utilitarianism and International Ethics', in T. Nardin and D. R. Mapel (eds), *Traditions of International Ethics* (Cambridge: Cambridge University Press, 1992).
Eppstein, J., *The Catholic Tradition of the Law of Nations* (London: Burns, Oates and Washbourne, 1935).
Esmein, A., 'La théorie de l'intervention internationale chez quelques publicists français du XVIe siècle', *Nouvelle revue historique, de droit français et étranger*, 24 (1900).
Fadner, F., *Seventy Years of Pan-Slavism in Russia: Karamzin to Danilevskii 1800–1870* (Georgetown: Georgetown University Press, 1961).
Farah, C. E., *The Politics of Interventionism in Ottoman Lebanon, 1830–1861* (London: Centre for Lebanese Studies in association with I. B. Tauris, 2000).

Field, Jr, J. A., 'American Imperialism: The Worst Chapter in Almost Any Book', *American Historical Review*, 83:3 (1978).

Finlay, G., *History of the Greek Revolution* (London: William Blackwood and Sons, 1861).

Finnemore, M., 'Constructing Norms of Humanitarian Intervention', in P. J. Katzenstein (ed.), *The Culture of National Security* (New York: Columbia University Press, 1996).

Fixdal, M. and D. Smith, 'Humanitarian Intervention and Just War', *Mershon International Studies Review*, 42:2 (1998).

Fonteyne, J.-P. L., 'The Customary International Law Doctrine of Humanitarian Intervention: Its Current Validity Under the U.N. Charter', *California Western International Law Journal*, 4 (1973–74).

Franceschet, A., 'Kant, International Law, and the Problem of Humanitarian Intervention', *Journal of International Political Theory*, 6:1 (2010).

Franck, T. M. and N. S. Rodley, 'After Bangladesh: The Law of Humanitarian Intervention by Military Force', *American Journal of International Law*, 67:2 (1973).

Ganji, M., *International Protection of Human Rights* (Geneva: Librairie E. Droz, 1962).

Geyer, D., *Russian Imperialism: The Interaction of Domestic and Foreign Policy, 1860–1914* (New Haven: Yale University Press, 1987).

Gong, G. W., *The Standard of 'Civilization' in International Society* (Oxford: Clarendon Press, 1984).

Gordon, T., *History of the Greek Revolution* (Edinburgh: William Blackwood, 1844, 2nd edition) [1832].

Gould, L. L., *The Spanish-American War and President McKinley* (Lawrence: University Press of Kansas, 1982).

Grewe, W. G., *The Epochs of International Law* (Berlin: Walter de Gruyter, 2000, translated from the German and revised by M. Byers) [1984].

Grimsted, P. K., *The Foreign Ministers of Alexander I: Political Attitudes and the Conduct of Russian Diplomacy, 1801–1825* (Berkeley: University of California Press, 1969).

Haggenmacher, P., 'Sur un passage obscur de Grotius', *Revue d'histoire du droit*, 51 (1983).

Hanioğlu, M. Ş., *The Young Turks in Opposition* (New York: Oxford University Press, 1995).

Harris, D., *Britain and the Bulgarian Horrors of 1876* (Chicago: University of Chicago Press, 1939).

Hartigan, R. S., 'Noncombatant Immunity: Reflections on its Origins and Present Status', *Review of Politics*, 29:2 (1967).

Heraclides, A., 'Humanitarian Intervention in the 19th Century: The Heyday of a Controversial Concept', *Global Society: Journal of Interdisciplinary International Relations*, 26:2 (2012).

Heraclides, A., 'Humanitarian Intervention in International Law 1830–1939: The Debate', *Journal of the History of International Law*, 16 (2014).

Herring, G. C., *From Colony to Superpower: U.S. Foreign Relations Since 1776* (New York: Oxford University Press, 2008).

Hinde, W., *George Canning* (London: Collins, 1973).

Hinsley, F. H., *Power and the Pursuit of Peace: Theory and Practice in the History of Relations Between States* (Cambridge: Cambridge University Press, 1963).

Hitti, P. K., *Lebanon in History* (London: Macmillan, 1967).

Hoffmann, S., 'The Politics and Ethics of Military Intervention', *Survival*, 37:4 (1995–96).

Holbraad, C., *The Concert of Europe: A Study in German and British International Theory 1815–1914* (London: Longman, 1970).

Jahn, B. 'Humanitarian Intervention – What's in a Name?', *International Politics*, 49:1 (2012).

Jelavich, B., *Russia's Balkan Entanglements 1806–1914* (Cambridge: Cambridge University Press, 1991).
Kant, I., 'Toward Perpetual Peace', in Immanuel Kant, *Practical Philosophy* (Cambridge: Cambridge University Press, 1996).
Keal, P., *European Conquest and the Rights of Indigenous Peoples: The Moral Backwardness of International Society* (Cambridge: Cambridge University Press, 2003).
Kingsbury, B. and A. Roberts, 'Introduction', in H. Bull, B. Kingsbury and A. Roberts (eds), *Hugo Grotius and International Relations* (Oxford: Clarendon Press, 1990).
Knudsen, T. B., 'The History of Humanitarian Intervention: The Rule or the Exception?', 50th ISA Annual Convention, New York, 15–18 February 2009.
Koskenniemi, M., *The Gentle Civilizer of Nations: The Rise and Fall of International Law 1870–1960* (Cambridge: Cambridge University Press, 2002).
Ković, M., *Disraeli and the Eastern Question* (Oxford: Oxford University Press, 2011).
Laberge, P., 'Humanitarian Intervention: Three Ethical Positions', *Ethics and International Affairs*, 9 (1995).
LaFeber, W., *The New Empire: An Interpretation of American Expansion, 1860–1898* (Ithaca: Cornell University Press, 1963).
Lauterpacht, H., 'The Grotian Tradition in International Law', *British Year Book of International Law*, 23 (1946).
Lederer, I. J., 'Russia and the Balkans', in I. J. Lederer (ed.), *Russian Foreign Policy: Essays in Historical Perspective* (New Haven: Yale University Press, 1967).
Lillich, R. B., 'Forcible Self-Help by States to Protect Human Rights', *Iowa Law Review*, 53 (1967–68).
Linderman, G. F., *The Mirror of War: American Society and the Spanish-American War* (Ann Arbor: University of Michigan Press, 1974).
Little, R., *Intervention: External Involvement in Civil Wars* (London: Martin Robertson, 1975).
Macfie, A. L., *The Eastern Question, 1774–1923* (London: Longman, 1996) [1989].
MacKenzie, D., 'Russia's Balkan Policies Under Alexander II, 1855–1881', in H. Ragsdale and V. N. Ponomarev (eds), *Imperial Russian Foreign Policy* (New York: Woodrow Wilson Center Press and Cambridge University Press, 1993).
Malanczuk, P., *Humanitarian Intervention and the Legitimacy of the Use of Force* (Amsterdam: Het Spinhuis, 1993).
Ma'oz, M., *Ottoman Reform in Geographical Syria and Palestine, 1840–1861: The Impact of the Tanzimat on Politics and Society* (Oxford: Clarendon Press, 1968).
Marriott, J. A. R., *The Eastern Question: An Historical Study in European Diplomacy* (Oxford: Clarendon Press, 1918).
McCartney, P. T., *Power and Progress: American National Identity, the War of 1898, and the Rise of American Imperialism* (Baton Rouge: Louisiana University Press, 2006).
Meron, M., 'Common Rights of Mankind in Gentili, Grotius and Suarez', *American Journal of International Law*, 85:1 (1991).
Mill, J. S., 'A Few Words on Non-Intervention', in J. S. Mill, *Dissertations and Discussions: Political, Philosophical and Historical* (London: Longmans, Green, Reader, and Dyer, 1867), vol. III.
Miller, K. E., 'John Stuart Mill's Theory of International Relations', *Journal of the History of Ideas*, 22:4 (1961).
Molen, G. H. J. van der, *Alberto Gentili and the Development of International Law: His Life and Times* (Amsterdam: H. J. Paris, 1937).

Morgan, H. W., *America's Road to Empire: The War with Spain and Overseas Expansion* (New York: John Wiley and Sons, 1965).
Mowat, R. B., *A History of European Diplomacy, 1815–1914* (London: Edward Arnold, 1922).
Nardin, T., 'The Moral Basis for Humanitarian Intervention', in A. F. Lang (ed.), *Just Intervention* (Washington, DC: Georgetown University Press, 2003).
Neumann, I. B., *Uses of the Other: 'The East' in European Identity Formation* (Minneapolis: University of Minnesota Press, 1999).
Nussbaum, A., 'Just War – A Legal Concept?', *Michigan Law Review*, 42:3 (1943).
Offner, J. L., *An Unwanted War: The Diplomacy of the United States and Spain Over Cuba, 1895–1898* (Chapel Hill: University of North Carolina Press, 1992).
Olson, W. C. and A. J. R. Groom, *International Relations Then and Now* (London: Routledge, 1991).
Orakhelashvili, A., 'The Idea of European International Law', *European Journal of International Law*, 17:2 (2006).
Pagden, A., *The Enlightenment and Why It Still Matters* (New York: Random House, 2013).
Parekh, B., 'Rethinking Humanitarian Intervention', *International Political Science Review*, 18:1 (1997).
Pavlowitch, S. K., *A History of the Balkans, 1804–1945* (London: Longman, 1999).
Pérez, L. A., Jr, *The War of 1898: The United States and Cuba in History and Historiography* (Chapel Hill: University of North Carolina Press, 1998).
Pitts, J., 'Boundaries of Victorian International Law', in D. Bell (ed.), *Victorian Visions of Global Order: Empire and International Relations in Nineteenth-Century Political Thought* (Cambridge: Cambridge University Press, 2007).
Pratt, J. W., *A History of United States Foreign Policy* (Englewood Cliffs: Prentice-Hall, 1965, 2nd edition) [1955].
Prokesch-Osten, A. von, *Istoria tis epanastaseos ton Ellinon kata tou Othomanikou kratous en etei 1821* [History of the revolution of the Greeks against the Ottoman state in the year 1821] (Athens: Athinas, 1868, trans. from the German by G. E. Antoniades) [1867].
Prousis, T. C., *Russian Society and the Greek Revolution* (DeKalb: Northern Illinois University Press, 1994).
Puryear, V. J., *France and the Levant: From the Bourbon Restoration to the Peace of Kutiah* (Hamden: Archon Books, 1968).
Ragsdale, H. and V. N. Ponomarev (eds), *Imperial Russian Foreign Policy* (New York: Woodrow Wilson Center Press and Cambridge University Press, 1993).
Ramsbotham, O. and T. Woodhouse, *Humanitarian Intervention: A Reconceptualization* (Cambridge: Polity Press, 1996).
Rieber, A. J., 'Alexander II: A Revisionist View', *Journal of Modern History*, 43:1 (1971).
Rodogno, D., 'The "Principles of Humanity" and the European Powers' Intervention in Ottoman Lebanon and Syria in 1860–1861', in B. Simms and D. J. B. Trim (eds), *Humanitarian Intervention: A History* (Cambridge: Cambridge University Press, 2011).
Rodogno, D., *Against Massacre: Humanitarian Intervention in the Ottoman Empire, 1815–1914. The Emergence of a European Concept and International Practice* (Princeton: Princeton University Press, 2012).
Russell, F. H., *The Just War in the Middle Ages* (Cambridge: Cambridge University Press, 1975).
Salibi, K. S., *The Modern History of Lebanon* (New York: Frederick A. Praeger, 1965).
Schmitt, C., *The Concept of the Political* (New Brunswick: Rutgers University Press, 1976 translated from the German with Introduction and notes by G. Schwab) [1932].
Schulz, M., 'The Guarantees of Humanity: The Concert of Europe and the Origins of the

Select bibliography

Russo-Ottoman War of 1877', in B. Simms and D. J. B. Trim (eds), *Humanitarian Intervention: A History* (Cambridge: Cambridge University Press, 2011).
Seton-Watson, R. W., *Disraeli, Gladstone and the Eastern Question* (London: Frank Cass, 1962) [1935].
Shannon, R., *Gladstone and the Bulgarian Agitation 1876* (London: Thomas Nelson and Sons, 1963).
Simms, B. and D. J. B. Trim (eds), *Humanitarian Intervention: A History* (Cambridge: Cambridge University Press, 2011).
Smith, E. K., '"A Question from Which We Could Not Escape": William McKinley and the Decision to Acquire the Philippines', *Diplomatic History*, 9:4 (1985).
Smith, J., *The Spanish-American War: Conflict in the Caribbean and the Pacific, 1895–1902* (London: Longman, 1994).
St Clair, W., *That Greece Might Still Be Free: The Philhellenes in the War of Independence* (Cambridge: Open Book Publishers, 2008) [1973].
Stavrianos, L. S., *The Balkans Since 1453* (London: Hurst, 2000) [1958].
Stojanovic, M. D., *The Great Powers and the Balkans, 1875–1878* (Cambridge: Cambridge University Press, 1939).
Sumner, B. H., *Russia and the Balkans, 1870–1880* (Oxford: Clarendon Press, 1937).
Susumu Y., 'Civilization and International Law in Japan During the Meiji Era (1868–1912)', *Hitotsubashi Journal of Law and Politics*, 24 (1996).
Sylvest, C., *British Liberal Internationalism, 1830–1930: Making Progress?* (Manchester: Manchester University Press, 2009).
Temperley, H., *The Foreign Policy of Canning 1822–1827* (London: Frank Cass, 1966) [1925].
Tesón, F., *Humanitarian Intervention: An Inquiry into Law and Morality* (New York: Transnational, 1997) [1988].
Tibawi, A. L., *A Modern History of Syria Including Lebanon and Palestine* (London: Macmillan, 1969).
Todorov, T., *The Conquest of America: The Question of the Other* (New York: Harper Perennial, 1992) [1982].
Trask, D. F., *The War with Spain in 1898* (New York: Macmillan, 1981).
Trim, D. J. B., '"If a Prince Use Tyrannie towards his People": Intervention on Behalf of Foreign Populations in Early Modern Europe', in B. Simms and D. J. B. Trim (eds), *Humanitarian Intervention: A History* (Cambridge: Cambridge University Press, 2011).
Tuck, R., *The Rights of War and Peace: Political Thought and the International Order from Grotius to Kant* (Oxford: Oxford University Press, 1999).
Varouxakis, G., 'John Stuart Mill on Intervention and Non-Intervention', *Millennium: Journal of International Studies*, 16:1 (1997).
Varouxakis, G., *Liberty Abroad: J. S. Mill and International Relations* (Oxford: Oxford University Press, 2013).
Vincent, R. J., *Nonintervention and International Order* (Princeton: Princeton University Press, 1974).
Walzer, M., *Just and Unjust Wars: A Moral Argument with Historical Illustrations* (New York: Basic Books, 1977).
Walzer, M., 'The Politics of Rescue', *Social Research*, 62:1 (1995).
Wheeler, N. J., *Saving Strangers: Humanitarian Intervention in International Society* (Oxford: Oxford University Press, 2000).
Williams, H., *Kant and the End of War: A Critique of Just War Theory* (Basingstoke: Palgrave Macmillan, 2012).

Woodhouse, C. M., *The Greek War of Independence* (London: Hutchinson's University Library, 1952).
Woodhouse, C. M., *Capodistria: The Founder of Greek Independence* (London: Oxford University Press, 1973).
Wortman, R., *Scenarios of Power: Myth and Ceremony in Russian Monarchy* (Princeton: Princeton University Press, 1995), vol. II.

Index

Abdulhamid II, Sultan 47–8, 102
　Balkan crisis (1875–78), Bulgarian case 157–8, 160
Abdulmecid, Sultan 47–8
　Lebanon/Syria massacres 138–40, 142–3
Abiew, Francis Kofi 162
Abraham, A. J. 138
abuse problem (in humanitarian intervention) 2, 5, 18, 22, 58, 63, 66, 68, 70–2, 124, 148, 214–15, 225–6
Adams, John Quincy 110, 199, 228
admission into family of nations and international law (recognition, entry) 34–5, 40, 42–3, 46
　China 37–8, 40
　Japan 37, 42–3
　Ottoman Empire 35–6, 43, 46–7
　see also family of nations; international law; standard of civilization
Adrianople, Treaty of (September 1829) 121
　see also Russo-Ottoman War (1828–29)
Aguinaldo, Emilio 209, 211
Ahmed Pasha 137–8, 140, 145n.34
Akarli, Engin Deniz 138
Aksakov, Ivan Sergeyevich 44, 173, 177, 180–1, 184, 186, 194n.81
Alexander I, Tsar 105
　acute dilemma for Russia 108
　against Greek struggle for independence 107–9, 111
　support for Greeks 108, 114
Alexander II, Tsar 171, 176, 182, 186, 188, 179, 192n.35, 193n.42, 228
　Balkan crisis (1875–78) 149, 170, 173, 175–7
　Bulgarians 174–7
　Pan-Slavism (against) 173, 175–6, 179

Russo-Ottoman War (1878–79)
　noble motives 175–8, 179
　noble motives questioned 187–9
　Serb-Ottoman War (1876) 173–5
Alexander III, Tsar 173, 175, 179
Alexandrowicz, Charles 31
Ali Pasha, Mehmed Emin, Grand Vizier 47, 139, 141
Ali Pasha, of Yannina, 107, 112
altruism 1, 101, 177, 178, 226
American Indians 15, 20, 21, 24n.12, 32, 200, 206
Amos, Sheldon 60 (table 4.1), 66
anarchy 5, 12, 20, 68, 82–3, 116, 209
Ancillon, Friedrich 44, 126n.29
Andrassy, Gyula
　Balkan crisis (1875–78) 149, 151, 156, 161, 172, 174, 178
Andrassy Note 149, 172
Anghie, Antony 2
Annan, Kofi, UN Secretary-General 3–4
April Uprising (Bulgarian) (April–May 1876) 150–1
　see also Bulgarian atrocities; Bulgarian case
Aquinas, Thomas 15
Argyle, Duke of see Campbell, George
Ariga Nagao 42
Aristotle 14, 24n.12, 27n.49
Arntz, Egide R.N. 59, 60 (table 4.1), 65, 67–8, 148
atrocity(ies), barbarity(ies), crimes, extermination, horror(s), massacre(s), slaughter 3–5, 12, 19, 38, 58, 63, 65–7, 71, 82, 87, 101, 124, 161–2, 214, 226–7
　against Christians by Muslims or Ottomans 44, 46–7, 124

Druzes or Muslims against Maronites and other Christians 137–40, 142
Ottomans against Bulgarians 45, 148, 150–5, 157, 172, 174–5, 183–5, 189
Ottomans (or Muslims) against Greeks 108–10, 114, 121, 123
against Muslims/Ottomans by Christians 47, 102, 124, 190, 226
Bulgarians against Ottomans 150–2
Greeks against Muslims/Ottomans 107, 109–10
Maronites against Druzes 137
Spaniards against American Indians 15, 20–2
Augustine, Saint 15
Austin, John 57, 87
Austria 44, 90, 105, 107–8, 112, 117–18, 120–1, 137, 141
see also Metternich, Klemens von
Austria-Hungary 71, 105, 135, 148–9, 151, 158, 161, 170, 179, 180, 205–6
see also Andrassy, Gyula; Andrassy Note
Avineri, Shlomo 85
'Awn, Bishop 137–8

Balkan crisis (1875–78) 45, 47, 148–51, 171–4
barbarians or barbarous (Asian and African peoples, states, countries, nations) 17, 20, 31–2, 34–6, 38, 58, 66, 72–3, 88–9, 189
see also civilized (states, nations, peoples); civilized–barbarians (uncivilized, non-civilized) dichotomy; civilized–barbarians (uncivilized, non-civilized)–savages distinction; civilizing mission; savages; uncivilized or non-civilized
barbarians (non-Chinese peoples) 39–41
Western barbarians 40–2
barbarization rumour (Greek case) 113–14, 122
see also Britain; Canning, George; Ibrahim Pasha; Lieven, Christopher; Russia; Stratford Canning
Baring, Walter 150–1
Barker, Ernest 27n.48
Barrington-Kennett, Vincent 156
Bass, Gary J., ix, x, 143, 162, 214, 226
Bazyler, Michael J. 162
Beautfort d'Hautpoul, General 140
Behuniak, Thomas E. 162

Beisner, Robert 210–11
belligerency (belligerents)106, 112
Bemis, Samuel Flagg 200, 202, 213
Bentham, Jeremy 33, 110, 228
Benton, Elbert 213
Berlin, Congress of (June–July 1878) 161–3, 179
Berlin, Treaty of (July 1878) 161–3, 179
Berlin Memorandum (May 1876) 149, 152, 172
Bernard, Mountague 60 (table 4.1), 64, 88, 135
Berner, Albrecht Friedrich 60 (table 4.1), 63
Beza, Theodore 19
Bismarck, Otto von 35, 149, 156, 161, 190, 228
Blaine, James 199, 201
Blake, Robert 155
Blanco, Rámon, General 204–5
Blanquière, Edward 117, 128n.76
Bluntschli, Johann Caspar 35, 41, 42, 52n.58, 57, 60 (table 4.1), 65–6, 72–3, 76n.59, 80n.160, 142, 148, 162
Bodin, Jean 17–18, 19–20, 21, 27n.61
Bonfils, Henri 34–5, 38, 60–1 (table 4.1), 66, 72, 148
Borchard, Edwin M. 61–2 (table 4.1), 68
Botev, Christo 150, 172
Brierly, James Leslie 62 (table 4.1), 70
Bright, John 33, 85, 155
Britain, British 33, 35, 38–41, 44–6, 48, 57, 71, 86, 105, 107–18, 120, 121, 123, 135–7, 139–42, 149–63, 170, 175–6, 183, 185, 206, 225–6
Balkan crisis (1875–78), Bulgarian atrocities 149–63
conflict with Russia 152–3, 156, 159–61
humanitarian aid to the Balkans and the Caucasus (1876–78) 156
intelligentsia and Bulgarian atrocities and Russia 155
public and press on Bulgarian atrocities and Russia 153–5, 159
support of Ottoman Empire 149, 151–3, 155–63
see also Derby, Lord; Disraeli, Benjamin; Elliot, Henry; Salisbury, Lord; Victoria, Queen
Greek War of Independence, 107–18, 121, 123
barbarization rumour 113–14

Index

British intellectuals and Greek War of Independence 110
  humanitarian concern 108–9, 113–14, 116
  see also Canning, George; Castlereagh, Viscount; London, Treaty of; Navarino, Battle of; St Petersburg Protocol; Wellington, Duke of
  Lebanon and Syria massacres 139–42
  see also Palmerston, Lord; Russell, Lord John
  territorial integrity of Ottoman Empire 44, 152, 158
Brownlie, Ian 123, 142, 214
Bryan, William Jennings 210–11
Bulgaria 175, 178–9, 182–3
Bulgarian atrocities 150–7, 162, 172, 175–7, 182–6
  see also Britain; Russia
Bulgarian case (1870s) 172, 175, 177–9, 182–5, 188, 190, 226–7
  Bulgarian autonomy 157, 160, 175
  Bulgarian independence 178, 182
  see also Britain; Russia
Bulgarian Revival 150
Burgess, John 201
Burke, Edmund 23–4, 33, 44, 83
Byron, Lord 110, 228
  Greek War of Independence 110, 112–14, 128n.76

Calhoun, William 204
Calvo, Carlos (Charles) 11, 57, 60–1 (table 4.1), 122
Campbell, George (Duke of Argyle) 153–4
Canning, George 105, 135, 228
  Greek War of Independence 111–17, 119–220
    ambivalence toward Greeks 111
    barbarization rumour 113–14
    gradual support for Greeks 111–17, 119–20
    London Treaty 116–17
    St Petersburg Protocol 114
  see also Britain
Cánovas, Antonio 198–9, 203–4
Capodistrias, Ioannis
  and Greek War of Independence 44, 105–6, 108–11, 117, 119–21, 191n.4
Carlyle, Thomas 153, 155, 183
Carnazza Amari, Giuseppe 38, 60–1 (table 4.1), 66, 87, 148

Carnegie, Andrew 200, 210, 213
Castlereagh, Viscount 44, 105, 107, 108–9, 111, 124n.3, 135, 228
  Greek War of Independence 107–9
Cavaglieri, Arrigo 61–2 (table 4.1), 68, 70, 87
Cavallar, Georg 84
Céspedes, Carlos Manuel de 198
Charles V, King and Holy Roman Emperor 21, 24n.12
Chateaubriand, François-René 44, 110, 115, 134, 228
Cherniaev, Victor 151, 173, 182
China 4, 33, 37–41, 73
  reaction to contact with the West 39–41
  see also barbarians (non-Chinese peoples)
Chomsky, Noam 2
Christian society of states (nations) 31, 35–8, 44, 59, 63, 72, 121, 136
Christianity 14, 18, 32, 34–6, 38, 42, 110, 185, 188
Christians 14, 18–20, 34–6, 44–7, 65–6, 69, 71–3, 87, 107–8, 115, 121–2, 124, 136–41, 143, 163
  Balkan (in Ottoman Empire) 152–3, 157–8, 162, 171–7, 189–90
  Catholic(s) 14, 154
  Christian Arabs 136–7
  Orthodox 106, 108, 155, 170, 181
Cicero 14, 17
civil war(s) 12, 59, 63, 65–7, 70, 84, 89–91, 105, 135, 226
civilization (European civilization) 31–3, 36–40, 43, 47, 110, 115, 122–3, 139–40, 169–70, 181, 185, 207–8, 226
  Christian 31–2, 35–6, 157
  European (and Christian) 34–6, 44, 124
  non-European
    Chinese 38–9, 41–2
  see also standard of civilization
civilized (states, nations, peoples) 31–8, 42, 89, 109, 177, 189, 227
civilized–barbarians (uncivilized, non-civilized) dichotomy 31–2, 66, 71–3, 89, 124, 189, 226–7
  see also barbarians or barbarous; civilized (states, nations, peoples); civilizing mission; uncivilized or non-civilized

civilized–barbarians (uncivilized, non-civilized)–savages distinction 32, 35, 227
  see also barbarians or barbarous; civilized (states, nations, peoples); civilizing mission; savages; uncivilized or non-civilized
civilized states' intervention in non-civilized states 65–6, 71–3
civilizing mission 31, 34, 38, 46, 89, 181, 190, 201, 208–10, 227
  see also barbarians or barbarous; civilized (states, nations, peoples); civilized–barbarians (uncivilized, non-civilized) dichotomy; civilized–barbarians (uncivilized, non-civilized)–savages distinction; savages; uncivilized or non-civilized
Clayton, Gerald David 154
Cleveland, Grover, President 203–4, 210, 213
Cobden, Richard 33, 44, 45, 81, 85–7, 89, 134, 135
  British Empire 33
  non-intervention 81, 85–7, 89, 134–5
  Ottoman Empire 44–5
Cochrane, Lord 115, 117
Codrington, Admiral Edward 115, 118–19
colonialism 17, 22, 33, 83, 85, 89, 210
Committee of Union and Progress see Young Turks
communitarianism/communitarians 2, 81, 87, 91n.4
Concert of Europe, 5, 46, 48, 162
  see also Congress system
Condorcet, Nicholas de 33, 134
Congress system 105, 106, 108
  see also Concert of Europe; Holy Alliance
Constant, Benjamin 33, 110
Constantinople, Conference of (December 1876–January 1877) 157–8, 162, 175, 176
  see also Ignatiev, Nikolay Pavlovich; Salisbury, Lord
cosmopolitanism/cosmopolitans 2, 81, 83, 86–7, 91n.3, 91n.6, 172
counter-intervention 64, 71, 86–7, 90, 134
Crawley, Charles William 117
Creasy, Edward Shepherd 60 (table 4.1), 66
Crimean War (1853–56) 43, 58, 137, 171, 178–80
crimes see atrocity(ies)
crimes against humanity 4, 5

Cuba 197–215
  struggle for independence 198, 201, 203, 206–7, 211–12
  against Cuban independence (US) 199, 203, 204–5, 207, 210, 212–13
  see also Estrada Palma, Tomás; García, Calixto; Gómez, Máximo; Maceo, Antonio; Martí, José
  see also Spain; US
Cubans 198, 200–1, 203–8, 210–11, 213, 226

Danilevskiy, Nikolay Yakovlevich 180–1
Darwin, Charles 50n.21, 155, 201
Davis, Cushman Kellogg 201, 208
Day, William R. 197, 208, 212
de Rigny, Admiral Henri, 115, 118
Decembrists 111, 114, 181
Delacroix, Eugène 109–10, 114
Derby, Lord 44, 149, 152, 156–61, 174
  Balkan crisis (1875–78), Bulgarian atrocities 149, 152, 156–61, 174
Despagnet, Frantz 61 (table 4.1), 68, 72, 137
Dewey, Commodore George 202, 207
Dickinson, Edwin DeWitt 62 (table 4.1), 72
Diderot, Denis 31, 33
Dilke, Charles 32, 159
disinterestedness clause (or self-denying clause) 58, 63, 69, 71–2, 101, 114, 122, 124, 140, 142–3, 207, 225
Disraeli, Benjamin 44, 149, 151–6, 158–61, 167n.106, 174, 176, 192n.35, 228
  Balkan crisis (1875–78), Bulgarian atrocities, 149, 151–6, 158–61
  Gladstone 154–5, 159
  Realpolitik 155
  Russia 152–3, 156, 159–61, 174, 176
  territorial integrity of Ottoman Empire 44, 152, 158
Dostoevsky, Fyodor 44, 183, 187–8, 190, 228
Douzinas, Costas 2
Drahomanov, Mikhail Petrovich 180–1, 188–9
Druzes 135–8, 141, 143, 145n.34
  see also Lebanon; Lebanon and Syria massacres
Dudley, Lord 116, 118
Dulles, Foster Rhea 208
Duplessis-Mornay, see Mornay
Dupuy de Lôme, Enrique 203, 205

Eastern Question, the 44, 69, 121, 149, 171, 175, 180, 181–2

Index

'effusion of blood', shedding of blood, bloodshed 58, 63, 71, 101, 116, 118, 122–3, 140, 174, 187, 207, 214, 225–6
Elliot, Henry 45, 151–2, 157–8, 165n.27
Ellis, Anthony 89
Engelhardt, Édouard Philippe 45, 60–1 (table 4.1), 67, 72
Esmein, Adhémar 18
Estrada Palma, Tomás 203–4, 211
ethnic cleansing 3–5, 190
Eurocentrism 31–2, 227
see also civilization; civilized–barbarians (uncivilized, non-civilized) dichotomy; civilized–barbarians (uncivilized, non-civilized)–savages distinction; civilizing mission; standard of civilization
extermination see atrocity(ies)

family of nations (international society) 32–3, 36–7, 39, 40, 42–3
see also international law; standard of civilization
Farah, Caesar E., 138
Farley, James Lewis 156
Fauchille, Paul 62 (table 4.1), 69, 71
Fenwick, Charles G., 62 (table 4.1), 69–70, 162, 197–8, 214
Ferguson, Adam 31
Field, David Dudley 38
Finnemore, Martha ix, 133n.179, 162
Fiore, Pasquale 36, 51.n.68 and n.69, 60 (table 4.1), 64–7, 73n.9, 87, 148
Fiske, John 201
Floeckher, Adolphe de 61 (table 4.1), 68, 72
Foner, Philip 202
Fonteyne, Jean-Paul L. 162, 214
France, French 2, 3, 18–19, 33, 38, 40–1, 43–4, 48, 83, 105, 107, 110–11, 113, 115–21, 123, 134–9, 140–3, 149, 153, 158, 161, 170–1, 205–6, 208–9, 225–6
Greek War of Independence 105, 107, 110–11, 113, 115–21, 123
Battle of Navarino 118
expeditionary force against Ibrahim 119–20
major figures supporting Greeks 110, 115
neutrality 107, 115
support of Greeks 116–17, 119–20
Lebanon and Syria massacres 138–42
expeditionary force 140, 143
humanitarian concern 138–9
instrumental motives 141–2
public and press 138–9, 142
see also Napoleon III, Emperor; Thouvenel, Édouard Antoine de
Franck, Thomas M. 142, 214, 227
Freeman, Edward Augustus 153, 155–6, 184
French Revolution (1789) 23, 82–3, 106, 134, 159
Froude, James Anthony 155, 183–4
Frye, William P. 201, 208
Fuad Pasha, Mehmed 47–8, 139–43
Fukuzawa Yukichi 42
Funck-Brentano, Théophile 60–1 (table 4.1), 66, 72

Ganji, Manouchehr 162
García, Calixto 198, 203, 211–12
Gareis, Karl von 60–1 (table 4.1), 68
Garnett, George 19, 27n.48
Garshin, Vsevolod Mikhailovic, 188, 196n.123
genocide 2, 4–5, 83–4, 226
Gentili, Alberico 15–18, 20–1, 29n.86, n.98, 31
just war 15–16
precursor of idea of humanitarian intervention 16
war against tyranny 21
Germany 41, 71, 148, 149, 153, 158, 161, 205–6, 209, 210
Gertsen, Alexander Ivanovich 180–1
Giers, Nikolay Karlovich 173, 179, 188
Gladstone, William 36, 45–6, 64, 152–5, 159, 165n.51 and n.59, 183–4, 228
Bulgarian atrocities 153–5
Disraeli 153–5, 159
morality in international politics 155
Ottoman expulsion from Bulgaria 154, 165–6n.59
Russia 159, 183–4
'Turks' 45–6
Glanville, Luke 17
Gobineau, Arthur de 32, 35
Godkin, Edward Lawrence 210
Gómez, Máximo 198, 203–4, 211–12
Gong, Gerrit W. 33
Gorchakov, Alexander Mikhailovich 139, 161, 171–2, 178–9, 191n.10, 192n.16, 228
Balkan crisis (1875–78) 149, 151, 153, 156, 158–9, 161, 170, 172–6
Britain 153, 156, 159
Pan-Slavism 153, 174, 178
Russo-Ottoman War 175–6
Serb-Ottoman War 173–4

Gordon, Colonel Thomas 109
Gould, Lewis L. 202
Greece 101–2, 111–12, 114, 119–23, 140, 151, 160–1, 171, 178
Greek case (1821–32) 47, 59, 69, 153, 176, 184, 226–7
Greek War of Independence 59, 65, 91, 105–24, 225
  Greek autonomy (tributary of Ottoman Empire) 110, 114, 116, 119, 121, 123
  Greek independence/independent Greek state 106–7, 111–13, 115, 117, 119, 121–3
  against Greek independence 117, 119, 121
  see also Alexander I, Tsar; Austria; Britain; Canning, George; Capodistrias, Ioannis; Castlereagh, Viscount; France; Mavrokordatos, Alexander; Metternich, Klemens von; Nicholas I, Tsar; Ottoman Empire; philhellenism; Russia; Ypsilantis, Alexander
Greeks 59, 106–15, 117–18, 120–3, 153, 176, 184
Greeks, ancient (Greek antiquity) 14–15, 17, 36, 110
Greeks as descendents of ancient Greeks 110, 116, 119, 121
Greene, General Francis Vinton 178, 209
Gregorios V, Patriarch 107–8
Grewe, Wilhelm G. 17, 22, 27n.61, 58, 162
Grotius, Hugo 15–18, 20–3, 28n.73, 29n.98, 31, 82
  just war 15–16
  precursor of idea of humanitarian intervention 16
  war against tyranny 17, 21–2
Guilleminot, Armand Charles 117, 119
Guizot, François 44–5, 134, 143n.2

Habermas, Jürgen 2
Haggenmacher, Peter 16, 29n.98
Hall, William Edward 12, 34, 41–2, 60–1 (table 4.1), 67
Halleck, Henry Wager 42, 60 (table 4.1), 64, 197
Hamilton, Captain G. W. 115, 117
Hamilton, Richard 202
Harcourt, William Vernon 60–1 (table 4.1), 64, 122–3, 155, 159, 184
Hastings, Captain Frank Abney 115
Hay, John 200–1, 208
Hearst, William Randolph 201, 217n.38

Heffter, August Wilhelm 34, 42, 60 (table 4.1), 63
Hegel, Georg 81, 84–5
Heiberg, Johan 60 (table 4.1), 63
Herring, George 200
Hershey, Amos S. 61–2 (table 4.1), 68, 197, 213
Higgins, Alexander Pearce 62 (table 4.1), 70
Hitti, Philip K. 138
Hoar, George Frisbie 210, 213
Hobbes, Thomas 1, 19
Hobson, John A. 33, 167n.102
Hodges, Henry Green 61–2 (table 4.1), 68
Holly Alliance 5–6, 8
  see also Alexander I, Tsar; Congress system
Holyoake, George 159, 167n.101
Hornung, Joseph 38, 60 (table 4.1), 67, 71
horrors *see* atrocity(ies)
Hotman, François 19
Hsü, Immanuel C.Y. 40
Hugo, Victor 110, 114, 228
human rights 35–6, 52n.69, 58, 72, 81, 83–4, 186
  systematic (or massive) violation of, 1–2, 4–5
Hyde, Charles Cheney 61–2 (table 4.1), 68

Ibrahim Pasha 112–15, 117–20
  barbarization rumour 113–14
  Greek campaign 112–15, 117–18
  onslaught against Greeks 114, 117–18
Ignatiev, Nikolay Pavlovich 44, 152, 157–8, 160, 170–6, 178–9, 191n.10, 192n.16
imperialism/imperialist(s) 1, 2, 17, 33–4, 42–3, 45, 85, 89, 208, 226–7, 229
  Russian 181
  US 200, 202, 208–9, 210–12, 214, 215
  anti-imperialism 208, 210–11
independence 2, 11, 23, 32, 42, 47, 58, 65, 71, 88, 148, 226
independent state(s) 23, 36, 44, 65, 67, 69, 70, 86
Innocent IV, Pope 17–18, 20, 22
Institut de droit international 34–8, 41, 43, 57
international law 2, 11, 12, 14–15, 23, 32–8, 40–3, 46, 48, 57–73, 68–9, 81, 87, 197, 213
  moral conscience of mankind 57, 73n.8 and 9
international law and humanitarian intervention 57–73, 225

Index

intervention
　collective intervention 5, 65, 69, 87, 123, 142, 225
　illegitimacy of 66–7
　legitimacy of 2, 4, 58, 63, 65–6
　right to 16, 65, 162
　see also non-intervention
Islam 45, 47–8, 135, 180
　see also Muslims
Italian independence and unification 58, 86, 135, 142
Italy 38, 46, 86, 149, 153, 158, 161, 172
Izzet Molâ 120

Japan 32–3, 37, 39, 41–3, 209, 210
　reaction to contact with the West 41–3
Jefferson, President Thomas 110, 199
Jomini, Alexander Genrikhovich 173, 176, 179, 183, 188
just cause (for war or intervention) 6, 14–16, 122
　unjust cause 16
just war, just war doctrine 5, 14–16, 187
　jus ad bellum 14
　jus in bello 14, 16

Kaneko Kentaro 43
K'ang Yu-wa 41
Kant, Emmanuel 11, 31, 33, 81–4, 85–6, 91n.3 and 6, 92n.8, 92n.19
　intervention in genocides implicit in Kant? 82–4
　non-intervention 81
　exception to 82
Karatheodori Pasha, Alexander 48, 161
Karavelov, Lyuben 150, 172, 182
Kebedgy, Michel 60–2 (table 4.1), 67, 71
Kent, James 34, 42, 60 (table 4.1), 197
Khurshid Pasha 137–8, 140
Kipling, Rudyard 208
Kireeva Novikova, see Novikova
Knudsen, Tonny Brems ix, 162, 214, 227–8
Komarovskiy, Leonid 60–1 (table 4.1), 66
Koskenniemi, Martti 57
Kosovo, NATO intervention 2–5, 226, 228
Kouchner, Bernard 2
Kung, Prince Yixin 40–1
Kuo Sung-too 40

Laberge, Pierre 83–4
Lafayette, Marquis de 115, 135
LaFeber, Walter 202, 217n.31

Lamartine, Alphonse de 44, 135, 136
Languet, Hubert 18–19, 27n.48
Lapradelle, Albert de 61–2 (table 4.1), 68, 214
Las Casas, Bartolomé de 15, 20–1, 24–5n.12, 31, 199, 206
last resort
　for humanitarian intervention 5–6
　for just war 5–6, 14, 16, 169
Latin America 111, 198, 202, 214, 227
Lauterpacht, Hersch 7n.12, 16, 22, 62 (table 4.1), 69–70
Lavalette, Charles Marquis de 138
Lawrence, Thomas Joseph 61–2 (table 4.1), 68, 123, 142
Layard, Austen Henry 45, 158, 166n.85
Le Fur, Louis 61–2 (table 4.1), 68, 214
Lebanon 47, 134–43, 225
Lebanon and Syria massacres (1860) 137–9
　European reaction 137–41
　local Ottoman authorities 137–8
　Ottoman reaction 139–41
　settlement 141
　see also Britain; Druzes; France; Maronites; Napoleon III, Emperor; Thouvenel, Édouard Antoine de
Lee, Fitzhugh 204, 212
Leo XIII, Pope 206
Levski, Vasil 150, 172
Liddon, Henry 154–5
Lieven, Christopher 108, 113–14, 116
Lillich, Richard B. 7n.19, 214
Lin, Tse-hsu 41
Linden, Harry van der 83
Linderman, Gerald 202
Lindsay, Robert Loyd (Lord Wantage) 156
Lingelbach, William Ezra 61–2 (table 4.1), 68
Liszt, Franz von 61 (table 4.1), 68
Lloyd George, David 46
Lodge, Henry Cabot 199, 201, 206, 209–10, 212
London ambassadors conference, London Protocol (March 1877) 158, 175–6
　see also Ignatiev, Nikolay Pavlovich; Russia; Shuvalov, Pyotr
London, Conference of (January–July 1827) 116
London, Treaty of (July 1827) 116–17, 119, 122, 225
　see also Britain; Canning, George; France; Greek War of Independence; Russia
Lorimer, James 35, 44, 46, 60 (table 4.1), 67, 72
Ludwig I, King 110, 121

Maceo, Antonio 198, 203
MacGahan, Januarius 151, 172, 175, 183
Madison, President James 110
Mahan, Alfred 201
Mahmud II, Sultan 47, 107–9, 112, 114, 117, 119–20
   Greek War of Independence
      Greek insurgents and *Rum* 107–9, 112, 117, 119–20
      Russia 107, 116, 120
Maison, General Nicolas 120
Mamiani, Terenzio 37–8, 60 (table 4.1), 63–4, 87
Mandelstam, André ix, 62 (table 4.1), 70, 162
Ma'oz, Moshe 138
Maronites 135–8, 140–2, 227
   see also Lebanon; Lebanon and Syria massacres
Marriott, J. A. R. 117
Martens, Fyodor Fyodorovich 36, 41, 46, 58, 60–1 (table 4.1), 65–6, 72, 74n.18, 76n.59, 148, 162, 177, 189
Martens clause 58
Martí, José 198–9, 203, 211, 218n.53
Martin, W. A. P. 41
Martínez de Campos, General Arsenio 198, 203
Marx, Karl 155, 166n.71
massacres *see* atrocity(ies)
Mavrokordatos, Alexander 112, 117
May, Ernest 202
Mazzini, Giuseppe 32, 44, 81, 86–7, 90, 134–5
   intervention 87
   nationalism, nationality principle 86
   non-intervention 86
McDougal, Myres S. 7n.19, 214
McKinley, William, President 200, 202, 204–9, 211, 213–14, 228
   Cuban question 200, 202, 204–8, 213
      against jingoism and war 200, 204–5
      humanitarian concern 200, 207–8, 213
      message to Congress for intervention 207
   Philippine question and reasons for annexation 208–9
mediation efforts 64, 91, 195, 124, 228
   Balkan crisis (1875–78) 148, 225
   Greek War of Independence 112–17, 119, 124
   Spain and Cubans 203, 215
Meron, Theodor 16, 21

Metternich, Klemens von 44, 105–8, 112, 117–18, 120–1, 190
   against Greek War of Independence 107, 112, 118
   support for Ottoman Empire against Greeks 44, 117, 120
Midhat Pasha, Grand Vizier Ahmed Shefik 48–9, 157
Miliutin, Dmitry 173, 175, 176–7
Mill, John Stuart 32, 35–6, 81, 86–91, 91n.4, 95n.97 and 103, 96n.132, 122, 134–5
   intervention, reasons for 89–91
      counter-intervention 90
      humanitarian reasons 90–1
      national liberation movements 88, 90–1
      protracted civil wars 90–1
   non-intervention, reasons for 88–9
Miller, Alexei 181
Miller, Orest 181, 184
Mirabeau, Victor 31
Molen, Gezina H. J. van der 16, 29n.98
monarchomach(s) 17–20
   see also Beza, Theodore; Hotman, François; Languet, Hubert; Mornay, Philippe de
Monroe, President James 110
Monroe Doctrine 110, 197–8, 214–15
Montenegro 102, 148, 151, 156–7, 160–1, 172–5, 178
Montesquieu 31–2
Moody, William Vaughn 210
Moore, John Bassett 61–2 (table 4.1), 197, 213–14
moral consciousness of humankind, shock to 15, 58, 69, 71, 228
More, Thomas 18
Moret, Segismundo 204–5
Morgan, H. Wayne 202
Mornay, Philippe de 19, 27n.48
Mowat, R. B. 226
Muhammad Ali Pasha (Mehmed Ali, Mehmet Ali) 112–13
Muslim(s) 34–5, 47, 71–2, 102, 107–8, 111, 113, 115, 122, 124, 136–8, 149–50, 160, 170, 184, 190, 199, 225
   infidels (non-Muslims) 44–5

Napoleon III, Emperor 135, 139–41, 171, 228
national self-determination 2, 86, 90, 135
nationality (nation) 86–7, 90, 171, 177
nationality(ies), principle of 86, 90, 106, 171, 180, 181

Index

natural law 14, 17–18, 23, 31–2, 36, 57
  positivism 31–2
Navarino, Battle of (October 1826) 64, 91, 117–20, 122, 149, 225
  reaction to 118–19
Nesselrode, Karl 105, 108, 114, 191n.4
Newman, Francis 33
Nicholas I, Tsar 114–16, 120, 228
non-Christian(s) (peoples, states, nations) 16, 3–6, 72
  infidels (non-Christians) 17–18, 20, 43
  see also Muslims
non-civilized see barbarians or barbarous; civilized (states, nations, peoples); civilized–barbarians (un-civilized, non-civilized) dichotomy; civilized–barbarians (uncivilized, non-civilized)–savages distinction; savages; uncivilized or non-civilized
non-intervention (principle) 11–12, 17, 23, 58–9, 63–6, 71, 81–2, 84–91, 105, 134–5, 197
Norton, Charles Eliot 210
Novikoff see Novikova, Olga
Novikov, Evgeny 141, 151, 174, 183
Novikova, Olga 154, 159, 183, 186
Nys, Ernest 35, 61–2 (table 4.1), 68–9, 73, 80n.163

Offner, John L. 202
Olney, Richard 203, 210
Oppenheim, Lassa F. L. 37, 61 (table 4.1), 68–9
Orford, Anne 2
Orientalism 35, 47, 170, 189, 227
Ortiz, Fernando 212
Ottoman Empire, Ottomans 32, 36–7, 39, 43–9, 52n.61, 55n.131, 71–3, 101–2, 106–21, 134–43, 148–52, 154–63, 170, 172–8, 180–3, 188–90, 226–7
  admission, inequality and intervention 36–7, 44–7, 72–3
  Bulgarian uprising and Ottoman onslaught 150–1
  Europe's options in dealing with Ottoman Empire 44–5
  Greek War of Independence 107–9, 110, 113–20
  Ottomans ('Turks') as the European 'Other' 43–4
  reaction to European initiatives in Balkan crisis (1875–78) 149, 157–8, 162
  reaction to interventions 47–8
  reaction to Lebanon/Syria massacres 139–41
  see also Abdulhamid II, Sultan; Abdulmecid, Sultan; Fuad Pasha, Mehmed; Mahmud II, Sultan; Pertev-Effendi; Tanzimat; territorial integrity

Palmerston, Lord 11, 86, 121, 135–6, 139, 228
  intervention 135
Pan-Slavism pan-Slavists, see Russian Pan-Slavism, Russian pan-Slavists
Paris, Conference of, Paris Treaty (US–Spain) (December 1898) 208, 210
Paris ambassadors conference, Paris Protocols (August 1860) 139–40, 225
Paris Peace Treaty (March 1865), Congress of Paris (February–March 1856) 35, 43–4, 46–7, 139, 151, 158, 172
  admission of Ottoman Empire in European family of nations 35, 43–4, 46
Pears, Edwin 152, 183
Pérez Jr, Louis A. 212, 217n.37
Pertev-Effendi 115, 117, 119, 120
philhellenism, philhellenes 109–11, 113, 115, 128n.84
  see also Greek War of Independence
Philippines, Filipinos
  Philippine independence, 211–12
  against Philippine independence see imperialism; US
  see also Aguinaldo, Emilio
  US (1898–99) 197, 202, 207–13
Phillimore, Robert 36, 60 (table 4.1), 63, 72, 76n.59, 135, 148, 154
Pillet, Antoine 61–2 (table 4.1), 68
Pipes, Richard 102
Pitts, Jennifer 33
Platt Amendment 211, 214
Polignac, Jules de 44, 116
political theory on non-intervention/intervention 81–91
Politis, Nicolas 62 (table 4.1), 70, 78n.131
Poros ambassadors conference (1828) 120
Porte (Sublime Porte) see Ottoman Empire
Portell Villá, Herminio 212
Potter, Pitman B. 62 (table 4.1), 70
Pradier-Fodéré, Paul Louis 60–1 (table 4.1), 67, 69, 72
Pratt, Julius W. 200, 202, 217n.31

Proctor, Redfield 205
Prussia 44, 71, 105, 107, 139, 141, 126n.29
publicists' and other scholars' assessment of character of interventions (humanitarian or not?)
  intervention in Bulgarian atrocities 162–3
  intervention in Cuba against Spain 213–14
  intervention in Greek War of Independence 121–3
  intervention in Lebanon–Syria massacres 142–3
Pufendorf, Samuel 23, 31
Pushkin, Alexander Sergeyevich 110, 171, 228
Pypin, Aleksander Nikolaevich 180–1

race(s) 32, 44, 45, 46, 71, 178, 189
  hierarchy of races 32, 50n.21
  inferior race(s) 32, 36, 38
  white (master) race 32, 200
    Anglo-Saxon race 200, 201, 208, 212
    Aryan (Germanic, Teutonic) race 32, 35, 50n.21, 201
Redslob, Robert 62 (table 4.1), 70
Reed, Thomas Brackett 206, 210
Reid, Whitelaw 201, 205, 208
Reisman, W. Michael 7n.19, 214
Renault, Louis 60–1 (table 4.1), 66–7, 69, 72, 148
responsibility to protect (R2P or RtoP) 4
Revue de droit international et de législation comparée 33, 35, 37, 43, 45, 57, 59, 66
Ribeaupierre, Count 115, 117
right intention (for war or intervention) 6, 15, 101
Rivier, Alphonse 36, 46, 61 (table 4.1), 68, 214
Rıza, Ahmed, 48–9
Rodley, Nigel S. 142, 214, 227
Rodogno, Davide ix, x, 55n.129, 136, 162, 165n.27
Roig de Leuchsenring, Emilio 212
Rolin-Jaequemyns, Gustave 57, 59, 60–1 (table 4.1), 65, 67–8, 72–3, 148
Roosevelt, Theodore 198, 200–2, 209, 211, 213
Root, Elihu 197, 206, 211, 215n.4
Rossi, Pellegrino 59, 60 (table 4.1), 143n.2
Rotteck, Herman Rodecker 60 (table 4.1), 63
Rougier, Antoine 12, 17, 61–2 (table 4.1), 68–9, 73, 80n.164, 101, 121–2, 137, 142–3, 162, 214
Rum (Rum millet) 106, 107–8, 119
Russell, Lord John 110, 139, 155

Russia 4, 38, 41, 44–5, 49, 90, 101, 105–21, 123, 136–7, 139–41, 148–53, 156–63, 169–84, 187–90, 191n.10, 192n14
  and 16, 193n.50, 194n.80, 215, 225, 226, 227
  Balkan crisis (1875–78), Bulgarians, Serb-Ottoman War, 148–53, 156–63, 169–84, 187–90
  Austro-Hungary, agreement with 151, 158
  Russian volunteers in Serbia (1876) 151, 173, 183, 185–8
  support for Balkan Slavs in Russian press 178, 182–4
  support for Balkan Slavs in Russian public 169–72, 174
  support for Balkan Slavs in Russian society 151, 169, 171–2, 180, 182, 184, 187
  Greek War of Independence 101, 105–21, 123
    see also Alexander I, Tsar; barbarization rumour; Capodistrias, Ioannis; Decembrists; Lieven, Christopher; Nesselrode, Karl; Nicholas I, Tsar; Russo-Ottoman War (1828–29)
  Russo-Ottoman War (1877–78)
    noble motives 175–8, 179
    noble motives questioned 187–9
    see also Alexander II, Tsar; Gorchakov, Alexander Mikhailovich; Ignatiev, Nikolay Pavlovich; Russian Pan-Slavism; Shuvalov, Pyotr
Russian Muslims 170, 190
Russian Pan-Slavism, Russian pan-Slavist(s) 44–5, 152–3, 170, 175–6, 179–82
  Balkan crisis (1875–78), Serb-Ottoman War, Bulgarians, Russo-Ottoman War 152–3, 163, 170–1, 173, 177–9
Russo-Ottoman War (1828–29) 120–1
  see also Adrianople, Treaty of
Russo-Ottoman War (April 1877–January 1878) 151, 156, 158, 176–8, 188, 190
  Britain, British public 158–60
  Russia, Russians 157, 160–1, 176–8, 188–9
  see also Alexander II, Tsar; Disraeli, Benjamin; San Stefano, Treaty of
Russophobia 155, 157, 170–1, 179–80
Rwanda genocide 3–4, 5, 226

Sabahaddin Bey, 48–9
Sadiq-Effendi 109, 112

Index

Sagasta, Práxedes Mateo 198–9, 204
Salibi, K. S. 138
Salisbury, Lord 156–7, 160–1, 175, 206
San Stefano, Treaty of (March 1878) 160–1, 163, 178, 179
  see also Ignatiev, Nikolay Pavlovich; Russo-Ottoman War (1877–78)
savages (African or Asian peoples) 32, 35, 38, 227
  see also barbarians or barbarous; civilized (states, nations, peoples); civilized–barbarians (uncivilized, non-civilized) dichotomy; civilized–barbarians (uncivilized, non-civilized)–savages distinction; civilizing mission; uncivilized or non-civilized
Scelle, Georges 46, 56n.142, 62 (table 4.1), 69, 78n.113
Schmitt, Carl 1, 22
Schurz, Carl 204, 210
Schuyler, Eugene 151, 175, 183
Séfériadès, Stélio 62 (table 4.1), 70
self-denying clause *see* disinterestedness clause
Seneca 17–18
Senior, Nassau William 59–60 (table 4.1), 122
Sepúlveda, Juan Ginés de 15, 24n.12
Serb-Ottoman War (1876) 148, 151, 156, 172–4
  see also Alexander II, Tsar; Cherniaev, Victor
Serbia (nineteenth century–1914) 102, 121, 148, 151, 156–7, 160–1, 172–5, 178, 182, 184, 186–7
  Serbian independence 151, 161, 163, 173, 182
  see also Serb-Ottoman War; Alexander II, Tsar
Serbia today 3, 4, 226
Shannon, Richard 153
Shaw, Stanford J. 137
Shelley, Percy Bysshe 110
Sherman, John 210, 212
Shuvalov, Pyotr 149, 151–3, 158–61, 174, 176, 178–9
Sidgwick, Henry 32, 155
Sino-Japanese War (1894–95) 42
  admission of Japan to family of nations 42
slaughter *see* atrocity(ies)

slaves by nature or natural slaves 14, 15, 24n.12
  see also Aristotle; Sepúlveda, Juan Ginés de
Slavic solidarity 180–1, 186, 187
  see also Russian Pan-Slavism
Smith, Adam 31–3
Smith, Frederick Edwin 61–2 (table 4.1), 68
Smith, Steven 84
social Darwinism 32, 50n.21, 201
Sorel, Albert 60–1 (table 4.1), 66, 72
sovereign, a (the) 12, 17–20, 22, 70, 84, 122, 176
sovereign right(s), power, authority 65–6, 82, 157
sovereignty, principle of, 2, 4, 6, 19–20, 23, 31–2, 46, 58, 65–6, 68, 71, 83, 123, 148, 226
Spain
  Cuban question 109–10, 115, 197–9, 200, 202–8, 211–12, 214
  Spanish (people, nation) and Cuban question 15, 17, 20, 198–9, 203, 207–9, 211
  US 197–215, 225–8
  see also Cánovas, Antonio; Sagasta, Práxedes Mateo
Spain, Renaissance 15, 20, 38
Spanish-American War (April–August 1898) 200, 207, 211
Spanish conquest of America 15, 20, 199
Spencer, Herbert 33, 89, 155, 201
St Petersburg Protocol (April 1826) 114–16
  see also Britain; Canning, George; Greek War of Independence; Lieven, Christopher; Nicholas I, Tsar; Russia; Wellington, Duke of
standard of civilization 31, 33, 39, 42–4, 73, 227
  see also civilization; civilized–barbarians (uncivilized, non-civilized) dichotomy; Eurocentrism
Stanley, Henry 33
Stead, William Thomas 153–4, 183–4
Stowell, Ellery C. 12, 18, 27n.61, 62 (table 4.1), 69–70, 76n.74, 137, 142–3, 162, 214, 228
Strangford, Lady 156
Strangford, Viscount 108–9, 112, 128n.84
Stratford Canning (Stratford de Redcliffe) 44–5, 114–15, 117–18, 120, 128n.84, 149, 154

Stroganov Grigoriy A. 108
Strong, Josiah 201, 212
Strupp, Karl 62 (table 4.1), 70
Suarez, Francisco 15–16, 18, 21, 31
successful outcome of intervention, prospect of 5–6, 71, 88, 226
Swinburne, Algernon Charles 155

Takashaki Sakue 42
Talleyrand, Charles Maurice 105–6
Tanzimat (reforms in Ottoman Empire) 45, 47, 136, 138
Taube, Michel 62 (table 4.1), 70
Tchaikovsky, Pyotr Ilyich 186
Teller Amendment 207, 215
territorial integrity (mainly of Ottoman Empire) 44, 47, 154, 158, 172
Tesón, Fernando 7n.19, 82–4
Thouvenel, Édouard Antoine de
  Lebanon and Syria massacres 135, 138–9, 141, 228
Tibawi, A. L. 138
Tocqueville, Alexis de 32
Tolstoy, Leo Nikolayevich 183, 185, 187–8, 196n.123, 228
Torriente, Cosme de la 212
Trim, D. J. B. ix, x, 19
Tsurutaro Senga 43
Tuck, Richard 22, 26n.40
Turgenev, Ivan Sergeyevich 183, 185
'Turks' (Ottomans according to Europeans and Americans) 43, 44–6, 52n.61, 108–9, 110–11, 115, 117, 122, 153–6, 159, 166n.71, 175, 177–8, 183, 185, 188–90, 217
Twain, Mark 210, 213, 228
Twiss, Travers 35, 46, 60–1 (table 4.1)
tyranny, against tyranny 12, 14, 16–23

Uchimura Kanzō 42
uncivilized or non-civilized (Asian and African peoples, states, countries, nations) 31, 34–8, 42, 66, 71–2, 227
  see also barbarians or barbarous; civilized (states, nations, peoples); civilized–barbarians (un-civilized, non-civilized) dichotomy; civilized–barbarians (uncivilized, non-civilized)–savages distinction
United Nations (UN) 2–4
  Security Council 2–5
    authorization by 2–5

US (United States of America) 2–4, 102, 110, 112, 197–215
  Cuba, motives for intervening 199–202, 212–13
    humanitarian 199–201
    instrumental 199, 201–2
  Cuban question, Spain 197–215, 225–8
    against Cuban independence (or limited independence) 203, 207, 212, 214–15
    anti-imperialism(sts), anti-expansionism(sts) 208, 210–11
    business circles, 200, 202, 205–6
    China market 201, 210, 217n.47
    expansionism(sts) /imperialism(sts), 200–2, 208–13, 215
    press 201–2, 205–6, 208, 217n.38
    public 200–1, 208–9, 211–13
    Senate and Congress (Capitol Hill) 205–7, 210
    see also Cleveland, Grover, President; Day, William R.; Hay, John; McKinley, William, President; Olney, Richard
  Greek War of Independence 109–10
  Philippine question 197, 202, 207–13
    anti-imperialists against acquisition 210–11
    expansionists (or imperialists) for acquisition 210
    see also Spain; McKinley, William, President; Philippines; Spain
Uspensky, Gleb 187
USS Maine episode 205, 208, 213

Valladolid debate (1550) 24n.12
Varouxakis, Georgios xi, 90, 95n.97 and n.103
Vattel, Emer de 11, 16, 23, 30n.116, 31, 41
Victoria, Queen 41, 139, 149, 152–3, 155, 159–60, 167n.106, 185, 192n.35
Vincent, R. J. 17, 22, 82, 86
Vitoria, Francisco de 15–16, 17, 20–1, 22, 28n.73 and 74, 31
  American Indians 15, 20–1
  just war 15–16
  precursor of idea of humanitarian intervention 16, 20–1, 28n.74

Walker, Thomas Alfred 61–2 (table 4.1), 68, 123
Walzer, Michael 2, 89–90, 96n.106, 214
war crimes 4, 5

Index

Wellington, Duke of 114, 116, 118–21
Westlake, John 37, 42, 46, 57, 61 (table 4.1), 68, 73, 80n.162, 214
Westphalia, Treaty (or Peace) of (1648) 11, 14, 23
   myth of 23
Weyler, General Valeriano 203–4
Wheaton, Henry 34, 41–2, 59–60 (table 4.1), 105, 121, 197
Wight, Martin 228
Williams, Howard 84
Williams, W. A. 202
Wilson, George Grafton 61–2 (table 4.1), 68–9, 213

Wilson Doctrine 198
Winfield, Percy H. 11, 62 (table 4.1), 70, 72
Wolff, Christian 11, 23, 31–3, 50n.16
Woodford, Stewart L. 204–5
Woodhouse, Christopher Montague 117
Woolsey, Theodore Dwight 41, 60 (table 4.1), 63, 67, 197
Woolsey, Theodore Salisbury 61–2 (table 4.1), 68, 213

Young Turks 48–9, 102
   foreign intervention 48–9
Ypsilantis, Alexander 106–7, 111

EU authorised representative for GPSR:
Easy Access System Europe, Mustamäe tee 50,
10621 Tallinn, Estonia
gpsr.requests@easproject.com

www.ingramcontent.com/pod-product-compliance
Lightning Source LLC
Chambersburg PA
CBHW071405300426
44114CB00016B/2194